THE ULTIMATE BOOK OF
VEGETABLES

THE ULTIMATE BOOK OF
VEGETABLES

Gardening * Health * Beauty
Craft * Cooking

The Reader's Digest Association, Inc.
New York, NY/Montreal

Contents

There is nothing that is comparable to it, as satisfactory or as thrilling, as gathering the vegetables one has grown.

– ALICE B. TOKLAS

A~Z OF VEGETABLES

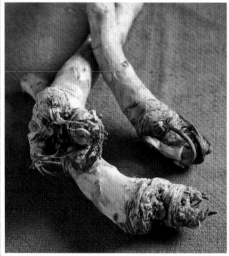

Vegetable directory

Artichokes

Both are called artichokes, but globe artichokes and Jerusalem artichokes are two very distinct plants. Globe artichokes grow like a giant Scotch thistle, and it is the unopened flower buds that are harvested. Jerusalem artichokes are tall-growing perennials in the sunflower family, and their roots are eaten.

Globe artichoke
Cynara scolymus

This classic antipasto vegetable has a distinctive, delicate flavor. Its striking silver foliage appears in winter, and in late spring it produces edible flower buds that, if you fail to harvest them in time, open as stunning purple thistle-like flowers.

The buds, or heads, are harvested in spring, before they start to open and when the stem is still flexible. The stiff outer scales are compressed around a shallow base, called the heart, which is the most desirable edible part. A thick cluster of silky hairs—the choke—is embedded in the heart. The choke must be removed, either before or after cooking, and the stiff outer scales removed before cooking. They are eaten freshly cooked or preserved in oil. The stem can be peeled and cooked, too.

BELOW: The unopened flower buds of globe artichokes (top) and the knobby roots of Jerusalem artichokes (bottom) are the edible parts.

Growing

Globe artichokes are hardy and drought-tolerant once established, but will produce more buds when grown in rich soil and watered well. Plant young plants or suckers in full sun in well-drained soil during spring. The plants will flower for two to three months. To keep the plants productive, divide clumps every three to four years in winter, when dormant.

Harvesting A plant will yield up to 20 buds. Pick the largest bud, or king head, first. Use pruning shears or a sharp knife; leave on a 12.5-cm (5-in) stem.

Varieties

There are a number of green budded varieties that grow to around 1.5 m (5 ft) high. Violetta has highly ornamental dusky purple–colored buds and only grows to 1.2 m (4 ft) high.

Buying and storing

Look for tightly closed heads with plump "leaves," or scales, that don't look dried or withered. Though best eaten the day they are purchased, they keep in a loosely sealed plastic bag in the crisper section of the refrigerator for up to four days.

ABOVE: The attractive unopened flower buds of Violetta globe artichoke.

The Jerusalem artichoke is a low-starch tuber. When roasted, it has a mildly sweet, smoky flavor reminiscent of a potato, artichoke, and water chestnut all rolled into one.

Jerusalem artichoke

Helianthus tuberosus

Also known as sunchoke

This hardy plant is grown for the edible knobby tubers of its root system. It has an interesting nutty flavor and can be eaten raw, boiled, roasted, stir-fried, or in soups. It is renowned for its ability to cause flatulence, although this unwanted side effect can be reduced by serving it with fennel. The flowers last well when picked for a vase.

Growing

This perennial is easy to grow and reaches up to 3 m (10 ft) high. It flowers in autumn with beautiful sunflower-like golden yellow flowers. These prolific flowers and its height make Jerusalem artichoke a good windbreak plant around tender vegetables.

Bare-rooted tubers are planted in winter in a sunny, well-drained position in reasonably fertile soil. It is often regarded as a permanent vegetable because any tubers left in the ground will reshoot. Be sure to dig up even the smallest tubers to prevent any unwanted regrowth in your garden.

Harvesting Dig up the tubers after the plants have died down in autumn. Handle with care, as the skins are thin. Brush off the soil and store in a dark, dry place. As with potatoes, it is important that you don't eat Jerusalem artichokes that have a greenish tinge.

Buying and storing

Choose firm Jerusalem artichokes with unwrinkled skins. Keep in a loosely sealed plastic bag in the crisper section of the refrigerator or in a very cool, dark place for up to a week.

Health benefits

A globe artichoke's health benefit is found in the plant's leaves: Research has shown that artichoke-leaf extract stimulates the gallbladder to release more fat-digesting bile acids. By boosting this cholesterol-rich bile, which is excreted from the body, it may help to reduce heart-threatening LDL cholesterol.

Jerusalem artichokes can cause gas, because they contain a hard-to-digest carbohydrate called inulin. Ironically, this substance has a beneficial effect on the gut: Inulin is a prebiotic that supports friendly bacteria such as *Lactobacillus* and *Bifidobacterium*, known to help protect against gastrointestinal disorders. Jerusalem artichokes are high in iron and also have a low GI, making them suitable for diabetics.

Artichokes with lemon butter for dipping

The edible part of a globe artichoke is the unopened flower bud, which has a slightly sweet taste. Each artichoke is composed of fleshy gold-green to purple "leaves" (scales, or bracts) surrounding a hairy, inedible "choke" on top of an edible, tender heart.

Remove tough outer leaves from 4 globe artichokes. Trim the stem so the artichoke sits flat. Rub with a squeeze of lemon juice. Bring a large saucepan of lightly salted water to a boil. Add artichokes and simmer for 15–20 minutes, until just tender—when a leaf from the middle pulls away easily and the heart is tender when pierced. Drain upside down.

Meanwhile, melt 125 g (4 oz) butter in a small saucepan and sauté 1 crushed garlic clove. Add the juice of ½ lemon, season with salt and freshly ground black pepper, and stir to combine.

Pour the lemon butter into a serving bowl and serve alongside the artichokes. Eat 1 leaf at a time (scraping the flesh off the leaves with your teeth), discarding the choke, and then eating the heart. **Serves 4**

Globe artichokes are generally pest-free, apart from slugs, snails, and aphids. Slugs, nematodes, caterpillars, and two-spotted mites can do minor damage to Jerusalem artichokes.

Royal favorite

Italian-born Catherine de Medici is credited with laying the foundations of French cuisine. Accompanied by a retinue of skilled Florentine cooks, she arrived in France in 1533, at the age of 14, for her wedding to the future King Henry II. The gastronomic innovations she brought with her included the fork (until then unknown in France) and a number of new foods that were to become staples of French dining, including parsley, haricot beans, olive oil, and globe artichokes.

Asian greens

Asian greens are easy to grow and add an authentic flavor to Asian cuisine. It is possible to keep your kitchen supplied with at least some of these varieties all year round. They all like to grow in a sunny position, in rich, fertile soil that is high in organic matter, and they are best grown quickly with ample water and fertilizer. Their main insect pests are snails and slugs, but given a good wash, leaves that have a few munched holes can still be cooked successfully.

Bok choy

Brassica rapa Chinensis Group

Also known as pak choy, buk choy, Chinese celery cabbage, Chinese white cabbage, mustard cabbage, celery mustard

There are many varieties of Asian vegetables, with new cultivars appearing all the time, and names vary between countries, states, and growers. Pictured clockwise from top left: a variety of choy sum, Chinese broccoli, baby pak choy with green stems, and Moonbuk, a dwarf variety of white-stemmed buk choy.

These small, non-heading members of the cabbage family have thick succulent leaf stalks, which are either green or white, and rounded dark green leaves. There are many different varieties, including dwarf or baby forms, and as a general rule, varieties with green stems are called pak choy and those with white stems are called buk choy. Young leaves and stems can be eaten raw in salads, but the most common use for mature plants is to steam, blanch, stir-fry, braise or add them to soups.

There is a deep red form, with pale green to whitish stems, which looks attractive in dishes and makes a very ornamental vegetable. Although usually considered a cool-weather crop, there are cultivars that can be grown all year round.

Growing

Grow from seed or seedlings and space around 20 cm (8 in) apart. Choose cultivars best suited to cool or hot weather, depending on when and in which climate zone they are to be grown.

Harvesting Outer leaves can be harvested as the plant grows, or harvest the whole plant at around eight weeks.

Tatsoi

Brassica rapa subsp. *narinosa*
Also known as Chinese flat cabbage

Similar to bok choy, tatsoi forms a flat rosette of succulent white or pale green stems with dark green rounded leaves. All parts of the vegetable are edible. Young leaves can be used in salads or added to soups or stir-fries as leaves mature, at around seven weeks. Thick stems should be trimmed, peeled, then steamed or poached. Yukina is a large form with a more upright habit, to 40 cm (16 in) high, and its large dark green leaves are heavily crinkled.

Growing

Grow from seed or seedlings and space around 20 cm (8 in) apart. This is a cold-hardy plant that can be grown as a winter vegetable.

Harvesting See bok choy.

Chinese kale

Brassica oleracea Alboglabra Group
Also known as gai larn, gai lan, Chinese broccoli, white flowering broccoli

This cool-season vegetable is harvested beginning at nine weeks after sowing. It grows to 60 cm (2 ft) high and produces white flowers, unlike the more common European forms of broccoli, which have yellow flowers. Both the stems and leaves are eaten. Steamed, blanched, or added to stir-fries, it has a crisp texture and a mild, slightly bittersweet taste.

Growing

Grow from seed or seedlings sown in autumn and space around 15 cm (6 in) apart to keep plants upright and stems thin.

Harvesting Harvest when young and tender; cut off stems with flower buds and young leaves. Unlike other broccoli, Chinese broccoli can still be harvested once a few flowers open.

Choy sum

Brassica rapa var. *parachinensis*
Also known as Chinese flowering cabbage

Choy sum has bright green leaves and yellow flower buds and grows to around 30 cm (12 in) high. The flowering stems with leaves are harvested up to eight weeks after sowing and can be steamed or blanched and drizzled with a little oyster sauce or added to stir-fries and soups.

Growing

Sow directly in the garden bed from spring to autumn and thin to 10–20 cm (4–8 in). It is frost-tender. High temperatures will result in tougher and fewer stems or bolting.

Harvesting See Chinese kale.

Tatsoi's flat rosette of glossy dark green leaves makes a handsome inclusion in the vegetable patch. With its peppery, mustardy flavor, this winter crop is good in soups.

Recipe

Asian greens with noodles, Malaysian-style

This recipe is a great way to use a variety of Asian greens. Belacan is a key ingredient in Nyonya (Peranakan) cooking, the unique fusion cuisine that developed in Malaysia when Chinese people settled there in the 16th century.

Preparation 10 minutes / **Cooking** 10 minutes / **Serves** 4

450 g (15 oz) hokkien (egg noodles)
1 tablespoon (10 g) belacan (Malaysian shrimp paste)
1 tablespoon (10 g) canola or peanut oil
1 long red chili pepper, seeded and finely chopped
1 large clove garlic, crushed
2 tablespoons small dried shrimp
1 tablespoon (20 g) palm sugar, shaved, or dark brown sugar
2 bunches (about 600 g/1 lb 5oz) Asian greens, such as bok choy, choy sum (Chinese flowering cabbage), Chinese broccoli (gai larn), or water spinach (kang kung), leaves separated and ends trimmed

Put the noodles in a heatproof bowl and pour boiling water over to cover. Let soak according to package instructions, then drain and set aside.

Press the belacan into a flat disc and put in the bottom of a wok or large frying pan. Heat gently until fragrant, then add the oil, chili pepper, garlic, and dried shrimp and stir so the belacan is distributed evenly and ingredients are well mixed. Cook 1 minute.

Stir in the palm sugar, Asian greens, and noodles and cook until the greens are wilted and stems are tender, about 5 minutes. If the noodles stick to the wok, add 3–4 tablespoons water. Serve immediately.

Note If belacan is not available, or if you find its flavor too strong, replace it with the same amount of fish sauce for a milder version of this dish.

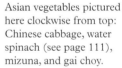
Chinese mustard greens can be grown as a green manure crop and are also used to cleanse garden beds of soil-borne root diseases.

Asian vegetables pictured here clockwise from top: Chinese cabbage, water spinach (see page 111), mizuna, and gai choy.

Recipe

Kimchi

This traditional Korean side dish of pickled vegetables can be stored in an airtight container in the refrigerator for up to three weeks.

Chop 1 Chinese cabbage (wombok or napa) and place in a colander over a plate; sprinkle with 5 tablespoons salt and toss to coat. Let stand for 30 minutes. Rinse and drain well. Transfer the cabbage to a very large glass container.

Add 1 peeled and sliced cucumber, 12 thinly sliced radishes, 4 chopped spring onions (scallions), 3 thinly sliced garlic cloves, and a 3-cm (1¼-in) piece of fresh ginger, peeled and sliced.

Combine 1 tablespoon salt, ¼ cup (60 ml) rice vinegar, 1 tablespoon chili paste, and 12 cups (3 liters) water in a large bowl and stir to dissolve the salt. Pour over the vegetable mixture.

Cover and refrigerate for at least two days, stirring occasionally, before serving. **Makes 10 cups (20 servings)**

Chinese cabbage

Brassica rapa Pekinensis Group

Also known as wombok, wongbok, napa cabbage, celery cabbage

Chinese cabbage has an upright, elongated shape with light greenish leaves and white fleshy stems and is similar to European cabbages. It takes up to 12 weeks to be ready for harvest. Eat raw in salads or cook in a variety of dishes—it retains its form even when cooked. The leaves are also used as an edible wrap and can be pickled.

Growing

Grow from seed or seedlings sown in autumn or spring and thin to around 20–30 cm (8–12 in) apart, depending on the variety, to help keep plants upright, with tight rather than loose inner cores.

Harvesting While mostly harvested as a complete head, it can be used as a cut-and-come-again vegetable if the inner core remains intact.

Gai choy

Brassica juncea
Also known as Chinese mustard greens

This is a fast-growing cool-season crop that is best planted in autumn or spring. Whereas the whole plant is ready for harvest in six to seven weeks, individual leaves can be picked from four weeks. Broad-leaved forms (*B. juncea* var. *rugosa*) include some giant (1 m [3 ft]) red varieties that are highly ornamental. The plant has a mustardy tang; it is more pungent than other greens such as kale or cabbage. Add to salads, stir-fry or steam as a side dish, or use in pickles. The plant can be used as a green manure or as a living mulch to prevent weed growth, too.

Growing

Grow from seed or seedlings sown in autumn or spring; space around 30 cm (1 ft) apart to keep plants upright and stems thin.

Harvesting Harvest leaves or the whole plant as required. For a milder flavor, pick leaves when young, as their flavor gets stronger with age.

Een choy

Amaranthus tricolor
Also known as Chinese spinach, red stripe leaf

This fast-growing vegetable reaches over 60 cm (2 ft) high, with bright green, oval-shaped leaves with a red central patch and veins. Leaves and stems are edible; use young leaves raw in salads and mature leaves cooked as a leafy green. Take care not to overcook when using in soups and stir-fries.

Growing

In warm climates sow all year round, but in cool climates it is best sown after the last frost. Young leaves should be ready for harvest in a month. Thin seedlings to 15 cm (6 in) apart and eat the thinnings. Een choy can be grown in trays as a microgreen, ready for harvest in as little as two to three weeks.

Harvesting Harvest young leaves regularly and pinch out the tips to encourage more bushy leaf growth. Een choy is best used fresh from the garden, although it will keep refrigerated for up to two days.

Mizuna

Brassica juncea var. *nipposinica*
Also known as Japanese mustard

This plant is used in Japanese cuisine as a salad green and has a pleasant mustard flavor, milder than gai choy. The plant forms a dense clump 50 cm (20 in) high with bright green, deeply incised leaves. Red-leaved forms such as Ruby Streaks are highly ornamental. Mibuna is very similar, although its leaves are long and have smooth rather than incised edges.

Asian vegetables pictured clockwise from top left: een choy, large bok choy, and one of the Asian varieties of English spinach.

Growing

Grow from seed or seedlings planted in spring or autumn; space around 30 cm (1 ft) apart.

Harvesting Pick young leaves from the outside of the plant as required, or harvest the whole plant when mature, at around six weeks.

Buying and storing

Greens should have bright, healthy-looking leaves that are not wilted and do not have any yellow, brown, or wet areas. Store in a plastic bag in the crisper section of your refrigerator for two days.

Health benefits

All Asian greens are nutritional powerhouses. For example, 1 cup (70 g) of cooked bok choy delivers 7224 IU of vitamin A (144 percent of your daily needs), while both Chinese kale and gai choy are low in calories and excellent sources of vitamins A, C, and K as well as folate and dietary fiber. Similarly, mizuna is rich in folate, iron, and vitamin C, which all boost the immune system. It also contains antioxidants called glucosinolates, which may help reduce cancer risk by ushering carcinogens out of the body before they can harm your DNA.

Asian greens are best cooked quickly and at a high temperature. Steam, blanch, or stir-fry them in a wok. Cook at the last minute, just before you're ready to serve.

The spears are harvested from the crown of the plant when it's at least two years old. Don't harvest the later shoots; instead, let them grow into ferns to replenish the crown.

WHITE ASPARAGUS
To get white spears, the asparagus must not be exposed to sunlight. Hill up extra soil to cover the crown; cut blanched spears 20 cm (8 in) below the soil surface as soon as their tips appear aboveground.

Asparagus
Asparagus officinalis

Once established, this tuberous-rooted perennial vegetable continues to produce for more than 20 years. Spears appear for about two months in spring and are best enjoyed straight from the garden, lightly steamed or stir-fried. Asparagus does not have pest or disease problems providing its growing requirements are met.

Growing

Grow in a sunny position in good, rich soil that has been well prepared with organic matter, mulched heavily, and fed well. Good drainage is essential, and acid soils should be limed. You can grow asparagus from seed, but it is better to purchase two-year-old crowns of male plants, as they are productive more quickly. Crowns are available bare-rooted in winter or in containers throughout the year.

Harvesting Asparagus must not be harvested in its first year and only sparingly in its second. The crown develops a strong root system and sets you up for full production in the third year. Spears appear from the soil in spring before any other foliage is visible.

Use a sharp knife to cut spears when they are 20 cm (8 in) long, cutting them below the ground and only harvesting spears that are more than 1 cm ($^1/_2$ in) thick.

Harvesting finishes in late spring. The mass of ferny fronds then grows to replenish food reserves to the crown. In autumn, cut the yellowing fronds down to 5 cm (2 in) high.

A common and curious side effect of eating asparagus was noted by the French writer Marcel Proust, who recorded that the plant "transforms my chamber-pot into a flask of perfume."

Artistic bunch
A painting of a bunch of juicy white asparagus by French Impressionist Édouard Manet is famous both for its technique and the story that accompanies it. The work was commissioned by collector Charles Ephrussi in 1880 for an agreed price of 800 francs. Instead, Ephrussi sent a check for 1,000 francs. Manet, in a wry response to the overpayment, painted a single asparagus spear on the same marble slab as the original bundle and presented it with a note saying, "There was one missing from your bunch."

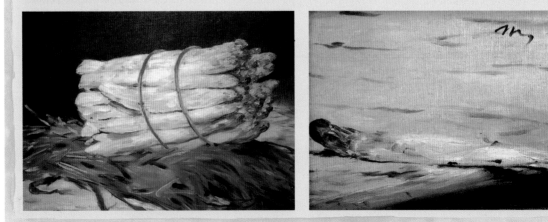

Varieties

✳ **Mary Washington** The most common variety

✳ **Purple asparagus** Produces rich purple spears

Buying and storing

Spears should be firm and plump from tip to end, with no wrinkling or withering. Check to make sure the tip looks fresh. Store in a loosely sealed plastic bag in the crisper section of your refrigerator for up to four days.

Health benefits

Known as *shatavari* in India's Ayurvedic healing tradition, wild asparagus (*Asparagus racemosus*) is said to support fertility, breast milk production, and a healthy urinary tract. Scientific research shows that asparagus is rich in saponins, which may help calm inflammation. Half a cup (90 g) of cooked asparagus contains just 20 calories but delivers a big dose of fiber (2 g) as well as 18 percent of the vitamin A and 12 percent of the vitamin C that you need daily.

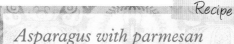

Recipe

Asparagus with parmesan

For a quick and easy side dish, gently boil asparagus spears until tender but still slightly crisp, about 2–3 minutes. Toss with shaved parmesan, a little olive oil, and some grated lemon zest and serve.

To prepare asparagus, wash it thoroughly in a bowl of cold water. Snap off the woody ends of the stalks. Cook in a large saucepan of lightly salted boiling water for about 3 minutes, depending on the size of the asparagus, then drain and serve.

ABOVE: All-purple varieties of asparagus are striking in the garden and on the plate. They generally have a finer flavor than green varieties and can even be eaten raw.

LEFT: White asparagus comes from a green variety that is blanched by preventing exposure to sunlight. The green variety here is Mary Washington, ideal for the home garden.

Avocados

Persea americana

Officially a fruit, avocados are used as a salad vegetable. Each pear-shaped, dark purple-black or green fruit contains yellowish green flesh of a creamy consistency around a large seed. This ripe flesh can be used in salads, sandwich spreads, guacamole dip, and even desserts.

Growing

The evergreen trees of the subtropics need excellent drainage and a deep, rich soil. Choose a frost-free, sheltered position, protected from wind. Plant in spring, when the ground is warm, and protect young trees from hot sun and strong winds for the first few years with burlap, shade cloth, or plastic.

In dry climates avocado trees require regular watering and like to be fed and mulched well, too.

Problems   Root rot is the biggest challenge for avocados. They can also be affected by fruit fly, thrips, scale, and aphids.

Harvesting   Avocados only begin to ripen after they've been picked, and ripening takes a few days to a week. Grafted cultivars will produce a small crop in three years, which hold on the tree well.

Varieties

You can grow avocados from seed, but they could take 10 years to fruit, and the fruit will be of variable quality. Grafted cultivars ensure reliable harvests. Even though these cultivars are self-fertilizing, growing at least two different varieties will ensure better harvests. Popular home garden varieties include Bacon, Fuerte, Hass, Reed, and Shepard.

Buying and storing

It is best to buy an avocado when it gives just slightly to gentle pressure at the stem end. Store at room temperature until it reaches desired ripeness—keep with bananas to accelerate ripening. You can use slightly firm avocado to slice or dice, or very soft, ripe avocado to mash or spread. Once cut, store in plastic wrap in the refrigerator for up to

Cukes (also known as cocktail or finger avocados) are mini avocados that are the size and shape of a small cucumber. They are just right for an individual serving.

The smooth, green-skinned Reed avocado (center) and the pebbly, purple-black Hass avocado.

To grow your own avocado tree, place four toothpicks in a seed and suspend it over a glass of water so that part of the seed is in the water. When roots and stem appear, plant in a pot in a sunny position with half the seed exposed. Water often.

three days. Leaving the stone in a cut avocado is said to help prevent discoloration of the flesh.

Health benefits

A quarter of the total calories found in avocado comes from oleic acid. This beneficial fat boosts the absorption of fat-soluble nutrients, including carotenoids, which help protect against heart disease. Adding a cup of avocado cubes (150 g) to a salad can increase the absorption of carotenoids from lettuce, baby spinach, and other vegetables by up to 400 percent. With its high concentration of monounsaturated fats and vitamin E, avocado also makes a soothing, moisturising ingredient in homemade skin-care and hair-care products.

Origins of the avocado

There is evidence of avocado cultivation in Mexico and Central America since 291 BCE, and there are avocados buried alongside mummies in Peru. The Aztecs called the fruit *āhuacatl*, meaning "testicles," in reference to the fruit's appearance when hanging from a tree. After the Spanish conquistadors invaded Mexico and Peru in the 16th century, avocados were transported to Europe and eventually other parts of the world. Over time, the Aztec word *āhuacatl* evolved into the Spanish *aguacate* and then into the word "avocado."

Recipe

Avocado wedges

With its creamy texture and mild, nutty flavor, avocado is perfect with the sweet tang of lime juice.

Peel and slice 1 avocado into wedges, sprinkle with a little salt and freshly ground black pepper, and dress with lime juice. For more bite, add a drop of Tabasco sauce.

This cluster of avocados is almost ready for harvest. Avocado trees grown from seed can take up to 10 years to start bearing fruit.

In Asian cuisines, the avocado is used in desserts; mashed and sweetened, it takes the place of cream.

Beans

There is an enormous range of green beans, broadly classified as bush beans, pole beans, and runner beans. They are warm-season vegetables sown after the risk of frost is over and are easy to grow. Yard-long beans are a tropical crop, while fava beans are cool-season vegetables.

Growing

All green beans need a sunny position in well-drained, alkaline soil with plenty of organic matter. Plant in a sheltered position to protect from wind damage. Sow seeds when the ground is warm in spring and summer, or all year round in subtropical and tropical areas. Water thoroughly after sowing, but then wait until germination before watering again to minimize the risk of the seeds rotting. Once the seedlings emerge, mulch—well away from the stems—to retain soil moisture and prevent weeds.

Problems It is important to protect emerging seedlings from snails and slugs. Whitefly, thrips, and mites can also cause problems. Fungal diseases can affect beans, depending on the climate and the seasonal conditions.

Harvesting Bush beans crop heavily for a relatively short period of three to four weeks, while pole beans can crop well for eight weeks, although they take a few weeks longer to start. It's best to make successive plantings of beans once every month to six weeks, for four to six months, depending on your climate and frosts. Harvest pods regularly to keep the plants producing. Pick when young and tender, at around 15 cm (6 in) long, before the seeds inside swell and make the pods lumpy. Many beans taste good eaten raw when they're picked young, although most are steamed, lightly cooked, or frozen for future use.

Bush beans

Phaseolus vulgaris
Also known as dwarf beans

These low-growing beans reach around 50 cm (20 in) high and do not require support. Plants start to crop heavily at around two months.

Varieties

There are many varieties available, so always choose one suited to your climate and the time of planting. Redlands is a reliable stringless variety with excellent flavor and good disease resistance. Bountiful Butter is a bean with tender, fleshy, golden yellow pods, a waxy sheen, and a sweet buttery flavor. Romano is a variety of wide, flat beans popular for fresh or dried use.

Pole beans

Phaseolus vulgaris
Also known as climbing beans

Climbing beans grow to at least 2 m (6 ft) high and need the support of canes, poles, trellises, tripods, or arches. They are more productive than bush beans, producing at least three times the yield per plant around three months after sowing.

Varieties

There are many varieties to choose from, so choose to suit your climate. Blue Lake is an old favorite with classic slender green beans, while Purple King produces attractive purple flowers followed by decorative and tasty purple pods, which turn green when cooked. Lazy Housewife is a hardy heirloom variety that can produce as much as 1 kg (2 lb) of beans per plant.

A tepee of strong canes provides a sturdy support for the substantial weight of pole beans as they grow, and it can also add height and interest to the vegetable garden.

ABOVE: Perennial, or runner, beans were originally grown in Europe for their beautiful red flowers. Trained over an arch or trellis, they won't look out of place in the flower garden.

LEFT: Beans come in a great array of colors, shapes, and sizes. Pictured in the bowl (from left to right) are green, cranberry, and wax beans; in the foreground (from left to right) are flat Romano, yard-long, and fava beans.

The winged bean (*Psophocarpus tetragonolobus*), also known as the four-angled bean or asparagus pea, is a perennial climbing legume best suited to the subtropics and tropics. All parts of the plant are edible—the bean pods, leaves, flowers, and tubers.

Runner beans
Phaseolus coccineus
Also known as perennial beans, seven-year beans

While perennial climbing beans can live for seven years, their vigor decreases over time, and it is best to replace them before then. They prefer cool climates. They emerge from a crown each spring as the weather warms, crop heavily in late summer and autumn, then die back before winter. The pods are broad and short but tender when cooked. They produce large, highly ornamental flowers, too.

Varieties

Scarlet Runner is popular because of its brilliant scarlet red flowers. There are also varieties that have scarlet-and-white and salmon-pink flowers.

Yard-long beans
Vigna unguiculata subsp. *sesquipedalis*
Also known as snake beans, asparagus beans

These stringless beans are better suited to warm climates, producing light green, rounded pods,

1 cm (¹/₂ in) thick, with an asparagus-like taste. Climbing forms produce pods up to 90 cm (3 ft) long; bush forms have pods 30 cm (1 ft) long.

Health benefits

As well as being a lean source of protein, green beans pack two surprising health benefits. They're a good source of silicon—a mineral that plays an important role in maintaining strong bones and healthy connective tissue. A cup (125 g) of cooked green beans contains about 3 mg of silicon. Even better, the silicon in beans is twice as absorbable as that in most other vegetables.

Green beans also contain the heart-healthy omega-3 fatty acid called alpha-linolenic acid (ALA). A cup has 111 mg—almost as much as 15 g (¹/₂ oz) of walnuts, one of the richest sources of ALA.

Yard-long beans grow quickly and vigorously. The beans are best picked when young and tender, at up to 40 cm (16 in) long, and are popular in Asian cuisine.

Pick the pods when they are finger length. You will need 2 kg (4 lb) of broad bean pods for a yield of about 500 g (1 lb) beans after they've been double-peeled.

Fava beans
Vicia faba
Also known as broad beans, tic peas

These hardy, cool-season plants grow to 1–1.5 m (3–5 ft) high, producing large pods in spring. They can be eaten whole only when very young. Usually they are shelled and double-peeled as the pods age. Fava beans are used as a green manure crop and are traditionally planted in beds where tomatoes will follow in spring.

An abundant food crop, the fava bean is also useful as a soil improver.

Growing

Fava beans are heavy feeders and do best in rich, fertile soil. Soak seeds overnight, then sow directly where they will grow—in autumn in mild climates, in winter and early spring in frosty areas. Pods will start developing in late spring or summer. Although the plants have a naturally upright habit, they need some support to avoid being damaged by wind or rain or flopping over under the weight of the pods. Plant in blocks or double rows, spacing seeds 20 cm (8 in) apart, and plant more each month to extend the harvest period. Pinch out 10 cm (4 in) of the tender new growth as the beans finish flowering to encourage good bean development. This growth can be cooked as a vegetable.

Problems   Flowers failing to set is usually due to cold weather or a lack of bees. Plants are frost-tolerant and prefer cool climates, but even so, frost does affect pod development. This will improve as it warms up but will stop again when temperatures get too hot. Misting the plants in the early morning will raise humidity and aid the setting of beans. Good air circulation will help prevent fungal diseases.

Harvesting   Whole pods are harvested when finger length and cooked whole if young and tender. If they are 10 cm (4 in) long or more, they are shelled and cooked, then their skins are removed. These can be eaten, blanched, and frozen for later use or dried for soups and stews. Dig the plants into the soil at the end of the season.

Varieties

There are dwarf and tall fava bean varieties, with either long or short, broad pods, and some varieties are more suited to warm climates. The white-and-black flowers are attractive. Crimson Flowered is a highly ornamental though less productive variety with stunning flowers.

How-to

Preparing fava beans

Fava beans grow in a much larger pod than regular green beans. Unless they are very young, you will need to shell fava beans and cook the seeds in boiling water for about 3 minutes. If the seeds are tender, you can eat them in their gray-green skins, but for mature fava beans, you "double-peel" the seeds to remove the skin before eating.

Split the pod and remove seeds with your thumb. After boiling for 3 minutes, pierce the skin encasing each seed—the inner bean will slip out. Gently reheat.

Some bean varieties are grown mainly for drying, then stored and, after soaking and cooking until tender, added to soups, stews, and winter casseroles. Their names can vary from country to country. Clockwise from top left: lima beans, cranberry beans, red kidney beans, cannellini beans, and soybeans (center).

Buying and storing

All fresh beans should be plump and brightly colored, with no blemishes, slimy areas, or wrinkles. They will keep in a loosely sealed plastic bag in the crisper section of your refrigerator for five days.

Dried beans can be stored in airtight containers in a cool, dark place for up to 12 months.

Health benefits

Fava beans are low in fat and high in protein. They are also a good source of fiber, vitamins A and C, potassium, and iron. Those with favism, a rare hereditary disease, should avoid fava beans.

Many beans can be eaten fresh and whole when young or allowed to grow, ripen, and dry on the plant. The pods are harvested, shelled, and the dried beans inside stored for future use in soups, stews, dips, and salads. Cannellini is the name given to any white-seeded bean that can be dried. Other traditional types grown for drying are cranberry beans, which have pink-and-cream–speckled pods and seeds; kidney beans, a climbing type with reddish brown beans; and lima beans, tropical climbing beans that have large, flat, kidney-shaped seeds. Soybeans are bush beans that grow in warm climates around the world and are a vital food crop.

Recipe

Soybeans with ginger and soy sauce

This simple sweet-and-savory Japanese recipe using dried soybeans can be stored in a container in the refrigerator for three to four days.

Preparation 15 minutes, plus 3–4 hours' soaking time / **Cooking** 2¼ hours **Serves** 4–6 as a side dish

150 g (5 oz) dried soybeans
⅓ cup (75 g) sugar
2 tablespoons soy sauce
5-cm (2-in) piece fresh
  ginger, quartered
Pinch of salt

Wash the soybeans and soak in a large bowl of warm water for 3–4 hours. Drain.

Bring 8 cups (2 liters) water to a boil in a large saucepan. Add the beans, reduce the heat, and simmer for about 2 hours, until almost tender.

Add sugar, soy sauce, ginger, and salt. Simmer 15 minutes, until most of the liquid has evaporated. The beans are ready when cooked through, al dente but not mushy. Serve at room temperature.

Beets

Beta vulgaris Conditiva Group

Also known as beetroot

A versatile vegetable, beets are easy to grow from plantings in spring, summer, and early autumn. The late plantings that mature through winter will be the sweetest because the roots store sugars during cool weather. It makes an attractive addition to the vegetable garden. Known for its edible roots, it also produces ornamental edible leaves with red, yellow, or white veins, which are good stir-fried, steamed, or raw in salads if picked young. There are two main types: globe and long-rooted. And whereas only the blood-red root was once available, now there are orange, gold, yellow, white, and even concentrically ringed roots of varying shapes.

Growing

As with all root vegetables, beets need well-drained, friable soil of a good depth for the root to develop properly. The soil should be rich in organic matter, and while aged manures can be used to improve the soil, be sure not to include fresh manures high in nitrogen, as these will cause the roots to fork, twist, and be "hairy." Beets prefer a soil pH that is neutral or slightly acidic.

Each seed is a compound, consisting of two or three seeds joined together. Soak seeds in water overnight before sowing into damp ground 10 cm (4 in) apart. Once the seeds germinate, gently separate them and replant the two extra seedlings in another row. As they grow, the roots can push themselves out of the ground, so hill up soil around them if necessary. Make a repeat sowing a month after the first sowing for a continuous supply.

Both the young foliage and the bulbous root of the beet can be eaten, but don't harvest too much foliage while the root is developing.

NATURAL FOOD COLORING

Juice squeezed from chopped fresh beets has been used as a food dye since at least the mid-1700s, when it appeared in an English recipe for pink pancakes. It still provides an alternative to synthetic coloring for cakes and icings in the home kitchen and to chemical dyes for fabrics such as cotton and wool. The beet's vibrant magenta hue comes from the pigment betanin, first identified in the 1920s and commercially extracted today for use by the food industry as a natural reddening agent for tomato pastes, sauces, jams, jellies, and ice creams.

Recipe

Rosolje—*Estonian beet salad*

This lovely pink salad is a hearty and uplifting addition to a festive table. Like all recipes that are a mixture of many flavors, *rosolje* gets better after a day or two in the refrigerator.

Cook 5 beets in a large saucepan of boiling water for about 30 minutes, or until tender. Drain and cool, then slip off the skins and dice the flesh. Meanwhile, peel 5 large red-skinned potatoes and cut into small chunks. Cook in a separate saucepan of boiling water for about 7 minutes, until tender. Drain and cool.

Put the beets and potatoes in a large bowl. Add 2 finely chopped sour dill pickles, 2 finely chopped pickled herring fillets, 2 chopped hard-boiled eggs, 1 diced red or green apple, and 250 g (8 oz) chopped cooked cold meat, such as beef or veal.

To make a dressing, stir 1 cup (250 g) sour cream and ½ cup (125 g) mayonnaise together in a small bowl until evenly combined. Add to the salad and turn gently to coat evenly. **Serves 8–10 as a side dish**

Problems Poor drainage can cause problems. Add boron to alkaline soils to correct any boron deficiency, which results in poor root development.

Harvesting Beets mature in two months in warm weather and three to four months in cool weather, and should be harvested when roots reach 5–10 cm (2–4 in) across. Young, or baby, beets are picked before they are fully grown and taste good raw or in a grated-beet salad, while older roots are best boiled, roasted, pickled, or preserved. Don't cut or twist off the leaf stems too close to the root, as this will cause the root to bleed, losing color and flavor during cooking. Beets can be left in the ground over winter until you are ready to use them as long as they are well mulched. However, leaving them in the ground for too long in warm weather will make them woody and tough.

Varieties

Gardeners love the red roots of Crimson Globe and Bull's Blood. For smaller beets planted closer together, try Mini Gourmet. There are a number of colored varieties, including golden forms with a reddish orange skin and sweet golden yellow flesh that doesn't bleed when cooked; white forms with extremely sweet white flesh and pale skin; and Chioggia, an interesting variety with red skin and concentric rings of red and white through the root.

Buying and storing

If leaves and stalks are present, fresh-looking leaves will indicate that the beet has been picked recently. Otherwise, look for firm, unblemished globes. Trim the leaves and stalks down to 2.5 cm (1 in) long if you won't use them within a day or two. Store in a loosely sealed plastic bag in the crisper section of the refrigerator for up to a week.

Health benefits

Beets are good for your brain. This is because they contain nitrates, chemicals that are converted into nitrites in the body. Research shows that nitrites help blood vessels stay supple and flexible, which can help keep blood pressure on an even keel and improve blood flow throughout the body, including the brain. Research shows that drinking around 2 cups (500 ml) of beet juice a day may help improve blood flow to the brain in older people, especially to the frontal lobe—a part of the brain that often experiences reduced blood flow in age-related dementia. Beets' brilliant hues come from pigments called betalains, which may help protect against some cancers.

Beets come in a variety of colors and sizes. Baby beets are sweeter and more tender and fine-textured than beets left to grow to full size. Pictured from top: red beets, baby beets, golden beets, and white beets.

Stone Age to space age

Wild beet is thought to have spread from the shores of northern Africa along the Mediterranean coast to the Caspian Sea. Our earliest ancestors gathered and ate the leaves. However, it was not until Roman times that the taproot, then much smaller than today's varieties, was first cooked and eaten, and only in the 15th century, when it appeared in an English book of recipes, did the root truly gain favor as a food. The vegetable reached new heights in 1975, when cosmonauts from the U.S.S.R.'s *Soyuz 19* welcomed the U.S.'s *Apollo 18* astronauts with a meal of borscht (beet soup) cooked in the zero gravity of space.

Swiss chard and rainbow chard are related to beets. They are a subspecies that failed to develop swollen storage roots and put their energy into leaf growth instead. See pages 101–102.

Brassicas

The brassicas that belong to *Brassica oleracea* include the classic cool-season vegetables broccoli, brussels sprouts, cabbage, cauliflower, kale, and kohlrabi. These are very hardy vegetable crops that are best grown in areas with a cool winter—in fact it is believed that frosts will actually improve the flavor of some brussels sprouts and kales. Some varieties have more heat tolerance. The Asian greens brassicas, classified as *B. rapa* and *B. juncea* (see pages 14–17) tend to be more tolerant of tropical or subtropical climates. Supermarkets may have cool-season brassicas for sale all year round, but it is during winter and spring that the home gardener can enjoy them at their flavorsome best.

Millennia ago, a kale-like, loose-leafed wild plant, native to the Mediterranean, was domesticated and became a cabbage-like vegetable. This was later developed into our modern brassica vegetables, which include cabbages.

Growing

Brassicas like a fertile, well-prepared soil that is well drained, high in organic matter, and slightly alkaline. Grow them from seeds or seedlings in late summer and autumn, with repeat plantings into winter.

Problems   The main problems for these plants are snails and slugs, which hide within their foliage; the caterpillars of the cabbage moth and cabbage white butterfly, which eat the leaves; and gray cabbage aphids, which hide in the heart of young seedlings. All are less likely to affect strong, healthy plants. Some soil-borne diseases can also affect these plants, but good crop rotation practices should eliminate them.

Caterpillars are more active in the warm weather of autumn and spring. You could pick off and destroy them or spray them with a biopesticide—always observe the withholding period before you harvest any produce—but exclusion is best. Net plants with floating row covers or cover them with movable frames of fine wire mesh. You can also distract butterflies from laying eggs on your produce by leaving half eggshells around. The butterflies lay their eggs on these instead—gather them up weekly, crush, and add to the compost. The usual insect predators of aphids are less active in low temperatures, when cabbage aphids are present. Squash them or spray off with a strong hose, or you may need to use a biopesticide.

Buying and storing

Broccoli and cauliflower should have clean, bright, tightly closed heads (broccoli may have a purplish tinge to the green). Cabbages and brussels sprouts should be tightly closed, with bright, unblemished leaves. Kale should have firm leaves with no sign of wilting or yellowing. Choose small kohlrabi, which will have better flavor than large ones, with unblemished skin. Store in loosely sealed plastic bags in the crisper section of the refrigerator for up to a week, or blanch and freeze for future use.

Health benefits

Applying cooked or raw cabbage leaves externally is a traditional remedy for breast engorgement in nursing mothers and for the pain of varicose veins and arthritis. When eaten, cabbage and other brassicas offer a wealth of protective compounds. These include glucoraphanin, gluconasturtiin, and glucobrassicin in broccoli and brussels sprouts and sinigrin in cabbage. These compounds have been shown to support the body's natural detox system and block enzymes that increase the risk of DNA damage, which can lead to cancer. The fiber in brassicas may help control cholesterol, too.

Territorial pests

The cabbage white butterfly and cabbage moth are territorial, and you can use this to your advantage to protect your crops. Cut out butterfly shapes from white plastic containers, such as empty yogurt or ice cream cartons, and nail these to low garden stakes. Insert these around your brassicas and the real butterflies will be less likely to visit your young plants. Threading small chunks of white Styrofoam on fishing line, each about 30 cm (1 ft) apart, and stringing this around your brassicas will have the same effect. The cabbage white butterflies and cabbage moths will see these adornments as other butterflies and moths that have already claimed that particular territory, and so they will leave your brassica patch alone.

Brassicas are also sometimes called cruciferous vegetables after the shape of their tiny, four-petaled, cross-like flowers.

Broccoli

Brassica oleracea Botrytis Group, Italica Group

Broccoli produces rounded green heads of unopened flower buds. It is usually lightly steamed or stir-fried, but it has a delicious taste when picked fresh and eaten straight from the vegetable garden.

Growing

Plant seedlings 40–50 cm (16–20 in) apart, allowing space for the heads to mature. For continuous supply, plant a few seedlings every four to six weeks until the end of winter, if space allows.

Harvesting The heads take from two to three months to develop and should be cut as required when they are firm and tight and before they start to flower, usually when they are around 10–15 cm (4–6 in) across. Once you cut the central head, the plant produces smaller side shoots and can keep producing for another four months.

Varieties

While most people are familiar with single-headed broccoli, with heads up to 20 cm (8 in) across, for home gardeners there are other varieties to choose from. These include sprouting broccoli, which produces many smaller heads of Broccolini-like shoots, and broccoli raab, or rapini, the traditional Italian vegetable whose leaves, stems and small, button-size heads have a more intense flavor. There are also purple varieties of both single-headed and sprouting broccoli, which not only look and taste good, but also are the original color of this winter vegetable. Another interesting variety is Romanesco, which produces lime-green heads of spiraled florets, themselves arranged in a spiral pattern.

New types of broccoli are released every year, and all taste great. Pictured here (clockwise from top left) are the familiar single-headed broccoli, the individual florets of broccoli sold as broccolini and purple sprouting broccoli.

Brussels sprouts

Brassica oleracea Gemmifera Group

These swollen leaf buds that form on the sides of a central stem look like mini cabbages and have a unique flavor, which is at its best when the vegetable is homegrown. There is a purple variety, Rubine, as well as typical green varieties. The outer leaves can also be used as a leaf vegetable, like cabbage.

Growing

Space seedlings 60 cm (2 ft) apart to give the plants space to develop. They can reach 75 cm (2½ ft) high and, given their height, can be damaged by strong winds. Either hill the soil up around the base of the plant as it develops or stake the thick plant stem. Remove the leaves from the bottom up as the sprouts start to form on the stem. Brussels sprouts are ideally planted in summer so they mature when the coldest—preferably frosty—weather occurs, although local conditions will determine planting times.

Harvesting Sprouts start to appear on the stem of the plant three months after planting and will continue to appear for several months. They start to mature from the bottom to the top, so pick the lower sprouts first. You can encourage sprouts at the top of the plant to swell by removing the cabbage-like head. Small sprouts have the best flavor, so harvest when they are tightly closed, immature and less than 2.5 cm (1 in) across.

Brussels sprouts look somewhat like baby cabbages as they develop up the stem of the plant.

There is no benefit in cutting a cross shape in the base of each brussels sprout. It does not reduce the cooking time, nor does it help to cook the sprouts more evenly. Instead, it is likely to make them soggy. One hypothesis is that the practice originated as a spell to "keep the devil out."

Recipe

Pan-fried brussels sprouts leaves with anchovies and garlic

Steamed, boiled, roasted, or pan-fried: no matter how you cook brussels sprouts, don't overcook them. Done correctly, they have a wonderful taste with a nutty overtone. Here, anchovies, garlic, and red pepper flakes add flair and flavor to this underappreciated vegetable.

Peel the leaves off 750 g (1½ lb) brussels sprouts and blanch in a large saucepan of boiling salted water for 30 seconds. Drain, refresh in cold water, and set aside.

Heat 2 tablespoons olive oil in a large nonstick frying pan over medium heat. Add 2 cloves thinly sliced garlic and 4 finely chopped anchovy fillets and cook, stirring, for 1 minute, or until the garlic is golden. Add the brussels sprouts and ½ teaspoon dried red pepper flakes and cook, tossing carefully, for 2–3 minutes, or until golden. Add 1 tablespoon lemon juice and season with freshly ground black pepper. Put in a large bowl and drizzle with extra olive oil to serve. **Serves 4 as a side dish**

Cabbages come in many shapes, including round, conical, and oval, and in many colors, including green and reddish purple.

Cabbages

Brassica oleracea Capitata Group

Cabbages are the classic brassica, with a wonderful, densely packed, rounded head that can weigh 1–6 kilograms (2–13 pounds). Once the head is harvested, secondary heads are unlikely, so you can pull the plant out. Cabbage is finely shredded and eaten raw in coleslaw or cooked as a vegetable.

Growing

Plant seedlings 40–60 cm (16–24 in) apart, depending on the variety, to allow space for the cabbage heads, or hearts, to grow. The heads of small varieties start to mature after 8 weeks, while large types take 14 to 22 weeks. For a continuous supply, plant seedlings every 4 weeks.

Harvesting Harvest when heads are firm and fleshy. Cut them off at the base with a sharp knife.

Varieties

Small or miniature cabbages, such as Sugarloaf, are a good choice in limited space. For ornamental value as well as good eating, choose one of the reddish-purple varieties, such as Red Drumhead, or try one of the savoy cabbages with their characteristically deeply crinkled leaves.

Sauerkraut contains more gut-friendly lactobacillus bacteria than live yogurt cultures.

Recipe

Sauerkraut with apple and bacon

Cabbage, sauerkraut's star ingredient, has a reputation as a digestive aid. This traditional Eastern European recipe uses canned sauerkraut for convenience.

Discard the first layer of cabbage leaves from a 1 kg (2 lb) cabbage and cut in half. Remove and discard the core section and any thick ribs. Shred the cabbage and put in a large heavy-bottomed saucepan with 1 tablespoon olive oil and 2–3 slices diced bacon. Add 1 teaspoon salt, 6 peppercorns, and 2 bay leaves. Cover and cook over low heat for 1 hour, until softened, stirring occasionally.
   Drain a 425-g (15-oz) can of sauerkraut, then add to the pan with 2 peeled and finely diced green apples. Stir to combine.
   Cover and cook, stirring frequently, for a further 30 minutes, until the apples are tender and the sauerkraut is very soft. Add 3 tablespoons soft brown sugar just before the end of cooking and stir to combine the flavors.
Serves 6–8 as a side dish

Where garden space is limited, grow a few heads of creamy white, green, or purple cauliflower in the flower border.

Cauliflower

Brassica oleracea Botrytis Group

No longer is cauliflower only available as a creamy white head. Now there are purple, orange and pale green varieties—the latter is sometimes referred to as broccoflower—all of which add visual interest to the vegetable patch. Like broccoli, cauliflower is mostly eaten cooked, but it also tastes delicious picked and eaten fresh from the garden.

Growing

Plant seedlings 50–60 cm (1½–2 ft) apart to allow space for the heads to mature. Heads take three to five months to mature, and the part you eat is the unopened flower head. Unlike broccoli, it does not resprout successfully after harvest, so once you pick a head, the plant needs to be removed. To obtain a continuous supply, plant seedlings every two to four weeks if space and time allow, or choose several varieties that take different times to mature.

Harvesting Start harvesting heads while they are tight and firm and before the flowers open, ideally when heads are around 20 cm (8 in) across.

Cauliflower and cheese sauce are a perfect match, but you can bring excitement to cauliflower's delicate flavor by adding spices or by roasting the florets.

Crispy spiced cauliflower

The coating on the cauliflower should be light, not a thick shell. Make sure you cut the florets into evenly sized pieces, not too large but not too small. They should be just tender when cooked.

Preparation 20 minutes / **Cooking** 1½ minutes per batch / **Serves** 6 as an appetizer or side dish

- 1 tablespoon cumin seeds
- 2 teaspoons coriander seeds
- ½ teaspoon ground paprika
- ½ teaspoon salt
- ⅓ cup (50 g) all-purpose flour
- 1 egg
- 1 egg white
- ½ cup (30 g) Japanese bread crumbs (panko)
- ½ cup (55 g) almond flour
- 1 cauliflower (about 1 kg/2 lb)
- Vegetable oil for deep-frying
- Aioli to serve

Heat a small frying pan over medium heat. Add the cumin seeds and coriander seeds and toast, stirring continuously, for about 30 seconds, or until fragrant. Transfer to a spice grinder or mortar and pestle, add the paprika and salt, and grind to a powder.

Put the flour in a plastic bag. Whisk the egg and egg whites together in a wide shallow bowl. Combine the bread crumbs and almond flour in another plastic bag.

Cut the cauliflower into florets and put in the bag with the flour. Hold the bag closed with one hand and shake to coat the cauliflower. Remove and shake off any excess. Add the cauliflower to the egg mixture and turn with your hands to coat—you don't need perfectly even coverage. Transfer to the bag with bread crumbs and shake to coat.

Half fill a large saucepan or deep fryer with oil and heat over medium-high heat. Cook a few florets at a time for about 1½ minutes, or until lightly golden—don't overcrowd the oil or the temperature will drop and the cauliflower will be oily. Lift out with a slotted spoon, drain, and transfer to a baking sheet lined with paper towels. Keep in a single layer.

When all the cauliflower is cooked, sprinkle with the spices and toss to coat. Season with a little more salt, if desired, and serve with the aioli.

Note There may be some larger pieces of coriander left after grinding the seeds, so sift the ground spices to remove them.

Cauliflower for the king

Louis XIV, who ruled France from 1643 to 1715, built the palace at Versailles as a symbol of his wealth and absolute power. The Sun King showed a fondness for the humble cauliflower, or *chou-fleur*, a vegetable not highly regarded at the time. The king liked it cooked in stock, seasoned with nutmeg, and served with butter.

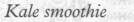

Kale smoothie

Remove the stem and shred 1 kale leaf (50 g) to yield ½ cup (35 g) firmly packed kale. Core and chop 1 green apple, slice 1 frozen banana, chop 3 dates, and grate a 1-cm (½-in) piece of peeled fresh ginger. Process in a blender with 1¼ cups (310 ml) coconut water. **Makes 2½ cups (625 ml)**

Gram for gram, kale has more than twice the vitamin C of an orange.

BELOW: The striking purple and white ornamental kales are popular as bedding plants. A spectacular addition to any garden design, especially a massed planting, they are not for eating.

ABOVE: Lacinato kale, or Tuscan kale, is a very popular variety for cooking. It is used traditionally in minestrone, a mixed vegetable soup of Italian origin.

Kale

Brassica oleracea Acephala Group
Also known as borecole

This easy-to-grow vegetable is often described by nutritionists and food lovers as a superfood due to the high levels of iron and antioxidants in the leaves. There are several varieties of this nonhearting cabbage, including some grown for purely ornamental purposes. The popular culinary types have ornamental as well as culinary appeal—the best-tasting leaves are harvested in winter. Kale can be eaten raw, straight from the plant, blended in a green smoothie, or lightly steamed, sautéed with garlic, or added to soups and stews.

Growing

Plant seedlings 60–75 cm (2–2½ ft) apart. They can grow to 1 m (3 ft) high and, due to their weight, can be damaged by strong winds. Hill the soil up at the stem base as the plant grows to help overcome this problem.

Harvesting A cut-and-come-again vegetable, kale can be harvested starting at eight weeks.

Varieties

Lacinato kale, often called Tuscan kale, is a chef's favorite, with elongated, crinkly, dark gray-green leaves. Red Russian has scalloped, wavy leaves, which are blue-gray with a purple hue and reddish stems. Curly kale has heavily curled and scalloped leaves that are thicker and tougher than the others but still cook beautifully.

Kohlrabi
Brassica oleracea Gongylodes Group
Also known as German turnip, turnip cabbage

This vegetable looks like it can't decide whether to grow under the ground or above it. Its name is German for "cabbage turnip," and its swollen base, which is actually the plant's stem, develops above the ground, making it ideal for gardens that don't have deep soils. Varieties with white, light green, or purple skins are available, and the foliage and base can both be eaten. The foliage is lightly steamed as a leaf vegetable. The base is peeled, and its white flesh, which has a sweet, nutty, turnip-like flavor, can be eaten raw, if picked young, or cooked.

Growing

Sow seeds thinly in rows and thin out to 25–30 cm (10–12 in) apart after germination. To grow a continuous supply, sow every four to five weeks.

Harvesting Kohlrabi is ready for harvest 8 to 10 weeks after sowing, before the swollen base is the size of a cricket ball. It is best to thin out some plants early to spread the harvest. If allowed to grow too big, kohlrabi becomes tough and woody. It stores well in the refrigerator for more than a week and can also be peeled and diced for freezing.

RIGHT: The striking purple and white bulbs of kohlrabi, or turnip cabbage. The flesh is white in all varieties.

ABOVE: Kohlrabi looks a little unusual, with its turnip-like base growing above ground and its cabbage-like foliage. It gives a relatively quick crop after 8 to 10 weeks.

How-to

Preparing kohlrabi

Kohlrabi is crunchy like a radish and tastes like a mild turnip or broccoli stems. Add it to a vegetable gratin or steam until just tender and drizzle with melted butter or olive oil, lemon juice, chopped fresh parsley, salt, and freshly ground black pepper.

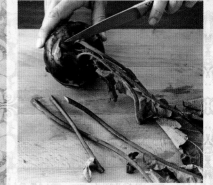

To prepare kohlrabi for cooking, cut off the leaf stems and trim the base and top.

Peel off the thick outermost layer thoroughly with a vegetable peeler or knife. Beneath the hard skin is another fibrous layer, which should also be peeled away. Peel until you reach the crisp flesh, then thinly slice or cut into pieces as directed in the recipe.

Carrots

Daucus carota subsp. *sativus*

The humble carrot is beloved by all. While usually thought of as a classic orange root vegetable, carrots have enjoyed a surge in popularity with the availability of heirloom varieties and other colors, including purple, yellow, and white. All can be enjoyed raw or cooked.

MAKING SOWING FINE SEEDS EASIER

Mix carrot seed with slightly damp sand in a jar. This mixture will be much easier to sow lightly into the prepared furrow, and the seedlings will need less thinning.

Carrots must be thinned twice to give the roots space to grow. Ideally, this should be done on cloudy days or in the evening, as the sun brings out the smell of the foliage, which attracts carrot flies.

DOCTOR CARROT guards your Health

During World War II, British children would very often eat the humble carrot as a substitute for the fruit that could no longer be obtained. The British government issued posters such as this one, as well as one with the slogan "Carrots keep you healthy and help you see in the blackout."

Growing

Carrots require well-drained, friable, deep soil that is light and easy for the root to push through. Soils that are heavy or rocky cause roots to twist and turn, while too much fresh manure or high-nitrogen fertilizer being dug in before planting will cause the roots to fork and be hairy. Avoid growing root crops in soil that is overly rich, because the plant will put its energy into above-ground leafy growth rather than into developing a good root.

If your vegetable patch doesn't have a good depth of light soil, grow baby or round-rooted carrots instead—they don't need the same deep soil. Alternatively, build up a section of the patch with a wooden frame, or even Styrofoam coolers with the bases removed, and fill this with good soil.

In the 1500s, during the reign of King Henry VIII of England, the feathery fronds of carrots were a fashionable hair accessory among ladies of the royal court.

Sow seed directly into shallow furrows in rows 30 cm (1 ft) apart and lightly cover with 1 cm (½ in) of light soil. Carrot seed needs light to germinate, so don't plant too deeply. Tamp down after sowing to ensure good germination. Carrots take two to three weeks to germinate, and the area must be kept moist until the seedlings emerge. You can cover it with a damp towel or burlap to retain moisture; check daily and remove as soon as the seedlings emerge. It is also important to keep the area free of weeds, which will compete with the young seedlings as they emerge. Once they start to germinate, thinning the seedlings is vital for the carrots to develop properly. Thin young carrot seedlings to 2.5 cm (1 in) apart when they are around 5 cm (2 in) high, and thin them out to 5 cm (2 in) apart when they are about 15 cm (6 in) high. The tender young carrots that you pull out with this second thinning are sweet-tasting baby carrots, too good to waste.

In mild areas you can sow carrots all year round, but in cool areas avoid growing them through winter. Carrots sown in late summer will mature in winter and taste sweeter due to the sugars that are stored in the roots.

Problems Soil-borne diseases and insect pests are reduced by crop rotation. Carrots grown without enough sun may attract aphids. Snails, slugs, and carrot flies can also be a problem.

Harvesting Pick carrots when the size suits you. Spread the harvest by pulling smaller carrots earlier and allowing the remainder to grow bigger. Most varieties take three to four months to reach full size. In cool climates carrots can be left in the ground, covered with straw mulch, until required.

Carrots qualify as a genuine superfood with potent medicinal uses and many health benefits.

Orange long-rooted carrots are most common, but the resurgence of heirloom vegetables means you can obtain seed for long-rooted carrots that are yellow, purple, and white as well as short-rooted and round-rooted orange carrots.

Varieties

Many varieties are worth growing. Baby carrots are quick to mature and great for kids. Round-rooted carrots are perfect for shallow soils or containers.

Buying and storing

Choose carrots that are firm, unblemished, and have a rich color. Store in a loosely sealed plastic bag in the crisper section of the refrigerator for up to one week.

Health benefits

When cooked and mashed, the soft pectin fiber in carrots makes them a soothing natural remedy for skin irritations and digestive upsets. Pectin has also been shown to help lower high cholesterol—one reason people who ate a quarter of a cup (39 grams) or more of carrots daily reduced their risk of cardiovascular disease by 26 percent in one study. Beta-carotene gives carrots their deep orange color, and may further protect your heart and arteries by disarming rogue oxygen molecules (called free radicals) that can damage cells. Carrot seed oil is used to moisturize the skin.

Recipe

Glazed carrots

Shiny and bright, glazed carrots bring a splash of color to the plate. Serve them sprinkled with a little fresh parsley for even more nutrients.

Peel 3 carrots and slice on a slight diagonal. Cook in a saucepan of boiling water over medium heat for 4–5 minutes, or until just tender. Drain, then return to the pan. Add 1 tablespoon butter and 1 tablespoon honey. Cook over low heat, tossing, for 2 minutes, or until well coated. Top with chopped fresh parsley or dill. **Serves 6**

Baby carrots taste sweetest raw. Simply rinse before eating. More mature carrots need to be peeled beforehand. For a snack, cut carrots into sticks or slices. Grate and add to salads and sandwiches, or use as an ingredient in cakes or muffins. To cook, lightly steam, roast, or stir-fry, or add to soups, stews, and casseroles.

Cassavas

Manihot esculenta

Also known as yuca, manioc, tapioca

Cassava is a tropical woody shrub, widely grown in South America, the West Indies, the Pacific Islands, and Africa, where its starchy tuberous roots are the third most important source of carbohydrates. The roots are also fermented to make liquor, while the leaves, which are high in protein—unusual for a leafy green—can also be cooked and used like spinach.

Growing

Cassava is hardy and easy to grow in frost-free areas and makes a good alternative to potatoes in tropical and subtropical climates, where potatoes don't grow. In autumn, propagate from woody cuttings of old, mature brown wood around 30 cm (1 ft) long. Lay cuttings horizontally on the soil surface and cover with a thin layer of soil, or half-bury them in the soil. Keep moist. By spring the plants that have shoots can be planted.

Harvesting   The plant grows to 1–3 m (3–10 ft) high and develops large lobed leaves at the ends of the branches, which are harvested and cooked as they reach maturity. Tubers are fully formed after 8 to 10 months and are harvested when the plant's leaves turn yellow and fall. Roots store well and are peeled and cooked like potatoes—boiled, fried, baked—or made into flour.

All parts of the cassava plant, a member of the Euphorbiaceae family, are poisonous and must be cooked before eating. Choose sweet root cultivars, as they have lower levels of toxins; boil roots for 20 minutes and cook leaves for 15 minutes.

Wood spirit root

In mythology cassava is portrayed as a savior that protects against starvation. According to one traditional story of the Tupi people of Brazil, long ago a woman was devastated as she watched her child starve to death. She buried the child's body under the floor of her hut. That night she was visited by a wood spirit, known as a *mani*, who changed the child's body into the roots of a plant, which subsequently became known as *mani oca*, meaning "wood spirit root." This plant became the chief staple food for generations of indigenous people of the Amazon and, in time, of inhabitants of the tropics throughout the world.

Buying and storing

Cassavas should have smooth, intact skin with no blemishes—if possible, avoid tubers with their ends trimmed off. Cassava is often sold coated in wax to stop it from drying out. Keep in the refrigerator or in a cool, dark, well-ventilated place for up to four days.

Health benefits

The starchy tubers of the cassava plant are a staple food for 500 million of the world's people, but before being eaten the tubers must be peeled, sliced, and boiled thoroughly. The cooking deactivates a substance called linamarin, which converts to deadly cyanide when ingested. Bitter-tasting varieties of cassava contain the most toxin. Traditional healers have long used cassava leaves and tubers to treat everything from fever to diarrhea to infertility. Cancer researchers are investigating linamarin's potential in targeted tumor-killing drugs.

A traditional remedy for headaches was a compress of pounded cassava leaves placed on top of the head.

Cassava is important in many Asian and Pacific Islands cuisines. It can be cooked in many ways. The soft-boiled root has a delicate flavor and can replace boiled potatoes in many situations: as an accompaniment for meat dishes or in purees, dumplings, soups, and stews. See our Cassava cake on page 303.

To prepare cassava roots for cooking, trim off the tapering ends, then cut into pieces and remove the thick skin with a sharp knife.

Celeriac

Apium graveolens var. *rapaceum*

Also known as turnip-rooted celery, celery root

This unusual plant develops a root that looks like a fattened, knobby turnip and has a nutty flavor reminiscent of parsnip and celery, with foliage like a shortened bunch of celery. The plant grows to 50 cm (20 in) high. The young foliage can be used as a celery substitute in cooking, while the root, its skin removed, can be grated and added raw to salads or sliced or diced for soups and stews. It has a flavor like celery, to which it is closely related, but a texture that is quite different.

Growing

Like all root vegetables, celeriac grows best in well-prepared, friable soil with good structure, depth, and drainage. Grow it in the cool weather to minimize its tendency to bolt to seed. Sow seeds directly into the ground in autumn, and the roots should be ready to harvest within four months. Thin seedlings to 20 cm (8 in) apart to allow the roots to develop properly. As with all root vegetables, make sure that the garden bed is weed-free before sowing to allow the proper development of the root and to prevent root disturbance from weeding while it is growing. Remove any side shoots as the plant grows.

Problems Snails and slugs can feast on the leafy above-ground growth, so check your plants regularly as they grow.

Harvesting The root can be harvested when it reaches 5–7.5 cm (2–3 in) across. It will keep in the refrigerator for a week. The flesh discolors once it has been cut or the skin has been removed; to prevent this, toss in lemon juice.

Buying and storing

Look for celeriac that is a good weight for its size and has no blemishes or soft spots. Store it unwrapped in the crisper section of the refrigerator for up to a week. It is best used all at once because it discolors once cut.

Health benefits

In ancient times, celeriac and its seeds were used in remedies for colds, flu, digestive complaints, and even water retention. Modern research suggests that this vegetable has real stomach-soothing properties. Extracts containing polysaccharides found in celeriac have been shown to keep the lining of the stomach healthy and may even reduce the risk of stomach cancer. Celeriac may also help with weight loss; a cup (155 grams) of cooked celeriac contains just 42 calories and 2 grams of stomach-filling fiber.

Celeriac is derived from wild celery, which has a small, edible root and has been used in Europe since ancient times.

The young foliage and the root of celeriac are used in cooking to add a sweet, celery-like flavor.

Recipe

Celeriac rémoulade

Celeriac has a subtle, celery-like flavor, with nutty overtones. It is the basis of the classic French dish *céleri rémoulade*—matchsticks of celeriac in a flavored mayonnaise.

Cut the skin off 1 celeriac (about 500 g/1 lb), then julienne, or cut into thin matchsticks. Toss in the juice of ½ lemon. In a medium bowl, combine 5 tablespoons mayonnaise, 2 tablespoons crème fraîche or sour cream, 1 tablespoon Dijon mustard, 2 tablespoons finely chopped fresh parsley, and 1 tablespoon finely chopped fresh mint, if desired. Season with salt and freshly ground black pepper, then fold into the celeriac. Thin the sauce with extra lemon juice if it is too thick. Set aside for 30 minutes for the flavors to develop. **Serves 4**

Use a sharp knife to top and tail the celeriac and remove the skin. Slice the root end off first to provide a steady base.

Celery

Apium graveolens var. *dulce*

Celery can be picked one crisp, crunchy stem at a time as required, or the whole bunch can be harvested. Excluding light from the celery stems, called blanching, reduces photosynthesis. This encourages the growth of crisper, longer, less stringy stems, which are also paler in color.

Celery seed is the dried fruit of *Apium graveolens*, which is related to, but not identical to, the vegetable celery. Celery seed's flavor is similar to that of fennel and anise.

Growing

This vegetable likes rich, well-drained soil with plenty of organic matter. While it can be grown from seed, it is slow to germinate. Even seedlings must be grown for more than two months before they reach planting size, but they are a better option.

Plant seedlings in spring in mild climates and late summer and autumn in hot climates. Seedlings should be spaced around 25 cm (10 in) apart. Celery doesn't like to dry out in summer, so be sure to water plants regularly. Nor does it like wind or extreme cold.

While celery can be grown without blanching, unblanched stems will be green and have a stronger flavor. If you want to have long, whitish-green stems, the bunch must be blanched three to four weeks before harvesting. Wrap newspaper or cardboard around each bunch to 40 cm (15 in) high and secure with string, or use empty milk cartons with the bottom cut out. Or plant self-blanching varieties in blocks so only the outside plants need shading.

Problems   Snails and slugs love the stems. Use liquid fertilizer to control pests; to control diseases, remove affected leaves. To avoid carrot flies, don't grow carrots and celery together.

Harvesting   Celery takes 17 weeks to develop to full size, though you can harvest individual stems earlier. If taking a few stems at a time, pick the outer stems first, twisting them near the base and leaving the young inner stems to keep growing.

Buying and storing

Buy whole or half bunches of celery with fresh-looking leaves (if still attached) and plump, firm stalks. To conserve space in the refrigerator, trim leaves from the top and the core from the bottom. Cut stalks to the desired length and store in a sealed plastic bag or an airtight container in the crisper section of the refrigerator for up to five days.

Health benefits

Celery has long been used in traditional Chinese medicine to treat high blood pressure. In the 1990s, researchers discovered that a compound in celery called 3-n-butylphthalide does, indeed, relax blood vessels and that it lowered the blood pressure of laboratory animals. Celery contains phytochemicals that help to reduce the production of certain prostaglandins, body chemicals that can cause inflammation. Celery seed and celery seed oil, meanwhile, are traditional remedies for rheumatism, gout, dizziness, and a poor appetite.

Both the stalks and the leaves of celery add flavor to cooked dishes and give a delightful crunch to salads.

Dice the tough outer stalks of a bunch of celery and use in soups, stews, or gratins. Use the more tender inner stalks raw in salads and juices. The leaves are flavorsome, too. Chop finely and add to soups and omelets, as you would fresh parsley.

Wild celery

Celery dates back to *selinon*, a wild plant mentioned in Homer's *Odyssey*. The ancient Greeks and Romans used it for the medicinal properties of its seeds, and it wasn't until the 16th century that celery began to be grown as a vegetable rather than a medicine.

Chayotes

Sechium edule

Also known as choko, chocho, christophene, vegetable pear

From the same family as cucumbers and melon, chayote is a highly productive, vigorous perennial vine that produces large, pale lime green to creamy white pear-shaped fruit. The skin is rough and sometimes prickly, and each fruit contains one long seed. Chayotes can be cooked as a vegetable or added to baked cakes and desserts. Young fruit can be eaten whole, while mature fruit must be peeled. The flavor is delicate and faintly nut-like. The plant's large, starchy roots taste like chestnuts, and new shoots, known as poor man's asparagus, are edible when 10 cm (4 in) long.

Growing

Chayotes are best grown in tropical or subtropical climates, where the vine is evergreen, and they crop all year round. When grown in cooler climates, they require six months without frosts and are deciduous. Plants need a sunny position sheltered from wind, with rich, fertile, moist soil and regular feeding. A sturdy frame is essential so the vine, which can grow up to 6 m (20 ft), is supported during fruiting. The vine will start full production after a year and can remain fully productive for five years. This is a hardy plant, attacked by few pests and diseases.

In autumn, choose a large fruit that is smooth rather than prickly and store it in light until spring. Plant it then, when the shoot is 5 cm (2 in) long, provided the ground has warmed up and the risk of frost has passed. Bury the lower two-thirds of the fruit on a 45-degree angle with the shoot end in the soil and the stem end above the soil surface.

Peel larger, older chayotes under running water, as they tend to have a sticky sap just under the skin.

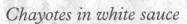

Chayotes grow on vigorous vines, which need a strong support or frame. Few plants are as productive.

Harvesting Harvest fruit when they are 5–7.5 cm (2–3 in) long. Fruit left to grow too large will become tough and lose flavor.

Buying and storing

Choose small chayotes with smooth, unblemished skin and no signs of sprouting. They can be kept unwrapped in the crisper section of the refrigerator for up to a week. They bruise easily, so take care not to put anything heavy on top of them.

Health benefits

Beverages made from the chayote plant are used as a traditional remedy for urinary problems, high blood pressure, and kidney problems on Mexico's Yucatán Peninsula and in the Philippines. On the Yucatán, chayote tea was used to ease urinary retention, burning during urination, and kidney stones. In the Philippines, chayote juice made by soaking the leaves and fruit overnight is used to treat high blood pressure. Does it work? Two small, unpublished studies suggest that chayote extract may help reduce high blood pressure slightly.

Recipe

Chayotes in white sauce

Chayote's rather bland flavor goes well with spicy ingredients and is ideal in Asian stir-fries. Chayotes can also be roasted, steamed, boiled, mashed or fried.

Peel, core, and quarter 4 chayotes. Cook in boiling salted water for 5–8 minutes, until tender. Drain. Meanwhile, melt 25 g (1 oz) butter in a small saucepan over medium heat. Add 1 tablespoon all-purpose flour. Cook for 1 minute, stirring constantly. Slowly pour in 1 cup (250 ml) whole milk, stirring continuously to combine. Cook, stirring, for 5 minutes, until the sauce thickens. Pour the sauce over the chayotes and sprinkle with freshly ground black pepper.
Serves 4 as a side dish

Grandma's chayote vine

The chayote vine's sprawling habit in warm climates made it an iconic feature of the Australian suburban backyard. It was often seen growing rampantly over fences, chicken houses, and outdoor toilets during the Great Depression, its harvest a frugal supplement in homemade apple pies.

Chicory, radicchio, and endive

Cichorium spp.

Chicory and radicchio (*Chicorium intybus*) and endive (*C. endivia*) are very closely related. Chicory has slender, serrated green leaves, sometimes with a reddish midrib and stem. The blanched young bud—the chicon—is called Belgian endive. Radicchio, also known as red chicory or red-leaf chicory, has broader reddish leaves; different varieties form either a hearted or loose-leaved head, like lettuce. There are two types of endive: those with plain leaves known as broad-leaved endive or escarole; and those with very frilly, serrated leaves that form a rosette, known as curly endive or frisée. All have a bitter taste, milder in young leaves, and are used in salads. Older leaves are better cooked as a side dish.

Growing

These vegetables prefer rich, well-drained soil and can be sown directly into the ground from spring to autumn. Thin the seedlings to 25–30 cm (10–12 in) apart after they germinate. The bitter taste of these vegetables gets stronger as the plants age or if they are stressed during growth, although this can be removed by blanching. To do this, cover the plant with a large plastic pot, a thick layer of straw, or a double layer of shade cloth three weeks before harvesting. If left to develop, the plants have tall flower spikes up to 1–2 m (3–6 ft) high with sky-blue, edible, daisy-like flowers.

Problems   These bitter-leaved plants are not troubled by insect pests or diseases.

Harvesting   Harvest individual leaves as needed or cut the whole head, leaving a small piece of stem above the roots so the plant can reshoot.

Buying and storing

All these leafy vegetables should look fresh and bright, with no discoloration, blemishes, or wilting. Keep in a sealed plastic bag in the crisper section of the refrigerator for up to three days. Keep Belgian endive in a brown paper bag for no more than two days.

Health benefits

Chicory's roots and leaves have a long reputation as traditional remedies for stimulating the appetite, treating upset stomachs and constipation, and even for addressing liver and gallbladder problems. The

The bitterness of these leaves makes them a perfect accompaniment for rich meat dishes. See our Bitter leaf salad **on page 228.**

Bitter salad greens (clockwise from left): chicory, curly endive (or frisée), broad-leaved endive (or escarole), a loose-leaved radicchio, Castelfranco radicchio, and (center) Treviso radicchio.

bitter taste comes from sesquiterpenes, shown by research to stimulate the secretion of fat-digesting bile acids from the gallbladder. No wonder chicory is often used in digestive bitter tonics. Endive and radicchio have these bitter compounds, too. They are good sources of inulin, an indigestible carbohydrate that feeds "good bacteria" in the digestive tract.

What's in a name?

Radicchio is also known as red or red-leaf chicory. The most famous variety is from Treviso and is called radicchio di Treviso, or simply Treviso. The Belgian word *witlof*, or *witloof* (literally, "white leaf"), is widely used for the blanched chicons of chicory. Although chicory leaves are popularly called endive in some places, true endive (broad-leaved or curly) is not Belgian endive, which is *witlof*.

Belgian endive is the white or pale pink conical chicon, or young bud, formed when a chicory plant's root is trimmed of its top then forced and blanched, or grown in the dark. The delicate flavor of Belgian endive has little of chicory's usual bitterness.

Corn is wind-pollinated. To ensure good pollination, it should be planted in a block of at least four to eight rows rather than in a single row.

See our recipe for Sweet corn chowder with cornbread on page 211.

Corn
Zea mays

The flavor of home-grown corn bears little resemblance to that of corn available commercially or in cans. Enjoy it cooked by itself, in stir-fries and soups, roasted in the oven, or grilled on the barbecue. Some varieties are so sweet they can be enjoyed raw when freshly picked.

Growing

Corn needs an open, sunny position with rich, fertile soil that has been well prepared with organic matter in the form of compost and aged animal manures. This tall, bulky vegetable is worth growing if you have the space. However, it is a heavy feeder and needs regular feeding with organic fertilizer. It also requires a lot of water to grow quickly and fruit well, and mulching is essential.

Corn can be grown all year round in the tropics and subtropics, where there is no frost, and sown in spring and summer in cooler climates. To ensure an extended season it is best to make successive plantings every three to four weeks.

Sow seeds directly into the soil once the risk of frost is over and the soil temperature is at least 10°C (50°F). Sow three seeds together, 5 cm (2 in) deep and 30 cm (12 in) apart, in a block of at least 20 plants to ensure good pollination. Once the seeds germinate and the seedlings have reached 20 cm (8 in) high, carefully remove the two smaller, weaker seedlings, leaving the strongest to grow to maturity. Once the plant reaches its full height of 1.5–2 m (5–6 ft) high, it will flower, with the tassel on the top (male flower) shedding its pollen over the silk (female flowers) below. Pollination can be aided by gently shaking the tassel on a calm morning.

Problems   Poor cob development resulting in many unswollen kernels is a sign of poor pollination; it can be avoided by sowing corn seed in blocks and assisting the pollen transfer from male to female

Amazing corn

In 16th-century England the word "corn" was used for any cereal crop. So when William Shakespeare wrote of "a green cornfield" and of "corn ready to reap," he was referring to oats or wheat. When the first English settlers in North America saw the plant the Native Americans used widely and called *mais*, they naturally gave it their own catchall term for a staple crop—"corn." Corn can be harvested and used at several stages during its ripening process, which greatly increases its value as a food crop for both humans and livestock. Shown here is Vincent van Gogh's 1888 painting "Corn harvest in Provence."

Barbecued corn, Mexican style

Preheat the barbecue or grill pan to medium. Remove husks from 4 corncobs and cut in half. Brush each corncob with olive oil (about 1 tablespoon in total). Cook on the barbecue, turning frequently, for 10 minutes, until tender.

In a medium bowl, combine 50 g (1³/₄ oz) cream cheese, ½ cup (125 g) mayonnaise, 1 teaspoon hot chili powder, and 2 teaspoons smoked paprika and season with salt and freshly ground black pepper. Dip each cob in the mayonnaise mixture and coat well. Put the corncobs on a serving platter and sprinkle with 2 tablespoons Parmesan cheese and sea salt.
Serves 4–6

There are numerous corn varieties available for home gardeners, including these classic yellow and white cobs.

flowers. Earworm can damage the cobs, but beneficial insects will help to keep their numbers down.

Harvesting   Corncobs, or ears, are harvested 11 to 14 weeks after sowing. They are ready to harvest when the silks on the end of a cob start to turn brown and the cob feels firm and plump. To check that it is ready, peel back the end of the husk and prick a kernel. If it exudes a milky liquid it is ready for harvest, while a watery liquid indicates the cob is not ready. No liquid indicates that the cob is overly mature, tough, and inedible. Harvest cobs by twisting them downward.

For the best flavor and freshness, eat corn immediately or within a few hours of picking, before the sugars start to turn to starch. Any excess harvest can be blanched on the cob, in slices, or as individual kernels and then frozen.

Varieties

❋ **Baby corn** Harvested when cobs are immature and used in Asian cooking. It can produce up to six cobs per plant; if left to mature on the plant, cobs can be harvested and dried for use as popping corn.

❋ **Bicolor** Mixture of yellow and white kernels on a single cob creates a speckled effect.

❋ **Golden Bantam** An heirloom favorite, with rich yellow kernels.

❋ **White varieties** Creamy white, sweet kernels.

Buying and storing

Corn is best purchased still in its husk—nature's packaging. Check to make sure the husk and silk protruding at the top of the cob look fresh and moist, not dry. Cobs should be plump and heavy. Store, unwrapped, in the crisper section of the refrigerator for up to two days.

Health benefits

The yellow corn silk at the top of an unshucked corncob makes a mild, light tea that promotes urination. This diuretic action explains corn silk's age-old use for urinary problems; it is also a traditional remedy for everything from malaria and obesity to bleeding during childbirth. Corn itself is a rich source of thiamine. One cup (164 grams) provides about a quarter of an adult's daily requirement of this B vitamin, which helps convert carbohydrates from food into energy. Getting enough thiamine may help reduce the risk of cataracts and could help shield the immune system from the effects of stress.

Cucumbers

Cucumis sativus

This refreshing salad staple will fruit easily and abundantly in summer and autumn. While the fruit varies in size and shape, all cucumbers are crisp, juicy, and taste great when grown well.

Growing

Plant seed directly into the soil in spring. In cool climates, raise seedlings under protection and plant when the ground has warmed and the risk of frost is over. Choose a well-drained, warm, protected spot with rich, fertile soil that is high in organic matter. Plant in full sun in cool climates or with some shade in hot, dry climates. Space plants 1 m (3 ft) apart; they should start fruiting within two to three months. A second planting in midsummer will keep you in cucumbers into autumn.

Some varieties are better as ground covers while others are ideal climbers. Elevating the vines over a trellis decreases humidity around the foliage, which reduces fungal problems as well as blemishes and insect damage. These plants have high water needs, so mulch well and don't let them dry out. Excessive heat or cold can also cause poor fruit formation.

Problems Minimize mildew problems by providing good air circulation for the vines. Mites can attack in hot, dry climates; reduce the risk of this by hosing underneath the foliage.

Harvesting Pick fruit regularly to encourage continued flowering and cropping for up to two months. Harvest with scissors or pruning shears, as pulling the fruit off can damage the vine.

Varieties

The fruit ranges in color from dark green to creamy white, golden, and brown and in length from 10 cm to 1 m (4 in to 3 ft). There are rounded, full fruit and ribbed and pleated fruit, with either smooth or prickly, rough skin.

✳ **Apple type** Lime green, cream, or white skin; rounded; pick when 10 cm (4 in) across.

✳ **Common green type** Harvest when 15–20 cm (6–8 in) long.

✳ **Lebanese** A small, slender cucumber with thin skin; pick when 10 cm (4 in) long.

✳ **Pickling varieties** The young fruit of any variety can be harvested for pickling; some varieties are grown for their small fruit.

Buying and storing

Look for plump cucumbers with no soft spots or wrinkling, especially at the stem end. Keep loosely wrapped in the crisper section of the refrigerator for up to three days. Once cut, cover in plastic wrap and keep in the refrigerator for up to two days.

Recipe

Summer refresher

Cucumber is 96 percent water, so this will help keep you hydrated.

Peel and seed 1 cucumber, reserving some ribbons for a garnish. Put the cucumber, 1 tablespoon honey, juice of 1 lime, ¼ cup (10 g) torn fresh mint leaves, and 1 teaspoon grated ginger in a food processor or blender. Process until smooth. Pour over ice and garnish with cucumber ribbons. **Makes 3 cups**

Health benefits

Putting slices of cucumber over your eyes may help reduce under-eye puffiness and relieve tension headaches. Like a cool, wet cloth, the cold cucumber slices shrink blood vessels slightly, reducing blood flow in the area and easing pressure and puffiness.

Adding cucumbers to your salad may have important health benefits. They contain polyphenols called lignans, which may help to reduce the risk of heart and blood vessel disease. Cucumbers also contain cucurbitacins. Laboratory studies suggest that these compounds may block the transmission of signals inside cancer cells, discouraging the growth of tumors.

Cucumbers come in all shapes and sizes, including (clockwise from top left) the Lebanese cucumber, telegraph cucumber, common green cucumber, pickling cucumbers and white apple cucumber.

Dandelion and other wild foods

There are many wild foods, made popular again by the food-foraging trend, that can be harvested as vegetables. Look for these along roadsides, in vacant lots—and in your own backyard. If you are new to foraging, take precautions to make sure plants are properly identified. Correct identification is essential before eating foraged foods, as many look similar to plants that are poisonous—you don't want to get them confused. Though wild foods are thought of as foods you forage for in the woods, you can also grow your own. Here are some of the best known.

Dandelion

Taraxacum officinale

Dandelions are known for their bitter leaves, which can be eaten raw when young and tender or cooked as they age to reduce their bitterness. Their uses are similar to those of chicory and endive. Raw leaves in a salad will be less bitter if they are picked before the flower stalk develops—you can add the flowers to salads, too. The long taproot is used in cooking and is roasted to make a caffeine-free coffee substitute. See page 161.

Fiddleheads

Pteretis pensylvanica

The fiddleheads of the ostrich fern appear for only a few days in spring and are an absolute delicacy, with a subtle flavor of asparagus, broccoli, and spinach. Be sure to get them identified, as the fiddleheads of some ferns are poisonous. Use in sautés, stir-fries, pasta sauces, and quiches. Rinse thoroughly before cooking, remove the brown papery coverings, and rinse again.

Garlic mustard

Alliaria petiolata

Also known as garlic root, Jack-by-the-hedge, poor man's mustard

On of the oldest spices to be used in European cooking but much maligned as a weed in the U.S., this biennial flowering plant can grow up to 1 m (3 ft) in its second year. Triangular leaves are slightly bitter and can be added to a salad or sauteed like spinach and other greens—but don't overcook or they will get mushy. The small white flowers are also edible, and the slender taproot can be used like horseradish.

Goutweed

Aegopodium podagraria

Also known as bishop's weed, ground elder, herb gerard, snow-in-the-mountain

Often found as a potted herb in Europe, goutweed is considered an invasive weed in the U.S. The serrated leaves, whose taste resembles that of parsley or celery, can be used dried or fresh and make a good addition to salads and soups.

Lamb's quarters

Chenopodium album

Also known as goosefoot, pigweed

This plant branches like a tree and often it appears dusty due to the white coating on the underside of its diamond-shaped leaves. Lamb's quarters are a European relative to spinach and are an excellent source of calcium, iron, and potassium. In early spring the whole plant can be eaten, but use just the leaves in spring and fall.

Nettles

Urtica spp.

There is an annual and a perennial form of this notorious plant, both oh which have fine hairs on the leaves that cause stinging. Cooking destroys the stinging hairs, and nettles make a nutritious soup and tincture (see page 160). Always harvest and handle nettles with gloves to avoid irritation.

CLOCKWISE FROM TOP LEFT: Dandelions, fiddleheads, garlic mustard, nettles, lamb's quarters, and goutweed.

Purslane

Portulaca oleracea

Also known as pigweed, little hogweed, moss rose

This annual succulent can withstand drought and poor soil conditions. Considered a weed in the U.S., purslane is widely used in East Mediterranean countries. It contains more omega-3 fatty acids than any other leafy vegetable, and it is also a good source of calcium, potassium, and vitamin A.

Rampion

Campanula rapunculus

This biennial plant produces a parsnip-like taproot, which is harvested in winter and can be eaten raw or roasted with other root vegetables. Its new shoots and young leaves can also be picked for salads.

Ramps

Allium tricoccum

Also known as wild garlic, wild leek, wood leek

Ramps can usually be found in deciduous forests throught the eastern U.S. and Canada. Both the leaves and the bulb of this member of the onion family can be used. This ephemeral harbinger of spring is much celebrated in Appalachia, where festivals abound from March to May, and where ramps are often fried with potatoes or scrambled with eggs and served with bacon, pinto beans, and cornbread. They can be used in place of onions, garlic, or shallots and are also a good candidate for pickling.

Salsify

Tragopogon porrifolius

Also known as vegetable oyster

This biennial plant has a long, slender, pale brown or white taproot similar to a parsnip, which is cooked, steamed, or baked as a root vegetable. In Australia Mammoth Sandwich Island is a popular cultivar, grown in temperate regions in the same way as carrots and parsnips. The root grows to 23 cm (9 in) long and 6 cm (2½ in) wide. The foliage can be blanched to reduce its bitterness and eaten as a leafy vegetable. Before cooking, scrub the root under cold running water, peel with a sharp knife, and

CLOCKWISE FROM TOP LEFT: Purslane, rampion, ramps, wood sorrel, scorzonera, and salsify.

place in water with a little lemon juice. Slice and sauté in butter as a side dish.

Scorzonera

Scorzonera hispanica

Also known as black salsify, black oyster plant

This perennial plant has a long, thin, parsnip-like root with purple-black skin and white flesh and a unique earthy flavor. It produces attractive purple daisy-like flowers, which are also edible. The skin is inedible, however. Boil the roots for about 20 minutes, then remove the skin to reveal the white inner core. Cook the peeled root with other root vegetables.

Wood sorrel

Oxalis stricta

Sour trefoil, stickwort, wood sour

Often confused with clover, wood sorrel can be identified by its heart-shaped leaves (versus clover's oval leaves). It can be found from spring to fall in lawns and along roadsides. Its lemony leaves go well with fish and steamed vegetables. Although unrelated to the sorrel you might see sold as an herb, the culinary uses are the same.

Health benefits

Wild plants have a long history of use as medicine, and a growing body of research documents their potential to improve health. Stinging nettles, for example, are an age-old remedy for muscle and joint pain, eczema, and anemia. Research now suggests that herbal formulas containing nettles can reduce hay fever symptoms and ease urinary problems related to benign prostatic hyperplasia. Dandelion has strong diuretic powers, and herbal formulas of the leaf are used for water retention and kidney disorders. Both the leaves and roots are thought to act on the liver and gallbladder and to stimulate bile to help cleanse the body of toxins.

The health benefits of other wild foods are only just starting to be explored.

Eggplants

Solanum melongena

Also known as aubergine, brinjal

These warm-season fruits, a staple of Mediterranean, Middle Eastern, Asian, and Indian cuisine, are thought to have originated in Asia. While those with shiny purple-black skin and white flesh are best known, there are white, red, orange, yellow, green, and bicolored eggplants, too. Shapes range from classic oval to round or cylindrical, and size varies, too. Eggplant can be fried, stuffed, roasted, grilled, marinated, or used in dips, curries, and braised dishes.

The classic eggplant shape is an elongated oval, seen here in shiny purple-black and striped purple and white. The finger eggplants are purple-black and a lighter rosy lavender.

Growing

Eggplants need a long, hot growing season of at least five months and can be perennial in frost-free areas, cropping for several seasons. They like fertile, well-drained soil. They can be grown from seed sown directly in the ground in spring, but because they take a long time to fruit, speed up the process by growing them on seedling trays eight weeks before planting time, then plant the seedlings when the ground warms up. Seeds may take two to three weeks to germinate. Space seedlings 45–60 cm (1½–2 ft) apart, taking care when transplanting, as they resent root disturbance. After transplanting, the plants take three to four months to fruit, but your patience will be rewarded with fruit for several months. Eggplants grow as compact self-supporting shrubs 40–90 cm (1⅓–3 ft) high; heavy-cropping tall varieties may need staking for support.

Problems   Aphids, caterpillars, fruit flies and two-spotted mites are the main pests. Eggplants belong to the Solanaceae family, as do tomatoes and peppers; all are prone to the soil-borne disease verticillium wilt. To reduce its spread, don't plant any of this family in the same site more than once every four years. Remove and destroy affected plants immediately.

Harvesting   Harvest when the skin is firm and smooth—fruit left on the plant for too long will start to wrinkle and taste bitter, tough, and coarse. Take care when harvesting, as the top of the fruit is quite prickly, and pick the fruit with pruning shears to avoid damaging the plant. Large-fruiting varieties will produce six to eight fruits per plant.

Eggplants can be grilled, roasted, or fried—cook them through completely, until soft. If stir-frying, ensure the oil is very hot, don't crowd the pan or wok, and turn the eggplant often to avoid burning.

See our recipe for Stir-fried pork with Thai eggplant on page 279 and Escalivada on page 240.

By any other name

The eggplant is believed to have originated in the Indian subcontinent, from which it spread along trade routes to western Asia. It gets its common name from varieties introduced to England in the 18th century, which were similar in shape and color to a hen's egg. In the western Mediterranean, the Arabic name, *al-badinjan*, evolved into the Portuguese *beringela*. This name, when taken southeast by Portuguese colonists, became *brinjal*, the name now used throughout southern Asia, and the Catalan *alberginia*, which was adopted into French as *aubergine*.

Varieties

The classic large, oval, pear- or teardrop-shaped fruit are European or Italian types. They grow 15–25 cm (6–10 in) long, and there are many varieties with purple-black, soft lavender, or pale green skin. Black Beauty is a popular and reliable variety with fruit 15–25 cm (6–10 in) long, while Listada di Gandia produces striking fruit striped purple and white.

The 10–20 cm (4–8 in) long, finger-like fruit are Asian or Lebanese varieties; fruit is borne in clusters of three to six and is ready for harvest at least a month before the larger oval fruits. Each plant can produce 40 to 50 fruit. In addition to the many different purplish black varieties, Thai Green produces slender, light green fruit up to 30 cm (1 ft) long.

Many varieties have elongated cylindrical fruit with skin of dark purple, ivory white, or light purple with white striping. Casper is a French variety with white-skinned, elongated fruit to 15 cm (6 in).

Thai Round Green is a popular variety in Asian cooking; its small, round fruit, striped in light green and white, grow up to 5 cm (2 in) across.

Buying and storing

Eggplant should be plump with smooth skin and have a good weight for its size. Choose moderately sized eggplants (for the type), as larger ones may be older and seedy inside. Keep unwrapped in the crisper section of the refrigerator for up to three days. Smaller eggplants can be stored in a loosely sealed plastic bag to keep them together.

Health benefits

For many centuries, the bitter taste of early eggplant varieties relegated this vegetable to ornamental status in European gardens. Eating it was discouraged because eggplant was said to cause leprosy, cancer, and insanity. Today, research provides health-promoting reasons to put eggplant on your plate. It contains phenols that, laboratory studies suggest, may play a role in maintaining good blood glucose and blood pressure levels. A flavonoid in eggplant called nasunin may help to keep cholesterol levels low.

How-to

To salt or not to salt

Salting an eggplant before cooking removes bitterness, but it is only necessary for some large varieties. Many varieties grown today do not need this precooking treatment.

Slice the eggplant, lightly salt slices, and leave for 15–30 minutes. Thoroughly rinse and dry the slices before frying or baking in olive oil. This reduces the amount of oil absorbed during cooking. Eggplant used in curries and braised dishes does not require salting, as it absorbs the flavors of the dish.

ABOVE: The shrubby eggplant bush, with its pretty flowers and shiny, richly colored fruit, makes a good-looking and versatile plant in the vegetable garden.

LEFT: Thai eggplants come in many shapes, colors and sizes. They include (from left) small green round eggplants about the size of a golf ball, which are sometimes called apple eggplants, and green pea eggplants, which are the size of a pea.

Fennel

Foeniculum vulgare subsp. *vulgare* var. *azoricum*

Also known as finocchio

This unusual vegetable is related to the herb fennel (*F. vulgare* subsp. *vulgare*). It forms a swollen, edible bulb of white leaf bases, unlike the herb and the weedy cousin, roadside or wild fennel (*F. vulgare* subsp. *vulgare* var. *vulgare*). The flesh is crisp and white with an aniseed flavor, which is stronger when eaten raw in salads and subtle when baked, braised, or fried. The feathery foliage, which grows 40–50 cm (16–20 in) high, is also edible; it looks pretty in the garden and will attract beneficial insects if allowed to bolt into flower.

Before cooking or using fennel raw in salads, remove the tough outer layer from the bulb.

All parts of the plant are said to aid digestion and prevent flatulence. Cooking fennel with either cabbage or Jerusalem artichokes is said to neutralize the gassy side effects of those vegetables.

The swollen base of fennel has a distinct aniseed flavor. The soft ferny foliage can also be used in the kitchen to add subtle aniseed flavor.

Growing

Grow in a sunny or semishaded position in friable soil enriched with plenty of organic matter to allow for proper development of the swollen base. Fennel is killed by frost, so in temperate climates plant in spring and autumn to harvest in 12 weeks. In tropical climates it is best grown during the dry season. Sow seed directly into the soil and thin when 5 cm (2 in) tall to 20–25 cm (8–10 in) apart.

Problems   Watch out for snails and slugs, which love the fleshy base.

Harvesting   Harvest two to three months after sowing, when bulbs are small—their flavor will be milder and sweeter than that of large bulbs. Cut just below the swollen base with a sharp knife or carefully pull the whole plant up and trim off the foliage.

Buying and storing

If the bulb has fronds, they should be bright green and not wilted. The bulb itself should be smooth, plump, and white, with no browning at the edge of the layers. Keep in a loosely sealed plastic bag in the crisper section of your refrigerator for four days.

Health benefits

The stalks and bulb of fennel are a good source of heart-healthy fiber and folate as well as blood pressure–lowering potassium. The seeds of this vegetable may also have benefits, but gardeners usually remove the flowers before seeds form to encourage the growth of thicker bulbs. As for the seeds of the herb fennel, they have been used for thousands of years. Research has shown that they have a mild hormonal action and a soothing ability to relax the smooth muscles of the respiratory system, stomach, and intestines. No wonder fennel seed—as a tea, extract, or even just crunched after a meal—is still a widely used traditional remedy for indigestion, digestive system cramps, and bloating in adults. Nursing mothers in many cultures have sipped fennel-seed tea to boost the production of breast milk—and to calm colicky babies. And fennel extract may have antiaging benefits for skin care.

It is not uncommon to come upon peasants carrying their bunch of fennel under the arm and, with some bread, making their lunch or dinner of it.

ALEXANDRE DUMAS,
DICTIONARY OF CUISINE, 1873

Fennel essential oil

Fennel has been used since medieval times to ward off evil spirits, while the ancient Chinese, Egyptians, and Romans believed it conveyed longevity, courage, and strength. Sweet fennel essential oil is distilled from the dried seeds of sweet fennel (*F. vulgare* subsp. *vulgare* var. *dulce*) and is used as a digestive aid. However, it is to be avoided during pregnancy.

Horseradish

Armoracia rusticana

This perennial root vegetable is popular as a garnish for meats and smoked fish and has many health-promoting qualities. Its foliage resembles that of spinach, growing to 60 cm (2 ft) high, and it forms a long, deep, white taproot.

Growing

Horseradish prefers well-drained, fertile, friable soil. It grows readily in the garden and has a tendency to take over, so grow it in a contained area or a large tub. Plant root cuttings 15–20 cm (6–8 in) in length in late winter or early spring, or plant a container-grown specimen at any time of the year.

Harvesting Harvest roots as needed, when 5 cm (2 in) thick, or dig up the whole patch when the foliage dies down in autumn. Any piece of root remaining will reshoot. The roots are peeled, grated, and used fresh. To preserve, either freeze the grated flesh in ice cube trays, then store in a resealable plastic bag, or make it into a condiment or sauce with vinegar, salt, and sugar. The root can also be dried.

Buying and storing

Choose firm pieces that have no withered areas or soft spots. Keep in a loosely sealed plastic bag in the crisper section of the refrigerator for up to two weeks. Once cut, it will keep for up to four days in the refrigerator, wrapped tightly in plastic wrap.

Health benefits

Pungent horseradish turns up in many old-time folk remedies, purported to help treat everything from urinary tract infections and kidney stones to bronchitis, gout, and joint pain. Eating a small spoonful boosts mucus production in your nose

LEFT: The horseradish root is harvested for culinary and medicinal purposes.

ABOVE: It is the thick stem at the base of the wasabi plant that is grated to make the classic Japanese paste.

Don't feed to horses

The "horse" in "horseradish" has nothing to do with the animal (its leaves are in fact toxic to horses), but is instead an old use of a word meaning "coarse, rough, or large for its kind." The pungent root acquired this name during the 1600s, when the habit of using it as a condiment reached England from Germany.

and sinuses, which may help clear out infection-causing viruses and bacteria. But there's another health reason to smother a roast beef sandwich with this spicy root. Being a member of the Brassica family, it contains compounds called glucosinolates, which may help remove carcinogens from your body before genetic damage can occur.

Recipe

Horseradish sauce and cream

Horseradish sauce Scrub, peel, and dice 1 horseradish root. Put in a food processor or blender with 1 teaspoon superfine sugar, ¼ teaspoon kosher salt, and ½ cup (125 ml) white vinegar and puree. Slowly pour in up to an additional ¼ cup (60 ml) white vinegar while processing until the mixture has the desired consistency. Transfer to a sterilized glass jar with a screw-on lid and store in the refrigerator for four weeks.
Makes 1 cup

Horseradish cream Put 6 tablespoons crème fraîche or sour cream, 1 teaspoon Dijon mustard, 1 tablespoon chopped fresh chives, and 3 tablespoons grated fresh horseradish in a bowl and stir to combine well. Keep in the refrigerator until ready to serve.
Makes ½ cup

Wasabi

Wasabia japonica
Also known as Japanese horseradish

This cool-climate perennial is renowned for the hot mustard- and horseradish-like flavor of its finely grated squat basal stems, or rhizomes. The leaves and flowers can be eaten as a salad green.

Growing

This plant's natural habitat is the valley floor of the forests of Japan, so grow it in shade, in a moist, well-composted soil, and keep it cool and moist over summer. It is not easy to cultivate.

Harvesting Start to harvest stems of wasabi as required after the plant is one year old. Young leaves can be harvested and enjoyed as a salad green.

Wasabi paste is made from the grated base stems of the wasabi plant and has a strong, hot, mustardy taste. The green paste is used as a condiment in sashimi, sushi, and many other Japanese dishes.

Lettuces and salad greens

A variety of lettuces and salad leaves can make a big difference in the taste and visual appeal of summer food, and they are among the easiest crops to grow. Colors range from pale green to dark and lime green, red, burgundy, and almost black. Then there is the plethora of shapes, textures and flavors. Even a tiny garden of containers can supply you with the fresh makings of a salad.

Lettuces
Lactuca sativa

The diversity is amazing, from traditional head lettuces to cut-and-come-again types. Use lettuce as a filler crop to make the most of your garden space.

Growing

Lettuce does best in enriched, fertile soil that is well drained but remains moist. It grows well in full sun but can also tolerate some shade in hot weather. Plants that are hungry or allowed to dry out will become bitter and bolt to seed, so be sure to water regularly, mulch well, and fertilize often.

Lettuce grows readily from seed; sow a few seeds in clumps 20–30 cm (8–12 in) apart on well-worked soil. Or plant seedlings to save around four weeks of growing time. When the seedlings are around 4 cm (1½ in) high, thin all but the strongest seedling. Leaf lettuces self-seed readily, but for a constant supply, sow every four weeks.

Problems   Snails, slugs, and earwigs relish fresh lettuce. Bitterness is caused by stress, so check watering, feeding, and poor soil conditions.

Harvesting   Cut head lettuces with a knife just above ground level, or pull up the whole plant and cut off the root. Pick leaves from leaf varieties as you need them, taking a few outer leaves at a time. In hot climates harvest in the morning, when leaves have a higher sugar content.

Varieties

Choose varieties most suitable to your climate and the growing season. Here are the three main types.

Crisphead and butterhead lettuces
These lettuces form a tight, solid head of foliage, which is harvested when the head reaches maturity at 8 to 10 weeks, before it elongates as it starts to flower. Once the head is cut off, the plant will not regrow. Varieties of crisphead lettuce include iceberg, red iceberg, and Great Lakes. Smaller lettuces that form soft, loose heads are called butterhead varieties; these include Boston and Bibb lettuces such as Buttercrunch and Mignonette. They can be harvested as a whole head, or the outer leaves can be picked as required.

Leaf lettuces   These repeat-harvest salad staples are sometimes called salad bowl lettuces. While some form a rosette, none has the dense head of butterhead and crisphead lettuces. They are a must for all vegetable growers, as you can harvest what you need when you need it. They take four to six weeks to mature, so you can harvest the whole head when fully grown and before it starts to send up its flower spike and set seed. Or take a few larger outer leaves from plants once they have five or six leaves and are growing well.

Common varieties include the green and brown oak leaf types; speckled forms such as Speckles and Spotted Trout; and the golden-leaved variety Australian Yellow.

Romaine lettuces   Grown well, these elongated lettuces with thick central midribs are sweet. You can harvest individual leaves as required, or wait for the whole head to be ready in 8 to 10 weeks. If you harvest the whole head, it will produce a second head, which is often bitter. These lettuces' upright nature allows for closer planting. Romaine, also known as cos, is the traditional lettuce used in Caesar salads. The dwarf compact Little Gem is a popular variety.

Iceberg is one of the most commonly available types of lettuce.

Lettuce is not only for salads. It can be cooked, too. Try it barbecued or sautéed, stirred into a soup, or added to a risotto.

Grow leaf lettuce in between slow-growing crops such as cabbages and cauliflowers. Planted at the same time, lettuce will be ready to harvest in eight weeks; the slower vegetables can then take that space to grow to maturity.

The forms and colors of lettuces make them a very attractive inclusion in the vegetable garden. Pictured here in the basket (clockwise from top left): Mignonette, green oak leaf, red oak leaf, green coral, red coral, butter lettuce, and baby romaine; and loose on the table (from top): romaine, baby frizzle, and red baby romaine.

The ancient Greeks believed that lettuce aided sleep and served it at the end of the evening meal.

Thirst quencher

Lettuce contains more than 90 percent water, and it is said that eating a whole lettuce quenches thirst better than water. It has long been a prized edible plant in the desert climates of western Asia, where, during the 7th century BCE, it was said to grow on the terraces of the Hanging Gardens of Babylon. According to the ancient Greek historian Herodotus, lettuce was served on the tables of the Persian kings around 550 BCE.

For an ornamental feature in the courtyard or on the balcony, grow mesclun in a pot. The idea is to create a leafy mixture that has a contrast of flavors, textures, and colors.

Salad mixes are perfect for small spaces. They thrive in containers, in a courtyard, or on a balcony. Choose varieties that will give a mix of bitter, sweet, and tangy flavors.

Mesclun

Mesclun is the name given to a mixture of salad leaves, including lettuces, that are grown, harvested, and eaten together. Many seed and seedling companies produce their own mesclun, consisting of various leafy vegetables that can be harvested when young, washed, and tossed in a salad with a good dressing. Treat them as cut-and-come-again varieties and harvest repeatedly.

The leaves in a mesclun mix will vary depending on the grower and can include the young or baby leaves of fine-leaved mustard greens such as Ruby Streaks, Flame Tree, and Lime Streaks; mizuna, mibuna, red Russian kale, chard, frisée, radicchio, beet greens, arugula, tatsoi, mâche, and miner's lettuce as well as some red and green leaf lettuces. Care and growing conditions are the same as for lettuce, but the leaves can be harvested at four weeks.

The nutty, peppery taste of arugula works well in salads or as a garnish. It is pictured here with the finer-leaved wild arugula (in the colander).

Arugula
Eruca sativa
Also known as rocket

The nutty, peppery taste of arugula is cherished in a mix of salad greens, as a last-minute addition to pastas, pizzas, and other cooked dishes, or simply by itself with a dressing of balsamic vinegar and a few Parmesan shavings. This quick-growing, repeat-harvest salad plant is ready to pick within three weeks; you can start taking a few leaves at a time when seedlings are around 15 cm (6 in) high. It is best to harvest arugula regularly when tender and young, as the flavor gets more pungent and bitter with age. Also, once you've planted arugula, it's likely to self-seed in your vegetable patch forever.

There are several varieties available—some with large-lobed leaves and some with smaller, more dissected leaves. Growing conditions are the same as for lettuce, although arugula is more tolerant of poor soils and dry conditions.

The creamy lemon flowers are also edible, combining a sweet flavor with a slightly peppery undertone. Or you can simply cut off any spikes of flowers to keep your plant producing more leaves.

Recipe

San choy bau

This is a classic Chinese starter that is perfect if you are preparing an Asian-themed meal. It's a great one to choose if you are feeding children—they love an excuse to eat with their hands.

Heat 1½ tablespoons vegetable oil over medium heat in a wok or large frying pan. Add 2 chopped garlic cloves and cook for 30 seconds, or until fragrant.

Add 500 g (1 lb) ground pork, breaking up any lumps with the back of a spoon, and cook for 5–6 minutes, or until slightly brown.

Meanwhile, combine 1½ tablespoons oyster sauce, 2 teaspoons soy sauce, and 2 teaspoons sugar in a small bowl. Combine 2 teaspoons cornstarch and ¼ cup (60 ml) water in a separate bowl.

Drain a 250-g (8-oz) can of water chestnuts and chop finely. Add the water chestnuts, 2 sliced scallions, and the oyster sauce mixture to the wok. Toss for 1 minute, then add the cornstarch mixture and stir until thickened.

Wash and drain 8 iceberg lettuce leaves. Trim the leaves with kitchen scissors to neaten them and to form a cup shape. Divide the pork mixture among the lettuce cups, then drizzle each one with a little hoisin sauce. Eat while hot. **Serves 4 (makes 8)**

Iceberg lettuce acquired its name because when transported to market in ice-filled railway wagons the massed lettuces bobbed like icebergs among the ice.

The secret to good lettuce is to grow plants quickly and provide them with plenty of water and nutrients.

Wild arugula

Diplotaxis tenuifolia
Also known as wild rocket

The fine leaves of this perennial plant have a flavor-filled, peppery taste. However, wild arugula can self-seed and become weedy, so check whether it is a problem in your area.

The beauty of leafy salad greens is that you simply pick a leaf as you need it.

Buying and storing

Choose lettuce and other salad leaves that are not wilted or slimy. Remove roots if present and pull leaves apart. Immerse in a large bowl or sink of cold water for five minutes, gently swishing with your hands occasionally. Lift out of the water (any grit will sink to the bottom), drain, then spin in a salad spinner. Put in a plastic bag and seal tightly, making sure the bag is slightly inflated to cushion the fragile leaves from damage. Prepared in this way, lettuces and leaves will keep for up to four days in the crisper or lower section of the refrigerator.

Health benefits

People who regularly enjoy a bowlful of leafy greens have above-average intakes of folic acid, vitamins C and E, cell-protecting lycopene, and alpha- and beta-carotene, although the nutrient content of the leaves varies. Starting a meal with salad is a smart weight-loss strategy, filling you up so that overall you may consume 7 to 12 percent fewer calories at that meal.

Mangel-wurzels

Beta vulgaris Conditiva Group

Also known as mangelbeet, yellowbeet, mangold, mangold-wurzel

This unusual heirloom vegetable is related to beets and Swiss chard. Initially grown only for stock fodder, mangel-wurzel is now prized for its culinary qualities. The large, edible orange-yellow roots are sweet and tender, with an earthy flavor. They are crunchy when eaten raw and can be grated into a salad, or they can be cooked just like beets—roasted, boiled, steamed, added to soups or dips, and pickled. The foliage is steamed or used in stir-fries, like Swiss chard.

Mangel-wurzels are widely grown as a fodder crop for pigs and cattle, but these highly nutritious root vegetables can also be grown for human consumption.

Growing

Mangel-wurzel is best suited to temperate climates, where it thrives in fertile soil with regular watering. Sow seed in spring after the last frost and thin out to 30–45 cm (12–18 in) apart in cool climates and 15–20 cm (6–8 in) apart in warm climates. While it likes to grow in a sunny position, it does better with some protection from the fierce summer sun in warm climates.

In cool climates mangel-wurzel roots can grow to weigh up to 20 kg (44 lb); in subtropical areas they only grow to 2–3 kg (4–6 lb). Mangel-wurzel is a biennial and does not flower until its second year, so be patient if you're planning on harvesting the seed. The root continues to grow over these 18 months.

Mangel-wurzel grows like a giant golden beet. The root's color changes from yellow to orange as it grows bigger.

Problems Water regularly; allowing the plants to dry out may cause the roots to split.

Harvesting The washed roots will keep in the refrigerator for several weeks, although the foliage is best used when harvested. Due to the long growing period (from 5 up to 18 months), mangel-wurzel can be left in the ground during winter in cool climates and harvested as needed.

Buying and storing

Mostly homegrown or purchased from farmers' markets, the roots are best eaten freshly picked. Store in the refrigerator for no more than a week, as they may become rubbery.

Health benefits

Like other beets, mangel-wurzels contain health-promoting compounds called betalains in the peel and flesh. These pigments give beets their deep red and yellow hues. But they're not just pretty colors. Betalains are compounds that help shield cells from DNA damage caused by destructive molecules called free radicals. Betalains also help to relieve chronic inflammation, which increases the risk of heart disease and diabetes.

Scarcity root

On the journey from its native Germany to the fields of British farmers, the yellowish orange beet known originally as *mangold-wurzel*, literally "root of the beet," had a name change to *mangel-wurzel*, meaning "scarcity root." It was an apt rebranding. A treatise from 1787, praising the plant for its prolific yield, noted that the root "in times of scarcity affords to mankind a salutary and agreeable food; and, when fodder is dear, presents, both in summer and winter, a copious and cheap nourishment for cattle."

Peel and shred the orange-skinned, sweet-tasting roots for salads or pickles. Diced and boiled, the roots become tender and are good mashed. They are also good in coconut milk–based curries with fresh ginger. The leaves contain oxalates and are more digestible when lightly steamed or stir-fried.

Melons

Melons may be better known as fruits but are considered to be culinary vegetables. Their juicy flesh varies in color, texture, and taste, but they are all sweet and thirst-quenching—a perfect choice in hot weather. Traditionally, watermelons have red flesh, honeydews have green flesh, and cantaloupes have apricot flesh. Now there are a number of heirloom varieties with flesh of different colors.

Sweet and refreshing, melons are eaten fresh, either alone or in salads, but also combine well with savory ingredients. Try watermelon with feta, cantaloupe with prosciutto, or honeydew with fish. And see our Watermelon, mint, and labneh salad on page 56.

Honeydew melon (top), watermelon (right) and cantaloupe (center) are grown from either seeds or seedlings, harvested, and then the plants are cleared from the field. Because of this, they are considered vegetables rather than fruit.

Watermelon
Citrullus lanatus

Nothing beats the juicy flesh of a homegrown watermelon. In addition to the large, classic, red-fleshed types, there are heirloom varieties with different-colored skins, smaller-size fruits, and orange, yellow, or even creamy white flesh.

Growing

Watermelons grow as a trailing vine, one that is less vigorous than a pumpkin vine. Their main requirements are warm temperatures, a long, frost-free growing season, and ample water. In cool areas they may benefit from being planted near a wall for extra radiant heat. These melons like well-prepared, enriched soil with excellent drainage. Build mounds of 1 sq m (10 sq ft), spaced 1 m (3 ft) apart; sow three seeds directly into each mound's warm soil and thin to the strongest seedling once they've germinated. In cool areas plant as advanced seedlings, but minimize root disturbance.

Problems　All melons are subject to the same pests and diseases as cucumbers and pumpkins. See pages 43 and 84.

Harvesting　Harvest watermelons when fully ripe. When they are ready, the tendrils closest to the fruit wither and brown, and the part that is in contact with the soil changes from pale green to pale yellow.

Varieties

Most varieties produce three to four fruits per vine and ripen in 10 to 20 weeks, depending on the type.

[Watermelon] is chief of this world's luxuries....
When one has tasted it, he knows what Angels eat.'

MARK TWAIN (1835–1910)

Home gardeners can produce mouthwatering melons, like the cantaloupe pictured above and the honeydews pictured at right.

Recipe

Watermelon, mint, and labneh salad

Here is a healthful twist on the classic combination of watermelon, feta, and fresh mint. Labneh is a Middle Eastern cheese made from strained Greek yogurt.

Remove the rind from a 1.5-kg (3-lb) seedless watermelon. Cut crosswise into slices, then into small wedges. Arrange in a large shallow bowl. Thinly slice 1 small red onion, then separate the rings and scatter over the melon. Top with ¼ cup (5 g) fresh mint leaves. In a small bowl whisk together 1 tablespoon each extra virgin olive oil and balsamic vinegar with a grind of black pepper. Drizzle over the salad. Crumble 100 g (3½ oz) labneh or soft goat cheese over the salad. Scatter a few extra mint leaves over the top and serve. **Serves 4**

Cantaloupe and honeydew

Cucumis melo

Also known as rockmelon, or sweet melon and muskmelon, respectively

These sweet-smelling melons are a delight to eat and taste even better when homegrown. The traditional cantalope has orange flesh; honeydews have green.

Growing

See watermelon.

Harvesting   Harvest 12 to 18 weeks after sowing. Cantaloupes separate from the stem when ripe, whereas honeydew must be cut from the vine.

See our Trio of melon sorbets **on page 299.**

Varieties

The range of heirloom varieties offers a choice of flavors, shapes, skin features, and flesh color. Depending on the variety, the vines will produce 3 large or up to 18 smaller fruit, and some keep for a number of months into winter.

Buying and storing

Whole melons should be smooth and firm, have a fresh-looking stem area, and be heavy for their size. Uncut melons will keep for a week in a cool place. If buying cut melon, look for evenly colored flesh with no dark areas and no yellow rind. Wrapped in plastic wrap, it will keep in the refrigerator for three days.

Health benefits

Traditional healers prescribed watermelon seed tea for fluid retention and a mixture of watermelon and pumpkin seeds to heal wounds. The colorful flesh of all these melons gives a clue to the health-nurturing micronutrients they deliver. Watermelon contains lycopene, which may help protect against heart disease and some forms of cancer. It's packed with citrulline—the body converts it to arginine, which can help healthy blood flow. Cantaloupe has 30 times more cancer-fighting beta-carotene than oranges; eating it regularly can help cool inflammation and reduce the risk of metabolic syndrome, which can lead to diabetes and heart disease. Honeydew is a great source of vitamin C and potassium.

Mushrooms

Mushrooms are surprisingly easy to grow at home, even though, unlike other vegetables, they're not grown in the ground. They *are* vegetables, however, though they don't use the sun's energy to grow. Instead, as fungi, they get their energy for growing from rotting organic matter. The edible part is actually the fruiting body. It emerges above the compost growing medium from a complex network of fine, root-like filaments called a mycelium, which appears as whitish-gray hairs covering the growing medium. Mushrooms have a delicate flavor, enjoyed raw or cooked, and are very high in nutrients.

Growing

For home gardeners, the best option is to buy a mushroom kit or farm in a box or plastic bag, which will produce mushrooms for several months if you harvest them regularly. Kits or farms are available for white button and cremini mushrooms. They contain everything you need to grow the mushrooms—

compost, inoculated with mushroom spawn, and peat soil, which becomes the covering layer known as casing. Oyster, shiitake, and other unusual types can be raised on logs bought already inoculated with the specific fungus. While there are edible wild or field mushrooms, many poisonous and even deadly mushrooms look similar; with a kit, you can be sure of what you're growing.

Mushrooms love cool, humid conditions and are best located in the shade, out of direct wind and sunlight, in an area with high humidity. Their ideal temperature range is between 15°C and 18°C (59°F and 64°F). They grow well in a cellar, under the house, in a cool shed, or even in the bathroom or laundry room. They need fresh air and shouldn't be grown in a cupboard with poor air circulation.

Follow the instructions after opening the kit: spread the casing layer over the compost, then keep the farm moist but not wet by regularly squirting it with a spray bottle of water. Within 10 to 15 days, a layer of white mycelium will cover the compost. Filaments then join together to form pinheads, which develop into mushrooms.

There are many varieties of mushrooms available at grocery stores and farmers' markets, though not all are readily grown at home. Top row, from left: slippery Jack, shiitake, pink oyster, enoki. Middle row, from left: cremini, oyster. Bottom row, from left: flat (outside box), white button, matsutake, yellow oyster, and portobello.

Herbed mushrooms with feta

Mushrooms are a versatile ingredient and a kitchen staple. They can be fried in butter and eaten on their own or added to omelets, soups, stir-fries, and stews. They also taste good roasted, barbecued, or broiled, as in this simple meal. For a more substantial dinner, serve the herbed mushrooms on top of a steak or with your favorite sausages. Include some thinly sliced garlic, a sprinkling of grated Parmesan, or some toasted pine nuts in the mushroom topping.

Preparation 10 minutes / **Cooking** 10 minutes / **Serves** 2

300 g (10 oz) flat mushrooms
1 teaspoon chopped fresh thyme
1 teaspoon snipped fresh chives
2 teaspoons olive oil
4 slices ciabatta
½ cup (75 g) crumbled soft feta cheese
½ lemon

Preheat the broiler. Trim the mushroom stems, leaving most of the stem intact. Put the mushrooms, stem side up, on a baking sheet. Sprinkle with the thyme and chives, then drizzle with the oil. Broil for 3 minutes, then turn the mushrooms over and cook for an additional 3 minutes.

Meanwhile, lightly toast the ciabatta. Put the mushrooms on the toast, then sprinkle with the feta. Squeeze lemon juice over and serve.

Do not wash mushrooms. Instead, wipe them with a clean damp cloth. Before cooking, trim the base of the stems. The more delicate the mushroom, the less cooking time it requires. Do not overcook any type of mushroom.

Problems Slugs, wood lice, mice, and cockroaches may also like your mushrooms, so position your kits up off the ground.

Harvesting Mushrooms appear around two to three weeks after the spawn is added to the growing medium if kept moist. Harvest mushrooms when they reach the desired size by cutting them off at the base of their stems with a knife. Do this regularly and further crops of mushrooms should appear for two to three months, until the compost has used up all its nutrients and is exhausted. (You can add this spent compost to your garden, but it can be quite alkaline, so don't use it if your soil's pH is high.) A kit can produce up to 1.5 kg (3 lb) of mushrooms if the conditions are right. They are best eaten fresh but will keep in the refrigerator, stored in a brown paper bag. The first crop is the largest, with all the subsequent crops being smaller.

Varieties

There are a number of commercially available varieties that can be grown by the home gardener. The most commonly grown is the white button mushroom (*Agaricus bisporus*). In its button stage, caps are 2.5–7.5 cm (1–3 in) in diameter, but if allowed to keep growing they will open out to flat mushrooms 10–17.5 cm (4–7 in) across.

Cremini mushrooms (*Agaricus bisporus*) and portobello mushrooms grow to a similar size but have a richer, arguably better flavor. Along with oyster mushrooms (*Pleurotus* spp.), all can be grown from commercially available kits of inoculated compost and casing.

Shiitake mushrooms (*Lentinula edodes*) can also be grown from a kit. Some suppliers sell kits that allow you to grow large field mushrooms from a shaded patch of inoculated ground outdoors.

There are many types of oyster mushrooms available for home gardeners, including the standard white and brown as well as blue, golden, pink, and a giant king oyster mushroom. Kits for the delicate enoki and other less well known types are available from specialty suppliers.

Growing a shiitake log

The shiitake mushroom from Japan is traditionally grown on wood. You can grow shiitakes at home by purchasing a kit that contains an inoculated log of wood. These kits have the potential to produce up to 500 g (1 lb) of fresh mushrooms in up to three flushes over a period of around six weeks. All you have to do is place the inoculated log in a shady spot in your garden, keep it moist, and wait for the mushrooms to sprout. Suppliers also sell plugs, or dowels, of spawn and special wax for sealing the spawn in a log.

Buying and storing

Choose unblemished mushrooms that have no very moist patches—which could become slimy—and that do not look dry and wrinkled. They should feel firm to the touch. There is no need to wash or peel mushrooms, but do brush off any dirt carefully. Instead of using plastic bags, store in a brown paper bag or special cloth mushroom bag in the crisper section of the refrigerator for up to three days.

Health benefits

For thousands of years, traditional healers have prescribed mushrooms to boost immunity. Today, research shows that exotic mushrooms such as reishi, hen-of-the-woods, shiitake, and *Cordyceps* species do contain potent, immune-enhancing compounds called proteoglycans and polysaccharides. The big news? Cremini mushrooms—common in supermarkets and produce markets—also have purported health benefits and may help cool chronic inflammation. And white button mushrooms, the most readily available type, have been shown in laboratory studies to boost the effectiveness of the immune system cells that ward off colds.

The ancient Egyptians believed the mushroom was the plant of immortality. The pharaohs decreed that mushrooms were food for royalty and that no commoner could ever touch them.

Fairy rings

Some species of fungi spread out through the soil from the original source of nutrients to form a circle, which can reappear, each time a little wider, for many years. In folklore these were places where fairies or pixies gathered at night to dance. The brown appearance of the nutrient-starved grass, which occurs before the fungi's fruiting body—the mushroom—breaks through, was thought to look as though it had been trampled by tiny feet. The largest known fairy ring is in northern France, near the city of Belfort—it is nearly a kilometer (around half a mile) across and has an estimated age of 700 years.

FAR LEFT: With their rich, meaty flavor, oyster mushrooms are common in stir-fries and also work well in hearty stews and vegetarian dishes.

LEFT: When growing these white button mushrooms at home, pick them before the membrane between the cap and stalk separates. For flat mushrooms, leave them until the cap has spread and the gills are revealed.

Ocas have a sweet, nutty flavor with a slight tang.

The skin and flesh of ocas are usually available in glossy shades of pink or orange, although in the Andes white, cream, red, yellow, and purple varieties are also grown.

Ocas

Oxalis tuberosa
Also known as New Zealand yam

Despite also being known as the New Zealand yam, where it is widely grown, this tuberous-rooted perennial originated in South America; there, it is popular as an alternative to potato. It can be fried, roasted, or boiled and has a unique flavor, sweeter and tangier than potatoes. The thin skin doesn't need peeling. The foliage can be cooked and eaten as a leafy green in place of sorrel.

Growing

Oca is grown like potato. It likes well-drained soil and is a better option than sweet potato in mild temperate climates if protected from severe heat and frost. It doesn't like tropical summers, so grow it as an autumn or winter crop in those areas. Oca forms a compact clump, 20–30 cm (8–12 in) high, of clover-like foliage on succulent stems, each with a single yellow flower. Underground, it produces a cluster of tubers 10–12.5 cm (4–5 in) long, which are usually pink, orange, or cream with a scarlet eye. Tubers are planted in spring in cool areas, 5 cm (2 in) deep and

Recipe

Honey-roasted ocas

The addition of manuka honey gives these ocas a distinctly New Zealand flavor. Serve with roast meat, chicken, or fish.

Preheat oven to 200°C (400°F). Wash and dry 500 g (1 lb) oca yams. Spread in a single layer in a roasting pan and drizzle with 1 tablespoon olive oil. Season with salt and freshly ground black pepper and toss to coat. Roast for 40 minutes, or until tender, tossing once or twice to prevent sticking. Drizzle with 1 tablespoon manuka or other monofloral honey and add 1 tablespoon grated fresh ginger. Toss to coat, then roast an additional 2 minutes, making sure the honey doesn't burn. **Serves 4**

3 cm (1 in) apart. If frost does affect the foliage, the tubers will reshoot and plants will still be productive.

Problems   Oca has no significant problems. Squash aphids if found occasionally on young leaves.

Harvesting   Tubers start forming after four months and are ready to harvest after six months, in late autumn or winter, when the foliage starts to die back. Tubers left in the ground will survive freezing and reshoot the following spring. Once lifted, leave tubers to dry in the sun for a few days to become sweeter, but protect them from frost. Ocas store well for a few months at room temperature. Keep some tubers in a box of dry sand or sawdust in a cool, dark place to replant the following spring.

Buying and storing

Choose firm yams. Store in a brown paper bag in a cool, dark place.

Health benefits

A traditional food from the mountains of South America, the oca has been called the lost crop of the Andes. The small tuber is a rich source of vitamin C and also delivers zinc, vitamin B_{12}, and iron. Recent research shows that proteins in the oca may have antibacterial and antifungal properties.

Kiwi spud

Although it was grown in Ireland in the 1850s as an alternative to the blighted potato crop, the oca is virtually unknown outside its homeland in the Andes Mountains—except in New Zealand, that is, where it has been taken up so enthusiastically that, like the Chinese gooseberry, which became known as kiwifruit, it has been adopted, in marketing terms at least, as native. Based on the success of New Zealand oca crops, scientists are working to develop varieties that are adapted to longer days and more hours of sunlight, opening the way for oca to become a commercial crop in warm temperate areas of Australia, North America, Japan, and Europe.

Okra

Ambelmoschus esculentus syn. *Hibiscus esculentus*
Also known as ladies' fingers, gumbo

Okra, sometimes known as ladies' fingers due to its long, tapering shape, is actually a seedpod. This once common, highly productive annual vegetable is making a comeback. It is a fast-growing summer crop, best suited to tropical or warm temperate climates. Plants grow to 1–1.5 m (3–5 ft) high and produce attractive, pale yellow, hibiscus-like flowers with red centers. The immature seedpods that follow are the edible part and can grow 7.5–10 cm (3–4 in) long. They are eaten raw, cooked as a side dish, or added to soups and stews. The new shoots of the plants can also be cooked and eaten.

Growing

Sow seed into warm soil in late spring or early summer once the risk of frost has passed, or grow in pots until seedlings are 10 cm (4 in) high, then plant 30–50 cm (12–20 in) apart.

Harvesting Flowering starts two months after sowing, once the plant reaches full size. Pods can be harvested three to four days after the flowers have opened, before the seeds become mature. Pick immature pods daily to ensure they are tender and to encourage continued cropping for many months. Pods left on the plant will get tough and woody. Okra is best used fresh, as it will only keep in the refrigerator for a few days. Plants will keep cropping for four to five months, from summer to autumn.

Problems Verticillium wilt and nematodes are the main problems.

Varieties

Several varieties are available. Clemson Spineless, with green pods, is one of the most easy to obtain, while Red Burgundy produces red pods on an attractive plant with bright, cherry-red stems.

Buying and storing

Okra should be evenly colored with no blackened areas or soft spots. Choose slightly small okra, as large ones will be woody and tough. Store in a paper bag in the crisper section of the refrigerator for up to two days. Freezing helps to retain nutrients, but only freeze those pods that haven't softened or begun to turn brown.

Health benefits

When cooked, okra releases a slippery, mucilaginous substance that forms the basis for many soothing folk remedies. It has been used to soothe irritated skin, ease urinary tract problems, and even treat venereal diseases. In India, a traditional remedy for itchy skin called for a paste made from okra and milk, while tea made from not-yet-ripe okra pods was said to treat gonorrhea. Okra contains high amounts of pectin, which helps decrease blood cholesterol levels by interfering with bile absorption in the gut and forcing the liver to use circulating cholesterol to make more bile.

To reduce okra's gummy texture, cook it whole with an acidic vegetable such as tomato. See our recipe for Creole-style gumbo **on page 283.**

Okra is a member of the same family as the hibiscus, as is clear from its pale-lemon flowers. The plants are an attractive addition to the vegetable garden.

How-to

Preparing okra

To defuzz okra, rub with paper towels or with a vegetable brush under running water. Pat dry or spread out to air-dry.

To trim okra, use a paring knife to carefully remove the outer layer of the stem without cutting into the pod. Alternatively, remove the thin layer of the conical stem with your fingers. If using okra in a gumbo, top and tail the okra before slicing.

Greek remedy

Greek cooks counter okra's slimy texture with a dose of vinegar. Use a sharp paring knife to trim the ring around the top of the okra, just under its stubby stem. Rinse and drain, then put the okra in a large bowl and sprinkle generously with red wine vinegar. Let stand for at least 30 minutes, rinse, drain, and cook according to the recipe.

Onions

There are many different members of the edible onion genus, and they make essential ingredients in the kitchen. Both the foliage and the bulbs can be used, depending on the type. While all are easy to grow, the hard part comes with deciding what types and varieties to grow. Their identification can be a little confusing because they are known by so many different names.

Growing

All members of this family like to grow in an open position in full sun with friable, well-drained soils. A bed that has been prepared with well-rotted organic matter, such as compost and aged manure, will not need further fertilizing. They must be grown free of root competition from weeds or other plants, so weed the bed thoroughly before planting and be sure to weed regularly, without disturbing the bulbs, during the growing period. All edible onions prefer cool, moist conditions at the start of their growing period and dry, warm conditions as they mature.

If you have plenty of space in your vegetable garden, onions such as the white, brown, and red varieties pictured here are a great crop to grow for a range of flavors and storage times.

Bulb onions
Allium cepa Cepa Group
Also known as globe onion, common onion

Growing

Bulb onions have been grown since ancient times and are a great winter food crop. There are many varieties, and it is important that you choose those that best suit your climate because bulb formation is triggered by day length, which differs between varieties. Early-maturing (short-day) varieties are best grown in winter, while late-maturing (long-day) varieties can be grown in spring.

In tropical areas grow only early varieties in late summer and autumn; in subtropical areas, grow early varieties in autumn; and in temperate areas you can grow early and late varieties from late autumn to early spring.

Choosing the wrong variety or planting at the wrong time may cause the plants to bolt to seed instead of producing a bulb. Early-maturing varieties are for short-term storage, while the later varieties can be stored for a longer time.

Bulb onions can be grown from seed sown directly into the ground or raised as seedlings. Sow seed into shallow furrows, cover lightly with soil, and water gently. Seedlings will emerge in one to two weeks and should be thinned early to 2.5 cm (1 in) apart and later to 7.5–10 cm (3–4 in) apart in rows 20–30 cm (8–12 in) apart.

It takes up to three months for seed sown in trays to be ready to transplant. Plant seedlings when they are around 10–15 cm (4–6 in) high. Separate individual seedlings and trim the tops and tails (roots) to 5 cm (2 in) long to make them easy to plant. Make a furrow 2.5 cm (1 in) deep and lay seedlings 7.5–10 cm (3–4 in) apart along one side of the furrow. Back-fill the furrow from the other side, lightly covering the roots with soil, and gently firm in. They will stand upright within a few days.

Onions can take six to eight months to mature. They need regular watering during warm weather and constant weeding as they grow, because they resent root competition from weeds. During this time the bulb itself sits on the surface and expands.

Problems Most problems are due to growing the wrong variety for your climate or for the time of year. In damp conditions downy mildew may affect onions, and they can also be infested with thrips, aphids, and onion nematodes.

Harvesting Mature globe onions are ready to harvest when their foliage dries and falls over. Lift plants out of the soil carefully and spread on the ground for a few days to cure before collecting them. This curing ripens the bulb, helps the outer skin to dry, and ensures longer storage. In very hot climates, it should be done on a rack in a shed. After curing, rub the bulbs with your hands to remove the foliage and roots and hang them to store in wire baskets, wire mesh, or string bags in a cool, dry

Scallions (left) have a thin white base. The bulb of spring onions (right) is more, but not fully, developed.

place. Be careful to avoid bruising, which encourages diseases.

Varieties

There are many bulb onion varieties. As well as yellow, brown, white, and red, onions are grouped into varieties suited for early-, mid-, or late-season planting, and into odorless and non-odorless. The latter are less pungent because of their lower sulfur content and can have a sweeter flavor. Some of these are referred to as sweet onions.

Bulb onions can be harvested at different stages in their development, before they reach maturity.

Scallions   These can be spring-grown bulb onions pulled when young, green, and leafy, before the bulb develops. They have thin white bases no wider than their long, straight, green stalks and a very mild flavor. The base and leaves are used raw in salads, as a garnish, or in cooking.

Spring onions   These are young bulb onions pulled in spring, when the bulbous base is just starting to form. They have green stalks, small white bulbs and a mild taste.

Pearl onions   At around 70 days, once the bulbous base has grown larger but is still not full-sized, many varieties can be lifted for cooking.

Buying and storing

Buy smooth, firm onions with no black sooty areas or signs of sprouting. Keep in a cool, dark, but well-ventilated place in a ventilated basket or box, not in a plastic bag. Contrary to common practice, potatoes and onions shouldn't be stored together, as the gases they produce can hasten spoilage. Check your stored onions regularly for signs of deterioration. They will keep for up to three weeks, depending on their age when purchased.

Whatever they are labeled in the shop, the white base of scallions, spring onions, and pearl onions should be firm and bright, with no browning. The tops should look fresh, green, and not wilted. For easier storage, trim the dark green part that you won't use. Keep in a loosely sealed plastic bag in the crisper section of the refrigerator.

When growing onions, it is important to keep the surrounding soil weed-free to avoid any root competition.

There is often confusion about onion varieties, some of which are nothing more than the same plant harvested at different stages of maturity. Terms vary between countries, regions, and even stores. Spring onion, green onion, and scallion are names often used interchangeably. The only real difference is the size of the bulb—all have a mild flavor and can be eaten raw or cooked.

Health benefits

The humble onion is a veritable medicine cabinet of traditional remedies. It's a star player in cough syrups, in poultices to soothe cold and pneumonia symptoms, and it even shows up in remedies for earache and convulsions. Modern science says onions contain a bouquet of compounds known as flavonols (including myricetin, apigenin, luteolin, kaempferol, and quercetin), which seem to cool inflammation and relax blood vessels—potentially reducing the risk of a stroke. This pungent member of the *Allium* genus is a source of diallyl disulphide, too, which may help protect against joint damage.

RIGHT: Shallots can look very similar to small onions. Here are small bulb onions (top), not to be confused with gold shallots (bottom) and Asian shallots (left).

ABOVE: Banana shallots are named for their elongated shape. They are larger and slightly milder than other types of shallots.

Shallots

Allium cepa Aggregatum Group

True shallots are the most delicately flavored of the onion genus; there are several types available.

Gold shallots are planted 10 cm (4 in) apart in spring. While growing, the foliage can be harvested and used as you would scallions. The main crop is lifted in summer, when the foliage dies down, and laid out to dry for a few days. A single bulb multiplies to produce 6 to 12 bulbs.

Gold shallots have a sweet, delicate, onion-like flavor prized by cooks. Asian, or red, shallots have

a purple or reddish skin color and a subtle flavor. Banana shallots are a cross between an onion and a shallot. They have an elongated shape—hence their common name—and are easier to use because their larger size makes them easier to peel.

Buying and storing

Shallots should be firm with unblemished skin. They will keep for up to two weeks in a cool, dark, but well-ventilated place in a ventilated basket or box— do not store them in a plastic bag.

Growers are developing sweeter, less pungent varieties of onions, which are good eaten raw in salads. There's the Vidalia onion in the US, while Australia has the Queensland Mild (right).

Sweet onion

A variety of onion grown on the Hawaiian island of Maui is so crisp, sweet, and juicy that it can be eaten like an apple. It flourishes in the rich volcanic slopes of Mount Haleakala, and it is said to be the unique combination of soil, temperature, and humidity that gives this onion its unusual sweetness. Each spring the island holds a raw onion–eating contest to prove the point and honors the winner with a lei of onions.

Potato onion
Allium cepa Aggregatum Group
Also known as multiplier onion

The potato onion multiplies underground, and both the foliage and bulb can be used in the kitchen to give a mild, sweet onion flavor. Plant small bulblets in autumn for a summer harvest; a large bulb will produce up to 12 bulbs per clump. Bulbs store well for four to six months. The small bulblets can be kept and planted for future crops.

Tree onion
Allium cepa Proliferum Group
Also known as Egyptian onion, topset onion, walking onion, self-perpetuating onion

The tree onion is grown from small sets of bulblets planted in autumn. Bulbs multiply in the ground, and bulbils also form on the top of the 1.5 m (5 ft) flowering stem. These stems bend down and form roots away from the main plant. Be sure to keep some offsets for replanting the following year.

Welsh onion
Allium fistulosum
Also known as bunching onion, ciboule

These quick-growing, slender-stemmed, perennial onions have been grown since ancient times. They have hollow stems and cylindrical hollow leaves, with no obvious swelling or bulb at the base. There are many cultivars, ranging in size from 15–50 cm (6–20 in) high; all have edible pale yellow flowers. The most commonly grown varieties have a white base with rich green leaves, but there are also varieties with a pink or red base. This group of plants is quite confusing, because although most are evergreen, some cultivars suited to growing in very cold climates die back and behave more like shallots, while some of the larger forms have blanched stems and look more like leeks.

The plant is pulled out and eaten 8 to 12 weeks after planting, and everything from the white base to the foliage tips are used—raw in salads or stir-fries or as a mild onion substitute in other dishes. Welsh onions can be sown in the ground at any time of year, in rows 5–10 cm (2–4 in) apart. Thin seedlings to 2.5 cm (1 in) apart, and use thinnings in the kitchen. Alternatively, separate clumps into individual seedlings or divide an old clump and replant. For a constant supply, make successive plantings every four to six weeks.

The onion is the basis for countless dishes in every cuisine, but we let it shine in its own right in our French-inspired savory onion tarts. See our recipe for Onion and shallot pastries on page 237.

Chives
Allium schoenoprasum

Although usually called a herb and not a vegetable, this perennial grassy foliage plant adds a mild onion flavor to any dish or salad. It forms a clump 20 cm (8 in) high, with edible mauve flowers in late spring, and makes an excellent border plant. The foliage dies back completely after the growing season and reshoots in spring. Clumps should be divided every two to three years.

Garlic chives (*Allium tuberosum*) have edible white flowers and coarser, flatter foliage with a mild garlic flavor.

Chives make an attractive border for beds in the vegetable patch or flower garden. Both the flowers and foliage can be used in the kitchen.

Buying and storing
Chives should be upright with no droopiness or slimy areas. Keep chives loosely wrapped in plastic in the refrigerator for up to three days.

Pictured from top to bottom: bunches of chives, which have a rounded hollow leaf, the flower stalks of garlic chives, and the flat leaves of garlic chives.

Leeks add a subtle flavor to many traditional soups, stews, and casseroles, or they can be steamed, braised, or fried as a side dish.

Leeks are a useful winter vegetable. They will withstand the coldest winters and will thrive in any well-drained soil provided it is well manured in the winter before planting.

Recipe

Buttered leeks

Don't be tempted to replace the butter with oil in this classic side dish. Leeks cook best in butter, slowly, over a low, gentle heat.

Trim and wash 500 g (1 lb) leeks to make 350 g (12 oz) trimmed weight. Halve leeks lengthwise, then cut into 2.5-cm (1-in) pieces. Melt 1 tablespoon butter in a small frying pan over medium heat. Add the leeks, season with salt and freshly ground black pepper, and stir. Reduce heat to low and cook gently for 5 minutes, stirring occasionally. **Serves 4**

Leeks

Allium ampeloprasum Porrum Group

This giant member of the *Allium* genus produces thick, fleshy stems topped with dark green foliage up to 1 m (3 ft) high. The edible part is called the shank; it can grow 5–6 cm (2–2½ in) thick and has a milder flavor than onions. The dark green tops are usually discarded, although they can be wrapped in cheesecloth with bouquet garni ingredients to give added flavor to soups and stews. Leeks are best grown from seed sown in containers, then planted into 10-cm (4-in)-deep holes, spaced 15 cm (6 in) apart, to ensure blanched stems. While they can take 8 to 10 months to mature fully, they can be harvested at any size.

Buying and storing

Leeks should look plump, especially the white part. Store unwrapped leeks in the refrigerator for up to five days.

Well loved he garleek, oynons, and eek lekes.
And for to drinken strong wyn,
reed as blood.

GEOFFREY CHAUCER (1343–1400)

How-to

Trimming leeks

To prepare leeks for cooking, wash thoroughly to remove the grit or soil that is often trapped between the leaves. Trim off the base.

Trim off the uppermost part of the leaves. If you want to keep the leek whole, slit along the outside layer and wash thoroughly. Or cut the leek in half and wash thoroughly.

Garlic
Allium sativum

This superfood is popular in the home garden due to the superior flavor of the fresh product and concern over the chemical treatment of overseas imports. It is loved for its culinary and medicinal qualities. A natural antibiotic, it is used to help prevent and treat infections and is a long-standing traditional cure for coughs and colds.

Plant individual cloves in autumn for harvesting six to seven months later. Push cloves 7.5 cm (3 in) deep in the soil, spaced 15 cm (6 in) apart, with the pointy end up. Harvest when the leaves start to yellow but there are still four or five healthy leaves on each stem. These can be plaited together and, if dried thoroughly in the sun then hung in a cool, dry place, can last for six months or more.

Buying and storing

Garlic should be firm and have good weight for its size. Avoid bulbs with any signs of sprouting. Store in a ventilated basket or box—not in a plastic bag—in a cool, well-ventilated place out of direct light.

Garlicky "butter of Provence"

The 19th-century Nobel Prize–winning French poet Frédéric Mistral, when praising the iconic food and sunshine of his Provençal birthplace, described the traditional local sauce called aioli—made with olive oil, lemon juice, egg yolk, and a generous quantity of garlic—as "fragrant, gilded like a thread of gold." For Mistral, aioli "epitomized the heat, the power, and the joy of the Provençal sun," adding that it had yet another virtue, thanks to the pungent odor—"it drives away flies."

Since garlic then hath powers to save from death,
Bear with it though it makes unsavory breath.

THE SALERNITAN RULE OF HEALTH,
A 12TH-CENTURY MEDICAL TEXT

There are many varieties of garlic, with white or pinkish skins, large or small cloves, and different keeping qualities.

Garlic is a great home crop, especially when organic garlic is expensive to buy. It doesn't take up much space and stores well.

Parsnips are grown for their creamy-white roots. They are harvested when fresh vegetables are scarce, and are a very hardy and undemanding crop to grow in the home garden.

Parsnips
Pastinaca sativa

These creamy white, carrot-like vegetables are grown for their long white taproots, which have a sweet, nutty flavor. Although parsnips can be grown in all climates, they are easiest to grow as a winter vegetable in cool or temperate climates, where frosts concentrate the sugars in the root. They are a popular winter vegetable for roasting, mashing, soups, and stews.

Growing

Like most root crops, parsnips are best grown from seed sown directly into well-prepared fertile soil, which has been worked to a depth of 30 cm (1 ft) so roots can develop properly. It is essential that you obtain fresh seed, as it loses its viability rapidly. Sow as you would carrots, sowing the fine seed thinly in a furrow 1–1.5 cm (^{1}/$_3$–^{1}/$_2$ in) deep in rows 30 cm (1 ft) apart. Soaking the seeds overnight before sowing helps germination. Cover seeds with light soil or compost, press firmly, and water gently. The seeds are slow to germinate, taking three to four weeks to appear, and it's important to keep the bed damp until the seedlings emerge. The seed must be kept moist; cover sown seed with a damp dish towel or burlap to retain moisture, check daily, and remove when the seedlings emerge. Once they are growing, thin seedlings to 10 cm (4 in) apart to allow for the development of large roots.

In subtropical areas sow in autumn and winter; in temperate areas sow from late winter till autumn; and in cool areas sow in spring and summer.

Problems Late sowing may produce small roots, and the plants may run to seed prematurely. Parsnips bolt to seed in spring, and their roots become woody at this stage. Forking and hairy roots are caused by adding fresh organic matter, such as manures that have not been aged, to the soil. Rotting is due to poor drainage. Inconsistent watering may also cause roots to split.

Harvesting Parsnips take four to five months to grow to full size. Start pulling roots early to spread the harvest, choosing the large roots first. When they are mature, the foliage starts to die back. Parsnips can be left in the ground over winter and harvested as required. To avoid damaging the roots, loosen carefully with a garden fork before lifting. They keep well in the refrigerator and can also be cut, blanched, and frozen.

Milk, butter, and nutmeg are perfect partners for sweet and creamy mashed parsnips.

Buttering up

The saying "Fair [or fine] words butter no parsnips" means that flattery and promises will not feed a hungry person and that a situation requires action, not words. It can be traced back to the 17th century, when it appeared in a 1651 verse by John Taylor, a Thames ferryman known as the Water Poet:

Great men large hopeful promises may utter;
But words did never Fish or Parsnips butter.

Parsnips feature in the poem because they were common in the English diet at the time. To make a more flavorsome dish, they were usually served with butter.

Buying and storing

Choose parsnips that have bright creamy skin with no brown areas. Check the very tips to make sure they look fresh and unwithered. Keep unwrapped in the crisper section of the refrigerator for up to five days.

Health benefits

Centuries ago, the English herbalist Nicholas Culpeper recommended wild parsnips to expel "the wind from the stomach and bowels, or colic." This beneficial action on the intestines is due to the vegetable's high fiber content. Parsnips can be a good alternative to potatoes if you're trying to lose weight—they're lower in calories, and the fiber helps to fill you up. They are a good source of vitamin C, potassium, and folate, a B vitamin that your body needs to create healthy cells.

Peruvian parsnip
Arracacia xanthorrhiza
Also known as arracacha, batata baroa

Although this herbaceous rooted perennial is not a true parsnip, it is in the same family as the carrot and parsnip. It forms a crown of large, creamy white tubers, each similar in size to a carrot. These starchy tubers with a crisp texture and delicate flavor are cooked in the same ways as potatoes, while the young stems can be eaten raw or cooked.

Growing

Like most root crops, Peruvian parsnip likes to grow in friable, well-drained soil. Take offshoots from the main root crown in spring, cutting back the foliage to help reduce wilting. Leave the offshoot for two to three days in a dry, sheltered place, then plant into a container of potting mix. Plant outdoors when it has taken root and established well in the container.

Harvesting While you can start to harvest young tubers after 4 months, they don't mature fully until 10 to 12 months.

A parsnip with potential
While tomatoes, potatoes, green beans, and chili peppers all found favor with the European colonists of South America, the equally useful and nutritious Peruvian parsnip was overlooked and not even given a scientific name until the mid-19th century, 300 years after the Spanish conquest. It is now a major crop in Brazil, grown in preference to the potato because of its lower production costs. Related to both the carrot and celery, it combines the qualities of both—young, pale-skinned roots can be boiled, roasted, or fried and are an ingredient in Latin American stews and soups, while the stems are eaten raw in salads or cooked as a side dish.

Recipe

Pear and parsnip soup
Heat 2 tablespoons olive oil in a large saucepan. Add 1 thinly sliced leek (white part only) and fry for about 5 minutes, until soft. Add 800 g (1¾ lb) peeled and chopped parsnips, cover, and simmer for 5 minutes.
  Add 4 cups (1 liter) water or low-sodium chicken or vegetable stock, reduce the heat, and simmer for about 10 minutes, until the parsnips are softened. Add 3 peeled, cored, and diced pears and stir to mix well.
  Puree the soup in a food processor or with a handheld stick blender. Bring back to a boil. Serve immediately, topped with plain yogurt, parsley leaves, and freshly ground black pepper. **Serves 4**

In times past, when sugar was not available, parsnips were used in sweet drinks, jams, and desserts.

Mature parsnips will be ready for harvest as soon as the leaves die back in autumn, but if you have frosts in your area, wait until then, as frost will improve their flavor.

Peas

Pisum sativum

This cool-weather crop is easy to grow and very rewarding. For those who have only eaten frozen peas, the taste sensation of eating fresh, home-grown peas will be a surprise. Tender shoots and pods can be used as well as the peas themselves.

Growing

Peas need a sunny position and like the "best of the best" when it comes to soil. Work the soil over to a depth of 30 cm (1 ft), incorporating well-rotted organic matter, and build up the bed if your soil is shallow. Good drainage is essential, as peas are prone to rotting. Also, if your soil is acidic, add lime. Peas are a legume and are actually able to improve the soil through nitrogen-fixing nodules on their roots. These nodules draw nitrogen from the air and return it to the soil for use by future crops. Grow leafy green vegetables in the soil after harvesting and removing pea plants, and they will flourish.

Europeans did not eat fresh peas until the 1600s, when petits pois became a favorite of the French aristocracy.

Climbing, twining pea plants have pretty flowers, and the flavor and freshness of homegrown garden peas is unbeatable.

Planting Peas can be sown from autumn to spring. However, in frosty areas, sow your crop so that it isn't in flower when frosts occur, as these can affect both flowers and pods. The ideal temperature range for flowering and harvesting is 20–25°C (68–77°F), while temperatures over 30°C (86°F) cause poor pollination, lower yields, and rapid development to overmaturity.

Peas are best sown directly into dark, damp soil. To do this, water the bed well the day before planting and sow seeds 2.5 cm (1 in) deep and 5 cm (2 in) apart. Press down firmly with your hand, and don't water again until shoots emerge within a week.

Being a climbing vine, peas don't take up much ground space and are easy to squeeze into even the smallest garden. If growing the true climbing types, sow them next to a fence or support at least 2 m (6 ft) high and weave their shoots through this as they grow. Be sure to loosely tie them to the support as they grow, because spring winds can pull the plants away just when they are in full flower. The dwarf types only grow to 60 cm (2 ft) high, but they crop better if their tendrils can cling to a low trellis, fence, or tepee of twigs for support.

Problems Protect the seeds and seedlings of all types of peas from rodents, birds, snails, and slugs until germination occurs and seedlings reach 10 cm (4 in) high. Also look out for caterpillar damage. Warm, humid weather in spring can cause powdery mildew and leaf and pod spot, so avoid watering from above. The peas inside the pod may be attacked by southern green stinkbug, clover springtail, and pea weevil.

Harvesting Peas will fruit best as the weather warms in early spring; their main harvest period is over just two to three weeks for English peas and five to six weeks for pod peas, so sow successive crops at two- to three-week intervals. Aim to pick the pods when the seeds (that's the peas) inside are well developed but before they mature fully. Pick pods every few days to keep the plants producing well. The more you pick, the more you encourage further flowering and cropping. When a plant has finished producing, cut it down to the ground, leaving the roots in the soil to boost nitrogen levels.

Pods of English peas will keep in the crisper section of your refrigerator for two to three days, but they are at their best when eaten right away. You can also blanch and freeze them. Pod peas store and freeze well, too.

In England and France pod peas such as sugar snap peas and snow peas are known as mangetout, meaning "eat all."

Varieties

Peas are broadly divided into three groups.

English peas   These are the traditional peas. The pods are discarded in favor of the sweet, juicy peas on the inside. Some pods can be left on the vine to produce dried peas for stews and soups. Varieties include the early-season dwarf Earlicrop Massey and Massey Gem, and the popular midseason Greenfeast, all of which grow to about 1 m (3 ft) high. Tall Telephone is a climbing midseason variety that reaches 2 m (6 ft) high. For something a little different, try purple-podded peas, a variety that has stunning purple-pink flowers followed by purple pods with green peas inside.

Sugar snap peas   These have crunchy, sweet, edible pods that enclose full-size peas. They are available as climbing varieties, which grow 2 m (6 ft) high, and dwarf types, which grow to 60 cm (2 ft) high.

Snow peas   These are best eaten when the immature pods are still young and flat. They are eaten pod and all. See page 72.

English peas (top) are picked when the pods have reached their full length and the peas inside are swollen; they are shelled to discard the pod, and only the peas are eaten. Snow peas (right) are picked when still flat and eaten whole. Sugar snap peas (bottom left) are eaten whole at any stage.

Young peas can be eaten with their pods. You can also harvest pea shoots, the top 6 cm (2½ in) of young seedlings' growth, and add them to a salad. Pinching out shoots encourages branching and stimulates the plant to flower and fruit more.

Snow peas should be picked every few days to encourage continual cropping and to ensure that they don't lose their flavor and tenderness.

Fresh, sweet snow peas require little preparation. Simply sauté in a little olive oil, add low-sodium vegetable stock, and simmer until tender-crisp.

Snow peas

Pisum sativum var. *macrocarpon*

Also known as mangetout, edible podded peas

These sweet, crisp peas are eaten whole when the immature pods are tender and still flat, before the peas inside start to swell. They are good eaten straight from the plant, used raw in salads, or lightly steamed or stir-fried. They can be sliced like beans. Growing conditions are the same as for English peas.

Harvesting The pods form about 7 to 10 days after flowering. For traditional varieties, harvest when they are about 7.5–10 cm (3–4 in) long and 2.5 cm (1 in) wide. Pick the pods regularly, at least every two to three days, using scissors or a sharp knife. Those that are left on the vine will start to thicken as the peas inside start to swell; they become tough and lose their unique flavor. Snow peas taste best when they are picked and used straight from the vine. While they will keep in a plastic bag in the refrigerator for several days, they do not freeze well.

Varieties

As well as climbing and dwarf snow pea varieties such as Bikini, there are some giant snow peas, such as Yukomo Giant and Mammoth Melting Sugar, which produce pods up to 14 cm (5½ in) long.

Golden Sweet is not a true snow pea, but like a snow pea, its golden yellow pods are best eaten when young—pod and all. It produces stunning two-tone purple flowers and is a prolific cropper as well as being highly ornamental.

How luscious lies the pea within the pod.

EMILY DICKINSON (1830–1886)

Recipe

Snow pea stir-fry

The inclusion of nuts adds protein to this stir-fry.

In a small bowl, whisk together 1 tablespoon soy sauce, 1 tablespoon sesame oil, 1 teaspoon cornstarch, ¼ teaspoon sambal oelek or chili paste, and ½ cup (125 ml) water. Set aside.

Heat 1 tablespoon vegetable oil in a wok or large frying pan over high heat. Add 1 sliced red onion, 1 sliced yellow bell pepper, 1 cup (150 g) raw unsalted cashews or almonds, and 1 tablespoon grated fresh ginger. Stir-fry for 2–3 minutes, or until the nuts begin to brown.

Add 500 g (1 lb) snow peas and 3 scallions sliced on the diagonal and stir-fry for 2–3 minutes. Add the soy sauce mixture and cook, stirring continuously, for 1–2 minutes, or until the sauce has thickened. Serve immediately.
Serves 4

Pease porridge

In Europe, peas were not eaten fresh until the 17th century, when green *petits pois* became a favorite of the French aristocracy. Instead, yellow peas in dried form were a staple food of the poor, usually eaten as pease porridge, a near-solid mix of boiled split peas. Besides satisfying hunger because of the time they take to digest, cooked dried peas help lower blood glucose levels. Shown here is Sir Samuel Luke Fildes's 1881 painting *Dolly*.

Warm mixed-pea salad

If you can, use freshly shelled peas and fresh-from-the-garden snow peas, or a mix of snow peas and sugar snap peas, for this pretty salad.

Cook 300 g (10 oz) fresh peas and 200 g (7 oz) trimmed snow peas in a saucepan of salted boiling water for 1–2 minutes, until tender-crisp, then drain. Heat 2 tablespoons olive oil in a small frying pan, then gently cook 8 sliced scallions for 4 minutes, until soft. Transfer to a bowl and mix in the warm peas and snow peas and 1 bunch (125 g/4 oz) arugula. Whisk 1 tablespoon lemon juice, 2 tablespoons olive oil, sea salt, and freshly ground black pepper in a small bowl to combine. Drizzle the dressing over the salad and toss gently to coat. Sprinkle with 1 teaspoon chopped fresh thyme or mint and serve.
Serves 4

Shell full-sized peas and discard the pods. Trim snow peas and sugar snap peas.

Buying and storing

English peas come in pods that should look smooth and firm. Ideally, the peas inside will fill the pod snugly—if the pod is bumpy it may mean the peas inside are large and possibly older and not sweet and desirable. Snow peas and sugar snap peas should have smooth pods without blemishes and be firm and crisp, not floppy. You can store all peas in a loosely sealed plastic bag in the crisper section of the refrigerator for two to three days.

Health benefits

If you're sensitive to sulfite preservatives, adding more peas to your diet could help. A cup (69 grams) of cooked dried peas contains 196 percent of your daily requirement of molybdenum; research suggests that low levels of this mineral could trigger sulfite sensitivity. Half a cup (80 grams) of green peas—a folk remedy for everything from an upset stomach to warts—contains 5 milligrams of coumestrol. In one study, people who got 2 milligrams or more of this polyphenol from food every day were at lower risk for stomach cancer. The high fiber content of peas helps keep blood glucose low after meals, too.

*Pease porridge hot,
Pease porridge cold,
Pease porridge
in the pot,
Nine days old;
Some like it hot,
Some like it cold,
Some like it
in the pot,
Nine days old.*

18TH-CENTURY
NURSERY RHYME

Whether you're growing climbing or dwarf peas, put in supports that are at least as high as the ultimate height of the variety you've chosen.

Peppers

These classic warm-season fruits from the tropical regions of the Americas look and taste good and are very high in vitamin C. Chili peppers are the hot cousins, while bell peppers are the sweet cousins. There is a tremendous variety of size, shape, and color, but all are compact, highly productive plants for the space they take up. This makes them a great value in even the smallest vegetable plot.

Growing

Growing conditions for peppers are similar to those of their relatives the tomatoes, except that peppers need warmer temperatures. In tropical and subtropical climates they can be grown all year round, sown or planted every two to three months to ensure continuous supply. However, in cooler climates they are planted in spring after the last frost has passed and enjoyed over summer and into autumn. They need a well-drained, enriched soil in a warm sunny position, protected from wind.

Grow from seed or buy seedlings to save time, but do not sow or plant them until the soil temperature has reached at least 23°C (73°F). If you have a short growing season, start plants off indoors or in a mini greenhouse. Sow seeds around six to eight weeks before you are ready to transplant them into the garden. Space plants 45–60 cm (1½–2 ft) apart and shelter them with temporary shade cloth in extreme heat, as temperatures over 38°C (100°F) will cause flowers to drop and fruit to scorch. Cold weather at the end of the season will stop flowering and fruiting. While they will reshoot after winter in frost-free areas, peppers are best grown as an annual.

These plants are heavy feeders and should be fertilized regularly during the growing period to keep them producing flowers and fruit. Also water them evenly and regularly to avoid plant stress.

Problems   Chili peppers are not susceptible to pests, whereas bell peppers are prone to fruit flies and southern green stinkbugs in summer and aphids in autumn.

The fruit of both can encounter growing problems. They can be sunburned in extremely hot weather if they protrude from their leaf canopy. The fruit is still edible, and the damaged patch can be cut off during food preparation. But to avoid sunburn, cover your plants with shade cloth or other shelter during extreme heat. Blossom-end rot causes a sunken brown patch on the end of the fruit; it is due to irregular watering in hot weather or to a lack of calcium. Water plants regularly and feed them well to help minimize this. And the best way to avoid soil-borne diseases is with strict crop rotation.

Harvesting   The quality of flavor and either heat or sweetness improves as the fruit matures. Because most store-bought peppers are unripe, they have a sharpness of flavor not found in homegrown, fully ripe produce. They take three to four months to mature. Cut off the fruit with a small piece of stem attached, taking care not to damage the plant, and harvest regularly to keep your plants productive.

Planting parsley near pepper plants is said to help deter garden bugs that often attack the plants.

Peppers come in many shapes, sizes, and colors. Pictured here are the giant bell types and long-fruited types.

Bell peppers
Capsicum annum
Also known as sweet peppers

Bell peppers are used in a wide range of cuisines—raw in salads or as a garnish, or roasted, grilled, stir-fried, stuffed, braised, pickled, or marinated. Most people are familiar with the red, green, and yellow varieties offered for sale, but there are also white, orange, purple, chocolate brown, and black varieties. Their shapes range from the standard large bell-shaped fruit to long, slender types, and there are miniature varieties just 5 cm (2 in) across, too.

Growing
Capsicum plants grow 60–90 cm (2–3 ft) tall. It is best to support them with stakes to minimize wind damage and keep the fruit off the ground so they stay clean and out of reach of snails and slugs. Insert stakes at planting time to avoid damaging the roots of established plants later.

Harvesting   Harvest from late summer to autumn at any stage from green to fully colored. Excess fruit can be preserved in the traditional way, by slow-roasting then storing in oil.

Varieties
※ **Giant bell types** Large red and green lantern-shaped fruit. For example, California Wonder has 10–15-cm (4–6-in)-long fruit, with thick flesh that tastes good when picked green but is sweet when harvested red.

※ **Mini bell types** Small, compact plants that produce large quantities of small fruit around 5 cm (2 in) across in a range of colors, including red, yellow, and chocolate brown.

※ **Long-fruited types** Grow 15–25 cm (6–10 in) long, with thin flesh, and are popular for roasting and frying. They are available as green fruit that ripen to red or yellow. Jimmy Nardello is a popular Italian variety that produces slender, slightly twisted red fruit to 25 cm (10 in). Other reliable varieties include Red Bull's Horn, Long Sweet Yellow, and Sweet Banana.

※ **Sweet Chocolate** Medium-size fruit to 10 cm (4 in), with a glossy dark green skin; ripens to chocolate brown with reddish-brown flesh inside.

Buying and storing
Choose firm, brightly colored peppers with no wrinkles or soft spots. Keep unwrapped in the crisper section of the refrigerator for up to a week. Once cut, wrap in plastic wrap and keep in the refrigerator for up to two days.

Health benefits
Helpful for strengthening the immune system, a red bell pepper has three times the vitamin C of an orange.

The immature fruit of bell peppers are green and unripe, though still edible. They are at their sweetest when fully colored and ripe.

> **HEIRLOOM VARIETIES**
>
> You will find the seeds of many heirloom varieties of bell peppers sold under different names. Look through suppliers' catalogues for the best type for your garden.

Recipe

Romesco sauce
This famous sauce from Catalonia, Spain, is a great accompaniment for barbecued chicken or seafood. It is also delicious as a topping for potatoes or quickly blanched broccoli and green beans.

3 red bell peppers, roasted, peeled, and seeded
4 cloves garlic
100 g (3½ oz) almonds, blanched and roasted
200 g (7 oz) day-old sourdough bread, cut into cubes
100 ml (3 fl oz) sherry vinegar
300 ml (10 fl oz) extra-virgin olive oil

Put peppers, garlic, almonds, bread, and vinegar in a food processor or blender and process until smooth.

Add olive oil slowly to obtain the desired consistency. Keep in the refrigerator for up to two days.

Makes 2 cups

All chili peppers are ornamental, but not all ornamental chilies are edible, so always check the plant label. The two plants at top left are ornamental and make an attractive addition to the garden. The plant in the foreground is a Thai chili, a hot pepper used in Southeast Asian cooking.

CAUTION
Always wear gloves or wash your hands thoroughly after picking or handling chili peppers. Accidentally touching your eyes or any delicate skin areas, such as those around the genitals, can be intensely painful.

Chili peppers

Capsicum annum, Capsicum chinense, Capsicum frutescens, Capsicum pubescens
Also known as chilies

There are hundreds of varieties of chili peppers, varying in intensity from mild to extreme. Chilies can be harvested and used fresh—usually cooked but also eaten raw—pickled or frozen for future use, or sun-dried on the plant then strung together. Colors range from the classic red and green to yellow, orange, and purple. Some varieties are extremely decorative and worth growing for their ornamental value. For example, Black Pearl, Black Prince, and Explosive Ember have dark purple to jet black foliage with black or violet purple fruit ripening to red, while Rainbow Thai has red, purple, and cream fruit all on the one plant. Some ornamental chili plants are not edible, so be sure to check the label.

Misnamed
Columbus is to blame for chilies also being called peppers. His intended destination on his great voyage of 1492 was India, and among the treasures he hoped to bring back were spices, including black and white peppercorns. Instead, he landed in the Americas, and he called the fiery pods that he found there and later brought back to Europe red peppers.

Growing Bushes are 45 cm to 2 m (1½–6 ft) high; some of the smaller varieties make great pot specimens. Most prefer full sun.

Harvesting You can pick chili peppers at any stage, but heat increases as they mature. They will not ripen after being picked.

Varieties
These popular varieties are rated on a relative heat scale of 0 to 10, with 0 meaning no heat, just sweetness—as found in bell peppers—and 10 being the hottest. Some varieties are off the scale.

❋ **Shishito**—rating 1 out of 10
A popular Japanese variety with fruits to 12–15 cm (5–6 in) long, which age from green to red. They are excellent for tempura and stir-fries.

❋ **Anaheim**—rating 2 out of 10
The fruit has a conical shape, like a bull's horn, and is 15–20 cm (6–8 in) long and 3 cm (1 in) wide. These chilies change from dark green to deep red when ripe but are picked green, when they are very mild. They are a common ingredient in Mexican cuisine, with their size making them popular for stuffing as well as using raw. They can be frozen successfully.

❋ **Jalapeño**—rating 5 out of 10
These chilies are horn-shaped with a blunt end, have a sweet-hot flavor, and are a regular garnish and condiment in Mexican cuisine. They grow 6–8 cm (2–3 in) long and are usually harvested before they turn from deep green to bright red.

❋ **Cayenne**—rating 6–8 out of 10
These classic 12–20 cm (5–8 in) thin chilies ripen from green to gold or red. They have a hot, tangy flavor and are dried and ground to make cayenne pepper, a popular seasoning.

❋ **Thai**—rating 8–9 out of 10
Loved for their use in Thai cuisine, these small upward-growing fruits are around 1.5–3 cm (½–1 in) long and age from red to green. Each plant can produce up to 200 fruits. There are many types of Thai chilies.

❋ **Habanero**—rating 10 out of 10
These fiery chilies are used in cooking or to flavor sauces and condiments. The dark green fruit ripens to red, orange, peach, mustard, yellow, white, or chocolate.

❋ **Bhut jolokia**—rating off the scale
Commonly known as the ghost chili, this scorching pepper is one of the world's hottest. The pimply green 6.5-cm (2½-in) fruit ripens to red, brown, purple, peach, or yellow.

The heat in chili peppers evolved as a cunning means of ensuring the successful dispersal of the seed. The peppery taste repels mammals but does not affect birds.

On the heat scale of 1 to 10, the red bhut jolokia, or ghost chili (top), from India, is one of the world's hottest, rating off the scale, while the green shishito chili (bottom) rates 1.

A variety of chilies (clockwise from top right): assorted red and green Thai chilies and green cayenne chilies (in bowl); green Anaheim chilies; red and yellow habanero chilies; a variety of red Thai chilies; and green jalapeño chilies.

Buying and storing

Buy chilies with firm, unwrinkled skins and no blemishes. Keep in a plastic bag in the crisper section of the refrigerator for up to five days. In a hot, dry climate, you could dry them on drying racks at room temperature. Once they are dry and there is no chance of mould, you can store them in an airtight container for up to six months.

Health benefits

It seems counterintuitive, but the chemical in chilies that gives them their unbearable heat can also be used to relieve pain. Native Americans rubbed chilies on their gums to ease toothaches, and after European explorers brought these plants back from the Americas during the 15th and 16th centuries, extracts found their way into ache-easing remedies in Europe, too.

Researchers have identified the active ingredient as capsaicin, which works by depleting a messenger chemical in the skin that sends pain signals to the brain. Studies show that capsaicin creams can reduce arthritic pain by 57 percent and nerve pain caused by diabetes by 58 percent. Prescription-only capsaicin patches can ease nerve pain.

Chili heat—how hot is hot?

The ingredient in chilies that gives them their heat is capsaicin, and it is nature's way of protecting the plant from grazing animals. The heat is in the whole fruit but is more intense in the seeds and internal white membranes. There is a common belief that the smaller the chili and the more upright it stands on the plant, the hotter it is; however, many of the varieties with larger fruits are also extremely hot.

Measuring the heat of chilies used to be done by human testers, who would quantify the parts of sugar water needed to neutralize the heat of a particular variety. This method, developed in 1912, rated the chilies in Scoville units.

Today, high-performance liquid chromatography measures the amount of capsaicin that a fruit contains to compare the different varieties. Capsaicin is not water-soluble, so drinking water, iced tea, or beer will give only fleeting relief after eating a fiery chili. Casein—found in milk, yogurt, and yogurt-based drinks—is the most effective way to relieve the heat.

Heat increases as a chili's fruit becomes fully ripe and colored.

Potatoes

Solanum tuberosum

The humble spud is a staple in many countries around the world. Whether you like them baked, roasted, boiled, mashed, fried, or added to cooked dishes, there is a perfect potato for the job. Today, potatoes aren't only white. Some have yellow, red, pink, or purple skin, and while most have white or creamy yellow flesh, there are some with purple flesh. The flesh varies in its starch content and waxiness, which is why certain varieties are better suited to particular methods of cooking.

Growing

Potatoes are highly productive and can yield 3–4 kg (6–8 lb) of tubers per square meter (yard) if grown well. They need fertile, well-drained soil that is high in organic matter. Prepare the bed a few weeks before planting by adding aged animal manures and compost. Fork the soil over thoroughly to remove any clods and make it easier for tubers to develop. Potatoes should be grown in full sun and protected from cold winds, with plenty of space and ample water while growing. They are related to bell peppers, chili peppers and eggplants, and all are prone to certain diseases. Don't grow potatoes in a bed where any of these vegetables have grown in the past four years.

Potatoes prefer mild temperatures of 16°C–22°C (61°F–72°F). In tropical and subtropical areas they can be grown all year round, although they are best planted in summer and autumn for harvest before the rainy season. In cold areas they are planted about four weeks before the last frost so their new foliage is not killed. In these climates they grow during spring and early summer, when there are 60 to 90 days of frost-free conditions. Ideally, the soil temperature should be 15°C (59°F). In milder areas you can plant an autumn crop.

Problems Proper crop rotation is essential to help reduce most pest and disease problems. Many insect pests can be avoided by keeping potatoes properly covered under soil, as the pests will damage only the exposed tubers. Irregular watering causes several problems, including soil cracking, which lets insects reach the buried tubers.

Harvesting Potatoes will be ready for harvest in 15 to 20 weeks, depending on the variety. New potatoes can be dug up as needed from 8 to 12

Never eat potatoes that have been exposed to light and have developed green patches, as they contain a toxic alkaloid known as solanine.

Potatoes are the underground tubers of bushes with lush foliage. Plants grow best in full sun, with plenty of water and ample space to develop.

weeks after the plant has flowered, once the foliage begins to yellow from the bottom leaves up. These new potatoes are best steamed whole and covered with butter and finely chopped fresh herbs such as parsley or chives.

For long-lasting potatoes that come to full maturity and are ready for storing, harvest two to three weeks after the top foliage has died off. Leaving them for those extra weeks allows their skin to harden off, or set, so that the skin doesn't rub off and the tubers don't break easily when rubbed.

Test one or two potatoes before lifting the entire crop. Use any damaged potatoes immediately and store the rest in a dark, dry place with good air circulation. Brush excess dirt off, but don't wash them; they are best stored with dirt on, as this helps exclude light and stop them going green. Always use a garden fork to harvest potatoes, as you're less likely to damage the tubers than if you use a spade. The dirt will fall between the prongs of the fork.

Potatoes will also store well in the ground as long as the weather is not too wet or warm.

ABOVE: The rich purple flesh of the Purple Congo variety will make a striking addition to the dinner plate.

RIGHT: There are many varieties of potatoes that you can grow or purchase. They are either sold washed or unwashed, although they keep better with dirt on them. Here on the platter (clockwise from top left) are Pink Eye, Russet Burbank, Bintje, Ruby Lou, Royal Blue, and Dutch Cream. On the table are Sebago (top right) and Purple Congo. In the round bowl (bottom right), Nicola and Desiree; and in the flat dish, small Kipfler (left) and full-size Kipfler.

Position three potato-growing bags in a space of about 1 sq m (1 sq yd) and grow a different variety in each. You can put the bags on concrete or paving. And expect to harvest between 30 and 50 potatoes from each bag.

If space is limited, growing potatoes in potato bags is a great option. The Velcro flap on the side of the bag lets you access the new potatoes from the sides as the plants—and tubers— are growing.

What to plant

It is best to start with certified disease-free seed potatoes every year. While it is possible to plant any potatoes that sprout, many nonorganic supermarket potatoes are sprayed with antisprouting chemicals. Certified seed potatoes are best planted whole. However, if they are very large, cut them into pieces that weigh around 50–60 grams (about 2 ounces) each and that contain at least two or three eyes. Leave the cuts to air-dry thoroughly. The eyes are the dormant buds from which the potato will shoot.

The seed potatoes and cut pieces need to sprout before planting. Spread them out in a warm, well-lit place such as a cupboard or above the refrigerator or freezer for up to a month, or until the sprouts are thick and around 1.5 cm (½ in) long. Discard any potatoes with shoots that are thin and long.

Though the potato is an excellent root, deserving to be brought into general use, yet it seems not likely that the use of it should ever be normal in the country.

DAVID DAVIES,
*THE CASE OF LABOURERS IN HUSBANDRY
STATED AND CONSIDERED* (1795)

Where to grow

There are a number of ways to grow potatoes, both in the ground and above the ground. The important thing to understand is that they yield about 80 percent of their crop above the level where the seed potato was originally planted. Each seed potato is capable of producing a tenfold harvest. This means that either you plant them deep in the ground in trenches and then mound the soil up around the plants with a rake as they grow or you plant them at soil level and then stack soil on top of them.

Planting in trenches Dig a trench 15 cm (6 in) deep, leaving the soil on the side for refilling. Space the trenches 75 cm (2½ ft) apart. Space the sprouted seed potatoes 30 cm (1 ft) apart along each trench. Cover them with 10–15 cm (4–6 in) soil. As the shoots emerge in three to four weeks, use the reserved soil to cover them, hilling it up over the emerging shoots. This encourages the formation of more tubers and ensures that they're not exposed to sunlight. You can also add a layer of straw mulch 5–10 cm (2–4 in) thick for the same purpose.

Planting the no-dig way To grow spuds the no-dig way, mix together aged animal manure, such as that from a cow or sheep, compost, and straw. Lay wet newspaper on the ground, then add a 15–20-cm (6–8 in)-layer of the bedding mix on top and lay out your seed potatoes on it, 30 cm (1 ft) apart. Cover them with 15 cm (6 in) of the bedding

You can plant your sprouted potatoes in individual 15-cm (6-in)-deep holes, spaced about 30 cm (1 ft) apart. The sprouts should be thick, not too thin or too long.

mix and water well. When the potato shoots have reached 20–30 cm (8–12 in) in length, cover them with another 15-cm (6-in) layer of bedding mix so that only their tips are visible. Continue to add extra layers of bedding mix throughout the growing season until you have a depth of around 60 cm (2 ft). A dose of seaweed-based plant tonic at planting and flowering time will also be helpful.

Raised towers This raised, no-dig planting method uses towers made from three stacked Styrofoam boxes with their bottoms cut out, stackable wooden frames, or wine barrels, even old ones on which the base has fallen out. You can also make a tower out of a ring of chicken wire or wire mesh supported by some wooden garden stakes or steel fence posts.

The potatoes are easy to harvest when the foam boxes or wire towers are taken apart, and there is no risk of damaging the tubers with a garden fork. Also, the compost, manure, and straw mix can be recycled elsewhere in the garden.

Potato bags Potato-growing bags made from laminated polypropylene are ideal for gardeners with limited space. They let you multiply 3 to 5 seed potatoes tenfold into 30 to 50 potatoes. These bags have a special Velcro flap in the side so it's easy to feel around and find new potatoes while the main crop is growing.

Recipe

Warm potato salad

For an elegant, flavor-drenched warm salad, boil nutty new potatoes and high-fiber fava beans, drizzle them with an herby vinaigrette, then serve on lettuce leaves.

Preparation 15 minutes / **Cooking** 15 minutes / **Serves** 4

500 g (1 lb) small new potatoes
1 kg (2 lb) fresh whole fava beans in the pod or
    300 g (10 oz) frozen fava beans
1 teaspoon sugar
1 teaspoon prepared mustard
1 teaspoon cider vinegar
3 tablespoons olive oil
3 large sprigs fresh thyme
Salt and freshly ground black pepper
100 g (3½ oz) beet greens or mixed lettuce leaves
4 tablespoons snipped fresh chives

Put the potatoes in a large saucepan of boiling water, bring back to a boil, then reduce heat, cover, and cook for 10 minutes. Drain. Meanwhile, if using whole beans, split the pods and take out the beans. Put the fresh or frozen beans in a separate saucepan of boiling water and cook for 3–4 minutes. Drain well. When cool enough to handle, remove the tough outer skins; pierce the skin encasing each bean and slip the inner bean out.

Whisk the sugar, mustard, and vinegar in a large bowl until the sugar has dissolved. Whisk in the oil and rub the thyme leaves into the bowl. Season to taste.

Make a bed of leaves on four plates. Gently toss the drained potatoes and beans in the vinaigrette. Sprinkle with chives and toss again. Top the leaves with the potato-and-bean salad.

Chips or fries?

Although cooks have been frying small slices of vegetables for centuries, the term "potato chip" did not come into use until the 1800s, when it began to appear in both recipe books and literature. Charles Dickens, in *A Tale of Two Cities* (1859), describes "husky chips of potatoes, fried with some reluctant drops of oil." It was beaten into print, just, by "French fried potatoes"—potatoes cut into thin slices and cooked in boiling fat—as detailed in Eliza Warren's *Cookery for Maids of All Work* (1856). During World War I American soldiers serving in Belgium and France popularized the term "french fries."

The harvest from a single sprouted tuber is impressive. When lifting a plant, insert the garden fork at least 15 cm (6 in) away from the stems to avoid impaling the potatoes.

Recipe

Twice-cooked fries

For perfect fries, the trick is to double-fry. Peel and cut baking potatoes into 1.5-cm (½-in) spears. Pat dry. Half fill a deep fryer or a large saucepan with oil and heat until hot (170°C/340°F). A cube of bread or small piece of potato skin dropped in should sizzle. Cook the potatoes for 5 minutes, until just starting to color. Remove and leave to drain and dry out on paper towels. Increase the oil temperature to 180°C (350°F). Cook again until crisp and golden, about 7–10 minutes.

Varieties

Growing a number of different potatoes not only gives you a variety of uses, qualities, and flavors, this diversity also reduces the likelihood of pest and disease problems.

Potatoes with a low starch content are waxy and hold their shape after cooking. Often referred to as boiling or waxy potatoes, they are the best choice for potato salad. Potatoes with a high starch content are ideal for baking, boiling, mashing, and frying; they're called baking potatoes. All-purpose potatoes have a medium starch content and can be used for most cooking methods.

Yellow-fleshed potatoes   These have a buttery flavor and waxy consistency when cooked, making them chefs' favorites.

❉ **Fingerling** Yellow-fleshed, elongated tubers with a finger-like shape and a firm texture.

❉ **Bintje** Knobby yellow skin and waxy yellow flesh. Keeps well; great for cooking and frying, and makes excellent potato salad.

❉ **Desiree** Elongated oval tubers with pale pink skin and creamy flesh. Excellent for all cooking methods except frying.

❉ **Dutch Cream** Large, oval tubers with creamy yellow flesh, thin skin, and a buttery taste. Good mashed, baked, or in salads.

❉ **King Edward** Oval tubers; smooth, dappled pink skin with creamy flesh and a floury texture. Great all-purpose potato, excellent mashed or baked, and makes great fries.

❉ **Kipfler** Small, finger-like tubers with yellow skin and creamy yellow flesh. Excellent all-purpose potato, although not ideal for frying.

❉ **Nicola** Small to medium tubers with elongated shape, yellow skin, and yellow flesh. Slightly sweet, buttery flavor is good in all cooking. Excellent in salads, boiled, mashed, or baked.

❉ **Pink Eye** Cream-and-purple tubers with a waxy yellow flesh. Great boiled, steamed, or baked.

❉ **Royal Blue** Oval tubers with rich royal blue skin and creamy yellow flesh. The blue skin fades to golden brown when cooked. Good mashed or baked, and makes great fries.

❉ **Ruby Lou** Oval tubers with shiny pink skin and creamy flesh of great flavor. Good all-rounder.

❉ **Spunta** Large, oblong tubers with yellow flesh. While good for baking and mashing, its large shape makes it popular for making fries.

White-fleshed potatoes These tend to have a more floury, starchy consistency when cooked.

✳ **Coliban** Medium-sized, round tubers with smooth skin and white flesh. Its floury texture is best suited to mashing, baking, or making fries.

✳ **Red Pontiac** Round, reddish-pink–skinned tubers with white flesh. Great for mashing, boiling, or baking, but not for frying, as they crumble.

✳ **Russet Burbank or Idaho** Large, elongated tubers with brown skin and white flesh. Good for baking, mashing, and making fries.

✳ **Sebago** One of the most common potatoes. Large, oval tubers with smooth white skin and white flesh. Good all-purpose potato and the main variety used for fries and potato chips.

✳ **Toolangi Delight** Round tubers with deep dimples, purple skin, and white flesh. Great for baking, mashing, or making fries and gnocchi.

Other potato varieties

✳ **Cranberry Red** Large red-fleshed tubers with good flavor. Good for mashing or baking.

✳ **Purple Congo** Elongated tubers with very dark purple skin and purple flesh, which turns a lovely lavender color when cooked. Good for mashing, steaming, boiling, microwaving, and salads, but not good for baking. A squeeze of lemon juice over the cooked potato can intensify the purple color.

Dig! Dig! Dig!

In Britain during World War II, the Dig for Victory campaign urged people to grow as much food as possible. Garden beds and public land were turned over to the cultivation of potatoes, carrots, cauliflower, and onions. A similar campaign of planting Victory Gardens was implemented in the U.S.

While many people are accustomed to white potatoes, the colorful flesh of the yellow and purple varieties has more nutritional benefits. The pigments come from carotenoids and flavonoids, currently being studied for their health benefits, including cancer prevention.

> *For me, a plain baked potato is the most delicious one.... It is soothing and enough.*
>
> M.F.K. FISHER (1908–1992)

Buying and storing

Potatoes should be firm and unblemished. Avoid any that show signs of sprouting or that have green areas. Keep in a cool, dry, dark place in a ventilated basket or box—do not store in plastic bags. And contrary to common practice, potatoes and onions should not be stored together, as the gases they produce can hasten spoilage.

Health benefits

Applied raw to the skin as a poultice, potatoes have long been used as a folk remedy for warts, wounds, and burns. A hot baked potato, held so the steam might enter the ear, was said to ease earaches, while steam from boiling potatoes was a remedy for eye disorders. Rich in vitamin C, they were also used to prevent and treat scurvy. Eating a white potato with the skin boosts potassium intake, which helps the body regulate blood pressure.

Recipe

Potato latkes

Latkes are often served with a dollop of sour cream or applesauce, but you can simply sprinkle them with salt and serve as part of a meal. Crisp on the outside but creamy inside, these grated-potato pancakes are especially good for breakfast.

Peel and grate 1 kg (2 lb) baking potatoes and combine with 1 finely chopped small onion. Take a handful of the potato-and-onion mixture and squeeze over a bowl to remove as much liquid as possible. Transfer to a clean bowl and repeat with the remaining mixture.

Add 2 lightly beaten eggs. Sift together ⅓ cup (50 g) all-purpose flour and 1 teaspoon baking powder and add to the bowl. Stir until well combined.

Heat 6 mm (¼ in) vegetable oil in a large frying pan over medium heat. Drop ⅓ cup of the mixture into the pan and flatten slightly with a spatula to about 7.5 cm (3 in) in diameter—you should be able to cook about four at a time, but don't overcrowd the pan. Cook for 3 minutes on each side, or until golden brown and crisp.

Drain on paper towels and keep warm while cooking the remaining latkes. Serve hot. **Serves 6 (makes 12 latkes)**

Pumpkin and winter squash

Cucurbita maxima, Cucurbita moschata, Cucurbita pepo

If ever there was an easy vegetable to grow, it is the winter squash. The only drawback is that the vines need space to roam. In many gardens the best crops are produced by plants that appear from the compost. There are so many wonderful varieties to choose from, in every shape and color. While most are grown for their edible and long-storing fruit, the shoots, tendrils, flowers, and seeds are also edible.

Growing

Pumpkins and winter squash are vigorous warm-season vines that take up plenty of space, so site them where they can grow as they want, even over a fence or shed. They do best in protected sunny positions where strong winds can't damage their large leaves. Where space is limited, grow small "bush" varieties, which are less vigorous and only spread to around 1 m (3 ft) across. Or grow small "nugget" varieties and train them up climbing frames.

These vegetables are grown from seed sown directly into well-drained, fertile soil. It is worth improving the 1 sq m (1 sq yd) surrounding the planting site with compost, organic matter, and well-rotted manure. Or simply make a mound of compost and sow into that. Sow three seeds per mound, and space mounds 2 m (6 ft) apart.

In tropical areas pumpkins and winter squash are grown during the dry season, while in cool or moderate climates they are grown in spring and summer for a late autumn or winter harvest. Be sure to sow after the last frost has passed and harvest before the first frost occurs, as frost will damage the fruit internally. In frost-prone areas, start seeds in seedling trays under glass. Transplant carefully to minimize root disturbance, which the roots dislike.

The plants produce male and female flowers on the same plant—usually more male flowers than female. Mostly, bees and other insects will pollinate the plants for you, but if weather conditions are not favorable to these pollinating insects or few appear in your garden, you, the gardener, can do the job. To hand-pollinate, pick several male flowers in the morning, remove their petals, and brush them against the female flowers. (Female flowers are closer to the vine on a short stem, and they have a miniature pumpkin at the base of the flower, while male flowers have longer, more spindly stems and are a greater distance from the vine. Male flowers also leave a trace of pollen on your hand when you rub them.) As the vine grows and reaches 60 cm (2 ft) in length, pinch out the growing tips to encourage lateral branches, which naturally produce more female flowers. The growth you pinch out can be cooked and eaten as a leafy vegetable.

Once the plant has grown and has several fruit on each vine, pinch out the growing tips again. This stops the plant, producing more fruit. Instead, it puts its energy into developing the fruit it already has.

Plants must be watered regularly and not allowed to dry out. On hot days their leaves may droop, but if the soil is moist they will recover in the evening. Mulch well to conserve soil moisture and to keep the base of the fruit clean.

Problems   Poor pollination is one of the biggest challenges for growers of pumpkins and winter squash. If the weather is too cold, wet, windy, or hot, pollinating insects will not be active. This means that the female flowers present won't be pollinated and so won't form fruit. Instead, the flowers appear to form fruit, but they then fall off. Also, in extreme hot weather, the pollen dries out quickly, before insects or gardeners have had a chance to pollinate.

Leaf-eating ladybugs and pumpkin beetles can attack vines and crops. Mildews can also affect the vines in humid conditions, and these can be treated with organic fungicides.

Golden Nugget squash is a good choice for small gardens. It has a more compact growth habit than other, larger varieties and can also be trained up a sturdy frame or support.

There are many pumpkin varieties you can grow for good eating. Here are some of the best (clockwise from top left): Jap, Butternut, Jarrahdale, Queensland Blue, and Golden Nugget.

Pumpkins cross-pollinate readily, so only collect the seed of varieties grown in isolation. Cut open the pumpkin one month after harvest and scoop out the seeds. Wash and dry them thoroughly on paper towels before storing for next year.

Harvesting Pumpkins and winter squash take 14 to 20 weeks to mature. Leave fruit on the vine for as long as possible while the vine still has green leaves, because it is still feeding them with nutrients. Harvest when the vine dies and the stalk on top of the fruit dries and hardens—the fruit is ready when a knock on the side makes a hollow sound. Pick the pumpkins or squash with a 5-cm (2-in) stalk. If you pick them with a shorter stalk, it can reduce their shelf or storage life. While you can harvest immature pumpkins as required, they won't store well.

Leave harvested pumpkins and winter squash outside for up to a week to harden, or cure, the skin. Store them in a single layer on racks in a cool, dry, airy environment to ensure good air circulation. Only store pumpkins and squash with intact skins; those with damaged areas allow rot to set in. Check them regularly, as rats and mice love to invade them. Some varieties can be stored for up to 10 months.

Cinderella's coach

Pumpkins found their way into European vegetable gardens in the 1500 and 1600s. They were grown as curiosities due to their striking size and shape, and as food for the poor. By 1697 French writer Charles Perrault had incorporated this New World arrival into his version of an old European folktale—"Cinderella." The French heirloom pumpkin variety Rouge Vif d'Etampes, flat-topped, deeply ridged, and with a glossy red-gold skin, bears a strong resemblance to the heroine's magical coach and is today known as the Cinderella pumpkin.

Heirloom varieties have interesting shapes and colors, as well as varied sizes and uses. Here (clockwise from top right) are futsu, Pennsylvania Dutch crookneck, and minikin pumpkins.

Varieties

There are many wonderful heirloom varieties of winter squash worth growing. Here are the most well known.

❋ **Blue Hubbard and Golden Hubbard** Large, pear-shaped squash with warty skin and exceptionally flavored orange flesh.

❋ **Butternut** Small, yellow, pear-shaped fruit weighing 1–2 kilograms (2–4 pounds) each, with a thin skin and deep orange flesh.

❋ **Golden Nugget** Bush pumpkin that produces 6 to 10 small, round orange fruit up to 12.5 cm (5 in) across with thin skin and pale orange flesh. Takes just 10 to 14 weeks to mature; stores well.

❋ **Kabocha** A gray-green shell and bright yellow flesh. It is reliable in the tropics.

❋ **Jarrahdale** A popular commercial variety, producing large, gray-skinned fruit with deep orange flesh. It is easy to peel and keeps well.

❋ **Queensland Blue** A popular variety, with large fruit weighing up to 3–4 kilograms (6–8 pounds) each, with green to gray skin and bright orange flesh. It has good flavor and keeps well.

I would rather sit on a pumpkin and have it all to myself than be crowded on a velvet cushion.

HENRY DAVID THOREAU, *WALDEN* (1854)

Roasted pumpkin seeds

Recipe

Next time you cook a pumpkin or carve a jack-o'-lantern, save the seeds for making a spicy snack. For a sweet version, omit the cayenne pepper and salt in this recipe and season with sugar, cinnamon, and nutmeg instead.

Preheat the oven to 150°C (300°F). Remove the seeds (about 90 g/3 oz) from 1 pumpkin and rinse in a colander to remove any excess pulp. Dry with paper towels. Toss the pumpkin seeds in a bowl with ½ tablespoon melted butter or oil, 1 teaspoon salt, and, if you like, 1 teaspoon cayenne pepper.

Spread the seeds out in a single layer on a baking sheet and bake for 40 minutes, stirring occasionally, until the seeds are a light golden brown color. Cool before eating.
Makes 1 cup

Butternut is a reliable winter squash, well suited to most climates. Its deep orange, very sweet flesh is good roasted or pureed in soups.

also ...

How to make a jack-o'-lantern for Halloween

Some pumpkin varieties are bred specially for lighting up Halloween. Or you can use any large, bright orange pumpkin.

Draw a circle or other shape around the stem of the pumpkin, making it large enough for you to be able to put your hand and a scraping tool inside. Cut along the circle, remove the lid, and set aside.

Using a knife, spoon, or scraping tool, scoop out the seeds, strings, and enough flesh to leave a thickness of about 2.5 cm (1 in).

Draw a face pattern on tracing paper and cut out the shapes. Tape the paper shapes to the pumpkin and, using a washable marker, draw the shapes on the skin. Remove the paper. Using a sharp knife, carefully cut the shapes out of the pumpkin. Put a small, lit candle or night-light inside.

Pumpkin and gramma pies

Pumpkin as dessert—baked in its shell with honey, eggs, and spices—was popular long before the addition of a pastry crust made pumpkin pie an American classic.

Pumpkins are credited with helping the Pilgrims survive their first harsh winters in North America in the 1620s and have ever since been part of Thanksgiving dinners. The traditional pumpkin pie, however, is said to have been developed in France in the 1650s and did not join the Thanksgiving table until the early 1800s. The similar Australian gramma pie, a Depression-era favorite, is traditionally made with an old-fashioned, elongated, pear-shaped pumpkin variety known as trombone pumpkin that has thin skin and sweet, deep orange flesh.

Buying and storing

Choose firm, unblemished pumpkins or winter squash with some stem present if possible. If buying cut pumpkin or squash (usually in plastic wrap), make sure it looks firm and bright, with no stringy or spongy flesh. Uncut, it will keep for up to three months in a cool, dark, well-ventilated place. Cut, it can be kept in the refrigerator for up to four days, wrapped tightly in plastic wrap.

Health benefits

Could stashing a pumpkin or winter squash under the bed ward off rheumatism? Will pulverized pumpkin seeds get rid of a tapeworm? And can pumpkin salve—a folk remedy for baldness—grow hair? Probably not. Today, these vegetables' claim to health-promoting fame is their treasure trove of nutrients. These include alpha-carotene and beta-carotene, which may bolster immunity; lutein and beta-cryptoxanthin, two carotenoids that may help protect eyes against vision-robbing cataracts and age-related macular degeneration; and potassium, which supports optimal blood pressure levels.

Sometimes, the term "pumpkin" may be used almost disparagingly for food fit for animal fodder, a reflection in part of the number of varieties grown and the suitability of the climate for growing this crop.

A trailing pumpkin such as this heirloom variety Lil' Tiger Stripe will spread out over the garden, producing around eight fruit or even more.

Beets, carrots, spinach, parsnips, cucumbers, lettuce, and green beans are said to grow well alongside radishes.

Some of the many types of radishes are pictured here. In the basket (clockwise from top left): pale green watermelon, elongated French breakfast, black, orange, cylindrical red, Korean, and micro red (center); and on the table, the long white daikon radish.

Radishes contain rich supplies of dietary fiber, vitamin C, folate, and potassium.

Radishes

Raphanus sativus

Spicy, peppery taste and crisp, crunchy texture—that's radish's reputation. But there are many types, which can be used in the kitchen in different ways.

Growing

Radish seed is sown directly into a shallow trench, in fertile, friable soil, which is easy for the roots to push through as they grow. Radishes require ample water and mulching over summer. Sow thinly, then thin seedlings to 5 cm (2 in) apart for summer radishes and 10–15 cm (4–6 in) apart for daikon radishes. The thinnings can be eaten, leaves and all. To keep up a constant warm-weather supply, it is best to make small sowings of summer radishes every few weeks in rows 20 cm (8 in) apart or in blocks 30 cm (1 ft) square.

Problems   Radishes grown slowly due to poor soil or a lack of water over the summer growing period will have split roots, hollow middles, or tough, pithy, or hot roots. Watch out for snails and slugs eating holes in the sides of tender exposed roots.

Harvesting   Radishes are harvested as needed; pull the largest roots first to allow the smaller roots to mature. Roots that are left in the ground become tough and excessively hot.

Varieties

Summer radishes, with their small round, oval, or elongated shapes, are the most familiar. Skin colors range from classic red and white to pink, purple, and violet. Although they can be grown all year round, they usually grow as a quick summer crop in as little as three weeks. Enjoy them in salads.

Roasted radishes

Roasting sweetens radishes, giving them a succulent, mellow flavor.

Preheat the oven to 220°C (425°F). In a medium bowl, toss 1 bunch of red and pink radishes, halved if large, with 1 tablespoon olive oil, a pinch of coarse salt, black pepper, and 1 teaspoon fresh rosemary leaves to coat. Spread in a baking dish in a single layer. Roast for about 25 minutes, stirring to cook evenly—crisp on the outside, soft inside. Serve warm. **Serves 4**

Daikon radishes (*Raphanus sativus* Longipinnatus Groups) are the large white radishes that grow up to 60 cm (2 ft) long and can be spherical or cylindrical. When sown in autumn, they take 9 to 10 weeks to mature in winter. There are white- and red-skinned varieties. They have a milder flavor and are used in cooking, salads, or pickles.

Winter radishes have black skin and white flesh and are grown in winter. They have a mild flavor and grow to the size of a beet.

Buying and storing

Radishes usually come in a bunch with leafy tops; these indicate freshness if they are bright and not too wilted. To store, discard the tops and keep radishes in a loosely sealed plastic bag in the crisper section of the refrigerator for up to four days.

Health benefits

Bite into a red radish fresh from the garden, and its spicy kick seems to bite back. The taste and smell of this cruciferous vegetable indicate the presence of sulfur-rich compounds called glucosinolates. Scientists now suspect that a diet that is rich in glucosinolate-packed foods may help lower the risk of some cancers. But hundreds of years ago, radishes had other uses: in honey-based syrup for coughs, as a poultice for joint pain, and as a juice to ease upset stomachs. That last use may have some basis in science. Radishes contain diastase, an enzyme that helps break down starches.

Summer radishes are ideally suited to container growing, as these rapid growers thrive in small spaces.

Little ginseng

Radishes were used in traditional Asian medicine. The restorative and cooling properties of the long white daikon radish are the stuff of Chinese folklore, earning it the nickname little ginseng. The healing qualities are clearly proclaimed by the ancient Chinese saying: "When white radishes are in season, doctors should take a break."

Rhubarb

Rheum × hybridum

This very attractive plant forms a clump of large, bold, dark green leaves up to 1 m (3 ft) high atop crimson red, edible leaf stalks. The red stalks become soft and succulent when cooked and have a naturally tart flavor, which most people sweeten with sugar or honey. Be warned, however, that the leaves are poisonous due to their oxalic acid content and should not be eaten.

Growing

Rhubarb is easy to grow in rich, moist soil with plenty of organic matter, as long as it is well drained. If drainage is questionable, build up the bed first. It doesn't like to dry out over summer, so grow it in semi-shade in hot, dry climates to avoid leaf scorch.

While rhubarb can be grown from seed, it is better to plant bare-rooted crowns, which are available in winter, or potted specimens. This will ensure that you grow a reliable variety and will take at least a year off the wait for your first crop. Space crowns 1 m (3 ft) apart. Don't harvest the plant in its first year of growth. Instead, leave the crown to establish properly, and only start picking stalks in the second year. Crowns can remain productive for many years, although they should be divided, and some decline in vigor after five years should be expected. Remove any flower stems; they appear because of a lack of watering or fertilizing and will rob the crown of energy.

Rhubarb is native to northern and central Asia and reached Europe in the 1300s with the Silk Road traders.

Harvest the fully grown outer stems of your rhubarb plants from the second year onward, pulling the largest stems from the outside of each plant as you need them.

Recipe

Fruitful decision

Benjamin Franklin is credited with introducing rhubarb to North America in the 1770s, and although it failed to achieve immediate popularity, by the 1820s it had gained steady acceptance, largely as a pie filling. Although rhubarb is, botanically speaking, a vegetable, its use as a fruit led to a New York court ruling in 1947 that it was a fruit and should be taxed accordingly. At the time, taxes were lower for fruits than for vegetables in the U.S. This resulted in reduced prices for rhubarb, which led to an increase in both its availability and consumption. Shown here is *Rhubarb* by Norwegian artist Nikolai Astrup (1880–1928).

Rhubarb is best covered with foil and baked or simmered in a little water or fresh orange juice in a saucepan that has a tight-fitting lid. Never cook it in an aluminum container, as it will react and give a metallic taste.

Problems The most common problem is crown rot, which causes the plants to suddenly collapse and die. Don't replant in the same position, and make sure that soil drainage is excellent.

Harvesting Stalks should be around 2.5 cm (1 in) thick when harvested. Harvest only from the second year onward. Start from the outside of the clump, and don't cut the stalks. Instead, pull down and twist, as this also removes the leaf collar from the crown.

Varieties

There are a number of varieties available. Acidity varies, as does stem color, from green to deep burgundy red, but all have good flavor.

Buying and storing

If the leaves are still attached to stalks, they should look fresh. Stalks should be vibrantly colored, firm, and plump, with no brown areas. To store, cut off the leaves and discard, then keep the stalks in a loosely sealed plastic bag in the crisper section of the refrigerator for up to a week.

Health benefits

Rhubarb root has been used in traditional Chinese medicine to treat constipation, diarrhea, digestive system ulcers, and high blood pressure. The roots and red stems contain tannins and anthraquinones—compounds that stimulate the intestines and act as a laxative. British researchers discovered that baking rhubarb for 20 minutes releases high levels of possible cancer-fighting polyphenols. Scientists are now hoping to use these results to study the effects that rhubarb's antioxidants may play in treating leukemia.

Rhubarb root also contains lindleyin, a compound that may have hormone-like effects. In one preliminary study rhubarb extract seemed to ease the severity and frequency of menopausal hot flashes for 109 women; more research is needed to confirm that this use is safe and effective.

Rhubarb and custard

Rhubarb and custard is an old-fashioned favorite that combines the silky tartness of rhubarb with the sweet creaminess of custard. If you'd like extra spice, you could add star anise, ginger, and grated citrus zest with the cinnamon.

Trim 1 bunch (500 g/1 lb) rhubarb and cut into pieces. Put ⅔ cup (160 g) sugar, 1 cinnamon stick, 1 tablespoon lemon or orange juice, and 2 tablespoons water in a medium saucepan. Stir over medium heat until the sugar dissolves, about 2 minutes. Reduce the heat to low. Add the rhubarb, cover, and simmer gently, stirring occasionally for 10 minutes, or until tender and not crunchy. Remove from the heat, discard the cinnamon stick, and set aside in a medium bowl, covered.

Put 100 g (3½ oz) superfine sugar and 5 egg yolks in a medium bowl and beat with an electric mixer until light and fluffy.

Put 2 cups (500 ml) milk and 1 split vanilla bean in a heavy-bottomed saucepan and bring to a boil over medium heat. Pour it onto the egg mixture, whisking continuously to combine.

Pour the custard into a clean saucepan. Cook over low heat, stirring continuously, until it starts to thicken slightly.

Spoon a little custard over the rhubarb and transfer the remaining custard to a ceramic jug for serving. **Serves 4**

Rutabagas and turnips

Brassica napus Napobrassica Group and *Brassica rapa* Rapifera Group

These round root crops have dropped out of culinary favor, yet they are quick and easy to grow and deserve greater recognition and popularity. Rutabagas, also called swedes, are a cross between a turnip and a cabbage. They have sweet, juicy, yellow or cream roots, are milder in flavor than turnips, and have purple skin on the top of the root. The young roots can be eaten raw or grated into a salad, while older roots are cooked for their earthy flavor—roasted, pureed, or included as a good filler in soups and stews.

Turnips are smaller. The top of the white roots can be white, yellow, green, or purple. When young, turnips are quite sweet. The roots are used as a side dish, added to soups or stews, roasted, or pickled, while the young foliage can be used as a leafy green—steamed, braised, or added to salads.

Growing

While they like to grow in full sun in well-drained soil enriched with compost, both vegetables will tolerate poorer soils and partial shade, conditions under which other vegetables would struggle. They are sown thinly in late summer and autumn for a winter harvest, directly into rows 1–2 cm ($\frac{1}{2}$–$\frac{3}{4}$ in) deep. Thin the seedlings to 15–20 cm (6–8 in) apart for rutabagas and 7.5–10 cm (3–4 in) apart for turnips. In cool climates they can also be sown in late winter and early spring.

Problems   Rutabagas and turnips are affected by the same pests as other brassicas. See page 28.

Harvesting   Roots are ready to lift and harvest after one to two months for turnips and three to six months for rutabagas. Use a fork and work carefully to avoid damage. In cold climates both vegetables can be stored in the ground over winter. Rutabagas store well in a cool place, while turnips only store well in the refrigerator.

Turnip jack-o'-lantern

At least one of the traditions associated with Halloween has its roots in the ancient Celtic festival of Samhain, held to mark the end of the harvest season. A feature was the hollowing out of turnips into lanterns, which were carried to ward off evil spirits. The holes initially carved to emit light came to depict scary faces. Immigrants from Ireland and Scotland carried the tradition to North America.

Rutabagas and turnips make delicious purees and also lend themselves well to roasting. See our recipe for Roasted potatoes and root vegetables **on page 257.**

ABOVE: Because turnips grow quickly and are best picked young, sow a few seeds every two to four weeks for a continuous supply.

LEFT: Rutabagas are usually harvested when much larger than turnips. Keep the ground well watered, or they may become stringy.

Add mashed rutabagas to mashed potatoes for extra color and flavor. Rutabagas are traditionally used in Cornish pasties.

Buying and storing

The roots of rutabagas should be plump, with smooth, unblemished skin. If turnips have tops, these should look fresh and reasonably unwilted, with the leaves green, not yellowed. The skin should be smooth and almost pearly. Store both in loosely sealed plastic bags in the crisper section of the refrigerator—rutabagas for a week and turnips for two days only.

Health benefits

All parts of the turnip plant have been used as kitchen "cures" for cancer—powdered seeds, roots boiled in lard, the stems and leaves, even the flowers. There's no evidence that these work, but research shows that turnips contain glucosinolates that help the body neutralize and whisk away harmful toxins and hormones that could raise cancer risk. One cup (156 grams) of cooked turnips delivers a healthy dose of potassium and vitamin C, which helps heal wounds, bolsters immunity, and protects cells from damage. Rutabaga is a particularly good source of potassium and magnesium, which help maintain optimal blood pressure levels. Its bitter flavor is a sign that this vegetable contains glucosinolates, too.

Recipe

Neeps and tatties

There is much debate about whether neeps are made from rutabagas or turnips. Whichever you use, this is a traditional Scottish accompaniment to haggis. It also goes well with corned beef or roast lamb.

Peel 500 g (1 lb) rutabagas and cut into 2.5-cm (1-in) chunks. Put in a large saucepan and cover with water. Add 500 g (1 lb) peeled and chopped baking potatoes. Bring to a boil, then cook for 20 minutes, until very soft. Drain well and return to a low heat to evaporate excess water.
  Mash the vegetables, then add 60 g (2 oz) chopped butter. Beat with a wooden spoon until almost smooth. Mix in 1 tablespoon chopped fresh chives and season with salt and white pepper. Serve garnished with snipped fresh chives. **Serves 4**

Spinach
Spinacia oleracea

Spinach is renowned for its health benefits. Calorie for calorie, it provides more nutrients than any other food. Raw, it has a mild sweet taste that is good in salads, especially if the young leaves are used. Its flavor becomes more robust when it is cooked. It grows to 25 cm (10 in) high with arrow-shaped flat leaves.

Growing

Spinach requires a rich, fertile, well-drained soil that is high in organic matter so it does not dry out in warm weather, as this will cause it to bolt and run to seed. Traditionally, it is grown as a winter vegetable, although it may need protection from extreme frost in cold areas. There are new varieties that can be grown in summer in mild climates. Sow seeds 1 cm (1/2 in) deep in rows 30 cm (1 ft) apart. As the seeds germinate, thin them to 15 cm (6 in) apart, and use the thinnings as baby spinach.

Problems Like many other leafy vegetables, spinach is bothered mainly by snails and slugs.

Harvesting Baby spinach is picked when young and tender. The plants are fully grown in 8 to 10 weeks, when you can either take the large outer leaves first—use a knife rather than just pulling— or harvest the entire plant.

Buying and storing

Spinach leaves are quite delicate, so any you buy may be slightly soft, but make sure they are not too wilted and not shriveled at all. Keep in a sealed plastic bag in the crisper section of the refrigerator for only a day or two, and wash just before using.

Health benefits

Contrary to popular belief, this leafy green is not extra rich in iron. It is rich in vitamins A, K, and health-promoting flavonoids, which has earned it a reputation as a superfood. In animal studies, spinach extracts have discouraged cancer growth and cooled inflammation. It also contains lutein and zeaxanthin, which can help protect eyes from macular degeneration.

Early-harvest baby spinach can be used raw in salads or lightly steamed. Mature spinach can be steamed or gently cooked by itself or added to soups, cream sauces, omelets, pasta dishes, and the classic Greek spanakopita, or spinach pie.

Spinach is a wonderful cool-season vegetable. It can be harvested when the leaves are small and young as baby spinach (right) or when the plants are fully grown (left).

Strong to the finish
Although it is popularly thought that Popeye's instant muscles came from the high iron content of the spinach that he adores, in fact it was the vegetable's vitamin A that the cartoon character cited as his reason for choosing this particular pick-me-up before a fight. "Spinach is full of vitamin A and that's what makes humans strong and healthy," he advised in 1932 as he popped open his first tin.

Other types of spinach

Many other leafy green vegetables share the name spinach, and they are similarly rich in nutrients and protein. However, they are also high in oxalic acid, so don't eat too much too often.

Amaranth
Amaranthus tricolor
Also known as Greek spinach, Chinese spinach, Indian spinach

This leafy vegetable features in the cuisine of Greece, Southeast Asia, Africa, and the Caribbean. The leaves have a sweet, tangy flavor. Young leaves are used in salads, and mature leaves are best cooked as a leafy vegetable.

Amaranth can be sown all year round in warm climates and after the last frost in cool climates. It grows to over 60 cm (2 ft) high and is remarkably drought-tolerant. The light green leaves with pinkish-red new growth and the stems are edible. Flowers, produced over a long period, look like drooping tassels. Red amaranth (*A. cruentus*) has ornamental appeal, with reddish-purple leaves, red tassel flowers, and red seeds. While the leaves of grain amaranth (*A. hypochondriacus*) are edible, its seeds are a staple cereal crop in South America. All forms will self-seed readily, but save some seed just in case they don't.

Ceylon spinach
Basella alba
Also known as climbing spinach, Malabar spinach, Indian running spinach

Ceylon spinach is grown throughout tropical Asia and is perfect in limited space, climbing to 1.5 m (5 ft) high or trailing as a ground cover. Perennial in the tropics, where it is grown from cuttings or seed, it is an annual in cooler climates, best sown from seed in spring 20 cm (8 in) apart along a climbing frame. It has green twining stems, glossy dark green leaves, and white flowers. The red-stemmed form (*B. rubra*) is attractive, with its purple-green leaves, pink flowers, and vibrant reddish-purple stems. A cut-and-come-again vegetable, a succulent texture and similar flavor to Swiss chard. Plants are ready for harvesting within two months, with young leaves used raw in salads and mature leaves cooked like spinach. If overcooked or used in soups and stews, it adds a mucilaginous consistency, perfect for thickening.

Egyptian spinach
Corchorus olitorius
Also known as West African sorrel

This fast-growing leafy green is used as a vegetable and an herb in Middle Eastern and African cuisine. It can be eaten fresh in salads when young or cooked as a vegetable as the leaves mature. The

CLOCKWISE FROM TOP LEFT: Amaranth, or Greek spinach, Ceylon spinach, Surinam spinach, Egyptian spinach—these quite different plants all share the name spinach.

plant is also harvested to produce the jute fiber used to make burlap and rope. Sown in spring and summer, it grows in a clump to 1 m (3 ft) high. It is best suited to tropical or subtropical climates, where it self-seeds readily and may become weedy.

Surinam spinach
Talinum fruticosum syn. *Talinum triangulare*
Also known as waterleaf

This bushy plant, native to Central and South America, is widely grown in West Africa and Southeast Asia. It reaches 30 cm to 1 m (1–3 ft) high, with bright green leaves and attractive small pink flowers. Its dark green leaves have a crunchy, tangy flavor and are used raw in salads or lightly cooked in stir-fries. Once established, it self-seeds readily, or it can be propagated from cuttings. It grows best in tropical climates, where it is perennial in moist semi-shade. In cold climates it is an annual.

Sprouts

Sprouts are not grown outdoors in the vegetable patch, but they are used as vegetables. Easy to grow inside, they take up very little space, can be grown all year round, and make a wonderful addition to salads, sandwiches, stir-fries, or garnishes. They are superfoods, exceptionally high in nutrients.

Growing

There are two main ways to grow sprouts. True sprouts are grown in a soil-free container, using moisture, air, and light, and the whole sprout with the attached seed is eaten. Microgreens are edible plants grown in shallow trays or containers of seed-raising mix, and the above-ground plant shoot is harvested when very young and eaten. To keep your household in a constant supply, you simply grow successive batches. And only use organic seed.

To grow true sprouts without soil, you'll need a specially designed sprouting jar, a multilayered sprout tower, and a sprout bag. Or you can make

Sprouted seeds are packed with vitamins, minerals, protein, and other nutrients.

your own sprout jar using a clean glass jar, a piece of cheesecloth, and an elastic band. Follow the instructions below and you will have a steady supply of your sprout of choice.

To grow microgreens in soil, use shallow trays or small containers of moistened seed-raising mix. Thickly sprinkle seeds over the mix, then cover seed with a fine layer of seed-raising mix. Moisten with a spray bottle and mist with water several times a day to keep moist. Green shoots will appear within 10 to 14 days, and the tiny, delicate plants are ready to harvest between 1 and 3 weeks, depending on the type. Cut shoots with scissors just above soil level and use immediately. Some will only give you one crop; others regrow and can be cut several times.

Varieties

True sprouts for jars or towers   These are common vegetable or cereal seeds for sprouting.

※ **Alfalfa (*Medicago sativa*)** Fine, thread-like sprouts have a nutty flavor.

※ **Broccoli (*Brassica oleracea* Italica Group)** Sprouts have a hot, strong, broccoli-like flavor.

※ **Fenugreek (*Trigonella foenum-graecum*)** Sprouts have a sweet, spicy, curry-like flavor.

※ **Mung beans (*Vigna radiata*)** Sprouts have thick white shoots, which are crisp, sweet, and juicy.

※ **Radish (*Raphinus* spp.)** Sprouts have a spicy, slightly hot, radish-like flavor.

Other popular varieties for sprouting include azuki beans, chia, red clover, red cabbage, kale, garlic chives, onion, and quinoa. While most sprouts can be eaten raw, you may prefer to lightly steam lentil, soybean, and chickpea sprouts.

Microgreens for soil   Wheatgrass, barley grass, buckwheat, pea and snow pea shoots, cress, white mustard, radish, broccoli, sunflower, and mesclun suit this method. Shoots are harvested when 3–10 cm (1–4 in) high, after the first true leaves appear in 7 to 21 days, depending on the variety. Many can also be harvested a few weeks later as baby salad greens. Some varieties can be grown as both a true sprout and a microgreen.

※ **Cress (*Lepidium sativum*)** Shoots have a mild, spicy flavor and are ideal for salads.

※ **Snow pea (*Pisum sativum* var. *macrocarpon*)** New, fresh shoots have a lovely sweet pea flavor similar to baby spinach.

※ **Wheatgrass (*Triticum aestivum*)** Grown for its nutrient-packed foliage, which is added to juices and smoothies, it prefers a warm position, where it will be ready for harvest in 6 to 9 days.

※ **White mustard (*Sinapis alba*)** Shoots have a mild mustard flavor. They are traditionally served with eggs.

How-to

Growing sprouts

All you need is a clean glass jar, a piece of muslin (cheesecloth) or other breathable fabric, a rubber band and the seeds you wish to sprout. Position the jar in a warm, light-filled environment but not in direct sunlight. Always follow the directions on the seed packet specific to each variety and only use organic seed for sprouting.

Pour a thin layer of you choice of sproutable seeds into the jar (top left) and cover with warm water. Secure the piece of muslin (cheesecloth) over the mouth of the jar with an elastic band and leave the seeds to soak for 6-12 hours, depending on the variety.

Drain through the muslin (center), then rinse well with warm water. (To rinse, half fill the jar with water. Replace muslin, swill seeds gently in the water, then drain.) Place the jar on its side in a warm, light place. When seeds start to shoot, rinse them every morning and night and drain.

Sprouts can be harvested in 3-10 days (top right), depending on the variety. The flavour of the sprouts often intensifies with age and they are at their best before they develop green leaves. Once they are the size you want, generally 1-10 cm (½-4 in), rinse thoroughly to remove any hard unsprouted seeds and seed coatings, drain and air-dry, then store in an airtight container in the refrigerator for up to a week.

True sprouts are grown in a soil-free environment, and both the seeds and sprouts are eaten. Top row, from left: Alfalfa sprouts (in large bowl), mung bean sprouts (in small bowl), and store-bought bean sprouts. Bottom row, from left: onion sprouts, broccoli sprouts, and quinoa sprouts.

Microgreens are aboveground plant shoots. Clockwise from top left: pea shoots, broccoli shoots, daikon shoots, white mustard shoots, sunflower shoots, and purple radish shoots (center).

Buying and storing

Sprouts should look bright and crisp, with no dryness or excess moisture. If they come in a plastic basket, store them in that. Alternatively, spread in a shallow airtight container, cover loosely with a paper towel, and seal tightly with the lid. Sprouts will keep in the refrigerator for up to four days.

Health benefits

Topping your salad or sandwich with a handful of crunchy broccoli sprouts could be good for your stomach. In one recent study, people infected with the ulcer-causing bacteria *Helicobacter pylori* who ate a third of a cup (70 grams) of broccoli sprouts daily for eight weeks had fewer of these bugs and less stomach inflammation than people who didn't eat the sprouts. Alfalfa sprouts contain saponins—plant compounds that may help lower levels of heart-menacing cholesterol.

Sprouts are considered a superfood because they are high in nutrients.

Recipe

Sprout salad with daikon radish and edamame

Bean sprouts are sold in many supermarkets and Asian grocery stores. Grow them yourself and add a wonderful fresh crunch to any salad.

Thaw a 400-g (14-oz) package of frozen shelled edamame.

Peel 90 g (3 oz) daikon and cut into julienne strips.

Cut 1 Lebanese cucumber or other small cucumber into ribbons.

Combine the edamame, daikon, and cucumber in a serving dish or salad bowl.

Add 90 g (3 oz) soybean sprouts, 30 g (1 oz) snow pea sprouts, and 60 g (2 oz) store-bought bean sprouts and combine.

Place the juice of 1 lemon, 1 teaspoon sesame oil, and 1 teaspoon olive oil in a jar and shake to combine.

Drizzle dressing over salad and serve immediately.

Serves 4

Summer squash
Cucurbita pepo

Summer squash are warm-season vegetables picked when tender and young and eaten fresh. Winter squash, their close relatives, are left until fully mature and stored like pumpkins, their close relatives. Some squash can be used when young or mature. Summer squash are prepared in a similar way to zucchini, another relative—lightly steamed, stuffed, or baked, or added to stir-fries, casseroles, or curries.

Growing

Summer squash are best grown from seed sown into seedling trays or small pots and planted in spring when the risk of frost is over. Space seedlings 1 m (3 ft) apart in rich, fertile soil in a sunny position and keep moist over the growing period.

Recipe

Summer squash stew

This colorful and adaptable stew is an excellent way to deal with a glut of ripe summer vegetables.

Heat 2 tablespoons olive oil in a shallow frying pan over medium heat. Add 1 chopped onion and 1 crushed garlic clove and cook for 5–8 minutes, until soft.

Top and tail 500 g (1 lb) mixed yellow, striped, and green pattypan squash and cut into quarters. Add to the pan with 1 tablespoon fresh thyme leaves, season with salt and freshly ground black pepper, and cook for 10 minutes.

Stir in 2 diced large tomatoes and cook for an additional 1–2 minutes. Stir in the zest of 1 lemon and 2 tablespoons fresh parsley leaves. Serve hot or warm. **Serves 4**

Pattypan squash are also known as button squash because of their shape. Depending on the variety, they can be pale green, striped, gold (above), or green (right). The flesh is slightly sweeter than that of zucchini.

The plants will start fruiting within two months of planting and will continue to do so over the summer.

Problems   Mildew can affect the foliage.

Harvesting   Cut fruit from the vine with a knife to avoid damaging the plant. Pick regularly once plants start fruiting, as the fruit can quickly become oversized, with tough skin and a loss of tenderness. Regular harvesting also promotes more flowering and a longer cropping period. Summer squash are best used fresh from the vine, but they can be kept in the refrigerator for up to two weeks.

Varieties

The most popular type of summer squash is the pattypan. These flattened fruit have scalloped edges, and come in golden yellow, creamy white, pale or dark green, or striped. Harvest when young and tender at around 7.5–10 cm (3–4 in) across; the flesh is white with a delicate nutty flavor.

There are many other varieties, including crookneck, straightneck, and spaghetti squash, which is also a winter squash, which produces 20–30 cm (10–12 in) oval fruit with spaghetti-like, stringy flesh. Yellow crookneck squash produce an abundance of small, golden yellow fruit with warty skin. They are planted in spring, harvested at 12 to 17 weeks, and can be used fresh or stored for use during the winter.

Buying and storing

Choose summer squash with firm, smooth, shiny skin and fresh-looking stem ends. Store in a loosely sealed plastic bag in the crisper section of the refrigerator for up to three days. These squash can bruise easily, so don't place them under harder vegetables, such as carrots.

Health benefits

The dried seeds of summer squash have been used as a folk remedy to combat intestinal parasites and ease urinary urgency in men with an enlarged prostate gland. But today, researchers have found a surprising property in this vegetable's tasty flesh: inflammation-quenching carotenoids, including beta-carotene, lutein, and zeaxanthin, which are not destroyed by freezing or cooking. A single cup (130 grams) of summer squash also delivers 2 grams of fiber—including pectin, which may help keep blood glucose and cholesterol at optimal levels. Pectin helps support beneficial bacteria in the digestive system, too.

The French name for pattypan squash, pâtisson, *derives from a Provençal word for a cake made in a scalloped mold.*

Recipe

Spaghetti squash

The flesh of spaghetti squash comes out in long strands, resembling the pasta for which it is named.

Preheat the oven to 190°C (375°F). Using a sharp knife, prick 1 spaghetti squash (1.5 kg/3 lb) all over. Put on a baking tray and roast whole for about 1 hour and 20 minutes, until a sharp knife can be inserted with only a little resistance. Do not overcook. Remove the squash from the oven and set aside until cool enough to handle. Halve lengthwise and scoop out the seeds. Scrape the squash with a fork to remove the flesh in long strands.
Serves 6 as a side dish

Gem squash is a type of summer squash from South Africa. It has creamy yellow flesh that is sweet when small and savory as it matures. It is prolific and ideal for small gardens.

Summer squash such as Early Summer crookneck grow as low bushes and fruit prolifically. Use them in the kitchen in a similar way to zucchini.

Sweet potatoes

Ipomoea batatas

Also known as kumara

This tuberous root vegetable from the tropical Americas is as versatile as the potato, with a subtle sweet flavor that makes it perfect for baking, mashing, and using in soups, stews, curries, and even cakes. It forms a vigorous twining vine at least 1.5 m (5 ft) long and produces attractive pink flowers and underground tubers, which are usually orange but can also be purple or white. The young leaves and shoots can also be cooked as a leafy vegetable, like spinach.

Ocean journey

The sweet potato originated in Central and South America, and it has been cultivated in Polynesia since 700 CE. But how did it get there? New plants grow from tuber cuttings, not from seed, so it couldn't have traveled by bird from South America or by floating on ocean currents. It's now thought that the Polynesians traveled to South America and back again to get the sweet potato. That's a distance of around 11,300 kilometers (7000 miles). These early sailors made the journey in small craft, through open sea, with no navigable landmarks other than the stars.

Growing

Sweet potato prefers a sunny position in rich, fertile, well-drained soil that has been enriched with added organic matter. It is best suited to warm climates but can be grown in cool climates as long as there are at least five months of warm days and nights and no frosts. Even though you can plant tubers directly in the garden bed, it is best to produce cuttings from sprouted tubers. As the weather warms in spring, put a tuber in a box of damp sand, cover with 5 cm (2 in) of sand, and leave in a warm protected position for the tuber to sprout. When the sprouts are 15–30 cm (6–12 in) long, cut them from the parent tuber, remove all side leaves except those on the tip, and plant these tuber cuttings outdoors. Space them 50 cm (20 in) apart in rows 1 m (3 ft) apart, and water them well until roots develop. The roots and edible tubers grow where the stem nodes touch the ground, and each plant can produce up to eight tubers. The vines can be grown over a climbing frame to maximize your space.

Sweet potatoes are high in beta-carotene and vitamins C and E.

Problems Crop rotation is essential to eliminate sweet potato pest and disease problems.

Harvesting Harvest tubers when the vines turn yellow and die back in autumn. The tubers often form well away from the base of the original plant, so lift carefully with a fork to avoid damaging them and leave to dry before gathering. Store clean tubers in a cool, dry place for up to five months.

Varieties

❋ **Beauregard** The most widely grown variety, with reddish orange skin and deep orange flesh.

❋ **Hawaiian Sunshine** Produces tubers with off-white skin and purple flesh.

❋ **Northern Star** Reddish purple tubers with creamy white flesh.

Buying and storing

Sweet potatoes should have smooth, intact skin with no blemishes—if possible, avoid those that have had their ends trimmed off. Keep in a cool, dark, well-ventilated place for up to a week.

Health benefits

Sweet potatoes have been used around the world as a folk remedy for anemia, diabetes, and high blood pressure as well as bug bites, fever, and stomach upset. Humans have been eating sweet potatoes for 10,000 years or more—and gaining health benefits from this vegetable's unique nutritional profile. Orange-fleshed sweet potatoes deliver a big dose of beta-carotene, which may reduce the risk of cancer and heart disease. Purple-fleshed sweet potatoes contain anthocyanins that may help neutralize toxins and damaging free radicals in the digestive system.

Candied sweet potato is a beloved addition to the Thanksgiving table. Sage makes a perfect pairing with mashed sweet potato. Use it as a topping for shepherd's pie instead of mashed potato. Sweet potato is also good in desserts and baked treats.

See our recipe for Spicy sweet potato cheesecake on page 304.

Sweet potato is a highly productive, easy-to-grow vegetable for warm regions. Pictured here (left to right) are a cream-fleshed and the classic orange-fleshed variety.

Swiss chard (top) has sturdy white midribs, while rainbow chard (bottom) has midribs in red, pink, orange, or gold. They have a deep, earthy flavor and a wonderful bittersweetness. The leaves are highly nutritious.

Swiss chard

Beta vulgaris Cicla Group

Also known as silverbeet, sea kale beet

Related to the beet, this cut-and-come-again vegetable is grown for its crinkly green leaves. It is often confused with spinach, which has flat leaves, and can be used as a substitute for it in cooking, although its flavor is stronger. The most common Swiss chard forms a clump 60 cm (2 ft) high with upright white stalks and midribs and deep green leaves. Rainbow, or colored, chard is becoming more popular for both its edible and ornamental value, with stalks and midribs in hues of gold, orange, pink, and crimson.

Growing

Swiss chard is easy to grow, preferring fertile soil that is rich in organic matter. It can be grown from seeds or seedlings planted in soil 25–30 cm (10–12 in) apart. Sow a few seeds in a clump, and once they've germinated, remove all but the strongest seedling. In mild climates you can plant or sow Swiss chard all year round. In colder areas, planting in late autumn or winter may cause the plant to run to seed.

How-to

Preparing Swiss chard leaves

To prepare Swiss chard for cooking, cut off the stems near the leaves and discard. Cut a V in the midrib and discard. Wash the leaves well and proceed with the recipe.

Swiss chard is easier to grow in warm climates than spinach. It is hardier and can better tolerate hot, dry conditions.

Swiss chard spanakopita

Swiss chard makes a tasty variation on the traditional Greek spinach pie. It must be as dry as possible so the pie doesn't become soggy.

Preheat the oven to 180°C (350°F). Heat 1 tablespoon olive oil in a saucepan over medium heat. Add 1 finely chopped onion, 1 tablespoon chopped scallions, and 2 finely chopped garlic cloves and sauté for about 5 minutes, until the onion is tender. Transfer to a large bowl and set aside to cool.

Blanch 1 kg (2 lb) Swiss chard leaves in batches for 10–20 seconds each, then refresh. Drain well and squeeze out any excess moisture. Coarsely chop and add to the onion mixture with 250 g (8 oz) coarsely crumbled feta cheese, 125 g (4 oz) ricotta, 1 tablespoon grated Parmesan, 1 tablespoon chopped fresh dill, and zest and juice of ½ lemon. Season to taste, then stir to combine.

Brush a 10-cup (2½-liter) ovenproof dish with melted butter. Layer 5 sheets of phyllo pastry over the base and sides, brushing each sheet with melted butter and allowing the pastry to overhang the dish.

Spoon in the spinach mixture and fold in the pastry edges, then cover with 7 sheets of phyllo, brushing each sheet with melted butter. Trim excess pastry and tuck edges into the sides of the dish. Brush the top with the melted butter, then score in a diamond pattern with a sharp knife.

Bake for 45–50 minutes, until golden and cooked through, covering loosely with foil if it browns too quickly. Cool for 5–10 minutes, then slice and serve warm. **Serves 6–8**

Cut off any flower spikes that are produced so the plant puts all its energy into growing foliage rather than flowering and seeding. Swiss chard plants will usually remain productive for 12 to 18 months, although their vigor and lushness may be reduced.

Problems   Caterpillars, snails, and slugs love to nibble on the foliage.

Harvesting   After about two months, take leaves from the outside first, twisting and pulling them off from the base. Always leave at least six inner leaves. Do this regularly to encourage further growth. Old leaves are tough and strong-tasting; add them to the compost or feed them to your chickens.

Health benefits

Swiss chard's stems and leaves contain nine different types of betacyanin pigments, which may help to reduce inflammation, protect DNA from damage by free radicals, and support the body's efforts to neutralize toxins. Leaves also contain syringic acid, a flavonoid that may help to tame blood glucose levels.

Buying and storing

Swiss chard leaves should be dark green and firm. Avoid any that look wilted or have brown or yellow areas. The stalks should be bright white with no browning. Swiss chard can be awkward to store; to save space, you could separate stems and leaves and store in a sealed plastic bag. Or tear the leaves into smaller pieces, wash and dry well, then seal tightly in a plastic bag that is slightly inflated so the air will cushion the leaves from damage. It will keep for up to four days in the crisper section of the refrigerator.

Cleaning leafy greens such as Swiss chard, kale, and collard greens can be difficult because the crinkly leaves hold on to sand and grit. Immerse them in a large bowl or sink of water. The leaves will float on the surface, while the sand and grit will sink to the bottom. Gently swish the greens in the water with your hands, then remove and repeat with fresh water until there is no sand at the bottom of the sink.

The strikingly colored stems and midribs of rainbow chard make an attractive feature in the vegetable garden.

Taro root

Colocasia esculenta

Also known as Tahitian spinach, elephant's ear, eddoe, dasheen

This perennial plant produces large, heart-shaped leaves on fleshy stems, forming a clump 1.5 m (5 ft) high. It is a highly ornamental plant. Its underground tubers are a staple root crop in the Pacific Islands, Hawaii, India, and tropical areas throughout Asia. The tubers are boiled, mashed, roasted, or fried. The leaves and stems are also edible once cooked.

Growing

Best grown in the tropics, where the long growing season guarantees large tubers, taro root can also be grown as an ornamental plant in cooler areas if it has frost protection. It likes nutrient-rich soil and plenty of water—it can be grown either in moist soil or boggy areas or hydroponically It grows in full sun or semi-shade. Plant from divisions in spring and summer or from tubers in spring.

Harvesting In the tropics taro root tubers can be harvested at any time, but in cooler climates they are best harvested in winter when the foliage yellows and dies down. They don't keep well once lifted and are best left in the soil until required. All edible parts of the taro root must be thoroughly cooked before eating to destroy the toxic calcium oxalate that this plant contains. The tubers should be peeled first.

Varieties

One of the most commonly grown varieties is Bun Long. Its creamy white, starchy flesh has purple flecks and becomes soft once cooked.

Celery-stem taro

Colocasia gigantea (syn. *Colocasia esculenta*)

Also known as bac ha, giant elephant's ear, Tahitian spinach, cocoyam, white taro

It is the young leaves and stems of this plant that are used in cooking for their celery-like flavor.

Buying and storing

Check for any blemishes or soft patches on the skin. Keep in a cool, dark, well-ventilated place and use within two days.

Health benefits

In Hawaii, taro root is called *kalo*, the king of medicinal plants. The root is sliced and rubbed onto cuts and wounds to halt bleeding. The leaves are turned into an asthma treatment, and the leaf stems are used to ease pain and stop insect bites from swelling. The tuber itself is used to ease indigestion and constipation. Today, taro root is better known for its nutritional benefits. One cup (132 grams) contains 7 grams of fiber—more than one-quarter of an adult's daily needs. Taro root is also a good source of potassium and magnesium, which help regulate blood pressure, as well as copper, manganese, and phosphorus.

Taro root is a staple root crop throughout Asia and the Pacific. There are also Chinese cultivars suited for growing in subtropical areas.

Recipe

Oven-baked taro root crisps

Serve with guacamole or hummus.

Preheat the oven to 200°C (400°F). Peel ¼ taro root (about 125 g/4 oz) and slice into thin rounds. Put on an oiled baking sheet in a single layer. Spray with oil and season with salt and freshly ground black pepper.

Bake for 12 minutes, until the edges of the taro chips are just starting to turn golden, shake well, then bake for approximately 3 minutes more. Cool until crisp.

Makes 2 cups

Taro root has a quite bland but slightly sweet flavor and is similar in texture to potato. It is used in both savory and sweet dishes. In Polynesia, it is often combined with coconut in puddings and cakes. It can also be roasted, fried, or added to soups, stews, and stir-fries.

Tomatoes

Lycopersicum esculentum

The tomato is one of the best crops to support the case for the grow-your-own movement. Nothing beats the taste of a tomato that is fully ripe and homegrown. Originating in South America, tomatoes have been adopted by countries and cuisines around the world, and there are now hundreds of varieties to choose from, not just the classic large red fruit. They come in all shapes, sizes, and colors, from classic tomato red to almost black, orange, yellow, green, and even striped.

The botanical name of the tomato means "wolf peach."

Growing

Tomatoes can be grown from seeds or seedlings planted in the soil as it warms up in spring. Ideally, the soil temperature should be at least 15°C (59°F), and the risk of frost must have passed. If the soil warms up but nights remain cold, cover tender seedlings with cloches—glass, plastic, polyethylene, or PVC covers. Or make your own out of plastic drink bottles with the bases cut off and the tops removed.

While it is often easier to grow seedlings than sow seeds, there are more varieties available—especially heirloom varieties—to gardeners who choose the latter option. In late winter sow seed into individual-cell plastic trays or biodegradable pots 6 to 8 weeks before you plan to plant. Keep in a warm, sheltered spot, such as a mini greenhouse. In cold areas, put seedlings into larger pots as necessary until the ground is warm enough.

Plant tomatoes 45–60 cm (1½–2 ft) apart, making sure that you bury each seedling up to at least the first set of leaves. The stem of the tomato plant will develop roots at the buried leaf node, helping to make the plant stronger.

It's important to provide a stake or other upright support for the plant and the weight of its ripening fruit. Regularly tie the growing plant to the support with soft ties.

Tomato puree

Passata di pomodoro is a fresh tomato puree made from tomatoes that have been strained to remove seeds and lumps. Traditionally, it uses up the glut of ripe tomatoes at summer's end and involves large family gatherings. The tomatoes are passed through a tomato press or a food mill to separate the skin and seeds from the pulp, which is put in sterilized bottles and cooked in a large pot of boiling water.

Position In the right position tomatoes will fruit for six months of the year, from summer to early winter.

Tomatoes can be grown in the ground or in a container. As a general rule they require full sun. In hot, dry climates, however, they may do better with the extra protection of shade cloth during the harsh summer months. In cooler climates they are best positioned against a wall or fence to maximize the sun's rays and radiant heat. Tomatoes need a growing season of at least three months, and this radiant heat will keep them warm for longer.

Protection While tomatoes like good air circulation, they should be grown in a sheltered position, protected from strong winds.

Soil Tomatoes need well-drained, fertile soil that has been well prepared with organic matter in the form of compost and aged animal manures. Crop rotation is essential to minimize soil-borne diseases. Do not plant tomatoes in the same bed where eggplants, capsicums, chilies, or any other member of the Solanaceae (nightshade) family has been grown in the previous three years.

Training Most tomatoes require at least some form of upright support, whether it is a garden stake, a tripod, a cylinder of wire mesh, or a trellis. Some gardeners like to pinch out the side shoots; however, studies have shown that while this does limit bushy growth, it also results in reduced yields.

Tomatoes are heavy feeders and do best when fed and watered regularly over the growing season.

Problems Many diseases that affect tomatoes can be minimized or overcome by practicing crop rotation and keeping your plants in optimal health. Sunburn appears as brown patches on exposed parts of the fruit, so be sure not to prune off plants' side branches in hot areas, as the extra foliage will protect and shade the fruit.

Blossom-end rot causes sunken brown patches at the base of the fruit due to a calcium deficiency or irregular watering. Flower drop can occur if there are high temperatures, especially at night.

Fungal diseases are reduced by ensuring good air circulation around foliage and avoiding overhead watering; only apply water to the base of the plant to avoid wetting the leaves. In hot, dry climates tomato russet mite can be a problem, causing the leaves to brown and die off from the bottom up. Treat with a miticide or hose under the foliage in the morning to reduce mite numbers—in hot, dry areas this will not cause fungal problems.

Whitefly can affect plants and can be controlled by using whitefly traps. Tomato hornworm can be controlled with a bioinsecticide, while fruit fly can be treated by exclusion with floating row covers or organic lures and sprays.

Popular tomato varieties include (from top left to right) Roma, perfect in sauces and puree; and the Hillbilly beefsteak and the Oxheart, both of which are all-purpose tomatoes packed with flavor and good for sandwiches and salads as well as for cooking.

Harvesting Pick tomatoes once they start to turn red, then fully ripen them indoors. Once ripe, they will keep in the refrigerator for several weeks.

At the end of the season, when the weather cools, tomatoes will fail to ripen outdoors. Carefully pull the whole plant out of the ground with as much soil as possible and hang upside down in a protected place, such as a shed or veranda. The fruit will continue to ripen despite the plant being uprooted. Alternatively, pick all the fruit and bring it indoors; the fruit that is green with a tinge of orange will often start to ripen inside within two to three days. Green tomatoes that fail to ripen can be used to make green tomato pickles, green tomato fritters, or even a green tomato cake.

Tomatoes contain high levels of lycopene, a known antioxidant that protects the heart.

Heirloom varieties have better disease resistance. They also crop over a longer period and have more intense flavor than the more recently developed modern hybrid tomatoes.

For a rich choice of color, shape, size, and wonderful flavor, check local seed suppliers for heirloom varieties such as (clockwise from top left) red and golden Mortgage Lifter, Schimmeig Creg, Black Krim, and Green Zebra.

Common varieties

* **Beefsteak tomatoes** Huge, meaty tomatoes, great for slicing; a single slice can cover a piece of bread from crust to crust. There are several varieties and a range of colors.

* **Grosse Lisse** A medium to large dark red beefsteak-type fruit, producing abundantly over a long period. Its name means "huge and smooth."

* **Mighty Red** A favorite globe type; disease-resistant, high yields, and fine flavor.

* **Mortgage Lifter** A famous tomato; prolific, often with massive fruit and great flavor.

* **Oxheart** Large, heart-shaped, orange-scarlet tomato. It performs well in hot, humid areas.

* **Roma, or plum, tomatoes** The traditional egg-shaped tomatoes used for cooking and sauces because of their dense flesh.

Heirloom varieties

* **Black Krim** A large-fruited, dark-skinned, and deep red–fleshed variety with a smoky flavor. It is ideal for cool climates.

* **Black Russian** A prolific variety with medium reddish-black fruit. Its black skin absorbs heat, making it perfect for growing in cool climates.

* **Burnley Bounty** A late-fruiting variety, tolerant of cool conditions. It will produce excellent large tomatoes in midwinter.

* **Green Zebra** Highly productive; striped green and yellow when ripe. One of the best tomatoes for taste and yield, it crops over a long period.

* **Tigerella** A highly productive, long-fruiting tomato with excellent flavor and a skin that shows orange stripes on a red background.

* **Tropic** Sweet-flavored fruit, well suited to hot, humid tropical and subtropical climates.

Cherry varieties

Cherry tomatoes are the easiest to grow and are usually the first to fruit, so get them in early to have them in your summer salads. There are both bush and climbing varieties, and all bear prolifically.

✳ **Black Cherry** Dark purplish, round tomato with very sweet, juicy fruit.

✳ **Cherry Roma** Miniature versions of the classic Roma tomatoes, with the classic elongated shape and a great flavor.

✳ **Tommy Toe** Plump, 3-cm (1¼-in) tomatoes, very juicy, available in a range of colors, perfect for salads. They consistently rate extremely well in tomato taste tests.

✳ **Currant** Varieties that produce long sprays of 10 or more tomatoes, which ripen evenly.

✳ **Yellow Pear** A popular variety with yellow, pear-shaped fruit and good sweet flavor.

Recipe

Gazpacho

This refreshing soup is always served cold.

Combine 4 cups (1 liter) tomato juice, 4 seeded and coarsely chopped Roma tomatoes, 1 peeled, seeded, and coarsely chopped cucumber, 1 seeded and coarsely chopped small yellow bell pepper, 3 finely chopped scallions, ¼ cup (60 ml) freshly squeezed lemon juice, ¼ cup (15 g) coarsely chopped fresh basil, and 1 crushed garlic clove in a large bowl. Add salt, freshly ground black pepper, and Tabasco sauce to taste.

Refrigerate for at least 1 hour before serving.
Serves 4

Dwarf varieties are suitable for growing in containers where space is limited. Tiny Tim grows 30–40 cm (12–16 in) high and produces masses of red cherry-size fruit.

Of the many different cherry tomatoes available, you could choose (clockwise from top left) Cuban Yellow Grape, Cherry Roma, Black Plum, currant tomatoes, Yellow Pear, grape tomatoes, or Zebrino.

Buying and storing

For immediate use, choose tomatoes that have bright red skin and that give slightly when you press them gently. Avoid any that have bruises, blemishes, or soft spots. Tomatoes will continue to ripen at room temperature, so if they are still firm and pale in color, leave them to ripen for a few days. Always store at room temperature, not in the refrigerator, and use them before they become very soft, unless you want them for cooking.

You'll find a great way to use semi-dried (sun-blushed) tomatoes in our Grilled vegetable terrine on page 239.

Health benefits

Sipping a hot cup of tomato "tea" is a modern folk remedy for colds. Modern-day science suggests that consuming tomatoes and tomato products regularly could help reduce risk for strokes, heart attacks, fracture-prone bones, and several types of cancer. But tomatoes haven't always been a popular health food. In 1628, one prominent Italian physician called these delicacies from the New World "strange and horrible things."

How times have changed. We now know that tomatoes are a rich source of lycopene, a powerful antioxidant and cancer-fighting agent that may play a role in heart health by lowering LDL cholesterol. Lycopene pills don't deliver the benefits found in real tomatoes, and cooked tomatoes have more lycopene than fresh.

Cherry tomatoes do well in containers of enriched potting mix. They can also look highly ornamental in a hanging basket. Be sure to water and fertilize regularly.

Love apple

In medieval times the tomato, a member of the nightshade family, Solanaceae, was considered either inedible or poisonous. Furthermore, it was suspected of having aphrodisiac properties—the French called it *la pomme d'amour*, or the love apple.

A world without tomatoes is like a string quartet without violins.

ANONYMOUS

Recipe

Semi-dried tomatoes

Traditionally, sun-blushed tomatoes and sun-dried tomatoes are fresh, ripe tomatoes that are placed in the sun to remove almost all their water content. Semi-dried tomatoes are like sun-blushed tomatoes, being slightly plumper and juicier than those that are sun-dried. They are easy to make at home and good if you have a bumper crop. Small or Roma (plum) tomatoes are best. Drain off the olive oil before eating.

Preheat the oven to 150°C (300°F). Cut 500 g (1 lb) tomatoes in half lengthwise. Arrange cut side up on a baking sheet lined with parchment paper. Sprinkle with salt and freshly ground black pepper. Bake for 2½ hours, or until the tomatoes dry around the edges but are still soft in the center. Set aside to cool. Transfer to a sterile, airtight jar and cover with olive oil. Store in the refrigerator for up to 2 weeks.

Arrange the tomatoes cut side up on the baking sheet.

Yams

Dioscorea spp.

Originating in Asia, these root vegetables have become the staple carbohydrate in many tropical regions, including West Africa, the West Indies, and Asia. Plants grow as vigorous twining vines and produce large tubers with a bland flavor, best baked, steamed, or boiled.

Growing

Yams grow well in the tropics and warm temperate regions where there is plenty of water throughout the growing season. They require soil rich in organic matter and will thrive in either full sun or semi-shade. Plant sprouting tubers as the ground warms up in spring. Being a vine, this plant will need a trellis or climbing frame for support.

Harvesting   Tubers can be harvested when the vine dies back in autumn. As with all root crops, take care when lifting tubers to avoid damaging them. They store well in a cool, dry place for a number of months. Keep some tubers for replanting next season.

Varieties

❋ **Dioscorea alata**—Greater yam, purple yam, white yam, water yam, winged yam, Guyana arrowroot
The vine produces extremely large, brown-skinned tubers with white or purple flesh and nutty flavor. Tubers reach 15–30 kg (30–60 lb) each.

❋ **Dioscorea bulbifera**—Aerial yam, air potato
In addition to tubers in the ground, it produces tubers in leaf axils on the vine that are large enough to harvest. It is less productive than *Dioscorea alata*, but plants can become weedy.

❋ **Dioscorea cayenensis**—African yellow yam, igname jaune
This is one of the main yam species grown in West Africa. The vine can grow to 10–12 m (30–40 ft), so it is not a good choice in small gardens. It is a cultivated yam available at farmers' markets and Caribbean groceries.

❋ **Dioscorea esculenta**—Chinese yam, lesser yam, potato yam, cinnamon vine
The vine produces small tubers with fine hairs and deliciously cinnamon-scented flowers. This variety will tolerate cool climates as long as it is watered well over the summer.

Buying and storing

Sweet potatoes are sometimes mislabeled as yams. True yams have rough skin, while sweet potatoes are smoother. Choose yams with unblemished skin and firm flesh. Store in a cool, dark cupboard at room temperature, not in the refrigerator. Once cooked, keep in the refrigerator for up to three days.

In tropical and subtropical areas, yams are a better crop for the home garden than potatoes. The tubers have tough brown skins, while the flesh can vary in color from white to yellow to purple.

Health benefits

Wild yam (*Dioscorea villosa*) is used in East Indian traditional medicine as a remedy for sexual and hormonal problems. Chinese herbalists use wild yam for rheumatism and asthma, while Native Americans and early American settlers used it for colic and coughs. Despite an initial flurry of interest, researchers today say that wild yam creams do not provide hormones that help menopausal symptoms.

The edible, cultivated yams found in the grocery store do have health benefits. One cup (136 grams) provides a significant amount of vitamins B_6 and C as well as 25 percent of the recommended daily intake of manganese. This important trace mineral is used by the body to manufacture sex hormones, connective tissue, bones, and blood-clotting factors.

While yams can be substituted for sweet potatoes in recipes, true yams have an earthier, starchier taste and a drier texture than sweet potatoes. Yams go well with strongly flavored meats such as venison and are often served with spicy sauces. They can be roasted, added to stir-fries, made into chips, steamed, mashed or pureed. Always peel yam tubers first and always cook them well before eating.

In Africa, yam is pounded into a dough-like paste called fufu. It is rolled into balls, dipped in a soup or stew, and eaten by hand.

Water plants

Edible aquatic plants are perfect for gardeners who want to combine their desire to grow produce with their wish to have a water feature. Some of these plants don't even need a pond. They'll grow well in a boggy or poorly drained area of the garden.

Growing

Site these plants in full sun in a preformed fiberglass pond, a flexible rubber liner in a hole dug in the garden, an old bathtub, or an old sink. Use a combination of potting mix and garden soil topped with gravel. It is important to keep the water ecosystem within the pond healthy by having a balance of oxygenating plants.

Arrowhead

Sagittaria sagittifolia

Also known as Chinese potato, duck potato, swamp potato

The cream-fleshed tubers of this aquatic plant are edible, as are the young shoots. Plant the tubers in early spring for an autumn harvest. Some *Sagittaria* species are weedy, but the forms grown for eating are nonflowering and therefore nonseeding.

Look for arrowhead tubers in Asian markets and food stores. Also sold as Chinese potatoes, they look like small onions without the layers. The tubers do not store well, so use them as soon as possible.

Fertility and purity

The lotus is renowned for its stunning large pink or white flowers, which have been immortalized in Asian art. It is a symbol of beauty and fertility in Hinduism and of spiritual purity and awakening for Buddhists. For ancient Egyptians, it was associated with rebirth.

Arrowhead tubers must be cooked before being eaten and can be fried, boiled, or baked—peel off the bitter skin before cooking. They have a nutty, potato-like flavor. Chicken soup with arrowhead is a Chinese New Year dish. Dice the peeled tuber and add it to your favorite chicken soup recipe. Crispy fried arrowhead is a variation on potato chips.

Arrowroot

Maranta arundinacea

Also known as West Indian arrowroot, prayer plant

Arrowroot prefers a well-drained position in a warm, frost-free climate. It has pretty foliage that closes up at night, as if in prayer. Plant tubers at the start of the spring and the clump will grow to 1.5 m (5 ft) high over 10 to 12 months. When the stems and leaves yellow and die off, the tubers are ready to harvest. The tubers can be eaten raw or cooked, although they are very fibrous. It is the starch in the tubers that is extracted to make commercial arrowroot, a powder used in desserts and to thicken soups, sauces, and gravy.

Canna lily

Canna edulis syn. Canna indica

Also known as Indian shot, canna

This hardy, clump-forming perennial spreads by edible underground tubers. It is highly ornamental, with 2-m (6-ft) stalks of large green leaves topped with red flowers. It prefers a warm, sunny position in a frost-free area; in cold regions lift the tubers over the winter and replant the following spring. While not a submerged aquatic, it likes a damp position with plenty of water. Tubers for eating are best harvested before they become fibrous, at around six months.

The tubers, which were a staple of the Incas, can be eaten raw but are usually peeled and added to stir-fries or boiled or baked as a potato substitute. They can also be ground to make a flour, often referred to as arrowroot (true arrowroot is described above). The young leaf shoots can be cooked and eaten as a vegetable.

Lotus

Nelumbo nucifera

Also known as sacred lotus

This aquatic perennial grows 1–1.5 m (3–5 ft) tall, with large circular leaves and exquisite flowers. The leaves, roots, flowers, and seeds are all edible. The lotus needs a long, warm growing period to flower, so it is best not grown in cool climates. Plant the rhizomes in winter, when they are dormant.

When buying lotus roots for cooking, choose those that are firm, and juicy, without blemishes or soft spots. Wash the whole root, place it in a sealed plastic bag with water, and keep in the vegetable drawer of the refrigerator for a week. Once cut, cover with fresh lemon juice before storing again.

Add sliced lotus root to any stir-fry to give it interesting shapes and texture.

Water chestnuts

Eleocharis dulcis

This aquatic plant has narrow, reed-like foliage and develops underground corms—the edible part—which are harvested when the foliage dies down at the end of autumn. These corms can grow up to 4 cm ($1\frac{1}{2}$ in) across. Plant corms 20 cm (8 in) apart, with 5 cm (2 in) of water above the top of the pot. This plant is extremely productive, with each individual corm able to produce over 1 kg (2 lb) of corms.

When purchasing water chestnuts for cooking, look for those that are firm, with unwrinkled skin and no soft spots. Unpeeled fresh water chestnuts will keep for up to two weeks in a plastic bag in the refrigerator. If peeled, store in cold water in the refrigerator and change the water daily.

Water chestnuts have a sweet flavor that can be enjoyed raw or cooked; their crunchy texture remains even after cooking. They are a staple of Chinese cuisine.

Watercress

Nasturtium officinale

Watercress is a hardy perennial aquatic creeper that grows naturally in gently flowing streams. It is fast-growing, with small white flowers all summer long. The young shoots and leaves are very nutritious and have a spicy, peppery taste. Sow the seed in spring or autumn.

Rich in nutrients, watercress can be used in salads, soups, and sandwiches. The

Recipe

Stir-fried water spinach

This simple stir-fry is a popular side dish in Chinese, Vietnamese, and Thai meals.

Preparation 10 minutes / **Cooking** 6 minutes / **Serves** 4 as a side dish

- 1 bunch water spinach (kang kung)
- 1 tablespoon vegetable oil
- 2 cloves garlic, sliced
- 1 teaspoon fish sauce
- ½ teaspoon sugar
- 1 red chili pepper, seeded and finely chopped

Separate the leaves of the water spinach and cut the stems into short lengths.

Heat the oil in a wok or large frying pan over high heat. Add the water spinach stems and stir-fry for 3–4 minutes.

Add the water spinach leaves, garlic, fish sauce, sugar, chili pepper and 1 tablespoon water. Toss until the leaves wilt and the stems are tender-crisp, about 2 minutes. Serve immediately.

Health benefits

Water plants have a special place in traditional medicine systems around the world. Canna lily, an ancient treatment for infection and rheumatism in subtropical and tropical regions, has been shown in a recent scientific study to have an anti-inflammatory effect. In traditional Chinese medicine, lotus root is believed to improve liver function and to strengthen the heart, spleen, and stomach. The spicy leaves of the watercress plant have been used to sweeten bad breath, ease coughs, promote urination, and improve digestion.

Modern research confirms that water plants deliver important health benefits. For example, one recent study found that consuming watercress regularly reduced genetic damage to blood cells. In another, 10 out of 11 women who ate a large helping of watercress daily for four weeks saw improvement in their skin, including a lessening of brown spots and redness.

Beware the weed potential of edible aquatics.

peppery crunch of watercress makes it a great companion for fish, in salads, and a perfect garnish for roast duck, venison, and lamb dishes.

Purchase watercress and other leafy water plants at their peak. Select bunches that show no signs of wilting, and avoid those with bruised, torn leaves or crushed stems. Before storing, remove any limp leaves. Rinse to remove soil, then dry thoroughly and put in an open plastic bag lined with paper towels. Store in the crisper in the refrigerator for three days.

Water spinach

Ipomoea aquatica

Also known as kang kung, swamp cabbage

This perennial trailing plant grows well in the tropics and subtropics and is popular in Southeast Asian cuisine. Sow from seed in spring and summer or grow from a runner. Its young leaves, stems, and tips are delicious in a stir-fry or steamed.

Like most water plants, water spinach is available from specialty growers, farmers' markets, or Asian grocery stores. Store it as you would watercress and keep for up to three days.

CLOCKWISE FROM TOP LEFT: Canna lily, arrowhead, lotus root, watercress, water spinach, and water chestnut.

Zucchini is one of the easiest and most productive vegetables to grow, but you can have a glut of them at the same time everyone else does. Have a good range of recipes ready so you can preserve or freeze them to enjoy when other crops slow their production.

Although the best-known zucchini have dark green skin, there are varieties with golden yellow or pale green skin, such as the Lebanese variety pictured here.

Zucchini

Cucurbita pepo

Also known as courgette, marrow

These easy-to-grow summer vegetables are so productive that many gardeners find themselves swamped with the output. In the UK, zucchini is often referred to as summer marrow, along with summer squash, tromboncini, and ornamental forms known as gourds. They are tastiest and at their best when picked young.

Growing

Sow seeds into warm, well-prepared, fertile soil in spring when the risk of frost is over. Plant two or three seeds in each hole and thin to the strongest seedling once they have germinated. Bush varieties take up less space, at around 1 sq m (1 sq yd) each, while the trailing varieties can be trained over a trellis or frames. One plant can produce large quantities of fruit over two months—you will need only one or two plants for a family. They can fruit in as little as 50 to 60 days, so midseason sowing will give you zucchini into autumn. The young fruit can be cut from the vine with the flower still attached and these zucchini flowers can be used in the kitchen for stuffing and other culinary delicacies.

Problems Zucchini are prone to powdery mildew, so ensure good air circulation; if watering overhead, water in the morning so foliage dries rapidly. Mites and whitefly can also affect plants under stress.

Harvesting The key is to harvest fruit regularly, every day or two, when young, soft, and tender and around 10–20 cm (4–8 in) long. Fruit left on the plant will rapidly achieve mammoth proportions. Allowing a plant to produce these large fruit could halt flowering and production of more fruit, but if grown in good soil, this is less likely. Young fruit can be steamed or stir-fried. Once they get big, zucchini become tough and are better stuffed or baked, made into pickles, or grated for use in cakes. Fresh zucchini will keep in the refrigerator for 7 to 10 days.

Varieties

Black Beauty is a popular home garden variety with very dark green, almost black skin, similar but more productive than Black Jack. Gold Rush has lovely golden yellow skin, while Lebanese zucchini are light green and slightly teardrop in shape. Costata Romanesco is an Italian variety with ribbed fruit, which makes star-shaped slices when cut across. There are also gray-skinned varieties and some that are round instead of long.

Gourds

Gourds belong to the Cucurbitaceae family. These annual vines produce interesting fruits in a range of colors, sizes, and dramatic shapes. They come in edible and ornamental varieties, which are allowed to mature fully on the vine and dry. Then they are picked and dried further indoors for long-term storage. They can be used in artwork or arranged in a bowl for a decorative display.

How-to

Preparing zucchini flowers

Zucchini has a delicate flavor and requires little more than quick cooking in butter or olive oil, with the skin left on. It can also be battered and fried, steamed, or added to soups, stews, and pasta sauces.

Zucchini flowers may be stuffed and baked or deep-fried, or they can be dipped in tempura batter and fried. They also make a lovely garnish or pizza topping.

See our recipe for Stuffed zucchini flowers on page 258.

To prepare a zucchini flower, hold the flower in your hand. Use your thumbs to make a split in the flower and open it. Then snap off the stamens inside the flower with your fingertips and discard them. Do this just before you're ready to fill the flower, as it will wilt quickly.

Zucchini flowers are harvested with the small developing fruit attached. Use a knife to cut through the zucchini stalk.

Tromboncino is an interesting vegetable with pale lime skin and a bulbous end. Although best picked when young and tender, at around 20–25 cm (8–10 in) long, it can grow up to 1 m (3 ft) long.

Buying and storing

Zucchini should have firm, smooth, shiny skin and fresh-looking, firm stem ends. Zucchini are crisp when freshly picked but become flaccid over time, so make sure they are still firm. Store in a loosely sealed plastic bag in the crisper section of the fridge for up to 3 days. Larger fruit with thicker, tougher skin will keep longer.

Health benefits

One cup (180 grams) of cooked zucchini provides 3 grams of fiber and just 29 calories—making this vegetable a filling, slimming choice if you're watching your weight. It also delivers a healthy dose of vitamins A, C, and K, along with essential minerals magnesium, potassium, copper, and manganese. The soluble fiber found in zucchini helps reduce LDL cholesterol by carrying it out of your body before it can be absorbed into the bloodstream. Zucchini also contains choline, a type of vitamin B that looks after cell membranes and helps nerve signals reach your muscles.

The word "zucchini" comes from an Italian word meaning "little squashes."

GROW YOUR OWN

Setting up a vegetable garden

When setting up a vegetable garden, there are many factors to consider, from the practicalities to design, from aesthetics to underlying principles, and from big-picture ideals to working practices.

Choosing the best site

Working out where to site your vegetable garden will actually determine its success or failure, so make sure you take some time and think it through fully. Here are some technical factors to consider:

Sun

Vegetables require some sun to grow well. Not enough sun will reduce crop quantity and quality, increase the likelihood of insect pests, and in the case of herbs, reduce their flavor. The angle of the sun can vary significantly at different times of the year. As a result some vegetable gardens grow great summer vegetables, but in winter, when the sun is lower in the sky, there is not enough light to grow good winter vegetables. The solution is to find a position for your vegetable patch where you get sun all year round. Alternatively, have two different areas, one for summer vegetable growing, one for winter.

In hot, dry climates some vegetables are best grown with a little protection from fierce summer sun. Do this by locating them where they will get gentle morning sun and afternoon shade, or by using shade cloth, either permanently or pulled across only on really hot days.

Heat

Radiant heat from walls, fences, and concreted or paved areas significantly increases air temperature, and this can cause vegetables to burn, be more prone to insect pests and diseases, or at least have higher water requirements in hot weather. In cool climates, however, this radiant heat can be used to great advantage for the late ripening of summer vegetables such as tomatoes.

BELOW: Climbing peas are a great crop to grow against a fence to make use of vertical space—a good tactic in small gardens. There is the added benefit of hiding the fence.

ABOVE: Fava beans require staking to prevent them being damaged by wind.

Wind

The main ways in which wind causes problems in the vegetable patch is that it blows over tender plants, breaks stems, and dries out plants in hot weather. You can provide protective windbreaks, which slow wind speeds while still allowing good air circulation and helping to prevent fungal diseases.

Other siting considerations

A vegetable garden should be as close to your house as possible so you can gather vegetables and herbs readily. It should be located near a tap and even, ideally, have its own rainwater tanks as its water source. Having a shed or storage area close by for tools and equipment is also handy, with an adjacent compost heap or worm farm so you can manage garden waste and access the compost easily. Finally, garden beds should be designed so that all produce is within arm's reach and you can harvest produce easily without having to stand on the garden beds.

Follow these planning principles to get your vegetable plot off to a good start and to ensure a rich harvest.

ABOVE: This neatly boxed garden is divided into plots, which makes it easy to keep track of what you've planted where.

POSITION
Choosing the right position makes the difference between success and failure when it comes to growing vegetables.

LEFT: Grass or lawn paths between vegetable beds are comfortable and soft to walk on and reduce radiant heat from hard or paved paths.

LEFT: You can incorporate food-producing areas into the rest of your garden so they harmonize with ornamental beds.

Alternatives to a garden bed

In some gardens and situations it's not possible to create the right conditions for vegetables in beds in the ground. But the good news is that a vegetable garden doesn't have to be planted in the ground.

Build up or choose containers

You can grow vegetables above ground in raised beds or in containers. Your decision to do this will be based on the quality of the soil, its drainage, and root competition. Raised beds are ideal for gardeners with mobility issues. Also, if your yard or courtyard is covered in stone or concrete, a raised vegetable garden can be built directly on top of this solid base.

A raised bed can be constructed from walls of brick, stone, or hardwood or concrete railroad ties; you can also use prefabricated kits of plastic panels or corrugated iron tanks. If choosing a tank, use galvanized iron or steel, as it will have a better life span than other corrugated metal products, which will corrode from the acids in the soil. You can also build a simple bed by edging straw-bale walls with plastic mesh to hold them in place, or use the no-dig method (see page 125).

Growing vegetables in containers is the perfect solution if space is limited or you want a portable or temporary option (see pages 134–135).

Free from root competition

It is important to position your vegetable garden away from trees and large shrubs, as their extensive root systems will compete for and rob your plants of water, nutrients, and soil space. If this isn't possible, build a raised bed on top of the soil surface, place a root barrier on the ground, then add the soil. Make sure you extend the root barrier outside the walls of the raised bed, because tree roots will follow any source of moisture and nutrients they can and take advantage of the smallest gaps to get at it.

Where to start— from the ground up

The thought of starting a vegetable patch from scratch is exciting, especially as it gives you the chance to get the soil right. Build your vegetable garden where you have, or can at least create, good soil. It is vital.

Getting the soil right

Getting your soil right is essential when growing vegetables. The quality of the soil will determine the quality of your produce—it even has an effect on the incidence of pests and diseases among your crops. Vegetables prefer to grow in well-drained, loamy soil that is rich in organic matter. It should have a friable texture, a light, crumbly consistency, yet look dark in color and smell sweet.

When starting a new vegetable garden:

Step 1 Determine the soil type in your garden: loam, clay, or sand. All soil types are improved by the addition of organic matter. Sandy soils can also be improved with an organic soil wetter and clay soils with annual dressings of gypsum in autumn.

Step 2 Identify the pH of your soil. The pH is the measure of the soil's acidity or alkalinity, and it affects the ability of plants to take up nutrients available in the soil. Vegetables prefer to grow in soil with a pH of 6.0–7.5, so test your soil with a pH testing kit for home gardeners. If the pH is too low (acid), it can be raised with dolomite or lime. If the pH is too high (alkaline), it can be lowered with sulfur, though this is a slow process.

Step 3 Improve and amend the soil in your vegetable patch. Use aged, well-rotted animal manures and compost to feed the soil, improve its structure, build up fertility, and supply plants with the nutrients they need to survive, thrive, and provide bountiful crops.

In the heavy-feeding world of the vegetable garden, soil improvement is an ongoing process.

Filling raised vegetable beds

When purchasing the soil to fill raised beds, always choose a good-quality blend suitable for vegetable growing and be prepared to add extra organic matter, such as compost or aged animal manure. If the raised bed is quite high and you plan to grow vegetables only, you'll need 30–45 cm (1–1½ ft) of soil. Fruit trees need greater soil depth. To bulk up a raised bed, fill the base with tightly packed bales of straw or hay. Even though this bottom layer will eventually break down, this should only lower the soil level by around 15 cm (6 in) in 12 to 18 months; by then, you'll need to add more compost anyway, which will raise the soil depth again. You could also use old bricks, gravel, or clean building rubble as the bottom level to save on soil.

Also ...

Community gardens

If you are unable to find the right position for a vegetable garden or you don't have the space, you can become part of a local community garden. There are many versions of community gardens, with models ranging from individual beds to shared plots. Whatever the model, all will give you the opportunity to grow food, meet people, share gardening knowledge, and cultivate vibrant communities. Contact your local government or local garden club to find one near you.

Becoming involved in your local community garden is a great option if you have limited space or your garden's situation is unsuitable for growing vegetables. Pictured here at the Turramurra Lookout Community Garden, on Sydney's North Shore, are (clockwise from top left): cabbages, kale, and other leafy greens; recently sown raised beds; fava beans growing with support; and healthy beet foliage.

Designing a vegetable garden

When you're working out the design of your vegetable garden, consider it from both an aesthetic and a practical point of view. And remember that your beds must be easy to access so you can nurture and harvest your crops.

Drawing up a plan

With so many design possibilities and gardening practicalities to consider, it's important to draw up a plan on paper first. Take a bird's-eye view and design a layout that works in the space and site you've allocated in a style that appeals to you. For example, will the vegetable garden be positioned in its traditional domain—the backyard—or will it feature in the front yard? Decide whether you want it to be aesthetically pleasing as well as productive.

While every vegetable garden is different, the common design styles fall into four broad categories: formal, informal, food forest, and small spaces.

The vegetable parterre at the historic property Heronswood in Dromana, Victoria, Australia, home of the Diggers Club, is highly productive yet still looks colorful and interesting.

Design styles

Formal

If you like things neat and orderly while also being aesthetically pleasing, create a formal vegetable garden using a geometric layout. The French-inspired *potager* (small kitchen garden) organizes beds in a formal pattern and then combines the diverse colors, textures, sizes, and forms of the vegetables to create a living patchwork.

Vegetables can also be grown in parterre gardens, where low hedges of box or a similar plant enclose beds that are usually filled with dense plantings of vegetables. Again, the vegetables are chosen for their variety and visual appeal, with those that are less attractive being positioned farther away and out of view.

Another way to design a formal vegetable garden is to start with a framework of structural plants, such as border plants or hedges of clipped rosemary or lavender, then add plants with architectural qualities as focal points, such as globe artichokes, cardoons, or rhubarb, then fill in the remaining space with those vegetables you want to grow and eat.

Informal

This is the traditional backyard produce garden, perfect for those interested purely in practicalities and those who want a workable, highly productive vegetable patch. It can be set up as raised beds or planted into the ground, usually with between four and six beds, depending on the available space. This makes it easy for the gardener to adopt a good crop rotation practice. An informal garden also works well when setting up a no-dig garden system (see page 125).

Food forest

This is a term often used to describe gardens that include fruit and nut trees along with vegetables to create an abundant harvest. There are few rules in such a garden, where vegetables are allowed to self-seed and grow where they choose. Those that must be sown or planted are positioned where there is space rather than where a deliberate order of rows and sections dictates.

Small spaces

If space is limited, grow vegetables in containers, in vertical gardens, or even among your ornamentals. Who says you can't underplant your roses with small vegetables? Growing tall vegetables—tomatoes, climbing peas, and beans—vertically on frames or stakes will create shade from the summer sun.

RIGHT: An informal layout should always have good pathways so you can sow, plant, maintain, and harvest without treading on the beds.

LEFT: An espaliered apple tree is productive without taking up too much space and acts as a fence around a vegetable garden.

Well-designed vegetable gardens are both productive and attractive.

WHAT ARE GREEN MANURES?

Green manures are annual leafy plants that are dug into the soil toward the end of their life cycle to add organic matter and nitrogen to the soil. See page 145.

LEFT: Clearly defined beds make it easier to practice crop rotation, although this can also be done by swapping plants within individual beds.

Crop rotation

This is an essential annual practice of planting unrelated groups of vegetables successively in the same location to avoid the build-up of soil-borne pests and diseases and to make better use of soil nutrients. It is based on the fact that many pests and diseases affect particular plant families, so moving these plants to different planting sites from year to year helps prevent these problems from persisting. Also, different plants take up different nutrients, and you can make the most of this with crop rotation. For example, legumes such as peas and beans add nitrogen to the soil, and a crop that needs nitrogen, such as lettuce, can follow them to take advantage of that added nitrogen.

Plants can be grouped into families. To prevent disease problems from persisting, plants from the same family—for example, eggplants, tomatoes, potatoes, bell peppers, and chilies, all of which belong to the Solanaceae family—should not be grown in the same spot in two consecutive seasons.

The main vegetable groups

* **Alliums** Chive, garlic, leek, onion, scallion, shallot

* **Brassicas** Broccoli, brussels sprout, cabbage, cauliflower, kale, kohlrabi, radish, rutabaga, turnip

* **Composites** Chicory, endive, lettuce, radicchio, salsify, scorzonera

* **Cucurbits** Cucumber, gourd, melon, pumpkin, winter and summer squash, zucchini

* **Legumes** Bean, fava bean, clover, pea

* **Solanaceae** bell pepper, chili pepper, eggplant, potato, tomato

* **Umbellifers** Carrot, celeriac, celery, fennel, parsley, parsnip

CLOCKWISE FROM TOP LEFT: Fava beans, a green manure, can be followed by heavy-feeding cabbages, nitrogen-producing beans, then light-feeding Swiss chard.

Four beds or one

For a vegetable garden with four beds, rotate the following principles over four rotations (or growing seasons) in each bed. For crop rotation in a single bed, rotate crops around different parts of the bed every year or plant alternate crops.

❋ **Rotation 1**
Grow a green manure crop or apply compost and a straw mulch and leave to rest.

❋ **Rotation 2**
Grow vegetables that are heavy feeders, such as cabbages and broccoli—they need plenty of soil nutrients to crop successfully.

❋ **Rotation 3**
Grow legumes that replace nitrogen in the soil, such as peas and beans.

❋ **Rotation 4**
Grow vegetables that are light feeders, such as beets and Swiss chard—they don't need plenty of soil nutrients to crop well.

Based on the fact that most vegetable gardens have two main plantings (that is, two rotations) a year—spring to summer and then autumn to winter—here are examples of heavy and light feeders and suggested nitrogen producers for these plantings:

Spring to summer planting

Heavy feeders The Solanaceae, cucurbits, and leafy greens.

Nitrogen producers Peas, beans, and green manure crops.

Light feeders Root crops such as carrots, parsnips, and onions.

Autumn to winter planting

Heavy feeders Brassicas such as broccoli, brussels sprouts, cabbage, cauliflower, plus spinach and Asian greens.

Nitrogen producers Peas and fava beans.

Light feeders Root crops such as onions, leeks, garlic, beets, and carrots.

ROTATION 1: broad (fava) beans

ROTATION 2: cabbages

ROTATION 4: Swiss chard

ROTATION 3: climbing beans

The practices of crop rotation and companion planting are simple techniques to increase natural biodiversity in the garden and reduce the incidence of plant pests and diseases among the vegetables.

ROTATION CHART SHOWING SUCCESSION OF PLANTINGS

	ROTATION 1	ROTATION 2	ROTATION 3	ROTATION 4
BED 1	Green manure	Heavy feeder	Legume	Light feeder
BED 2	Heavy feeder	Legume	Light feeder	Green manure
BED 3	Legume	Light feeder	Green manure	Heavy feeder
BED 4	Light feeder	Green manure	Heavy feeder	Legume

Permaculture

This philosophy for productive gardens aims to provide food self-sufficiency by imitating nature and creating diversity. The term was coined from the two phrases "permanent agriculture" and "permanent culture" (or lifestyle). The principles of sustainability that cover the design and management of productive gardens in permaculture systems are as relevant to a home garden as they are to a farm. The principles are:

✻ **Uphold ethics** Have consideration for the earth, people, and fairness.

✻ **Support diversity** Provide food for humans and provide habitat and food for other species that coexist in the garden.

✻ **Eliminate waste** Reconsider energy use, redistribute excess food, recycle, and use renewable materials and sustainable organic products (fertilizers).

✻ **Adaptation, not manipulation** Turn problems into solutions, seek advice, and make changes slowly.

The smell of marigolds can deter insect pests from nearby zucchini and kohlrabi. Roots of French marigold exude a substance that breaks the cycle of root-knot nematodes.

Companion planting

Companion planting is a holistic way of gardening in which plants are grown together for a healthier garden. Choose a range of plants so you have flowers throughout the year to attract birds and beneficial insects such as hoverflies, ladybugs and lacewings to your garden, where they will devour insect pests that would otherwise trouble your vegetables. Herbs with flowers that attract beneficial insects include basil, bergamot, borage, bronze fennel, chamomile, coriander, dill, lavender, mint, oregano, parsley, rosemary, thyme, and yarrow. You could also add some ornamental annuals such as alyssum, Queen Anne's lace, and daisies. These flowers will also attract pollinating bees and wasps.

Include some plants that repel insect pests with their strong scent. Site them near desirable plants to keep the pests at bay. Feverfew, garlic, lavender, marigolds, marjoram, oregano, rosemary, and wormwood are effective pest deterrents.

Plant diversity is also important for a healthy vegetable garden. A mixture of different sizes, structures, foliage, and forms, as well as different flowers, provides garden guardians with a range of plants in which to shelter. Covering the soil with mulch also gives shelter to certain beneficial insects.

Building beds the no-dig way

This simple garden-building technique can be used on top of an existing piece of lawn or garden as well as on hard rocky ground or heavy clay and even on top of concrete. It sits above the ground and doesn't contain soil but plenty of organic matter, ideal for growing vegetables and herbs. If you will be using it to grow vegetables, it needs to be in a sunny spot.

Making a no-dig garden is simple but it does involve some preparation. You need newspapers; wood chips or bark mulch; green garden waste; pea straw, alfalfa hay or straw; chicken, cow, sheep, or other animal manure; lime; compost; and blood and bone or other organic fertilizer.

If you are constructing your no-dig garden on hard rocky ground, put down coarse material such as old leaves, sticks, garden trimmings, or wood chips to improve drainage. Then put down a base of newspaper up to 5 mm (¹/₄ in) thick, ensuring that the wads of newspaper overlap completely.

On top of this base, add eight layers, each 10 cm (4 in) thick unless stated otherwise below, watering each layer thoroughly before proceeding to the next.

The eight layers:

First layer Newspapers and wood chips or bark mulch, followed by a dressing of blood and bone.

Second layer Green weeds or grass clippings with no seeds or runners, followed by a dressing of lime.

Third layer Dry deciduous leaves or straw, followed by more blood and bone.

Fourth layer Sheep manure—you could also use cow or chicken—laid 5 cm (2 in) thick, followed by lime.

To keep the layers of your no-dig garden in place, you could edge it with logs or railroad ties.

Fifth layer Alfalfa, then blood and bone.

Sixth layer More sheep or cow manure laid 5 cm (2 in) thick, then lime.

Seventh layer More alfalfa, then blood and bone.

Eighth layer Compost around 5 cm (2 in) thick— the icing on the cake.

After building these layers, the no-dig garden bed should be about 60 cm (2 ft) above the ground. It will settle to half this size over a week or two, so ideally wait until this happens before you plant. Top up the bed with more compost, alfalfa, and manure as it breaks down over the ensuing months to ensure that it stays around 30–45 cm (1–1¹/₂ ft) high.

Also ...

Bees

The great pollinators

Bees carry pollen from flower to flower, which helps with fertilization in many plants.

Bees and other pollinating insects are essential if the fruit is the part of the plant that is eaten and the plant is insect-pollinated. Vegetables in this group include cucumbers, pumpkins, winter and summer squash, zucchini, and all the melons. Without bees or some other insect pollinator, the vines will grow but they won't set fruit—unless there's human intervention by hand-pollination, which is time-consuming.

To avoid harming bees and other precious pollinating insects, try to avoid using any sprays, including organic and homemade options. If you must use them, spray in the evening or early morning, before these pollinators are active.

Choosing the right plants

Mixing flowers and herbs among your vegetables not only adds color, it attracts bees. Bees are particularly attracted to blue flowers, such as borage and campanulas, and herbs such as basil, comfrey, and thyme. Remember not to harvest all your herbs but leave some to flower.

Zucchini have separate male and female flowers and would not produce a crop without bees carrying the pollen from the male flowers to the female.

Also ...

Some vegetables, such as (from left to right) the Jerusalem artichoke with its bright yellow flowers, the globe artichoke with its showy purple flowers, and scarlet runner beans add spectacle to the vegetable garden when they are in bloom.

The vegetable garden in flower

Vegetable gardens can be pretty as well as productive. Look for vegetables with different-colored foliage, varying leaf sizes, shapes, and textures, and attractive or intriguing flowers.

Aboveground, Jerusalem artichokes look like a thick hedge of tall sunflowers, which can double as a windbreak in the vegetable garden—the lovely blooms also make a good cut flower. The unopened buds of the globe artichoke are the edible part, but if you miss harvest time, the buds will open into stunning thistle-like flowers, which turn into equally attractive fluffy seed heads. Scarlet runner beans were once grown purely for their ornamental value, thanks to their arresting red flowers, which develop into the edible pods.

Edible flowers

Some vegetables have attractive flowers, and some of these are edible, so including them in your garden will give you bounty with beauty. The flowers of chives and the flowers and leaves of nasturtiums can be used in salads or as a garnish. The vivid yellow zucchini flowers have a delicate flavor; they can be lightly battered and deep-fried or stuffed. Many herbs and some ornamental plants also have edible flowers—borage, chicory, calendulas, marigolds, heritage roses, sage, society garlic, and violets can all be used to decorate or flavor food. Why not plant some of them in among your vegetables?

Planting vegetables that produce attractive flowers not only gives you an edible garden but one that is also beautiful and visually sustaining.

The pretty edible flowers of some vegetables, herbs, and ornamentals can be used in salads, cooking, or as a garnish. CLOCKWISE FROM TOP LEFT: Zucchini, chive, calendula and nasturtium flowers offer both color and flavor.

Vegetable gardening in small spaces

Although we might aspire to have a large vegetable garden, as housing becomes more high-density, the reality for many of us is that we only have a small area available in which to grow our vegetables. But even if the space you have for gardening is limited, it is still possible to create a highly productive garden of fresh, full-flavored vegetables. Whether it's a tiny courtyard, a small patio, a balcony or even a rooftop, here are some ways to enjoy a bountiful harvest in small spaces.

Plant selection is critical

With so many vegetables to choose from, it is easy to get swept away with ideas of what you want to grow. However, when gardening in a small space, it is essential that you choose "good value" vegetables that have the ability to be highly productive. Look at vegetables that are repeat harvest or cut-and-come-again; varieties that climb and take up little ground space; vegetables that have a long fruiting period; root crops that can be harvested and enjoyed at various stages of development; compact varieties, so more plants can be squeezed into the available space; and plants that have several edible parts, such as leaves, stems, and roots.

RIGHT: Many types of lettuce and salad leaves will thrive in containers if watered and fertilized frequently.

Avoid vegetables that take a long time to mature or take up a lot of space—such as large-headed cabbages, cauliflower, and broccoli. Instead, choose compact-headed or resprouting varieties.

Of course, the number one consideration when you're deciding what you grow is to make sure they are vegetables that you love to eat. There is no excuse for leaving it on your plate if you grew it.

Succession planting is also important so you maximize the space you do have. When one plant finishes or its crop is harvested and it will no longer produce, remove the plant, improve the soil, then put in new seeds or seedlings so there is never any vacant space and your vegetable garden keeps working. For this to work well, you must feed your soil continuously and improve it with organic matter such as compost or aged animal manures.

With creative and efficient use of the available space, you can grow a surprising amount of food in a small area.

RIGHT: It is possible to have a highly productive garden in a small space by growing vegetables in pots and containers and cleverly making the most of vertical space.

ABOVE: Lacinato kale growing along a pathway in front of green kale looks attractive as a border and is highly productive.

LEFT: Clever planning makes the most of small spaces. Here the timber walls of the raised beds double as seating space.

Tight spaces

Many garden areas are narrow and awkward, yet despite this they can still be productive if you understand the conditions and choose the right plants. Usually, the biggest challenge is the limited amount of direct sunlight or the lack of it at those times of the year when the sun is low. One way to overcome this is to grow climbing productive plants, which will grow up to the sun. Another is to choose plants that like shade or that grow with limited sun, such as leafy green salad vegetables or parsley, mint, and some other herbs. You may also only be able to use certain areas during specific seasons, when the plants' growing conditions are met. A garden bed that gets enough summer sun will grow summer vegetables well, but if it gets no winter sun, don't locate winter vegetables that need sun to develop properly there.

Other challenges in tight spaces can include reflected heat and wind. Reflected heat multiplies the heat of the sun. In hot, dry climates radiant heat from hard surfaces, such as walls, stones, and concrete, can create intense temperatures up to

50°C (122°F). This is too hot for most vegetables, and if they don't die they will often burn, have increased water needs, and be prone to more pest and disease problems. Reflected heat is more challenging for plants growing in pots than for those in the ground, as they don't have a large quantity of soil to act as a moisture reservoir.

Some tight spaces have a combination of limited sun and reflected heat, where the plants receive extremely harsh sunshine and reflected heat for just a few hours a day. To overcome this, create shade with permanent or temporary shade cloth, a sail, or even deciduous vines and climbing vegetables growing over a structure.

Narrow spaces can channel the wind and form wind tunnels, which adversely affect plant growth. If this is the case, consider how you can create a windbreak to protect your vegetables. You could use a solid barrier, wind mesh, or even a hardy, fast-growing climber over a trellis.

If your small space is completely paved and there is nowhere to make a vegetable bed, use pots, troughs, and planter boxes where space permits.

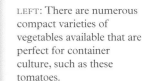

LEFT: There are numerous compact varieties of vegetables available that are perfect for container culture, such as these tomatoes.

BELOW: With the right orientation to the sun, some wind protection, and good care and maintenance, a balcony can become a highly productive vegetable garden. Shown here is a balcony on the 17th floor of a city apartment.

Containers and pots

If your garden space is a small patio, a balcony, or a rooftop, you can grow your vegetable garden in pots, troughs, planters, and tubs. The quality of the growing medium you choose will determine the quality of the produce. Buy the best you can afford, and for optimal results, be ready to amend it with compost or aged animal manure. For ultimate flexibility, keep large, heavy planters and pots on wheels, so you can move them around easily and get the best growing conditions for the plants over the changing seasons. See also pages 134–135.

Balcony gardens

If you have a balcony, you can make a vegetable garden of pots and troughs. First check if your balcony can take the extra load and also if the co-op board or building management has any restrictions on balcony fixtures. The main factors that will affect your success are sunlight, radiant heat, and wind. Consider how much sun your balcony gets every season—some balconies have great summer sun but none in winter, when the sun's angle changes. Also work out how hot the balcony gets in summer with the direct sun and radiant heat from surrounding walls and windows. Understanding these factors will help you choose vegetables to suit your conditions.

ABOVE: Broccoli can be grown in window boxes to make the most of limited space. Water carefully to minimize runoff.

LEFT: Specially designed rooftop gardens are a great place to grow vegetables, although it's important to take the sun, radiant heat, and prevailing winds into account and provide appropriate protection.

Vegetables can be grown successfully on the roof. This productive garden was specially engineered and uses special lightweight growing media.

Rooftops

If your rooftop has a courtyard, balcony, or flat area, add some large but light containers full of good-quality potting mix to grow your fresh produce. If you'd like more space, you may be able to create a "real" vegetable garden of raised beds on the roof.

Such gardens are sometimes designed into new buildings. Alternatively, get a builder's advice about whether one can be retrofitted to your existing structure. You'll need to check the load-bearing capacity of the structure and use lightweight growing media. Raised beds of varying heights will create visual interest, and their different soil depths will let you grow a range of both vegetables and fruit trees, which need deeper soils. Well-designed raised beds can also incorporate seating, workbenches, and storage space. Once constructed, simply sow and plant the raised beds and treat them the same as you would a vegetable garden at ground level, although make sure that you pay close attention to watering. The evaporation rates are much greater at roof height because of the exposure to sun and wind.

Look up—growing produce up and on the walls

When space is limited and you are looking for somewhere to grow your vegetables, think up. Adding a vertical dimension to your vegetable garden will multiply the available space enormously—and it looks great, too.

LEFT: The colorful salad vegetables and herbs planted in blocks on this green wall make a living picture.

Climbing plants

By growing climbing productive plants on frames, trellises, or poles, or by creating wall gardens, you can increase your growing area and maximize your harvest in a small space. Tomatoes, climbing beans, peas, cucumbers, and small squash all like to climb and are ideal for small gardens. Frames and trellises can be made from welded metal mesh, galvanized reinforcing mesh, wood, lattice, or wire stretched between two upright posts. The climbing frame can also have multiple purposes. For example, curve two frames together to form an arch, which also makes a shaded seating area and offers protection to nearby plants.

Supports can range from a single hardwood garden stake or a tripod of hardwood or bamboo stakes to a purpose-built metal climbing frame.

RIGHT: Climbing spinach (Ceylon spinach) clambers up a trellis. Pick off the flower buds to keep the tasty leaves and shoots producing.

Wall gardens

While the concept of creating a vertical wall garden is relatively new, it is a great option for those with limited space. There are a number of commercially available systems for creating wall gardens, or you can make your own from basic materials, such as a wooden pallet lined with landscaping fabric, filled with potting mix, and planted. You could also attach plastic pots or troughs to a wall-mounted frame and plant each pot individually—make sure you keep each pot moist and fertilize with a liquid foliar feed.

Many vegetables grow well in wall gardens, but success ultimately depends on its position and your level of care. Edible wall plantings can include loose-leaved lettuces, leafy salad greens, Asian greens, winter brassicas, trailing herbs such as marjoram, oregano, rosemary, and thyme, and hanging crops such as strawberries and tomatoes.

Building a pallet wall garden

Line all sides of the inside of a wooden pallet with woven plastic landscaping fabric. You can staple or nail the fabric to the outside of the pallet, but lining the inside looks nicer and it gives the wall garden more support once it's filled with soil. You may need two or three sheets of fabric to fully line the pallet, depending on its structure.

Leaving the top end open, fold the edges of the mat over to prevent fraying and secure it to the pallet with a staple gun or nails. The aim is to form a bag inside the pallet.

Place the pallet upright, in position, and secure it firmly to the supporting vertical surface. If it is being put against a wall or fence, place a waterproof barrier in between so the moisture from the pallet garden does not damage the wall or fence. Fill with good-quality potting mix combined with compost to improve its water-holding capacity, as it will tend to dry out quickly. Water well and top with potting mix until the soil level is stable. Using a very sharp knife, cut holes in the landscaping fabric and insert a plant in each hole. Then plant the open top. Regularly feed and water well—always start at the top.

Note An alternative to landscaping fabric is polyethylene film with drainage holes punched in the bottom or burlap. Landscaping fabric lasts longer.

ABOVE: There are various ways to build a pallet wall garden. Here, wooden pallets are converted to make a simple vertical garden of potted plants.

This colorful and productive wall garden features salad vegetables, herbs, and flowers interplanted to great effect.

ABOVE: A great container for edible gardening in urban spaces, PVC pipes can be used vertically or cut in half and used horizontally. It's a creative way to grow strawberries, lettuces, or Asian greens.

LEFT: You can use all kinds of recycled containers for growing salad greens and herbs. Here, mint and coriander grow in plastic drink bottles, and the coconut baskets create a charming display.

Other ways to grow up

The options are limited only by your imagination. Use large hanging baskets or even columns of hanging baskets, stacks of pots or the hanging canvas or plastic growing bags that are available commercially and hold up to 10 plants. Build plant towers from rings of reinforcing mesh lined with weed mat, plastic downpipes or stormwater pipes, or even concrete pipes. The main challenge with wall gardens is making sure plants don't dry out. If they do, your crops will be reduced.

Planted walls will bring a third dimension to your vegetable garden. They can function as a decorative wall or a space divider.

RIGHT: Wooden planter boxes attached to a vertical timber support make interesting shapes, textures and use of space.

Vegetables in pots and containers

Any container that will hold a growing medium is capable of producing a crop of fresh vegetables. Indeed, containers offer more flexibility and versatility than fixed garden beds, and as for portability—they win hands down.

Ensuring success

There are numerous reasons for deciding to grow vegetables in containers. These include the problem of limited space; the available space is covered with hard surfaces such as concrete rather than soil or garden beds; or you need to keep your vegetable garden portable because you're renting or moving. Also, if your growing conditions aren't ideal—your garden has terrible drainage or overly acid soil—containers will solve that. Whatever the reason, there are a few basic principles to follow.

BELOW: Given the right position and growing medium and appropriate maintenance, vegetables and herbs do well in pots.

The quality and success of any crop is directly related to the quality of the soil, so always use a premium-quality potting mix suitable for growing vegetables. Make sure that it drains freely, and in dry climates with hot summers, be ready to add extra compost to the mix to improve its ability to retain moisture.

Choose the right size container. It is better to choose large pots over small ones because they won't dry out as quickly and have a better volume of soil for your vegetables' root systems to develop. What size container you choose ultimately comes down to what you are growing in it. Tall-growing plants, such as tomatoes, should be grown in containers at least 50 cm (20 in) high and wide. Root vegetables need a reasonable depth of soil, so the pot must be at least 50 cm (20 in) high.

Position your potted vegetables appropriately. Even though most vegetables grow best in full sun, containers have a tendency to heat up, and the plants' root systems become more stressed than the same plants would be when growing in the ground. The temperature in a pot can reach 60°C (140°F).

Be prepared to water frequently. Most vegetables grown in containers will require daily watering in the summer months. Letting them dry out will result in poor-quality or reduced crops with inferior flavor. In the case of lettuces, allowing the plants to dry out causes them to become bitter rather than tender and sweet. Water stress can also lead to increased pest and disease problems.

ABOVE: A good way to hide unattractive plastic pots: paint a recycled wooden crate, then stand your pots of vegetables inside it.

Be prepared to feed generously and often. Even if the potting mix you use already contains fertilizer, the nutrients will be leached out or taken up by the plant in a relatively short period due to regular watering. For best results, feed your container-grown produce regularly so that it keeps growing actively and remains in optimal health. If using a liquid fertilizer, apply every two weeks, while solid organic fertilizers, such as blood and bone or pelletized chicken manure, should be applied every six to eight weeks during the growing period.

Choosing a container

There are so many different types of containers that are suitable for growing vegetables. Plastic, glazed, and terra-cotta pots all work well and look great, but always make sure they have enough drainage holes. Half barrels are another option because of their size; they will last longer if you seal the inside with bitumen sealant.

You can also grow small vegetables in window boxes and hanging baskets. Large troughs give you more flexibility, as they hold a large volume of soil, which means you're less limited in terms of what you can grow.

There are also a number of purpose-specific containers, such as potato-growing bags. These are a very clever idea for those with small garden spaces, letting you build the soil level up as the potato plants grow and even harvest new potatoes through special Velcro flaps on the side.

Styrofoam boxes used for transporting fruit and vegetables are a good way to get a reasonable amount of planting space quickly and cheaply. Just be aware that they can become brittle as they age and may only last a season or two.

What to plant

When you have only a limited amount of space to grow vegetables, it is essential to grow what you like eating as well as those crops that aren't readily available at the greengrocer or supermarket. It is also important to choose compact-growing varieties of vegetables whenever possible.

If you're using larger containers such as half barrels, plant groups of vegetables that will be used for the same purpose in the same barrel. Create a salad bowl for leafy salad greens in summer; a summer bounty of tomatoes and basil or bell peppers and eggplant; a soup pot of Swiss chard or rainbow chard, kale, broccoli, a few carrots, beets, and small cabbages for winter; and a year-round herb or garnish pot of parsley, arugula, and chives.

Squeeze parsley, coriander, chives, lettuces, and scallions into any available space, as these fast growers make fine fillers.

ABOVE: Growing vegetables in pots allows you flexibility to move them around according to what grows best in different situations, what is ready for harvest, and what makes a good display. It also gives you the opportunity to respond when the sun is too hot and harsh.

Get creative and recycle
Recycled containers that can be used for growing vegetables come in all shapes and sizes. The only limits on your imagination are that they must be able to hold soil while letting water drain freely. Avoid anything made of a material that will leach toxins or that held chemicals. The drum of a top-loading washing machine, bathtubs, kitchen or laundry sinks, sieves, wheelbarrows, tractor and truck wheel rims, metal buckets and cans—all of these could contain your crops.

Top 12 herbs for your vegetable garden

Growing herbs is a natural extension of growing vegetables. They require the same conditions, and the two complement each other in the kitchen as much as they do in the garden.

Herbal benefits

There are real benefits to including herbs in your vegetable garden. The first is that fresh herbs bring a wonderful flavor to homegrown vegetables, whether added during cooking or used raw in salads or as a garnish. And if the recipe only calls for two sprigs of thyme or a tablespoon of torn basil, there's no waste. Herbs grow well in the ground or in containers. Some are perennial and live for years, while annual or biennial herbs need to be resown.

Herbs such as basil, coriander, dill, mint, oregano, parsley, and thyme provide an excellent source of food for beneficial insects when they are left to flower. Bringing insect guardians into your vegetable garden allows nature to take care of many of the insect pests that would otherwise cause problems. This is biological control at its best.

FAR RIGHT: The herbs in these biodegradable fiber pots are ready for planting. There's no need to even take them out of their pots.

BELOW: This walled herb garden features culinary herbs such as chives and medicinal herbs such as echinacea.

Here are the top 12 herbs that you should try to include in your vegetable garden:

Basil
Ocimum basilicum

The unique flavor of this annual herb has made it an essential ingredient in both Italian and Asian cooking. Sweet basil is grown most commonly. It has large, soft green leaves, which are used for their distinctive scent and flavor. Fresh basil leaves are the principal ingredient in pesto and the perfect partner to tomatoes. The plant grows to 40 cm (16 in) high. Even though the flowers are attractive and edible, it is best to prune them off to encourage more leaf growth. This tender annual is best planted in spring for summer and autumn harvesting. Try the attractive dark purple leaf forms or those with lacy dissected foliage to add extra ornamental value to your veggie patch. Perennial basil will persist through winter in frost-free areas, but the flavor is stronger and not as sweet. Basil likes well-drained, rich soil that is kept moist.

Always tear basil leaves rather than chop them, as chopping bruises the leaf and causes it to darken. If using basil in hot dishes, stir it in just before serving to preserve its flavor.

Bay
Laurus nobilis

This classic Mediterranean herb has glossy, dark green, leathery leaves, which are used fresh or dried to give a distinctive flavor to a wide range of soups, stews, sauces, and stocks. Throw some sprigs of leaves in with roasted vegetables for added flavor. Bay is best grown in full sun to have good flavor. Because it eventually forms a very large shrub or small tree, it is often grown in a large container—this prevents it from getting too big and causing root competition in the vegetable garden. It will grow successfully like this in a large container for a long time. Bay trees respond well to pruning and make excellent topiary specimens.

CLOCKWISE FROM TOP LEFT: Sweet basil, bay, dill, and coriander, like all fresh herbs, add their unique aroma and flavor when used in cooking. Many herbs are well suited to growing in containers; they need good drainage.

Coriander
Coriandrum sativum

All parts of this plant are used to flavor cooked dishes, salads, or salsas—the fresh foliage, also known as cilantro, and the seeds and roots. The leaves have a sharp taste and are used in Asian, Indian, and Middle Eastern dishes, while the seeds and roots are dried and ground for use in curries and spice pastes. This annual herb grows to around 50 cm (20 in) high. To keep a plentiful supply, sow seed every few weeks in well-drained fertile soil. Prune off all flowers to encourage the plant to produce more leaves. In hot areas, choose slow-bolt varieties that are suited to leaf production and delay flowering.

Dill
Anethum graveolens

This annual herb has fine, feathery foliage, which is used fresh as a classic partner with eggs, soft cheeses, white sauces, vegetables, seafood, and chicken dishes. It has a parsley-caraway smell to its foliage. If adding the fresh herb to cooking, do so just before serving, as the flavor diminishes with heat. It grows to 1–2 m (3–6 ft) high, and seed can be saved for future planting. It prefers a sunny position in moist soil with good drainage.

CLOCKWISE FROM TOP LEFT: Lemongrass and mint are a feature of Southeast Asian cuisines, especially that of Vietnam and Thailand. Parsley and oregano are common in the cooking of the Mediterranean.

*How could such sweet and
wholesome hours
Be reckoned but with herbs and flowers?*
ANDREW MARVELL (1621–1678)

Mint
Mentha spp.
A use can be found for this versatile herb in every kitchen, but it must be planted wisely in the garden due to its invasive nature. Most people find it best grown in a pot with a saucer or stones underneath so it cannot make direct contact with garden soil and escape. It likes to be kept moist and thrives in shaded or semi-shaded positions. There are many different varieties with different qualities of scent and flavor; most are low-growing, spreading perennials to around 45 cm (18 in) high. Use fresh leaves with spring vegetables, in salads or fruit drinks, as a garnish, or in mint sauce and mint jelly, served traditionally with roast lamb. Fresh or dried leaves can be used to make a refreshing herb tea.

Oregano
Origanum vulgare
The fresh or dried leaves of oregano have a sweet, mild, spicy flavor and are used on bruschetta, in seasonings, and in Greek, Italian, Spanish, and Mexican dishes, especially those including meat, pasta, and tomato. Oregano has a distinctive flavor that is at its best when harvested only after the small purple flowers start to appear. It is a hardy perennial that grows to 45 cm (18 in) high and does best in a sunny position in well-drained soils. Being a Mediterranean herb, it is drought-tolerant once established. Its cousin sweet marjoram (*Origanum majorana*) has a milder, sweeter flavor and is also used in Italian cooking. There are golden-leaved forms of both oregano and marjoram, which have great ornamental value. These perennials do best with a hard prune at the end of autumn.

Lemongrass
Cymbopogon citratus
This strappy-leaved, grass-like herb is a frost-tender perennial that grows into a striking clump, adding an architectural element to the vegetable garden. The edges of its arching leaves are razor sharp, so position it where it will not cut passersby. It is used in a number of ways to add a lemon flavor to Asian cooking. Whole stems are bruised then tied together and added to a dish in the same way as a bouquet garni—to infuse while cooking—then they are removed before serving. Or the whitish bulb and tender white base of the stem are sliced very finely and added directly to dishes as they cook.

Parsley
Petroselinum crispum
The most widely grown culinary herb, parsley is added to cooking or used fresh as an ingredient or as a garnish. It is wonderful in salads and is the main ingredient in tabbouleh, and it can also be used with vegetables, fish, eggs, meats, stews, and soups. For the best flavor, add to hot dishes just before serving. There are two forms: curly parsley grows to 30 cm (12 in) high, and the more strongly flavored flat-leaf, or Italian, parsley grows to 50 cm (20 in). Parsley likes a fertile, well-drained soil in sun or partial shade. It flowers in its second year and will self-seed naturally. It makes a good border plant.

Rosemary
Rosemary officinalis

This Mediterranean perennial shrub can grow up to 2 m (6 ft) high. There are also a number of dwarf and ground-cover forms available. Rosemary has pale blue flowers and aromatic, needle-like leaves that are used fresh or dried in cooking. It is the classic herb to accompany lamb, but it also works well with chicken and other meats. It adds a lovely flavor if sprigs are thrown over your vegetables when you roast them. Rosemary needs to grow in full sun and is very drought-tolerant once established. It can be clipped to make a fragrant hedge around your vegetable patch, or use one of the ground-cover forms down an embankment or wall or as part of a vertical planting.

Sage
Salvia officinalis

While there are many ornamental forms of sage, culinary sage—also called garden sage or common sage—forms a rounded shrub up to 1 m (3 ft) high and has gray-green foliage and soft blue flowers. The leaves are used in cooking, often accompanying fatty meats such as duck. Sage is also added to poultry seasonings, casseroles, and soups. There are several culinary varieties that have great ornamental value because of their attractive foliage—tinged purple, marbled gold and green, or variegated pink, white, and green. Sage requires a sunny position in well-drained soil and is drought-tolerant once plants become established.

Tarragon
Artemisia dracunculus

This sun-loving herbaceous perennial herb is an essential part of French cooking. Its leaves have a complex flavor that combines basil and sweet anise with resinous undertones. It is used fresh or dried with fish, poultry, veal, eggs, cheese, and salads, although only a small amount is required to give your dish its distinct flavor. Tarragon grows 60 cm (2 ft) high and does best when its old foliage is cut down to ground level at the end of autumn. It likes to grow in a sunny position and requires excellent drainage.

Thyme
Thymus spp.

The many different forms of this Mediterranean herb range from creeping, flat ground covers to low, rounded shrubs growing up to 30 cm (1 ft) high. The leaves, occasionally with their stalks, are used fresh or dried in soups and stews and poultry, meat, and fish dishes. Different varieties have different flavors—lemon, caraway, and bitter orange as well as true thyme—and so add different qualities to the food they are cooked with. As the flavor is quite strong, add the sprigs at the start of cooking. Foliage colors vary, while flower colors range from pure white to pink and purple. Thymes are highly ornamental and make excellent border plants or ground covers between paving stones or stepping stones. All require a sunny position in well-drained soil and are very drought-tolerant once established.

Thyme's antimicrobial properties make it a powerful remedy for the treatment of colds and flu.

CLOCKWISE FROM TOP LEFT: Rosemary, sage, thyme, and tarragon are all intensely aromatic culinary herbs. The first three originated in the Mediterranean and are widely used in the different cuisines of that region.

Essential tools and equipment

Having the right tools for the job makes gardening easier and more enjoyable, especially when you're hard at work in the vegetable patch. Here are the essentials.

Choosing and using gardening tools

When purchasing tools, invest in quality. Don't be guided purely by price, as usually the cheaper products don't perform or last. Good-quality tools can last a lifetime if you look after them well. Make sure that you never leave them out in the rain or caked with soil, and take time each year to do some maintenance on them, whether oiling wooden handles or cleaning and sharpening blades. Choose from reputable brands that offer a manufacturer's warranty on materials, workmanship, repairs and replacement parts. While you may start out with just a few items, over time it's a good idea to expand your collection to include the following:

Spade

A light, strong spade with a sharp edge is a garden essential, used for digging, dividing plants, and cutting edges. Be sure to choose a spade that has a comfortable handle in a size that feels right for you. The main maintenance issue is to keep the bottom of the blade sharp.

Shovel

Gardeners are often confused about the difference between a spade and a shovel. A shovel has a large scooped blade designed for moving soil, mulch, compost, or anything else you can think of, while a spade has a flat blade for digging or cutting. Choose a shovel size that you can manage—a heavy load of soil in a large shovel may be too heavy.

Garden fork

Select a strong yet light fork to handle digging and cultivating jobs, from turning heavy-textured soil to lifting mulch, aerating compost, and lightly raking leaves, grass clippings, and weeds.

Hand trowel and hand fork

A hand trowel and fork are must-haves for every gardener, even if your garden consists of just one pot on a balcony. Make sure they are of good quality, because the cheap ones are renowned for bending or breaking at the neck.

Hand hoe

Some gardeners claim that these are their handiest garden tool in the veggie patch. It is used for weeding, tilling, or harvesting vegetables. Choose one that is lightweight and made from durable materials.

Sharpening digging tools

While this can be done by using a sharpening stone or grinder, a simple way is to plunge spades, shovels, forks, and the like in a bucket filled with sand and enough vegetable oil to make the sand moist but not wet. Plunge the tools in and out of the sand to remove any dirt and help to keep the edges of the tools sharp. The oil helps prevent the tools from rusting, and the sand acts as an abrasive. Always clean tools after use and never leave them lying outside in the weather.

Cheap tools are for fools.

ANONYMOUS

Metal rake
While not essential, metal garden rakes are handy in the vegetable bed for leveling soil with the back edge as well as raking with the prongs.

Pruning shears
Pruning shears are a necessary tool in the general garden, but while handy in the vegetable patch, they are not essential. If you do decide to purchase some, choose a good-quality pair that can be sharpened, are comfortable to use—this will help prevent hand fatigue—and are easy to maintain. Left-handed pruning shears are available for left-handed gardeners.

Gloves
Gardening gloves are a very personal choice. Many gardeners like to work in the soil with bare hands, but tasks such as handling animal manures, animal-derived products, fertilizers, potting mixes, and sprays or chemicals must be done with gloves. Whether they are fabric, rubber, or leather, make sure the fit and grip are comfortable and that the gloves can be used for both general gardening work as well as jobs for which you need movement and sensitivity.

Wheelbarrow
A good wheelbarrow will help with many jobs in the garden, from carting soil, compost, and mulch to moving bags of fertilizer and old vegetable plants headed for the compost. You may also end up using it to carry in the harvest. Choose one that is light, stable, and easy to maneuver and empty. In small gardens, use a bucket or a small tarpaulin instead.

Floating row cover
Net plants with floating row cover, a flexible mesh that prevents moths and butterflies from landing on your plants and laying their eggs—you can simply use it as a "throw-over," and you don't need a frame. It can also help protect your plants from extremes of heat and frost.

Garden stakes
You need a variety of these on hand, ranging from small bamboo stakes to thick, tall hardwood stakes. You can purchase handy fasteners to secure stakes together as an alternative to simply tying them together with garden twine.

Harvest essentials
Finally, for the fun part, have a basket or trug for collecting your homegrown produce—it can also be handy for carrying basic hand tools—and an old sharp knife for harvesting.

Having the things you need nearby will make gardening easier and help yield delicious harvests.

Store tools in a dry place where they are safe, protected from the weather, and easy to access.

Planting

Once the work of building and preparing your vegetable beds is done, it's time for the fun and rewarding step: planting. Now you will transform a tiny seed or flimsy seedling into food.

Growing from seed or seedling?

There are a number of things to consider when deciding whether to grow from seed or seedlings.

Availability Seeds are readily available via mail order and the Internet and can be sent to country areas and remote locations.

Variety The range of seedling varieties that are available is limited. Many heritage or unusual varieties can only be grown from seed.

Transplanting Some crops do not like the root disturbance involved in transplanting. Root vegetables such as carrots, beets, rutabagas, parsnips, and turnips do best when their seed is sown directly into the soil where they will grow. If you transplant these seedlings into the ground, they will suffer a setback.

Value Seeds are better value than seedlings, as you get more plants for your money.

Time Buying seedlings saves time, usually up to six weeks of growing time. Always remove the seedlings from their containers very carefully so they don't get damaged or suffer transplant shock.

Keep seedlings moist, and in dry climates water gently once a day or as required until they are well established.

Sowing very fine seeds
When sowing fine seeds, such as carrot, radish, and onion, add 1 packet of seed to ½ cup of sand and mix well. Sow this seed-and-sand mix 10–15 mm (⅓–½ in) deep. Cover with compost and tamp down firmly. Cover with an old dish towel, damp newspaper, or shade cloth and water gently. Check daily and remove as soon as seedlings emerge. Sowing with sand helps to thin out the seeds physically so there is less thinning once they germinate.

Needs of specific vegetables Some vegetables, including potatoes, sweet potatoes, and Jerusalem artichokes, are best grown from cuttings of tubers. Others, such as asparagus, globe artichokes, and rhubarb, are best grown from crowns, which are advanced plants that are already a year or two old.

Sowing seeds

Always have your soil prepared well. Most seeds germinate best in light, friable soil, so ensure that you have worked the soil over well, to a fine tilth, before sowing. Mark out a shallow furrow. Use a string line, garden stake, or the handle of a rake as a guide to keep your row straight.

Large seeds, such as beans, peas, sweet corn, pumpkins, and winter squash, are best pushed directly into the soil. Some gardeners like to plant several seeds in one hole. This is because one or two seeds may not germinate, but you will be left with at least one that does. If more than one germinates, thin them to leave only one seedling to grow properly.

Some seeds, such as radishes, are quick to germinate. You will see the first green leaves in as little as five to eight days, with small roots ready for harvest in four weeks, although they are fully grown in six to eight weeks. Other seeds, such as parsnip and parsley, will take much longer to germinate.

When sowing seeds or planting seedlings, always follow the directions and recommended spacing on the seed packet or plant label. Always insert a label at the end of each row identifying the vegetable and the variety.

Planting seedlings

Plant seedlings into well-prepared soil, water them, and make sure they are kept moist by rain or supplementary watering. Apply a seaweed-based plant tonic to minimize transplant shock. You'll need to water new seedlings more frequently in hot weather until they harden up and their root systems get established.

Protect them from snails, slugs, and insects that may attack the tender new shoots. Birds and rodents may also go for the seeds or shoots, so cover them with netting or row covers.

ABOVE: If you harvest your own seeds, air-dry them then store in paper packets in a dry place until you're ready to sow again.

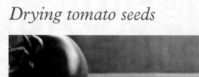

Seed collection

Many varieties of vegetables will naturally self-seed. If you have an informal garden layout or are using permaculture principles, you can to some extent let the plants decide where they will grow. If you prefer a more ordered approach, harvest seeds once they are dry and store them in labeled paper packets ready for next season's planting. Even simpler is to harvest the seeds just as they are about to fall and scatter them where you want that particular vegetable to grow.

Watering

Water vegetables regularly, depending on your climate, the weather, and how the plants are looking. It is better to give them a good soak once or twice a week rather than a light sprinkle every day. The soft, leafy nature of many vegetables means they have high water requirements, so don't let them dry out or their quality will suffer greatly.

Mulching

It is important to keep your garden beds weed-free, because weeds will compete with your vegetables for space, light, water, and nutrients. Weed, then mulch lightly with straw or alfalfa hay. Don't put mulch over areas that have been sown until the seeds have shot and are 5 cm (2 in) high. Add extra mulch as the seedlings get bigger.

The love of gardening is a seed that once sown never dies.

GERTRUDE JEKYLL (1843–1932),
ENGLISH GARDEN DESIGNER

How-to

Drying tomato seeds

ABOVE: A straw mulch over these beds of cabbages helps keep the soil evenly moist. It's critical if you want to grow the best cabbages possible.

Tomato seeds are coated in a gel sac that must be broken down by fermentation before the seed can be dried.

Add water to seed pulp and leave for a few days. The seeds will sink. Carefully pour off the water before sieving the seeds under running water to clean them. Let the seeds dry completely before storing them in an airtight container in a cool, dark place.

Compost, mulch, and fertilizers

Organic matter in the form of compost and well-rotted animal manures is an essential addition to all vegetable-garden soils. Whatever type of soil you have—clay, sandy, loam—it will be improved by adding these soil conditioners.

Compost

Making your own compost is simple and a great way to recycle the green waste your household produces. You can use a purpose-built compost bin or build your own 1 x 1-m (3 x 3-ft) bin from wood, iron, or even straw bales. Use mesh as a base for open bins to stop vermin. Then add your kitchen vegetable scraps and shredded garden prunings along with dry material such as straw, deciduous leaves, shredded paper, and even garden soil. Add composting worms to hasten the breakdown.

The key to success in making compost is to achieve a balance between fresh or wet materials (described as green) and dry materials (brown). It is also vital that you keep the pile sufficiently moist during hot weather and turn it regularly to aerate it. After initially working compost through your soil to a fork's depth, you don't need to dig subsequent annual applications into the soil. They can simply be laid on top, like a mulch.

Worm farms are another way to recycle kitchen waste. They produce a liquid leachate that can be diluted to the color of weak tea and used as a liquid soluble fertilizer. The solid matter known as worm castings or vermicompost can be applied directly to the soil as a soil improver.

If you keep chickens, feed them your kitchen scraps, then use their manure, rotted down and mixed with straw, in your compost system.

If you have the space, build your own compost bin with lumber—the closer to the vegetable garden the better. You could cover the heap to prevent moisture loss while also keeping the rain out.

Things you can use

* Weeds and plants (cut seed heads off first)
* Coffee grounds and tea leaves
* Eggshells
* Lawn clippings
* Manure
* Shredded paper and cardboard
* Straw and hay
* Horse-stable litter
* Spent potting mix
* Uncooked kitchen vegetable waste, such as fruit and vegetable peelings
* Dead flowers
* Shredded twigs and branches
* Plant trimmings

Things you should avoid

* Glossy paper or magazines
* Detergents and chemical products
* Diseased plant material
* Perennial weeds
* Scraps of food that will attract vermin, such as meat
* Thick paper or cardboard unless shredded

ABOVE: Poultry manure is alkaline and should always be rotted before use. Its smell can make it unsuitable for city gardens or apartment living.

Green manure crops

Green manures are a great way to improve the
fertility and productivity of your soil. Sow seeds of
different legumes such as fava beans, clover, rye,
and annual grasses in autumn for a lush winter crop,
then dig this into the soil as the plants start to
flower, before they become woody. Their deep root
systems retrieve mineral nutrients from the subsoil
and bring them closer to the surface, and they also
fix nitrogen. Once dug in, they make good quantities
of high-protein organic matter and nitrogen
available for your next crop. Dig them in at least
four weeks before planting vegetables in the bed and
turn the bed over again if necessary to hasten their
breakdown. These green manures also cover the soil
and suppress weeds in the winter months while at
the same time keeping the soil active and "sweet."

Mulch

Mulch helps to reduce the number of weeds and
insulates the soil, which keeps plant roots cool and
soil microbes happy. Mulch also conserves soil
moisture and reduces the need for watering in
summer. Always use organic mulches in the vegetable
garden, as they help improve the soil's organic
content. You can sift your compost and use the coarse
parts as mulch or buy straw or alfalfa mulches.

Fertilizer

Feeding your vegetable garden regularly is essential
if it is to be highly productive, because veggies are
heavy feeders. While there are many different
fertilizers, the two main groups are organic-based
fertilizers and inorganic or artificial fertilizers.
Organic fertilizers are manufactured from naturally
occurring products such as animal manures or
animal waste by-products; they provide nutrients
while also improving the soil. Inorganic fertilizers
are manufactured from minerals or chemicals and
feed crops more directly with particular nutrients,
though they do nothing for the overall soil structure.

Fertilizers are either liquid or solid in form. The
main difference is that liquid products are best used
on your vegetables every two to three weeks, while
the solid, pelleted products are applied every few
months or at least seasonally, as they break down
slowly to give a sustained, slow-release effect.

ABOVE: This green manure crop is a mixture of grasses and legumes.

LEFT: Organic mulch acts as insulation on the soil surface. It stops the soil from drying out quickly and helps to keep the soil organisms happy and healthy.

Keeping your plants healthy

While most aspects of vegetable gardening are fun, pests and diseases can be frustrating and disheartening. Providing your plants with the conditions for strong, healthy growth will significantly reduce your problems.

Prevention is better than cure

Prevention is the best cure for pest and disease problems in the vegetable garden and is most easily achieved by keeping your plants as healthy as possible. Crop rotation and companion planting are essential parts of this. Also, plants that are under stress from heat, drought, waterlogging, lack of nutrients, or root competition are far more likely to be affected by insect pests or diseases than the same plants grown without such stress.

Pests—what to do when something goes wrong

The first step is to correctly identify the problem. If unsure, take a sample to your local nursery or garden center. Then work out whether you need to intervene or whether naturally occurring beneficial insects, birds, and other creatures will control the problem for you, and if so, how long this will take. Finally, if you do need to act, decide what you can use that will have the least damaging environmental effect.

Basil is grown with tomatoes as a companion plant, to help bring in beneficial insects and ward off pests.

THE MAJOR INSECT PEST GROUPS

INSECT PEST	NATURAL PREDATORS	HOLISTIC TREATMENTS	ORGANIC TREATMENTS
APHIDS	Ladybugs, hoverflies, lacewings, parasitic wasps, damselflies, dragonflies, small birds, bats	Squirt off with hose	Insect repellent sprays; horticultural oil; insecticidal soap sprays; pyrethrum sprays
BEETLES, BUGS, AND WEEVILS	Chickens, ducks	Suck off with hand vacuum; knock into a bucket of soapy water	Insecticidal soap sprays; rotenone; diatomaceous earth (garden quality)
CATERPILLARS	Birds	Remove by hand	Bioinsecticides (*Bacillus thuringiensis*, spinosad)
CUTWORMS, EARWIGS, SLATERS, MILLIPEDES	Chickens, ducks	Physical barriers such as plastic cups or bottles with the bases cut out; physical traps	Diatomaceous earth (garden quality)
MITES	Predatory mites, hoverflies, ladybugs, lacewings	Hose up under foliage	Soap sprays; horticultural oil; sulfur sprays
SNAILS AND SLUGS	Ducks, lizards	Remove by hand; barrier of ash, crushed eggshell, or shell grit; copper tape barrier; beer traps	Copper sprays; iron-based snail pellets
WHITEFLIES	Ladybugs, hoverflies, lacewings	Yellow sticky traps	Insect repellent sprays; horticultural oil; insecticidal soap sprays

Horticultural oil

Oil sprays work well as pesticides for a wide range of insects, including aphids, leaf miners, leafhoppers, mealybugs, mites, scales, and whiteflies. They smother the insect pest, causing it to suffocate. Consequently, these sprays are only effective if you are able to get good coverage of the pest target. Use plant-based horticultural oils rather than petroleum-based products.

To make your own:

Add ¼ cup (60 ml) of dishwashing liquid to 1 cup (250 ml) of vegetable oil in a glass jar. Cover with the lid and shake well. Label the bottle clearly; it will store for a few months.

To use, simply dilute 2 tablespoons of the emulsion in 4 cups (1 liter) of water and spray as required.

Oil sprays can cause burning on sensitive plants. If you're not sure, spray a small part of the plant first and wait two to three days. They should never be used on ferns or palms or applied when the temperature is more than 29°C (84°F) in the shade. Also be sure not to apply oil sprays within four weeks of a sulfur-based spray.

Garlic insect repellent spray

Garlic spray helps to deter insects such as aphids.

To make your own:

Crush 3 garlic cloves and soak in 1 tablespoon of vegetable oil in a screw-top jar for up to a week. Strain and stir into 4 cups (1 liter) of water with 1 teaspoon of liquid soap. Use regularly.

You can also make a similar spray with chili peppers or horseradish.

Diseases—what to do when something goes wrong

Again, the first step is to correctly identify the disease affecting your plant. Then work out whether you need to intervene.

Milk spray

Milk spray is an effective fungicide for powdery mildew, although it does need to be reapplied weekly because it gets washed off by rain or watering.

To make your own:

Mix 1 part whole milk to 10 parts water. Spray affected plants in the early morning to slow the spread of the fungal problem.

Homemade organic garden sprays are easy to make as well as cost-effective.

Weeds

When it comes to weeds in the vegetable garden, weeding by hand is the best option. Once the weeds have been removed, make sure to mulch the area well to stop them from reappearing. For paths and larger areas under fruit trees, try sheet mulching. First, mow or trample down the weeds, generously sprinkle with organic fertilizer, and water well. Then put down layers of newspaper or cardboard (but no shiny paper or card stock) at least 5–15 mm (¼–½ in) thick, making sure to overlap them well. Then top with a thick layer of weed-free mulch.

THE MAJOR DISEASE GROUPS

DISEASE	HOLISTIC TREATMENTS	ORGANIC SPRAYS
LEAF SPOTS ON PEAS AND BEANS	Improve air circulation; avoid watering foliage from above.	Organic fungicides; milk spray
MILDEW	Improve air circulation; avoid watering foliage from above; pick off any affected leaves.	Organic fungicides; milk spray
TOMATO DISEASES SUCH AS WILT AND TOBACCO MOSAIC VIRUS	Crop rotation	Organic fungicides; milk spray

HEALTH AND BEAUTY

Vegetables not only improve your health, they also boast many beauty benefits. Make the most of them with the teas, treatments, and tips on the following pages.

Health and beauty

There is no doubt that a diet rich in fresh produce leads to a healthy, vibrant body. Now researchers have gone further, identifying hundreds of active ingredients, known as phytochemicals, that give plants their beneficial health-enhancing properties. Here we show you how to make the most of them.

Nature's healing storehouse

Fruits and vegetables are more than simply food—they are packed with nutrients that the body needs to stay healthy and avoid disease. Traditional healers and herbalists sensed this principle centuries ago and developed complex systems of medicine that used various foods to treat certain ailments. But it was not until relatively recently that science began to uncover the active components in plants and understand how they work.

The first breakthrough was vitamins—scientists discovered how essential they are for the proper functioning of the body. As more research has been carried out, they have identified hundreds of plant chemicals that actively take part in body processes, from fighting cancer to improving your mood.

In this chapter you'll find the foods to eat to lower your chances of heart disease and cancer, plus natural remedies for fighting ailments such as colds, headaches, and insomnia. You'll even find some sumptuous homemade recipes to beautify your hair and skin.

Vegetables and health

When it comes to staying healthy and preventing disease, no food group surpasses the amazing power of vegetables. The colorful and mouthwatering bounty of a farmers' market, supermarket produce department, or your own garden offers hundreds of nutrients that not only taste good but also have medically proven health benefits.

Start your day with a breakfast of scrambled eggs with bell peppers, onions, and spinach, followed by a lunchtime salad—or plenty of crunchy lettuce and tomatoes in your sandwich. An afternoon snack of red bell pepper slices and baby carrots can keep you going until dinner, and a plate brimming with a rainbow of savory produce, from roasted asparagus and baked sweet potatoes to three-bean chili, fresh corn, winter squash, or thick vegetable soup.

Traditionally, glass teapots are used to brew infusions and serve decoctions. Ceramic is suitable, but metal is not if the tea is for medicinal purposes, as the metal may leave a residue in the liquid.

Also ...

Health-boosting advantages of a vegetable-rich diet

As well as being rich in a wide variety of vitamins and minerals, vegetables are an excellent source of fiber and are full of precious antioxidants. The health-boosting advantages of a diet with plenty of vegetables include:

Brighter moods When researchers from Dartmouth College and the University of Warwick in the UK surveyed 80,000 people, asking questions about their emotional state and their food choices, they found a fascinating correlation. Those who ate seven servings of vegetables a day were happier than those who skimped. French researchers recently found a similar food-mood trend. Why? Perhaps because vegetables are packed with antioxidants that are known to keep a lid on inflammation, which can have a negative effect on mood.

Lower risk for heart disease and strokes In two landmark studies of more than 100,000 women and men, Harvard School of Public Health researchers found that those who ate eight or more servings of produce a day were 30 percent less likely to have a heart attack or stroke compared with those getting fewer than two servings daily. All types of vegetables helped, but green leafy vegetables—such as spinach, Swiss chard, lettuce, and mustard greens—and brassicas such as broccoli, cauliflower, and cabbage seemed to offer the greatest protection.

Better blood pressure Vegetables are a rich source of potassium, magnesium, and calcium—three minerals the body needs to help regulate blood pressure. It's no surprise, then, that one of the world's most effective blood pressure-lowering eating plans, the DASH Diet—short for Dietary Approaches to Stop Hypertension—calls for plenty of vegetables. Getting a good amount of potassium can also help balance the effects of sodium in the diet, which may raise blood pressure for some people.

Protection from type 2 diabetes When scientists from the University of Leicester, UK, tracked the health and eating habits of 22,000 people, they found that those who munched through one and a half daily servings of leafy greens had a 14 percent lower risk for diabetes than those who ate fewer greens. No other single vegetable had this effect—although eating a vegetable-rich diet in general helps protect against blood glucose problems.

A helping hand against cancer According to findings of the World Cancer Research Fund and the American Institute for Cancer Research, piling plenty of leafy greens, brassicas, onions, garlic, bell peppers, tomatoes, and other nonstarchy vegetables onto your plate every day probably protects against cancers of the mouth, throat, larynx, esophagus, and stomach.

A shield against vision loss Corn, kale, squash, spinach, and other deep green, yellow, or orange vegetables may be a special treat for sharp eyes. They contain two antioxidants—lutein and zeaxanthin—that are stored in the eyes, where they neutralize vision-robbing free radicals. This action may help protect against the development of cataracts, which cloud the lens of the eyes, and also against age-related macular degeneration, which damages the retina.

A tool for achieving and maintaining an ideal weight Packed with satisfying fiber, most vegetables are also low in calories, making this food group a great choice if you're trying to lose weight, maintain a lower weight after a successful diet, or avoid weight gain. Researchers at Pennsylvania State University report that the high fiber and water content and low calorie levels in most vegetables discourage overeating. Eat them as a starter—in a salad or vegetable soup—and, as volunteers in several studies discovered, you may go on to eat smaller portions of higher-calorie foods at that meal. You'll be less likely to want a between-meal snack later on, too.

Researchers say eating your vegetables can make you a happier person.

Some of the vegetable-based health remedies and beauty treatments used throughout history include (front row, left to right) avocado and olive moisturizing cream, refreshing carrot mask, tomato tonic, fennel and buttermilk cleansing milk, cucumber cleanser, cucumber-lemon shampoo, and dandelion tea, along with (back row, left to right) lavender oil, dried lavender, and cornmeal scrub.

Also ...

Alert: Vegetables some people should avoid

If you have certain health conditions or take certain medications, your doctor may have told you to be careful about some vegetables. These may impair the action of your medication or worsen your condition. Common examples include:

Leafy greens and blood-thinning drugs
If you take a blood-thinning drug such as warfarin (Coumadin), it's important to maintain steady blood levels of vitamin K. Sudden increases may lessen the effects of the drug. That means it's important to be consistent with your vegetable intake, since this is where most of your vitamin K is coming from. Try to keep to similar amounts of vegetables every day, and if you like and eat vegetables that are particularly high in vitamin K, such as kale, Swiss chard, spinach, mustard greens, and turnip greens, stick with half a cup a day, eaten at about the same time daily.

Oxalate-rich vegetables and kidney stones
One in five people who form calcium oxalate kidney stones (the most common type) have high levels of oxalates in their urine. If you have a history of kidney stones, limit oxalate-rich foods, such as rhubarb, spinach, beets, and beet greens.

Ancient remedies, modern medicines

Before there were drugs, food was medicine. Traditional healing systems around the world have used vegetables as raw ingredients in remedies for thousands of years. Practitioners of traditional Chinese medicine, for example, use winter squash to support the healthy functioning of the stomach and spleen. In Ayurveda, India's ancient healing system, tomatoes are considered blood purifiers and a cure for a poor appetite. In the Andes Mountains of South America, tubers such as ulluco were used to ease the pain of childbirth, while in Europe, midwives and herbalists have long recommended fennel seed tea to stimulate milk production in nursing mothers. In many places throughout the world, onion and garlic are treasured remedies for everything from a stuffy nose to digestion problems and fungal infections.

Today, many people still turn to vegetables to maintain good health or to address health concerns. For anyone getting over an illness or infection, there is nothing more nourishing than homemade soup brimming with vegetables. In the following pages, you'll find many traditional remedies to add to your arsenal—from a syrup of onion and honey for coughs to a raw potato poultice for bruises.

As science looks more deeply at the health-promoting properties of fresh garden produce, it is finding more and more active ingredients with the potential to have an impact on specific and serious medical conditions. For example, scientists are looking closely at a compound derived from broccoli and brussels sprouts that may be a potential treatment for a common and aggressive form of breast cancer. In test tube studies, another broccoli compound—sulforaphane—was recently shown to selectively target and kill prostate cancer cells. Lycopene, an antioxidant found in tomatoes, may help protect cells from damage that could lead to the development of cancer, according to the findings of a 2011 study. And the same chemical that gives chilies their fiery zing—capsaicin—is now the active ingredient in over-the-counter creams and prescription-only patches that ease debilitating joint and nerve pain.

Real food vs. pills These successes and ongoing inquiries do not mean, however, that pills will be replacing vegetables anytime soon. In many cases, research has proved that the benefits of eating a real vegetable cannot be duplicated in a supplement packed with high doses of a single chemical. Consider beta-carotene, for example. It's a powerful, cell-protecting antioxidant found in carrots, winter squash, and other yellow and orange vegetables. In food studies it appears to protect against cancer. But when researchers gave pure beta-carotene in the form of a supplement to smokers, they were shocked to find an increase, not a decrease, in cancer risk. So it seems that the benefits are only gained when you get your beta-carotene from vegetables.

Or consider lycopene. It may help reduce the risk for some types of cancer, but researchers now believe it works as a team with other tomato ingredients. In one laboratory study, tomato powder given to rodents lowered their cancer risk while lycopene supplements did not. The bottom line? There is no replacement for whole foods. Your mother was right: eat your vegetables!

Are we eating enough?

Most Americans munch three or fewer servings of fruit and vegetables a day. The average European eats 220 grams daily. Not bad, but all fall short of the five servings of produce a day recommended by US and UK health authorities.

How can you eat more? Start lunch and dinner with a salad and take a double portion of vegetables at meals. You can tuck more vegetables into wraps, sandwiches, and burritos and toss extra vegetables into soups, stews, sauces, and casseroles. Cut up vegetables and eat them with a healthful dip as a snack—carrot with peanut butter or bell pepper and zucchini strips with hummus.

If you find some vegetables bitter, you may be what scientists call a "super taster"—a person whose tongue has a higher density of taste buds and so a greater sensitivity to bitter flavors in some foods. If this applies to you, bring out the sweetness in vegetables by roasting them, cooking vegetables such as cabbage in fruit juice, or diluting bitter vegetables with sweeter or blander vegetables. For example, cut rutabagas or kohlrabi into a fine dice and mix them with peas and corn kernels.

Include plenty of vegetables of different colors in your diet. The phytochemical compounds that give vegetables their characteristic color provide significant, specific health benefits.

Also ...

Easy ways to get more vegetables into your diet

* Stir pureed cooked vegetables such as carrot, bell pepper, zucchini, and eggplant into pasta sauces, casseroles, and shepherd's pie.
* Bulk up soups with peas, corn kernels, and diced carrots.
* Add spinach to lasagna.
* Spice up a toasted cheese sandwich with some chopped onion and tomato.
* Top pizzas with chopped vegetables such as mushrooms, grilled bell peppers, thinly sliced squash, zucchini, or eggplant.
* Add chopped spinach or mushrooms to scrambled eggs.
* Roast chickpeas or red kidney beans until crisp and eat as a fat-free snack instead of nuts.
* Mix in grated carrot and zucchini when making burger patties.
* Include at least two vegetables in your lunchtime sandwich. Try chopped celery and parsley with chicken and mayonnaise, or sliced beets and baby spinach with roast beef.
* Use iceberg lettuce leaves instead of bread to make wraps and soft spring rolls.
* Add grated pumpkin, carrot, or zucchini to a nutty cake.
* Make your own dips with pureed grilled vegetables and legumes; add herbs and spices and low-fat yogurt for a creamy effect.

Research report

Vegetables that prevent disease

Research shows that certain vegetables contain more health-enhancing active chemicals than others. It makes sense to include more of these superfoods in your diet. Here we outline the foods to pile up on your plate.

Leafy greens

Health advantage Help prevent type 2 diabetes. Lower the risk for heart disease and possibly cancer.

Maximize the benefits Have a small amount of fat with your greens—such as olive or canola oil, chopped nuts, or slices of avocado—to increase the absorption of nutrients.

Research report Enjoying leafy greens more often—as a crunchy salad, a crisp stir-fry, a side dish of sautéed spinach or Asian greens, or by tossing strongly flavored green kale or watercress into soups, stews, and casseroles—could lower your risk for type 2 diabetes by 14 percent. No other single vegetable family has this power to help keep your blood glucose in the healthy zone, say scientists from the diabetes research team at the University of Leicester in the UK.

What's so special about greens? Plenty. These versatile vegetables contain beta-carotene, vitamin C, and polyphenols, all of which support your body's antioxidant defenses and fight against the damage that triggers diabetes. Greens also contain the

Eat these seeds!

Don't throw away the seeds that you'll find at the center of a whole winter squash. They're rich in zinc—a mineral that supports wound healing—and manganese, which helps antioxidants protect body tissues. To eat the seeds, first remove the strings attached to them, then rinse and dry the seeds. Spread on a baking sheet and roast in the oven at 180°C (350°F), stirring occasionally, for 20–30 minutes. Cool. You can shell the seeds or remove the shells as you eat them.

mineral magnesium, which helps your body process blood glucose in a healthy way. Surprisingly, greens have a small amount of good fats, which help make your cell walls responsive to the blood glucose–controlling hormone insulin. But that's not all. Getting your greens can also help with weight control because most of them have 40 calories or less per cup.

Greens are good for your whole body. Every additional daily serving that you add to your diet could lower your risk for heart disease by as much as 23 percent, say researchers at the Harvard School of Public Health. Why? All the benefits listed above, plus more: greens also provide vitamin C and fiber, which can help lower cholesterol and control body weight. Cell-protecting compounds in greens may be the reason these goodies could help lower your risk for cancers of the mouth, throat, larynx, esophagus and stomach, according to the American Institute for Cancer Research.

Pumpkin Winter squash

Health advantage Reduces risk for cancer, heart disease, diabetes, and vision loss.

Maximize the benefits Having just a teaspoon (3–5 grams) of vegetable oil with a serving of squash will help your body absorb more of the vegetable's fat-soluble beta-carotene.

Research report Bursting with vitamin C, colorful and tasty squash is a top source of the disease-fighting carotenoids alpha-carotene and beta-carotene. These compounds protect against cancer and lower your risk for heart disease, diabetes, vision problems, and more. Your body uses carotenoids as antioxidants to neutralize cell-damaging oxygen molecules called free radicals. It also converts carotenoids into vitamin A, which bolsters immunity.

Diets that are high in beta-carotene are

associated with low cancer risk. Getting this compound from food—not from pills—is crucial; research suggests that beta-carotene supplements do not protect against heart disease and cancer and may even increase the risk of cancer in people who smoke.

While squash is low in fat, it does deliver a respectable 340 milligrams of alpha-linolenic acid (ALA), a good-for-you omega-3 fatty acid. This plant-based fat is emerging as a health hero. Getting 1 gram per day lowers heart attack risk by 60 percent. Getting about 3½ grams per day could reduce levels of heart-threatening LDL cholesterol by 7 to 13 percent. While flax seeds and walnuts are richer sources of ALA, adding squash to your diet can help.

A bonus: Squash also contains polysaccharides that help regulate blood glucose. And this family of vegetables is a great source of lutein and zeaxanthin—carotenoids that accumulate in the retina of your eyes, where they act as sunglasses, filtering out damaging ultraviolet rays and so protecting against cataracts and age-related macular degeneration.

Tomatoes

Health advantage Protect against cancers of the lung, stomach, and prostate. Keep your heart, arteries, and bones healthy. Cut the risk of stroke. May also lower the risk of cancers of the cervix, breast, mouth, pancreas, esophagus, colon, and rectum.

Maximize the benefits Enjoy cooked tomato products, such as tomato soup or sauces, several times a week. One cup (125 ml) of cooked tomato puree delivers 12 times more of the cancer-fighting antioxidant lycopene than a cup of chopped fresh tomatoes.

Research report In one Harvard School of Public Health study that followed 47,000 men for 12 years, those who ate tomato products two or more times a week were 25 percent less likely to develop prostate cancer and 34 percent less likely to develop aggressive prostate cancer than men with the lowest intakes.

Lycopene may also discourage the proliferation of cancers of the breast, lungs, and endometrium (lining of the uterus), according to the American Institute for Cancer Research. But skip supplements. Experts suspect lycopene works in concert with other nutrients found in food. Studies of pills and capsules containing lycopene on its own have found few, if any, benefits.

More reasons to love tomatoes: Recent research suggests that they may bolster bone health and help reduce levels of heart-menacing LDL cholesterol.

Brassicas
Cruciferous vegetables

Health advantage May help reduce the risk for cancers of the colon, rectum, mouth, oesophagus, stomach and lungs.

Maximize the benefits Steaming, microwaving, or stir-frying brassicas (rather than boiling them) retains more health-protecting glucosinolates, folate, and vitamin C. Steaming also enhances the ability of the fiber in broccoli to whisk cholesterol-rich bile acids out of your digestive system, helping to keep levels of heart-threatening LDL cholesterol low.

Research report Researchers at Johns Hopkins University made a breakthrough discovery back in 1992: sulforaphane, isolated from broccoli, slowed the growth of cancer cells in test tube studies. Since then, scientists have discovered additional cancer-fighting phytochemicals in broccoli and the other brassicas. These include carotenoids, coumarins, dithiolethiones, flavonoids, glucosinolates, and isothiocyanates. One way in which they help is by switching on genes that soothe inflammation and help protect cells from cancer-causing damage.

Some studies suggest that people who eat lots of brassicas have lower risk for lung, colorectal, stomach, breast, and prostate cancers. Researchers at Florida A&M University are investigating a brassica compound called C-substituted diindolylmethane as a potential treatment for triple-negative breast cancer. This fast-growing cancer accounts for 15 to 20 percent of all breast cancers. But not everyone responds to the beneficial substances in broccoli, cabbage, brussels sprouts, and other members of this diverse vegetable family. About 50 percent of us lack a gene that helps the body retain and use these compounds. Right now there's no test to see if you're a brassica-responder, but even so, these high-fiber, low-calorie, vitamin-rich vegetables are still worth eating regularly.

Chili peppers

Health advantage Capsaicin-containing creams and ointments can help ease the pain of osteoarthritis, rheumatoid arthritis, diabetic neuropathy, post-herpetic neuropathy, and possibly nerve pain related to HIV/AIDS.

Maximize the benefits Be patient. It may take several weeks for over-the-counter capsaicin creams to effectively ease aches and pains.

Research report Chilies have a long history as a home remedy for pain. In 1979 a new era began when researchers discovered that capsaicin—the ingredient that gives chilies their heat and zing—has a unique talent: it can deplete a chemical messenger in nerve cells that carries pain signals to the brain.

In one study at Case Western Reserve University, 101 people with osteoarthritis or rheumatoid arthritis had their pain reduced by up to 57 percent after four weeks of applying capsaicin cream daily. When a group of 252 people with diabetes-related nerve pain (diabetic neuropathy) used capsaicin cream or a placebo for eight weeks in another study, the capsaicin users reported a 58 percent improvement in pain relief.

Latest breakthrough: A prescription-only capsaicin patch is showing promise against tough-to-treat pain associated with HIV/AIDS and with shingles infections.

Legumes

Health advantage May help reduce the risk for heart disease, high blood pressure, and high cholesterol. Can help keep blood glucose at optimal levels.

Maximize the benefits Minimizing the gassy aftereffects of beans could help you eat more of these healthful vegetables. Types that produce less gas include azuki and mung beans, lentils, and black-eyed, pigeon, and split peas. Soaking legumes overnight before cooking, then chewing them thoroughly, also helps break down gas-producing sugar molecules called oligosaccharides.

Research report Forget those flatulence jokes. Fitting in four quarter-cup (47-gram) servings of dried beans or peas a week could reduce your risk of coronary artery disease by as much as 21 percent, say researchers from Tulane University. And when people with type 2 diabetes ate a cup (190 grams) of beans every day for 12 weeks in a University of Toronto study, their blood glucose control improved significantly.

Beans are a great source of soluble fiber, which helps lower cholesterol levels by whisking cholesterol-rich bile acids out of the body in bowel movements. This fiber also helps keep blood glucose lower and steady.

Sweet potatoes

Health advantage Can help control blood glucose.

Maximize the benefits In any recipe where you would use white potatoes, you can use antioxidant-rich sweet potatoes instead.

Research report Compared with white potatoes, sweet potatoes have a higher fiber content and a lower glycemic load. In addition there are compounds in sweet potatoes that may help people with type 2 diabetes better control their blood glucose. In a study conducted at the Medical University of Vienna, people with diabetes who received a sweet potato extract increased their blood levels of adiponectin, a hormone that plays a role in the way the body uses insulin. Their blood glucose levels also improved.

Whether white, purple, or orange, sweet potatoes are a good source of fiber and vitamin C as well as antioxidants such as beta-carotene and anthocyanins, which may protect against inflammation, heart disease, and cancer.

Vegetables are naturally good and contain vitamins, minerals, and phytochemicals that not only help keep you healthy but also help protect against some diseases.

Remedies

Vegetables can be used to treat all manner of ills. There are potato poultices for easing swelling and cough syrups made, surprisingly, from onions. Most of the remedies described here have been handed down through generations, mainly because they work.

Imbibing a cure

Many of the remedies take the form of infusions or decoctions, both of which are taken as a tea. Most infusions have a pleasant taste, while decoctions tend to be bitter. You can always add a spoonful of honey to improve the taste.

How to make an infusion

Most, if not all, vegetable teas are infusions. They're made in the same way that you'd brew a cup of tea with a tea bag—by pouring freshly boiled water over the vegetable and letting it steep. The resulting infusion extracts active, water-soluble compounds from the vegetable and gives you a soothing hot beverage to sip.

Wash all vegetables thoroughly. Also try to use organic produce or ingredients if at all possible. If gathering ingredients such as stinging nettles from the wild, don't source from places where car pollution or herbicide sprays may be an issue.

To make an infusion, you'll need:

* Vegetable material called for in your recipe (lettuce is used here)
* Tools for slicing, chopping, or peeling (sometimes dried leaves or flowers are used)
* A glass or china teapot or clean coffee press
* A tea strainer
* A teacup

An old folk remedy called for half an onion to be placed on the bedside table or headboard to relieve congestion or nighttime coughing.

1   Put the recommended quantity of prepared vegetable material into a prewarmed glass or china teapot. A coffee press may also be used, but it must be very clean.

2   Pour a small cup (200 ml) freshly boiled water over the vegetable matter and stir. Put the lid on the teapot or press to trap the steam and prevent evaporation. Let the mixture steep as directed in the individual recipe.

3   Stir the mixture again before pouring through a tea strainer into your tea cup. Sip. Refer to individual recipes for the recommended number of cups per day.

Infusions do not store well. So it is best to prepare a fresh pot for each cup.

To make 2 cups of a lettuce infusion, chop 3–4 lettuce leaves—Boston lettuce is good—and 2–3 mint leaves.

Put the lettuce and mint leaves in a warmed glass or china teapot and pour 2 cups of boiling water over them.

Put the lid on and steep for 5 minutes. Strain and sip 1–2 cups of the infusion before bed to help with sleeplessness.

Peel and finely grate 1–2 large onions for a poultice that can be wrapped around the upper body to cover the chest area.

Fold a long piece of cheesecloth in half. Place the grated onion on top, then fold the cheesecloth over several times to enclose.

Use your hands or a spatula to spread the onion inside the cheesecloth to form a long, flat poultice that will cover the chest.

How to make a poultice

A poultice is a convenient way to apply a vegetable remedy directly to the skin and keep it there to aid in healing. Vegetable-based poultices are often used in traditional and folk medicine to draw out impurities and infection, aid in recovery from respiratory infections, and even to cure warts. Some vegetable poultice remedies call for the vegetable material to be put directly on the skin then simply covered, so be sure to follow the individual recipe.

To make a poultice, you'll need:

❋ Vegetables prepared specifically for use in a poultice. Refer to the individual recipe; some vegetables are chopped or grated, others are cooked first (onions are used here)

❋ A piece of cheesecloth three to four times larger than the area you wish to cover

❋ A gentle oil such as almond or olive oil

❋ Plastic wrap and a second long piece of cheesecloth (optional) to hold the poultice in place

1 Prepare vegetables according to the poultice recipe you are using. (Onions are grated here.) Prepare sufficient vegetable material to cover the affected body part.

2 Fold the piece of cheesecloth in half. Place the poultice mixture on it, then fold the cheesecloth over again to encase it. Use a spatula or the back of a large spoon to spread the material out so that it will cover all of the affected body part.

3 Rub oil onto the affected body part to prevent the poultice from sticking. Apply the poultice.

4 Cover the poultice with plastic wrap. If you'd like to hold it in place more securely, wrap with a second piece of cheesecloth (not too tightly) and tie. Follow individual recipe directions to determine how long to keep the poultice in place.

Onion poultice

Grated raw onion or mashed steamed onions are good for chest complaints. Prepare a poultice as above and place on the chest area for 1 hour.

Cabbage poultice

Homeopathic physicians say cabbage, when applied to the skin, is warming, stimulating, and detoxifying.

To make the simplest cabbage poultice, you'll need:

❋ Several large leaves of green cabbage
❋ A rolling pin

1 Wash and dry whole cabbage leaves. Lay each leaf on a table, counter, or cutting board and bruise by rolling over it with a rolling pin.

2 Lay bruised cabbage leaves on the chest. Cover with cheesecloth or a small towel. Leave in place for 1 hour, then replace with fresh leaves.

Variation Chop or shred green cabbage. Boil, steam, or microwave until soft, then use the warm cabbage to make a poultice, following the directions at left. Apply to the chest for 1 hour, then replace with a fresh poultice as required.

Also ...

Other uses for cabbage

Cabbage poultices are used by traditional healers to ease arthritic pain and soothe varicose veins. Cabbage leaves can also ease the pain of breast engorgement in nursing mothers. In this instance, slip a whole leaf inside the bra so that it cups the breast. Either green or red cabbage will be effective.

Colds, coughs, and other respiratory ailments

Vegetable-based remedies have long been used to ease respiratory symptoms, and there are recipes for easing congestion and for soothing coughs, too.

Hot tomato tonic

This popular cold chaser mixes vitamin C–rich tomato juice and lemon juice with immune-boosting garlic. Hot pepper sauce contains the pepper compound capsaicin, proven to reduce sinus inflammation and thus ease congestion.

To make a portion of tonic, you'll need:

* 1 cup (250 ml) tomato juice
* 1 tablespoon lemon juice
* 2 cloves garlic, peeled
* Tabasco or other hot pepper sauce to taste

1 Combine tomato juice and lemon juice in a small saucepan. Add garlic and heat until warm. Add drops of Tabasco sauce to taste.

2 Pour into a mug and sip slowly. Breathing in the garlic-infused steam may help you breathe easier, too. Drink as often as needed.

Onion and honey soother

Honey is a proven cough stopper. Onions contain sulfur, which may help fight infection (and also trigger the tears that come with chopping onions). Together, these ingredients are the foundation for an age-old cough syrup that can also ease the pain of a sore throat.

To make the soother, you'll need:

* 1 red or yellow onion, thickly sliced
* ½ cup (175 g) honey, or more if desired

1 Place 1 onion slice in the bottom of a glass bowl and cover with honey. Repeat onion and honey layers until all the slices are covered.

2 Cover the bowl with a lid or plate. Place in the refrigerator for 12–15 hours or overnight.

3 Take a spoonful of soother as needed. Store in an airtight container in the refrigerator for up to 2 days, then discard.

Hot tomato tonic can be garnished with a stick of celery. Celery is a traditional Chinese-medicine remedy that is thought to help lower blood pressure. Four stalks of celery a day are recommended.

Soothe coughs, congestion, and respiratory illnesses with (from left to right) onion and honey soother, ginger, onion, and carrot juice, and hot tomato tonic.

How to make a decoction

Teas that are made by boiling the plant material in water—rather than steeping it, as you would a tea bag—are called decoctions. Boiling brings out the active components and is used with vegetables that are dense, tough, or need more contact with heat to release their beneficial compounds. Espresso coffee is actually a vegetable decoction.

To make a decoction, you'll need:

✽ Vegetable material called for in your recipe (garlic is used here)

✽ Tools for slicing, chopping, or, in the case of garlic, crushing

✽ A medium non-aluminum saucepan with a lid

✽ A strainer or sieve large enough to catch all the vegetable material

✽ A teacup or mug

✽ Honey and lemon to taste

1 Place prepared vegetable material and water in the saucepan. Cover and bring to a gentle boil, then simmer for the recommended time. (This will vary with the vegetable used.)

2 Strain the liquid into the cup. Flavor with honey and lemon if desired.

Garlic tea

Garlic's antibacterial and antiviral properties make it a natural for fighting off the viral infections that trigger cold and flu symptoms. Some natural healers recommend swallowing a chopped garlic clove, mixed with honey, at the first sign of a cold. But you may find this refreshing tea—a decoction in which the garlic is boiled in water, not steeped—a more pleasant option.

To make two cups of tea, you'll need:

✽ 2–3 cloves garlic, peeled

✽ 2 cups (500 ml) water

✽ 1 teaspoon honey, or to taste

✽ Juice of ½ lemon, or to taste

1 Crush garlic with the flat side of a knife.

Also ...

Herbal tea brews

There are two ways to prepare water-based herbal tea extracts: infusions and decoctions. An infusion is a tea or tisane that is made by pouring boiling water over fresh or dried herbs (see page 156). A decoction is used when the herbs are hard or woody, so it is suitable for bulbs, roots, bark, and seeds. The plant material is boiled in water for several minutes using an enamel saucepan (never use an aluminum pan, as this will taint the decoction).

2 Put water and garlic in a saucepan. Heat until bubbles form around the side of the pan, then cover and simmer 5 minutes.

3 Strain garlic tea into a cup and flavor with honey and lemon to taste.

4 Sip slowly. Enjoy several cups a day whenever respiratory ailments strike.

Ginger, onion, and carrot juice

This spicy drink has excellent decongestant properties. The ginger and wasabi will help clear the sinuses, and the carrots provide beta-carotene, which helps maintain the mucous membranes and may also reduce inflammation.

To make a glass of juice, you'll need:

✽ 2.5-cm (1-in) piece fresh ginger, peeled and sliced

✽ ¼ onion, roughly chopped

✽ 2 carrots, roughly chopped

✽ ¼ teaspoon wasabi

Using a juicer, process ginger, then onion, carrots, and wasabi. Pour into a glass and drink.

Peel and crush 2–3 garlic cloves. The number of cloves will depend on personal taste and the particular garlic's strength.

Add garlic cloves to 2 cups of water in a saucepan—enamel is ideal. Bring just to a gentle boil, then simmer gently 5 minutes.

Use a funnel or strainer to strain the tea into a clean glass storage vessel before pouring it into a teacup.

Strained tincture liquid should be poured into brown tincture bottles and stored in a cool, dark place. This nettle tincture is high in iron and good for an energy boost.

Roman soldiers would slap their bodies with fresh nettles. The stinging sensation was invigorating and brought heat to the skin during the cold months of battle and marching.

How to make a fresh plant tincture

Alcohol can be used instead of water to extract the active ingredients of vegetables; it is often better than water because it removes more of the medicinal compounds. Alcohol-based preparations are called tinctures and may take a few weeks to mature.

To make a tincture, you'll need:

❊ Fresh or dried plant material
❊ Alcohol—at least 80 proof (40 percent alcohol); vodka is often recommended
❊ Chopping board and sharp knife
❊ A glass jar with a tight-fitting screw-on lid
❊ A piece of fine cheesecloth
❊ A glass bowl
❊ Dark glass tincture bottles with tight-fitting lids

1 Measure 250 g (8 oz) fresh leaves (nettles are used here). Wash thoroughly to remove any dirt, air-dry, and chop finely. Alternatively, use 125 g (4 oz) dried herbs. Pack a glass jar three-quarters full with plant material.

2 Add 2 cups (500 ml) vodka, leaving some space at the top of the jar. Screw on the lid and store in a cool, dark place for 14 days, shaking 2–3 times a day. Taste the liquid after 2 weeks. It should have the flavor and aroma of the plant material. Soak longer if necessary, up to 8 weeks. If it still tastes weak, strain off the liquid, discard old plant material, and add new material to the jar. Return the liquid to the jar and repeat soaking and shaking process for 2–3 weeks.

3 Strain the mixture through cheesecloth into a bowl, then tightly squeeze the plant material inside the cloth to extract every last drop.

4 Pour the liquid into dark tincture bottles. Seal and label with the plant material's name and the date. Store in a cool, dark cabinet for up to 3 years and use as directed for the specific plant tincture. Makes about 2 cups (500 ml).

Finely chop 250 g fresh nettle leaves. Nettles have stinging hairs, so wear a pair of rubber gloves to protect against them.

Firmly pack nettles into a glass jar until three-quarters full. Add 2 cups vodka to cover nettles, but don't fill right to the top.

After leaving for 2–6 weeks—taste to test when tincture is ready—strain the liquid through cheesecloth into a glass bowl.

Insomnia

Getting a good night's sleep can make all the difference in staying healthy. It's hard to fight off illness when you are tired. If you are having trouble sleeping, try this simple remedy.

Lettuce tea

Some types of lettuce contain a compound with sedative properties. That's why herbalists suggest brewing a pot of scented lettuce leaf tea to help overcome sleeplessness. Experts disagree about which modern lettuce varieties work best, but there's some evidence that Boston lettuce may be among the best.

For two cups of tea, you'll need:

✳ 3–4 Boston lettuce leaves
✳ 2–3 fresh mint leaves for extra flavor
✳ 2 cups (500 ml) boiling water

Chop lettuce and mint leaves. Follow directions for making an infusion on page 156. Steep lettuce and mint in the boiling water for 5 minutes. Strain and sip 1–2 cups before bed.

Digestive discomforts

Certain vegetables are known to calm the digestive tract; others act as a tonic, improving digestion and boosting your metabolism.

Fennel seed tea

A traditional remedy for infant colic, fennel seed has been shown in research studies to reduce gas and intestinal cramping while increasing movement within the small intestine.

For a cup of tea, you'll need:

✳ 1 teaspoon fennel seeds
✳ 1 cup (250 ml) just-boiled water

Follow the directions for making an infusion on page 156. Steep fennel seeds in the just-boiled water for about 10 minutes. Strain and sip.

Note To help infant colic, breast-feeding mothers may pass along fennel's soothing benefits by sipping a cup of this tea up to three times a day. Do not give fennel tea to a baby without consulting your doctor. For adult digestive discomforts, add other soothing herbs to the tea, such as chamomile, peppermint, or lemon balm.

Dandelion leaf tea

Dandelion tea is a traditional digestive tonic. It may help reduce fluid retention.

To make a cup of tea, you will need:

✳ 1–2 teaspoons dried dandelion leaf
✳ 1 cup (250 ml) boiling water

Follow the directions for making an infusion on page 156. Steep dandelion leaf in the boiling water for 15 minutes. Strain and sip. Drink 3 cups a day.

Lettuce tea (left rear) can help with soothing you to sleep. Fennel seed tea (front) and dandelion leaf tea (back right) are infusions that can be used to improve digestion.

Dandelion tincture

Bitter compounds in dandelion root stimulate the release of bile acids, which the body uses to digest and absorb fats and fat-soluble vitamins. You can purchase dandelion root tincture at a health food store or online, or follow the directions on page 160 to make your own. To use, stir 1 teaspoon into $1/2$ cup (125 ml) water and sip 15–20 minutes before a meal.

Nettle tincture

Nettle leaves are considered to be higher in iron than spinach, and are used as a tonic for the blood. Nettles can also be used to cleanse the digestive tract, promote healthy digestion, and ease stomach problems. Follow the directions on page 160 to make your own nettle tincture. Take 1 medicine dropper of tincture twice a day.

Also ...

Leafy greens for a restful sleep

Tryptophan in protein helps us to sleep, but to achieve optimal absorption of the tryptophan, you need to combine it with foods dense in carbohydrates. Other compounds in food also make a difference to sleep. For example, magnesium, found in leafy green vegetables, helps to relax muscles and calm nerves. Including such foods in a light evening meal may help you prepare for a restful sleep at night. Other vegetables that can help with insomnia include potatoes, sweet potatoes, corn, peas, winter squash, beets, cauliflower, broccoli, brussels sprouts, spinach, kale, asparagus, and celery.

Ayurvedic medicine uses an infusion of nettle tea as a spring tonic and rejuvenator.

Pick-me-ups and energy boosters

Plants of the deepest green give the most energy. Drinking a cup a day of nettle infusion, for example, will increase your energy without wiring your nerves.

Nettle infusion

Put 25 g (1 oz) dried nettle leaf in a teapot. Fill to the top with boiling water. Steep for at least 4 hours, or overnight. Strain and drink. Refrigerate the remainder and drink within 36 hours. After that, use leftovers as a hair rinse or to fertilize houseplants.

Spinach, carrot, and orange juice

This spinach-based drink contains fatigue-busting iron. Combined with the vitamin C in the orange juice, which enhances iron absorption, and the vitality-packed beta-carotene in the carrots, this is a powerful tonic.

To make a glass of juice, you'll need:

❋ 2½ cups (125 g) firmly packed spinach or baby spinach leaves
❋ 1 carrot, roughly chopped
❋ 1 orange, seeded and roughly chopped

Using a juicer, process spinach, then carrot and orange. Pour into a glass and drink.

Other combinations of vegetables for juicing

You could add carrots or beets to any of these combinations for extra flavor in the juice.

❋ Spinach, baby spinach, celery, lettuce, cucumber, and green apple
❋ Kale, celery, carrot, cucumber, chili pepper, and lemon
❋ Cucumber and celery
❋ Kale, celery, and grapefruit

Process the combination of your choice in a juicer.

Constipation

To help the gut work well, make sure you have an adequate intake of fluid and fiber, and keep active.

Spinach, cucumber, and carrot juice

Spinach juice is a home remedy for constipation. Here spinach combines with carrot to add a touch of sweetness and balance the strong spinach flavor. Cucumber is used for its high water content.

To make a glass of juice, you'll need:

❋ 1 carrot, roughly chopped
❋ 1 cucumber, roughly chopped
❋ 2 cups (100 g) firmly packed spinach or baby spinach leaves

Using a juicer, process carrot and cucumber, then spinach. Pour into a glass and drink.

Alert!

Juices are not a substitute for a balanced, healthful diet. Juicing removes the valuable fiber, leaving behind a concentrated dose of tooth-eroding acids and sugars as well as oxalates (in some vegetables) that can cause kidney stones. By all means, have a small serving of juice once a day as part of your vegetable intake, but any more than that won't give you extra benefits and could actually do you more harm than good.

Also ...

Coleslaw salad

This coleslaw is a good choice as part of your evening meal for a large dose of the fiber that will keep you regular. It calls for about 1 cup each of green apple, cabbage, carrot, and cucumber.

For the coleslaw, you'll need:

❋ 1 small green unpeeled apple, diced
❋ 1 tablespoon white wine vinegar
❋ 1 cup (75 g) finely shredded green or red cabbage
❋ 1 large unpeeled carrot, grated
❋ 1 small cucumber, diced
❋ ½ cup (60 g) raisins
❋ 2 tablespoons (15 g) flax seeds, ground if preferred
❋ 1 tablespoon extra virgin olive oil

1 In a small bowl, toss apple in vinegar to prevent browning while preparing other vegetables.

2 Put cabbage, carrot, cucumber, raisins, and seeds in a large bowl. Drain apple, reserving vinegar. Add apple to bowl and mix to combine.

3 Whisk reserved vinegar and oil together. Toss through the coleslaw to coat well, then serve.

Variation You could lightly steam or blanch the cabbage or use sauerkraut. For a creamier dressing, whisk 1 tablespoon low-fat plain yogurt with the vinegar and oil in step 3.

A cup or glass of (from left to right) spinach, carrot, and orange juice or spinach, cucumber, and carrot juice will give you iron for energy and help you meet your daily vegetable requirement.

Diuretics

Vegetables cannot take the place of diuretic drugs, often prescribed to help control blood pressure and congestive heart failure. But natural compounds found in vegetables such as asparagus can gently increase urine production—which may help reduce mild fluid retention and play a role in strategies to keep chronic urinary tract infections at bay. Try these plant-based teas.

Celery seed tea

Celery seed has been used in Ayurvedic medicine for thousands of years to combat water retention.

To make a cup of tea, you'll need:

❋ 1 teaspoon (about 2.5 g) celery seeds
❋ 1 cup (250 ml) boiling water

1 Crush celery seeds in a mortar and pestle or spice grinder.

2 Follow the directions for making an infusion on page 156. Steep crushed seeds in boiling water for 10 minutes. Strain and sip up to 3 cups a day.

Corn silk tea

A traditional remedy for bladder inflammation and painful urination, corn silk tea is still recommended by herbalists as a soothing, gentle diuretic.

To make a cup of tea, you'll need:

❋ 2 teaspoons dried or 3–5 strands fresh washed corn silk
❋ 1 cup (250 ml) boiling water

Follow the directions for making an infusion on page 156. Steep the corn silk in boiling water for 10–15 minutes. Strain and sip. Have 1 cup up to three times a day.

Note You can also use corn silk tincture. Purchase at a health food store or make according to tincture directions on page 160. Have 1 teaspoon (5 ml) three times a day.

Eat fiber-rich foods, drink plenty of water, and exercise daily to avoid constipation.

Also ...

Traditional remedies

Some food plants have played and continue to play an important part in traditional health care practices.

Native Americans put slices of raw potato or dabs of potato juice on warts. In Irish folk medicine, a potato carried in the pocket was believed to aid rheumatism. This was a less painful alternative to another traditional remedy—applying stinging nettle leaves. Native Americans used ground corn in poultices to treat bruises, swellings, and boils; for toothache, they made a poultice of horseradish leaves. Mayans used chili peppers to clear the sinuses. In Central Australia the needle-like leaves of dead finish (an acacia species with edible seeds) were used to treat warts, and a liquid from its soaked bark was taken for coughs.

In traditional Chinese medicine, dried and ground rhubarb root is taken internally to treat constipation and diarrhea, while onions are used to treat respiratory disorders. Dandelion root features in the traditional medicine of many cultures as a remedy for a range of complaints from constipation to gout.

Garlic can be used to prevent or treat infection. It also has an antiseptic effect on the digestive and respiratory systems and is an immune stimulant, making it useful in warding off coughs and colds.

Recipe

Garlic breath?
Sip this spinach tonic

If you love garlicky food or use garlic to boost immunity or fight cold symptoms, you may not love the side effects: pungent and sometimes unpleasant breath. Scrub it away, from the inside, with juice made from spinach and parsley. Natural healers say this combination can neutralize compounds responsible for the unfortunate fumes. You need:

1 large handful fresh spinach, washed
1 large handful fresh parsley, washed

Whirl together in a blender, food processor or juicer, then sip.

Immune boosters

Garlic supplements

In one study, people who took garlic pills for three months came down with fewer colds than study volunteers who received placebos. You can reap garlic's benefits by adding it to soups, stews, pasta sauces, and salad dressings or by taking some every day as you would a dietary supplement. There are five ways to do this:

Fresh garlic Mix 1 finely crushed garlic clove with 1 teaspoon honey. Have up to four times a day.

Aged garlic extract Aim for 600–1200 mg daily, divided into two to four doses.

Freeze-dried garlic Have two 200-mg tablets three times a day. Look for standardized products that contain 1.3 percent alliin or 0.6 percent allicin or say they contain 10–12 mg/g alliin and 4000 mcg of total allicin potential (TAP).

Liquid garlic extract Have 1 teaspoon daily.

Garlic tincture Have 4 teaspoons daily.

Warming sweet potato soup for winter

In traditional Chinese medicine, this slightly sweet, warming soup is recommended in cold, dry weather to protect against colds and coughs and to help when you have dry skin, chapped lips, or a dry cough.

For 4 servings, you'll need:

❋ 8 red Chinese dates, pitted
❋ 1 dried snow fungus
❋ 1 orange sweet potato, peeled and diced
❋ 1 Asian pear, unpeeled, cored, and
   cut into 8 pieces
❋ 1 lotus root section or 100 g (3½ oz) canned
   lotus root, diced
❋ ½ small red papaya, peeled, seeded, and diced
❋ 4-cm (1½-in) piece fresh ginger, sliced
❋ 1 tablespoon slivered almonds for garnish

1 Soak dates and white fungus in water for
   2 hours. Drain and cut fungus into pieces.

2 Gently simmer dates, white fungus, sweet
   potato, pear, lotus root, papaya, ginger, and
   4 cups (1 L) water in a large saucepan for
   30 minutes.

3 Discard the ginger. Ladle the soup into four
   bowls, sprinkle with almonds and serve.

Warming sweet potato soup for winter is used in traditional Chinese medicine for the nutritional and protective health benefits of its ingredients.

For a glassful of greens, process some sliced fresh ginger with a little water, then add chopped lemon and puree.

Add 2 cups water, kale, dandelion or other leafy greens, celery, cucumber, garlic and turmeric to the food processor or blender.

After processing the ingredients until they are smooth, pour the vibrantly green liquid into a glass and drink.

Mushrooms 'n' more soup

This recipe delivers immune-boosting mushrooms plus other strengthening ingredients.

For 4 servings, you'll need:

* 5-cm (2-in) piece fresh ginger, thinly sliced
* 1 large onion, chopped
* 2 cups (150 g) shredded cabbage
* 2 carrots, sliced
* 2 cups (180 g) sliced mushrooms of your choice
* 3 cups (450 g) diced winter squash
* 2 nori (dried seaweed) sheets (5 g), shredded
* 4 cups (1 L) low-sodium chicken or vegetable stock

Combine all ingredients in a large saucepan. Bring to a boil, then simmer for 1 hour. Have a bowlful every other day. This soup keeps in the refrigerator for about 3 days; freeze the rest in single portions.

Beet super juice

This combination of vegetables provides a good serving of antioxidants to help strengthen your ability to fight infection and disease.

To make 1 glass, you'll need:

* 2 carrots, chopped
* ½ beet, chopped
* 1 stalk celery with leaves, chopped
* ⅔ cup (30 g) spinach or baby spinach leaves
* 3 sprigs fresh parsley

Using a juicer, process carrots, beet, and celery. Add spinach and parsley and process until well combined. Pour into a glass and drink.

Soup is a typical vehicle for remedies in traditional Chinese medicine.

A glassful of greens

Natural healing experts say greens can boost immunity, perhaps by shifting your body's acid–alkaline balance toward the alkaline side, which is less inviting for invading germs. This recipe also delivers garlic, ginger, and turmeric, which research suggests support a healthy immune system.

To make 2 glasses, you'll need:

* 5-cm (2-in) piece fresh ginger, sliced
* ½ unpeeled lemon, roughly chopped
* 1 handful (30 g) chopped kale
* 1 handful (20 g) chopped dandelion greens or other leafy greens
* 1 stalk celery, roughly chopped
* ½ small cucumber, peeled and roughly chopped
* 1 clove garlic, roughly chopped
* ¼ teaspoon ground turmeric

1 Puree ginger and 1–2 tablespoons water in a food processor or blender. Add lemon and puree.

2 Add 2 cups (500 ml) water, kale, greens, celery, cucumber, garlic, and turmeric and process until smooth. Pour into a glass and drink.

Green drinks are fashionable—and an easy way to get more vegetables into your diet.

Also ...

Cucumber compress

Cooling cucumber slices do more than reduce under-eye puffiness. They may ease the pain of a tension headache by constricting blood vessels and reducing blood flow and pressure.

Apply cucumber slices to your eyes or forehead.

Lie down and relax for up to 10–15 minutes. Replace warm or dry slices with fresh, cool ones.

Natural beauty

Why visit the beauty salon when everything you need to pamper yourself is in your vegetable garden or refrigerator at home? Homemade beauty products are not only cheaper than commercial ones, you also know exactly what's in them.

Wash all vegetables thoroughly before using on your skin.

Active ingredients

Cucumber shampoo? Carrots in lip balm? A facial cleanser based on pumpkin (winter squash)? Tomatoes in pimple cream? These days, vegetables are taking on starring roles in a wide variety of skin care products and cosmetics.

It's one of the hottest trends in beauty. In magazines, on TV, and online, humble vegetables are acquiring a glittering new reputation. Reports call squashes gorgeous gourds, describe the new allure of tomatoes as tomato glam, and refer to cucumbers as "the perfect treat for summer skin."

Two forces explain this new vegetable appeal. First, vegetables have a long history of use in homemade beauty products. These traditional kitchen potions are enjoying new popularity as people search for natural products. At the same time, science is uncovering evidence that denizens of the vegetable patch—including potatoes, carrots, and fennel—have properties that make delightful and effective additions to creams, oils, shampoos, conditioners, and more.

Why not take the trend one step further—by creating all-natural vegetable-based beauty products in your own kitchen? It's easy, fun, and will save you money.

Inner and outer loveliness

Vegetable-based beauty is more than skin deep. To keep looking your best, you need to work from the inside out. Scientific research suggests that eating a wide range of produce can have benefits for your appearance. Here are some examples.

Vegetable compounds may improve skin texture and moisture In a study conducted by Germany's Witten/Herdecke University, people were asked to consume a proprietary vegetable-and-fruit extract or a placebo for 12 weeks while the quality of their skin was measured. Researchers found that the group that got the real extract had 9 percent better hydration and 16 percent better skin density than the placebo group.

Produce eaters are rated as more attractive Scientists from the UK's University of St. Andrews followed the produce-eating habits and skin tone of 35 volunteers for six weeks and got a surprise. Those who increased their intake of fruit and vegetables saw improvements in skin color, while the skin of those who cut back on produce became paler. Outside observers rated the produce eaters' skin as more attractive, too. The researchers think compounds called carotenoids—such as the beta-carotene in yams, winter squash, and spinach and the lycopene in bell peppers and tomatoes—were especially responsible for that healthy glow.

Vegetables help fight skin damage
In a study conducted by Australia's Monash University, researchers analyzed the skin and long-term eating habits of 323 women and men. They specifically looked at wrinkling caused by sun exposure and found that those who ate the most vegetables, legumes, and olive oil had 32 percent fewer signs of this sun damage than those who ate the least.

Why? Two reasons. Protective chemicals called polyphenols in plant-based foods may guard skin cells from the destructive effects of the sun's ultraviolet rays. And good fats, found in olive oil, avocado, and to a lesser degree in leafy greens and other vegetables, seem to bolster the skin's natural defenses. The researchers titled their study, which was published in the *Journal of the American College of Nutrition*, "Skin Wrinkling: Can Food Make a Difference?" The answer, they say, is yes.

Also ...

A long tradition

Vegetables really aren't newcomers to the beauty scene. In the centuries before the development of commercial products, they were widely used ingredients in home formulas for skin and hair around the world. Thousands of years ago, the Egyptians, Greeks, and Romans used olive oil as a skin moisturizer. Meanwhile, the Maya, Aztec, and Inca people reportedly prized avocado for its luxurious, skin-nourishing fats.

Cucumber pulp was used to freshen the appearance of freckled and dull skin, according to the extensive American folk remedies archive of the University of California, Los Angeles. Tomatoes—sliced, fried, green or salted—were applied to skin problems such as boils. Winter squash was thought to ease baldness and soothe burns. Carrots, when eaten, were thought to make hair curly and cheeks rosy.

Today, modern science has uncovered many properties of vegetables that help explain these traditional uses. Here are some examples:

Tomatoes contain malic and citric acids; both are similar to the alpha hydroxy acids used in commercial skin peels and may help whisk away dead skin cells.

Cucumber contains antioxidants that may help shrink swollen blood vessels and help reduce under-eye puffiness.

Pumpkin (Winter squash) is a rich source of antioxidants; University of California at San Francisco researchers now say antioxidants in skin preparations do have protective properties.

Carrots contain gel-like pectin—the sort used as a soothing ingredient in many commercial personal care products.

Beauty is close at hand. You need look no further than the crisper section of your refrigerator or the veggie patch in your garden. Get started with the recipes on the following pages.

Tools of the trade

The basic tools for making your own hair and beauty products are very simple. It's a good idea to keep them separate from the utensils you use for cooking, as plastic and wood absorb flavors and smells, metallic bowls and spoons can oxidize when they come into contact with vegetable juices, and substances such as vegetable wax and beeswax are difficult to clean thoroughly from surfaces. Here's what you'll need:

* Measuring cups and spoons
* Kitchen scales
* Non-aluminium or non-copper saucepans and double boiler
* Glass bowls
* Cheesecloth squares
* Glass eyedroppers or medicine droppers
* Wooden spoons and spatulas
* Chopping board

* Food processor or blender
* Vegetable peeler or kitchen knife
* Potato masher
* Kitchen thermometer
* Plastic mesh strainer
* Whisk
* Coffee or spice grinder or mortar and pestle
* Airtight glass jars and bottles with nonmetallic caps

Dry and dull skin

Dry skin is often thirsty and rough. It may feel tight and itchy or even look dull. Make sure you are drinking plenty of fluids, then try these vegetable-based products to help lubricate and rehydrate your skin.

Cucumber cleanser

Widely used in commercial cleansing and toning products, cucumber's high moisture content and ability to soothe and protect cells make it a go-to vegetable for dry skin. Yogurt contains natural acids that can brighten skin. Be sure to use a full-fat yogurt for this recipe.

For two applications, you'll need:

* 1 small cucumber (130 g/4½ oz), peeled if not organic
* 1–2 tablespoons Greek-style plain yogurt

1   Finely grate cucumber into a bowl. Transfer to a plastic mesh strainer set over a bowl. Let stand for 5 minutes to drain off excess liquid. Discard the liquid and put cucumber in a clean bowl.

2   Stir in enough yogurt to form a paste.

3   Wet your face with warm water. Using your fingers, gently massage the cleanser into your skin. Rinse off. If your skin needs extra soothing, leave the cleanser on for 15 minutes before removing. Refrigerate leftover cleanser in an airtight jar for up to 3 days.

Makes ½ cup (110 g)

Softening radish mask

Spicy radishes have a reputation among practitioners of natural, home-based skin care for softening dry skin. You'll enjoy the clean, nongreasy feeling, too.

If thick Greek-style yogurt is not available, use any plain, unflavored full-fat yogurt instead.

For one application, you'll need:

* ⅓ small cucumber (40 g/1½ oz), peeled if not organic
* 1 radish (15 g/½ oz), peeled if not organic
* 1 egg yolk
* 1–2 tablespoons Greek-style plain yogurt

1   Finely grate cucumber into a bowl. Transfer to a strainer set over a bowl. Let stand for 5 minutes to drain excess liquid. Discard the liquid and put cucumber in a clean bowl. Finely grate radish into the same bowl.

2   Stir in egg yolk and enough yogurt to make a thick paste.

3   Apply the mask to your face and neck. Leave on for 15 minutes, then rinse off with warm water. Cover any unused mixture and store in the refrigerator for up to 3 days.

Makes ⅓ cup (75 g)

Clarifying pumpkin (winter squash) mask

A popular do-it-yourself beauty treatment, this mask relies on the soothing qualities of pumpkin (winter squash). Some skin experts say pumpkin's antioxidants, natural acids, minerals, and potential anti-inflammatory properties work together to make a mask that softens the skin and imparts a healthy, natural glow.

For one application, you'll need:

* 4 tablespoons pureed pumpkin (winter squash)
* 1 teaspoon honey
* 1 egg yolk, beaten
* 1–2 teaspoons buttermilk

1   Put squash, honey, and egg yolk in a small bowl. Use a fork to mix thoroughly. Drizzle in small amounts of buttermilk and mix until the mask is spreadable but not runny.

To make a skin cleanser, finely grate a small cucumber into a bowl. If using a nonorganic cucumber, peel it first.

Tip cucumber into a strainer—preferably a plastic mesh strainer—set over a bowl. Let stand 5 minutes to drain off excess liquid.

Put drained cucumber into a clean bowl. Stir in up to 2 tablespoons thick plain yogurt, just enough to make a paste.

To make a pumpkin mask, combine 4 tablespoons pureed pumpkin with 1 teaspoon honey and 1 beaten egg yolk.

Add a little buttermilk at a time and mix well after each addition until you have a mask that is spreadable but not runny.

If possible, use organic vegetables to minimize pesticide residues in your skin-care products.

Rub olive oil on rough elbows. It contains squalene, an unsaturated fatty acid also found naturally in human skin. Replenishing squalene restores suppleness to skin damaged by wind and sun. It works on dry feet, legs, arms, and hands, too.

2 Apply the mask to clean, dry skin. Relax for 15–20 minutes with it on your face. Rinse off with warm water, gently using a wet washcloth to remove any dried mask if necessary. Pat dry. Discard any unused mixture.

Makes: ⅓ cup (85 g)

Note Steam the pumpkin until just tender to ensure it keeps all its nutrients and does not become too soggy. Cool and puree before mixing with the other ingredients.

Carrot seed oil moisturizer and makeup remover

Extracted from tiny carrot seeds, this oil soothes irritated skin and may help discourage wrinkles from forming. Its nongreasy feel is pleasant.

To make a small batch, you'll need:

❋ 3 tablespoons (60 ml) almond oil
❋ 3 tablespoons (60 ml) jojoba oil
❋ 1 teaspoon carrot seed essential oil

1 Mix almond, jojoba, and carrot seed oils. Store in a small airtight bottle with a tight-fitting lid.

2 To remove makeup, dab a little on a cotton ball. To use as a moisturizer, apply a fine coating to your skin at night. It will keep in a cool, dry place for up to 2 weeks.

Makes ½ cup (125 ml)

Carrot-seed lip balm

Help prevent chapped lips with this soothing balm.

To make a batch, you'll need:

❋ ½ tablespoon (10 g) shea butter
❋ ½ tablespoon (7 g) cocoa butter
❋ 1½ tablespoons (25 g) coconut oil
❋ 1 tablespoon (7 g) grated cosmetic-grade beeswax, beeswax pearls, or carnauba wax
❋ 3 drops carrot seed essential oil
❋ ¼ teaspoon (1 ml) vitamin E oil or 2 vitamin E capsules, punctured and squeezed

1 Put shea and cocoa butters in a double boiler or a small heatproof bowl set over a saucepan of barely simmering water. Stir in coconut oil and heat over low heat for 20 minutes, stirring occasionally. Use a kitchen thermometer to check that the temperature of the mixture doesn't get higher than 79°C (175°F).

2 Add beeswax or carnauba wax and stir well. After it has melted completely, remove from the heat and add carrot seed essential oil and vitamin E oil. Stir until smooth. Transfer to a lip balm tube or tin and allow to set for 3 hours. Use as required. It will store for up to 1 month.

Makes 2 tablespoons (55 g)

Also ...

Ways to be water wise

Drinking water is a great help for headaches because dehydration is a common cause. Not only that, but water is great for your skin. It won't happen overnight, but after just a week of drinking an increased amount of water, you may notice a healthy glow. You also get water from food. The top five vegetables for water content are cucumber, zucchini, bell pepper, celery, and tomato.

Drink at least eight cups of water a day to provide your skin with the moisture it needs from within.

Oily skin

Oily skin may be prone to breakouts, clogged pores, and too much shine. But certain vegetables will lift excess oil, tighten pores, and discourage pimples—without using irritating chemical additives.

The acidity found in tomatoes will help dry up blemishes. Tomatoes contain vitamins K, C, and A. The latter two are commonly used in prescription and over-the-counter treatments for acne.

Fennel and buttermilk cleansing milk

Gentle yet effective, this cleanser combines the natural acidity of buttermilk with the antiseptic and astringent properties of fennel. Oily skin is clarified without harsh chemicals, while fennel seeds tighten the pores and discourage the growth of bacteria that can cause blemishes.

For a week's supply, you'll need:
* 2 tablespoons fennel seeds
* ½ cup (125 ml) buttermilk
* 2½ cups (625 ml) distilled water

1 Crush fennel seeds using a mortar and pestle or a clean coffee or spice grinder.

2 Combine crushed fennel and buttermilk in a double boiler or a small heatproof bowl set over a saucepan of barely simmering water. Gently heat mixture for 20 minutes.

3 Transfer to a saucepan that is not aluminum or copper. Add distilled water. Boil for 10 minutes. Let cool. Strain into a bottle with a tight-fitting lid and store in the refrigerator for up to 1 week.

4 To use, pour cleanser into your palm or onto a soft cloth and apply to face, rubbing gently. Leave for 1–2 minutes, then rinse off.

Makes 2¼ cups (560 ml)

Tomato protects skin from inflammation and soothes at the same time. If you have an angry-looking pimple, cut a tomato in half and rub the cut side on your face.

Cornmeal scrub

Cornmeal is a coarse kind of flour that is ground from dried corn. Its slightly gritty texture is perfect for exfoliating even the most sensitive oily skin. Oats, milk, and lavender have a soothing effect.

To make a batch, you'll need:
* ½ cup (70 g) rolled oats, ground to a fine powder
* 2 tablespoons (15 g) dried lavender flowers or dried mint for a refreshing aroma
* 2 tablespoons (20 g) powdered milk
* 1 teaspoon cornmeal

1 Combine ingredients in a glass bowl. Pour into a container with a tight-fitting lid. Store in a cool, dark place for up to 6 months.

2 To use, pour 1–2 tablespoons of scrub into your palm. Mix with water to make a paste and massage gently into your skin. Rinse off.

Makes ¾ cup (110 g)

Tomato toner

The acids and astringent compounds in "love apples" brighten the skin, shrink large pores, remove excess oil, and soothe blemishes. Lime juice is a refreshing addition to this toner.

For one application, you'll need:
* 1 small (90 g) ripe tomato or 1 tablespoon canned tomato juice
* 2–4 drops lime juice

1 If using fresh tomato, process the fruit in a juicer, food processor, or blender. Strain off solids, reserving the juice.

2 Combine 1 tablespoon tomato juice and the lime juice in a small bowl.

3 Soak a cotton ball in the toner and dab onto your skin. Leave for 15 minutes, then rinse off. Store unused toner in refrigerator for 3 days.

Makes 1 tablespoon (20 ml)

To make a cleansing milk with fennel and buttermilk, crush 2 tablespoons fennel seeds using a mortar and pestle.

Combine fennel and ½ cup buttermilk in a heatproof bowl set over a saucepan of simmering water. Heat for 20 minutes.

Put fennel and buttermilk mixture in an enamel saucepan, stir in 2½ cups distilled water, and boil for 10 minutes.

Tomato pimple cream

Apply this treatment once or twice a week if you suffer an outbreak.

For one application, you'll need:

❊ ½ tomato
❊ 2 teaspoons (15 g) cosmetic clay or oatmeal
❊ 2 teaspoons full-fat plain yogurt

1 Finely chop tomato until it is the consistency of pulp. Combine 1 tablespoon pulp with cosmetic clay or oatmeal and yogurt in a small bowl to form a smooth paste.

2 Use immediately, dabbing on pimples. Rinse off. Discard any unused mixture.

Makes 2 tablespoons (30 g)

Normal and aging skin

Stress and neglect can leave your skin looking less than glowing, but you can give it an instant makeover with these gentle treatments. Aging skin is especially in need of some TLC, because with age it loses some of its elasticity, and its ability to repair itself diminishes.

Carrot, oats, and milk cleanser

This gentle cleanser helps skin in three ways. Milk contains lactic acid, which beauty experts say helps slough off dead skin cells—be sure to use whole milk. Oats help soften and moisturize. Carrots have beta-carotene, which nourishes skin, and pectin, which is soothing.

For one application, you'll need:

❊ ½ cup (70 g) rolled oats, ground to a fine powder
❊ 1 carrot, finely grated
❊ Approximately ½ cup (125 ml) whole milk

1 Combine carrots and oats in a bowl. Stir in enough milk so the mixture has the consistency of wet cake batter.

2 Spread cleanser gently on your face, rubbing lightly. (Be careful around the eye area.) Let it rest on the skin for 1–2 minutes, then rinse off with barely warm water. Pat dry. Discard any unused cleanser.

Makes ½ cup (125 ml)

Refreshing carrot mask

The honey in this delightful, relaxing mask helps tighten your skin's pores, while carrots nourish.

For one application, you'll need:

❊ 2 large (360 g/13 oz) carrots, chopped
❊ 2 tablespoons honey

1 Steam carrots until very soft. Transfer to a bowl and mash until smooth. Allow to cool a little. Stir in honey.

2 Apply the mask and leave in place for about 10 minutes. Rinse off with barely warm water. Discard unused mixture or store in refrigerator for up to 3 days.

Tip Steaming the carrots rather than boiling them ensures that they keep all their nutrients and don't become too soggy.

Makes ¾ cup (240 g)

Potato spot remover

Potatoes are said to be natural skin whiteners that can help to even out skin tone, lightening age spots and marks left behind by blemishes. Here are three ways to incorporate spuds into your beauty routine:

Simple mask Cut a potato into very thin slices. Lay slices over spots, blemishes, and areas with uneven skin tone. Remove after 10 minutes and rinse gently.

Pure potato juice Process a potato in a juicer. Alternatively, grate the potato, put in a plastic mesh strainer, and press out the juice into a small bowl. Dab potato juice on spots. Store unused juice in a covered jar in the refrigerator for 2–3 days.

Steam bath Steaming your face gently and carefully over a pot of hot potato water is said to open pores, cleanse, and help lift away impurities. The next time you boil potatoes for dinner, strain off the hot water into a bowl and lean over it so you can feel the steam. Be careful not to get too close. Add a handful of nasturtium petals for an extra toning boost.

Whatever your skin type, you can create products to suit it, such as (from left to right) cornmeal scrub, tomato toner, and refreshing carrot mask.

 Make a simple rejuvenating face mask: Mash a cucumber, cover your face with the pulp, and let it dry for 15 minutes; then wash your face with clean, warm water.

Remove berry stains from your hands by rubbing them with a piece of raw potato dipped in lemon juice.

Hair care

There is a multitude of hair-care products on the market, but many of the commercial brands contain chemical additives, some of which can strip out your natural oils or irritate a sensitive scalp. These recipes offer alternatives that are gentle on your hair and your wallet.

Potato rinse to cover gray hair

Looking for a natural way to darken and disguise graying hair? Look no farther than your kitchen. Beauty experts say this potato rinse can temporarily darken gray hair so that it blends in.

For one application, you'll need:

✳ 2 cups (180 g) or more potato peelings from washed potatoes

1 Put 4 cups (1 L) water in a saucepan and bring to a boil. Add the peelings, lower the heat, and simmer 5 minutes. Strain and reserve the water. Let it cool.

2 Shampoo and rinse your hair as usual, then rinse with the cooled potato water. Store any unused rinse, covered, in the refrigerator for up to 3 days.

Makes 3 cups (750 ml)

Tip Use any clean, light-skinned potato. You will need 1 kg (2 lb) potatoes to obtain enough peelings.

After-swim hair rinse

Copper oxide and copper sulfate, found in swimming pool water, can discolor blond hair. Natural acids in tomato juice help copper molecules loosen their grip on the hair so you can wash them away.

For one application, you'll need:

✳ 2–6 tomatoes (200–600 g/7–21 oz) or 1–3 cups (250–750 ml) canned tomato juice

1 If using fresh tomatoes, process them in a juicer, food processor, or blender. Strain off solids, reserving the juice.

2 Rinse your hair with water. Slowly pour fresh or canned tomato juice onto your hair. Work it through with your fingers so all hair is in contact with it. Leave in place for 1–2 minutes. Rinse off with warm water, then shampoo and condition as usual. Discard—or drink—any unused juice.

Makes 1–3 cups (250–750 ml)

Note The amount of juice you need will depend on the length of your hair. Two medium ripe tomatoes (200 g/7 oz) will give you 1 cup (250 ml) of juice.

Avocado and olive moisturizing treatment

Fats in avocado oil and olive oil give dry, flyaway hair a deep conditioning treatment. The yogurt and honey thicken this treatment so that it stays in place, allowing your hair to be in contact with the moisturizing vegetable oils for longer.

For one treatment, you'll need:

✳ 2 tablespoons avocado oil
✳ 2 tablespoons extra virgin olive oil
✳ 2 tablespoons honey
✳ Approximately ⅓ cup (95 g) full-fat Greek-style plain yogurt

1 Combine avocado oil, olive oil, and honey in a small bowl using a whisk or fork. Or process in a food processor or blender until smooth. Stir in yogurt until the treatment reaches the desired consistency—make sure it's not too runny.

2 Spread treatment through clean, dry hair. Cover with a shower cap or plastic wrap and leave in place for 10–20 minutes. Rinse off with warm water, then shampoo and condition as usual. Store unused mixture, covered, in refrigerator for up to 3 days.

Makes ¾ cup (210 g)

Coax your hair into health with a nutrient-rich diet and gentle hair-care products for your specific hair type.

Avocado and olive moisturizing treatment is made with an equal amount of extra virgin olive oil, avocado oil, and honey.

Whisk until completely combined and smooth—or process in a food processor—before adding plain yogurt.

The yogurt should be full-fat and thick, or Greek-style. Whisk to combine, adding a little at a time to get the right consistency.

Nettle shampoo for dandruff

Liquid castile soap is made from vegetable oils and contains no animal fats. It is available online, from organic markets and health-food shops, and from some department stores.

To make a batch, you'll need:

* 1 cup (250 ml) pure liquid castile soap
* ½ cup (125 ml) green tea, cooled
* ½ cup (125 ml) nettle tea (see page 156), cooled
* 1 tablespoon olive oil
* 1 teaspoon honey

1   Combine ingredients in a bottle and shake well.

2   Massage the shampoo into your hair and scalp. Rinse thoroughly. Store the bottle in a cool, dry place for up to 1 week.

Makes 2 cups (500 ml)

Nettle hair rinse for dandruff

Due to its astringent, slightly antiseptic properties, nettle has long been used as a tonic for hair and an anti-dandruff agent. Add a drop of tea tree oil, also a powerful antimicrobial agent, for an effective and natural treatment. If you dislike the scent of tea tree, substitute lavender oil.

For one treatment, you'll need:

* 1 cup (250 ml) nettle tea (see page 156), cooled
* 2 drops tea tree oil

1   Combine nettle tea and tea tree oil in a jug.

2   Shampoo and rinse your hair as usual. Carefully rinse with the nettle rinse, massaging it into the scalp. Do not rinse out. Use treatment two or three times a week.

Makes 1 cup (250 ml)

Cucumber-lemon shampoo

The cucumber in this shampoo conditions your hair, while the lemon acts as an effective cleanser. It is especially good for oily hair.

For one application, you'll need:

* ½ Lebanese or other small cucumber (60 g/2 oz), peeled
* 2 tablespoons (40 ml) lemon juice
* ½ cup (125 ml) hot water
* 1 teaspoon baking soda

1   Process cucumber and lemon juice in a food processor or blender until smooth.

2   Put hot water in a small bowl. Add baking soda and stir to dissolve, then pour into food processor and pulse for 1 second. Allow to cool.

3   Gently massage the shampoo into your hair and scalp, then rinse thoroughly. Discard any unused mixture.

Makes about ½ cup (125 ml)

Vegetable glycerine and vinegar conditioner

Vinegar hair rinses are an age-old way to add shine. Vegetable glycerine, sold in health-food shops and crafts stores, softens hair.

To make a batch, you'll need:

* 3 eggs
* 2 tablespoons grapeseed oil
* 2 tablespoons vegetable glycerine
* 1 cup (250 ml) spring water
* 3 teaspoons cider vinegar

1   Puree all ingredients in a food processor or blender until frothy. Pour into a plastic container with a tight-fitting lid.

2   Shampoo and rinse your hair as usual. Shake the bottle well, then pour conditioner onto your hair and massage thoroughly. Leave in place for 10 minutes, then rinse with warm water.

3   Store any unused conditioner, covered, in the refrigerator for up to 3 days. Shake well before each use.

Makes 3 cups (750 ml)

Make sure your vegetable shampoo is not too hot when you use it.

The avocado and olive moisturizing treatment (left) will give dry hair a deep conditioning. Cucumber-lemon shampoo (right) cleans and conditions oily hair.

Always rinse your hair thoroughly with warm water, then comb out any residue and rinse again.

Well-being

In our busy, stressful lives, it's a good idea to take time out for a little pampering. The recipes below are designed to work with your senses to make you feel refreshed and renewed. Spend a little prep time in the kitchen, then retire to the bathroom for some serious relaxation.

Cucumber or potato eye soothers

Puffy, tired eyes meet their match in slices of cool, comforting cucumber or potato. Both help by reducing puffiness. Use organic vegetables if possible.

For one application, you'll need:

✳ 2 thin slices of cucumber or potato

Wash the cucumber or scrub the potato to remove any dirt. Cut off 2 thin slices. Lie down, close your eyes, and put a cucumber or potato slice over each eye. Relax for 10–15 minutes. Remove slices and discard. Gently bathe eyelids with cool water.

Use almond oil on a cotton swab as a gentle cleanser for the delicate area around the eyes.

Add these treatments to your home day spa. Clockwise from front left: softening bath sachet with lettuce, carrot seed oil cuticle treatment, pumpkin spice skin scrub, and cucumber eye soothers.

Softening bath sachet with lettuce

Oatmeal plus a surprising addition—shredded lettuce—lend bath water a delicious softness.

For one bath, you'll need:

✳ 1 cup (140 g) rolled oats, ground to a fine powder
✳ 1 cup (60 g) shredded lettuce
✳ Handful of dried lavender flowers (optional)

1 Put oats and lettuce in a cheesecloth sachet bag. Add lavender, if desired, for a refreshing scent.

2 Put sachet in bathtub as it fills with water, then have a long soak. Discard the sachet after use.

For a sachet bag that's a little more special than a piece of cheesecloth, use a ready-made organza drawstring bag and decorate it with an embroidered motif.

Pumpkin spice skin scrub

The sugar in this scrub gently removes dry skin, while pumpkin helps moisturize. The spices are a spa-quality treat for your senses.

For one treatment, you'll need:

* 1 cup (260 g) pumpkin puree
* 1 cup (220 g) granulated sugar
* ⅛ teaspoon each ground cinnamon, cloves, and ginger

1 Put all ingredients in a small bowl and stir until just combined.

2 Immediately, before the sugar crystals melt, rub the scrub onto feet, legs, and arms, using a soft brush, washcloth, or your hands. Rinse off in the shower. Discard any unused mixture.

Makes 1½ cups (440 g)

Tip You will need a 400-g (14-oz) piece of pumpkin, peeled. Steam pumpkin until just tender to ensure it keeps all its nutrients and does not become too soggy. Cool and puree before adding other ingredients.

Carrot seed oil cuticle treatment

Rejuvenating carrot seed oil is found in many skin-care products. Herbal healers say it soothes rough, irritated skin—making it a perfect choice for ragged, dry cuticles.

For several applications, you'll need:

* ½ tablespoon grapeseed oil
* ½ teaspoon carrot seed oil
* ½ teaspoon wheat germ oil
* 1–3 drops of orange, cedarwood, or geranium essential oil (optional)

1 Combine grapeseed, carrot seed, and wheat germ oils in a small airtight jar. Add essential oil if desired to give the treatment a fragrance.

2 Shake well before using. Use a cotton swab to rub 1–2 drops of treatment into cuticles. If you use it at bedtime, wear cotton gloves to keep it in place for an overnight treatment.

3 Store in a cool, dry place for up to 1 week. Shake well before each use.

Makes 3 teaspoons (15 ml)

According to an old folk remedy, you can treat frostbite or sunburn by applying raw grated potato or potato juice to the affected area.

Also ...

First aid

Accidents happen around the home, especially bumps, bruises, and stings. When they do and you need a soothing remedy in a hurry, you could try a little vegetable-based first aid. Here are some easy-to-make remedies for common accidents.

Raw potato poultice

Raw potato is a traditional soother for inflammation and bruising. It is said to ease pain and swelling.

To make a medium-sized poultice, you'll need:

* 1 raw potato
* 1–2 tablespoons chilled milk

1 Wash the potato thoroughly, and peel if any dirt remains on the skin. Grate potato and combine with just enough milk in a medium bowl to form a paste.

2 See page 157 for directions on how to prepare, wrap, and apply the poultice. Store unused mixture in the refrigerator up to a week. When poultice feels warm or dry, replace with fresh mixture.

Note You can also use fresh potato peelings as a poultice for bruises.

Raw onion sting relief

Sliced onion is a traditional remedy for the pain and swelling caused by honeybee, wasp, and hornet stings. Doctors warn that this remedy cannot reverse allergic reactions, which need immediate medical attention. However, it is worth trying to relieve the discomfort of stings. Carefully remove the stinger first.

You'll need:

* Slices of fresh onion

1 Put 1 onion slice over the site of the sting. Either hold in place or wrap with plastic wrap to keep in place.

2 When the slice becomes warm or dry, replace with a fresh slice.

Garlic footbath and swab

Garlic's natural antifungal properties account for its traditional use in combating athlete's foot. In 2000, researchers put it to the test, pitting twice-daily applications of a liquid garlic solution against a popular athlete's foot drug in 50 people with this foot problem. After two months, everyone in the garlic group was free of foot fungus, compared with 94 percent of those who used the prescription product. The best way to introduce your feet to garlic? Try a footbath.

For one footbath, you'll need:

* A basin large enough for your feet
* Warm water
* 3–5 cloves garlic, peeled

1 Fill the basin with enough warm water to wet the bottoms of your feet and cover your toes.

2 Crush 3–5 garlic cloves into the water. Stir, then soak your feet for 30 minutes once a day.

Note You can make a garlic paste to treat this problem by mixing a finely crushed garlic clove with 1 tablespoon olive oil. Apply the paste to areas of your feet where fungus is a problem, such as between the toes.

THINGS YOU CAN MAKE

Photoprint place mats

Modern technology makes it easy to create your own iron-on transfers and make one-of-a-kind decorator items from photographs.

What you'll need

* 4 good-quality digital photographs from your collection
* 8½ x 11-in photo transfer paper suitable for your printer
* 40-cm (16-in) width of white homespun or calico fabric
* 50-cm (20-in) width of thin fusible batting
* 40-cm (16-in) width of matching backing fabric for each photograph
* Iron and ironing board
* Fabric scissors or cutting mat, ruler, and rotary cutter or fine craft knife
* Sewing machine and sewing thread to match backing fabrics
* Basic sewing supplies

1 Choose one of the four digital photographs and do a test print on ordinary paper to get an idea of the results. Following the manufacturer's instructions, print each photograph onto a sheet of transfer paper, shrinking or enlarging it to fill the whole page if necessary. Note that the image will be reversed when you iron it onto fabric, so if there are words or faces in your photograph, you will need to use photo-editing software to flip the photograph before you print it.

2 Place the images facedown on the white fabric, leaving at least 5 cm (2 in) between each image and more than 2.5 cm (1 in) around the outer edges of each printed area. Following the manufacturer's instructions, iron the images onto the fabric. Carefully peel away the backing paper, leaving the image on the fabric.

3 Cut out the printed images, leaving 2.5 cm (1 in) of unprinted fabric around the edges. Cut the fusible batting into four rectangles of at least 25 x 35 cm (10 x 14 in) each for 8½ x 11-in size prints. Following the manufacturer's instructions, carefully fuse the batting to the back of the fabric using a warm iron.

4 Trim the batting and fabric so that there is a 1.5-cm (½-in) border around all four sides of the image. Measure the size of the rectangle. It should be about 23 x 32 cm (9 x 12½ in). Cut a piece of backing fabric 2.5 cm (1 in) bigger than this rectangle on all sides (about 28 x 37 cm/11 x 14½ in). Pin the photo and batting in the center of the backing fabric and machine-stitch around the edge of the photo, sewing through all layers using thread that matches the backing fabric.

5 Trim off the corners of the backing fabric diagonally, 6 mm (¼ in) from the corner point of the photo and batting rectangle. Without ironing over the photo, press a 6-mm (¼-in) hem diagonally across each corner, then press a 1-cm (⅓-in) hem along each of the four straight sides of the backing fabric. Turn the hem edges of the backing fabric over so they line up with the line of machine stitching and pin in place.

6 Using the matching sewing thread, hand-stitch the hem edge of the border to the machine stitching, using invisible hemstitch.

7 To make matching napkins, cut 40-cm (16-in) squares of the leftover backing fabric and turn a 6-mm (¼-in) double hem on each edge. Machine-stitch using the same matching sewing thread as for the place mats.

Carefully peel the backing paper away from the printed fabric, leaving the image on the fabric.

Trim the corners of the backing fabric diagonally, 6 mm (¼ in) from the point of the corner. Turn over a 6-mm (¼ in) hem.

TIPS

* You will be able to hand-wash the place mats and napkins and iron them carefully, from the back only, using a warm iron.

* You will need four different backing fabrics for your four photos. Choose fabrics that match and complement the colors in the photos,

Show off the bounty of your vegetable garden by printing photographs on place mats. They will make a perfect backdrop for plates full of your fresh vegetables.

Garden kneeling pad

Sturdy outdoor fabric and useful handles make this foam kneeling pad look smart while being easy to clean and store.

What you'll need

- ✳ Foam rubber pad
- ✳ 2 pieces of weatherproof fabric, 1 patterned (for the top) and 1 plain (for the base)
- ✳ Pair of leather handles with stitching holes, from crafts stores or fabric shops
- ✳ Strong sewing thread
- ✳ Pinking shears or fabric scissors
- ✳ Sewing machine with heavy-duty (denim) needle
- ✳ Heavy-duty hand-sewing needle, pins, and sewing supplies

1   Buy a foam rubber kneeling pad from a gardening or hardware store, or have one cut to size at a foam rubber supplier. The one shown on these pages is a ready-made pad measuring 20 x 40 x 2 cm (8 x 16 x ¾ in) thick.

2   Cut the pieces of plain and patterned fabric to the same width as the foam pad, plus half the pad's thickness and a 1-cm (⅓-in) seam allowance on each side. Cut it to the same length as the pad, adding 12 cm (4¾ in) at each end. Our fabric pieces are 24 cm (9½ in) wide and 64 cm (25 in) long. Use pinking shears if you have them, as they will prevent the edges fraying without adding bulk in the seams.

3   Place the right sides of two pieces of fabric together and pin a 1-cm (⅓-in) seam down both long sides. Machine-stitch the seams. Press the seams open—check the manufacturer's instructions for the iron setting. Fold and press a 6-cm (2⅓-in) hem at each open end of the tube of fabric. Turn the fabric tube right side out.

4   Slide the kneeling pad into the tube with the long-side seams centered at the long sides of the pad. Pin the top and base fabrics together at each end and machine-stitch through all layers close to the outer edge and close to the kneeling pad (about 4–5 cm/1½–2 in from the edge). You might need a zipper foot on the sewing machine for this.

5   Position a handle at each end of the kneeling pad, making sure that each handle is centered at equal distance from the side edges of the cover at each end. Pin the handles in place and attach them using strong sewing thread and a heavy-duty sewing needle to stitch through the holes.

REMOVABLE COVER OPTION   The kneeling pad is washable; just hose it down or give it a light scrub with detergent and water, then let it dry completely. If you want to make the cover removable, machine-stitch around the hem at the ends and hand-stitch the handles to the top fabric only, then add two heavy-duty snaps at the base of the handles.

Gorgeous water-resistant fabric covers a foam kneeling pad for a useful gardening accessory.

With the foam pad inside, pin the top and base fabrics together and machine-stitch through all layers close to the outer edge and then close to the kneeling pad.

Reversible gardening hat

Vegetable print fabric gives this reversible gardening hat a groovy twist.

What you'll need

✳ 30-cm (12-in) width of vegetable print fabric
✳ 30-cm (12-in) width of contrasting fabric for lining
✳ 40-cm (16-in) square of stiff interfacing
✳ Thin cardboard for template
✳ Water-soluble fabric marker or tailor's chalk
✳ Sewing thread to match fabrics
✳ Sewing machine and basic sewing supplies
✳ Small button (optional)

1 Enlarge the template shape on page 205 by 200 percent on a photocopier, then transfer the shape onto thin cardboard and cut it out. Note the template doesn't include seam allowances; you need to add 6-mm (¼-in) seam allowances around the outside when you cut out the pieces.

2 Use a water-soluble fabric marker or tailor's chalk to trace around the template onto the fabric: Trace six shapes onto the vegetable print fabric and six shapes onto the lining fabric and cut them out, leaving a 6-mm (¼-in) seam allowance all around outside the traced line.

3 Working with the lining fabric segments, pin two segments with right sides together along one long edge. Machine-stitch together, stopping about 1 cm (⅓ in) from the point. Clip the curves of the seam, then open the two segments out and finger-press the seam allowance open. Take another segment and pin and stitch it, right sides together, to one side of this piece, repeating the clipping and finger-pressing.

4 When you have stitched all six pieces of the lining fabric together, join the two unstitched edges together and pin, stitch, clip, and finger-press the final seam. You will now have a wrong-side-out hat lining.

5 From the stiff interfacing, cut a circle with a diameter of 35 cm (14 in). Draw another circle, with a diameter of 20 cm (8 in) in the center of this circle, and cut it out. A simple way to do this is to fold the interfacing in quarters, then measure 17.5 cm (7 in) along the sides from the center point and draw the curve, then cut through all layers. Measure 10 cm (4 in) along the sides and draw the curve for the inner circle, then cut it out. You should have a ring of interfacing about 8 cm (3¼ in) wide. Lay the hat lining wrong side up on a flat surface so that the brim is spread out and the crown is sitting up, then lay the interfacing ring over the lining and pin them together around the outer edge. If you need to adjust the interfacing slightly to fit the lining, cut the ring into four equal segments and spread them 2–3 mm (about ⅛ in) apart or overlap them as required. Baste the interfacing to the lining fabric.

6 Repeat step 3 with the vegetable print fabric to make an outer hat. Turn this outer hat right side out and slip it inside the lining so the right sides are together. Pin the two pieces together around the outer edge, matching the seams.

7 Stitch a 6-mm (¼-in) seam around the outer edge of the hat brim, leaving one of the segments unstitched for turning. Trim the seam allowance and clip the curved seams. Turn the hat right side out through the open segment and press the seam around the edge of the brim. Turn under the raw edges of the unstitched segment and pin them together. Remove any basting that is still visible on the lining side.

8 Thread the sewing machine with thread that matches the outer fabric and put thread that matches the lining fabric in the bobbin. Topstitch 2–3 mm (about ⅛ in) inside the outer edge of the hat brim. (This will also close the unstitched segment.) Work another row of topstitching about 1 cm (⅓ in) inside the previous row, and repeat this six or seven times until you reach the part of the hat where it starts to curve up.

9 Ensure that all the points of the segments are pushed inside the crown of the hat and work a few small stitches through both the outer fabric and lining to secure the two pieces together. You could add a small button if you like.

TIP

If your fabric has a small all-over print or is plain, you can save time by tracing and cutting the shapes from doubled fabric. If you have a large vegetable motif or a directional pattern (such as stripes), it's better to trace each shape separately on the right side of the fabric so that you can control the position of the vegetable motifs or the direction of the stripes.

This hat is constructed from six fabric segments. The brim is stiffened with interfacing to provide protection from the sun.

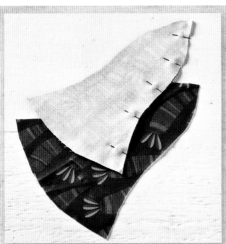

Pin and machine-stitch two segments with right sides together along one long edge. Repeat to join all segments.

Fold the interfacing in quarters, measure along the sides from the center point, and draw an arc between the two points.

Topstitch through all layers of fabric and interfacing around the brim edge, spacing rows of stitching about 1 cm (1/3 in) apart.

Appliqué apron and oven mitt

It's a piece of cake to make a plain apron and an oven mitt or a pot holder look tasty, using easy appliqué. You can make your vegetables in realistic colors, or let your imagination run wild.

What you'll need

✳ Plain fabric apron and oven mitt or pot holder
✳ Approximately 30 cm (12 in) double-sided fusible interfacing
✳ Scraps of fabric in your choice of suitable colors
✳ Embroidery thread to match fabrics
✳ Pencil and scissors
✳ Iron and ironing board
✳ Crewel embroidery needle

1   Wash, dry, and iron the apron, oven mitt, or pot holder.

2   Trace the appliqué templates on page 204 separately onto the paper side of the fusible interfacing, leaving at least 1 cm (¹⁄₃ in) between each shape and making sure to include the extra fabric (dotted lines) for overlapping. The pieces need to be traced in reverse because you will iron the interfacing onto the back of the fabric, so we have reversed the designs for you. It will help if you write the numbers on the interfacing shapes as well.

3   Cut around each shape about 5 mm (about ¹⁄₄ in) outside the traced line and lay it on the back of the fabric you will use for that part of the design. Fuse the interfacing with an iron, following the manufacturer's instructions. Now cut out the shapes along the traced line.

4   Lay the cut-out fabric shapes on the apron, mitt, or pot holder and arrange them until you are happy with their position. Use the pencil to lightly mark the position, then remove all the shapes and set them aside.

5   Fuse the shapes in place one at a time, starting with the lowest layer (numbered 1). To do this, remove the backing paper, position the fabric shape on the apron, mitt, or pot holder, and press with an iron according to the manufacturer's instructions. Allow it to cool before applying the next shape in the same way.

6   When all the shapes have been fused in place, thread a crewel needle with embroidery thread and work blanket stitch around the outside of each shape. You can also add details such as leaf veins and shadows. Press once more from the back, then use your apron, oven mitt, or pot holder with pride.

Simple appliqué using fusible interfacing and fabric scraps turns plain aprons, oven mitts, and pot holders into eye-catching works of art.

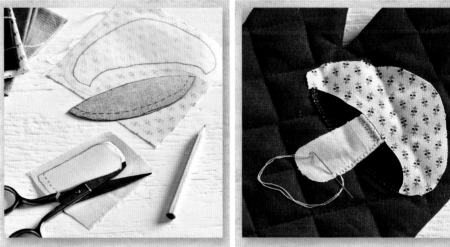

Fuse the interfacing to the fabric and cut around each shape along the traced line. Dotted lines indicate overlap areas.

Thread a crewel needle with embroidery thread and work blanket stitch around the outside of each ironed-on shape.

Painted vegetable pots

Make your own chalkboard paint to decorate the pots that you want to place on your balcony or in your courtyard or vegetable patch.

What you'll need

* Clean unglazed ceramic pots, such as terra-cotta
* Clear waterproof sealer
* Acrylic undercoat
* Acrylic paint in the color of your choice
* Superfine white grout powder
* Paint container and stirrer
* Paintbrush and masking tape
* Chalk sticks

1   Prepare the pots by cleaning them thoroughly if they've been used before. Make sure they are completely dry. Paint the inside of each pot with clear waterproof sealer. This will prevent moisture from the soil leaching through the ceramic and causing the paint to lift off.

2   Cut masking tape into short lengths, about 4–5 cm (1½–2 in) long, and apply them around the rim of the pot, overlapping the ends.

3   Paint the outside of the pot with undercoat and allow to dry completely.

4   Put ½ cup (125 ml) of colored paint in a container and add 1 tablespoon of grout powder. Mix well to ensure the grout is evenly distributed through the paint. Use immediately.

5   Paint the outside of the pot with the chalkboard paint mix and allow to dry. Repeat once or twice until you have an even, opaque covering.

6   When the paint is completely dry, carefully remove the masking tape. Plant the vegetable of your choice and write the name with chalk on the painted pot. You might need to refresh the chalk label regularly if you need to be reminded what's growing in the pot. Simply wipe the pot clean with a soft cloth and rewrite the name whenever it starts to fade.

TIP

Half a cup of paint will be enough for several pots, depending on their size. Once the chalkboard paint is mixed, it doesn't store well, so plan to do lots of pots at the same time and use it all up.

Chalkboard paint means you can write plant labels directly onto the pots when you plant the seeds or seedlings. After the harvest, simply wipe them clean, ready for your next vegetable crop.

Use masking tape to cover any areas you don't want to paint, then apply undercoat and chalkboard paint mix.

Clay plant tags

Remind yourself what's planted where with these easy-to-make clay plant tags.

What you'll need
* Air-drying clay
* Alphabet rubber stamp set
* Plastic wrap or black plastic sheeting and masking tape
* Bamboo skewer
* Colored twine

1   Cover the work surface with plastic wrap or plastic sheeting and tape down the edges so that it will stay smooth.

2   Open the packet of clay and tear off a small amount by pinching it between your finger and thumb. Roll it between your palms to make a ball about 2 cm (¾ in) in diameter.

3   Using your fingers, flatten the ball on the plastic surface and spread it out into an even, smooth round disk about 2–3 mm (⅛ in) thick. (For longer plant names, make the disk into more of an oval shape.)

4   Use a skewer to make a hole about 1 cm (⅓ in) in from the top edge.

5   Press the plant name into the clay disk using alphabet stamps. Begin with the middle letters and work outward.

6   Allow the clay to dry overnight. Thread twine through the hole.

7   Tie the label to the plant pot, a garden stake, or even to the stem of the plant itself.

TIP
If the clay starts to dry out as you work and small cracks form around the edges of the disks, use a damp cloth to gently smooth them over.

Use a bamboo skewer to make a hole near the top of each disk. Press the plant name into the clay using rubber stamps.

Use colorful garden twine to tie the tags to small stakes, ready to be put in the garden.

Dyeing with vegetables

Using only ingredients from your kitchen and garden, you can change the colors of the world.

What you'll need

✳ Item to be dyed (made of natural fibers, such as wool or cotton)
✳ Vegetable of choice (see dyeing tips below)
✳ White vinegar or salt for mordant
✳ Rubber gloves
✳ Old saucepan and colander
✳ Large glass or stainless-steel bowl
✳ Old wooden spoon

1   Choose a vegetable and its corresponding color from our list below, or choose your own vegetables and experiment to find your own colors. Chop the vegetable roughly (if using onions, peel and use only the skin) and put in an old saucepan. (Even though you won't be using any toxic chemicals, the saucepan may retain some of the color, so you don't want to use your shiny new cookware.) Cover the chopped vegetable completely with water, allowing about 4 cups (1 liter) of water to every 1 cup of chopped vegetable matter—the larger the item you're dyeing, the more water and vegetable you'll need. Bring to a boil, cover, and simmer for 1 hour.

2   Meanwhile, prepare the item to be dyed; how you do this depends on whether you plan to use vinegar or salt as a mordant. (A mordant is a substance that helps to fix the dye in the fibers, and we use either vinegar or salt here.) If you're using vinegar, soak the item in a solution of 1 part vinegar to 4 parts water for 1 hour. Wring it out, but don't rinse it before dyeing. If you're using salt as the mordant, simply wet the item, wring it out, and leave it damp.

3   Strain the hot dye water from the saucepan of simmering vegetable through a colander into a glass or stainless steel bowl that is large enough to hold the item you want to dye. If you're using salt as the mordant, add about ¹⁄₂ cup (150 g) of salt for every 4 cups (1 liter) of dye water and stir thoroughly to dissolve.

4   Carefully lower the item into the dye bowl, using an old wooden spoon to submerge and agitate it gently. Continue to stir gently and submerge the item for about 15 minutes, then let it soak for at least 1 hour. The longer you leave it, the stronger the color will be.

5   Remove the item from the dye bowl and rinse it in cold water until the water runs clear. Wash and dry the item.

Also ...

Dyeing tips

Vegetables provide a natural as opposed to chemical dye, so don't expect strong colors, and be ready for some variation. It's a good idea to experiment first to see what colors you can achieve.

Vegetable	Mordant	Color
Beet	Vinegar	Dark pink
Beet	Salt	Golden yellow
Yellow onion skin	Salt or vinegar	Orange-brown
Carrot	Vinegar	Pale yellow
Mushroom	Salt	Mushroom brown
Red cabbage	Vinegar	Pale pink
Red cabbage	Salt	Blue-purple
Red onion skin	Salt or vinegar	Pinkish brown
Spinach	Vinegar	Green

TIP
Keep any kitchen implements or equipment you use for making craft projects separate from your cookware. Do not use them for handling or cooking food.

In general, wool takes up color better than cotton. In each pair pictured here, the cotton is on the left and the wool is on the right. Be aware that these natural colors may fade over time.

COTTON and WOOL undyed

RED ONION with salt

RED ONION with vinegar

BROWN ONION with salt

BROWN ONION with vinegar

BEETS with salt

BEETS with vinegar

RED CABBAGE with salt

RED CABBAGE with vinegar

SPINACH with salt

SPINACH with vinegar

Knitted market bag

This bag is knitted with wool and cotton yarn, then dyed with the vegetable dye of your choice—we used beet. The cotton helps the bag keep its shape, while the wool gives strength.

What you'll need

❄ 250 g (8 oz) 12-ply (bulky/chunky) wool yarn
❄ 150 g (5 oz) 8-ply (DK) cotton yarn
❄ 10 mm (US size 15/UK size 000) circular knitting needles, 100 cm (40 in) long
❄ Wool needle
❄ Scissors

1. Create the base

This knitting project has a recommended gauge of 11 stitches and 18 rows to 10 cm (4 in). The exact gauge is not important but may affect the quantity of yarn you use. The bag is knitted in one piece, in garter stitch (every row knit). It is knitted flat, but you'll need a circular needle to hold all the stitches.

Holding one strand of each yarn together, cast on 88 stitches. Knit 10 rows of garter stitch.

2. Make a handle

Increase one stitch at each end of next two rows (92 stitches).

Cast on 28 stitches at the beginning of each of the next two rows (148 stitches). Knit 10 rows.

Cast off 28 stitches at the beginning of each of the next two rows (92 stitches).

Decrease one stitch at each end of the next two rows (88 stitches).

3. Make another handle

Continue to knit on these 88 stitches for 10 cm (4 in) (approximately 20 rows), then repeat the instructions in step 2 to make a second handle. Knit 10 more rows and cast off. Weave in the ends.

4. Finish the bag

Fold the bag in half and join the sides and the tops of the handles using your preferred method of sewing up. We used mattress stitch for a secure, flat seam.

Dye the bag using the vegetable dye of your choice (see page 188).

We used red and yellow onion skins to dye the crocheted market bag (right) and beet to create the pink shade of the knitted market bag (left). Because the wool takes the dye up more easily than the cotton in the knitted bag, you will get a lovely variegated effect.

Mattress stitch makes a secure, flat seam when you sew together the bag side seams and handle seams.

Crocheted market bag

Crocheted in cotton yarn, this new take on the traditional string bag will scrunch small on the way to market, then stretch to carry all your purchases home.

What you'll need

* 100 g (3½ oz) 8-ply (DK) cotton yarn
* 4.5-mm (US/UK size 7) crochet hook
* Scissors

1. Create the base

Round 1 Beginning with a slipknot, make a magic loop or a six-chain ring, and work 6dc into the ring.

Round 2 1ch, 2dc in each stitch (12 stitches).

Round 3 1dc in next stitch, 2dc in following stitch, repeat to end of round (18 stitches).

Round 4 1dc in next two stitches, 2dc in following stitch, repeat to end of round (24 stitches).

Round 5 1dc in next three stitches, 2dc in following stitch, repeat to end of round (30 stitches).

Round 6 1dc in next four stitches, 2dc in following stitch, repeat to end of round (36 stitches).

Round 7 Slip stitch into first stitch of previous round, 4ch (counts as 1tr, 1ch), work 1tr, 1ch into each stitch. Slip stitch into third chain to complete the round.

2. Work the sides of the bag

Round 8 1dc into first space of row below, 3ch, (1dc, 3ch) in each space of row below. Do not slip stitch to complete the round. Instead, simply continue around.

Round 9 1dc into first chain loop, 5ch, (1dc, 5ch) into each chain loop. Continue in this manner until bag is approximately 40 cm (16 in) deep from the edge of the base. Finish with a dc.

3. Make the bag top

Round 1 (3ch, 1dc) in each chain loop of previous round. Slip stitch into last dc of previous round.

Round 2 1dc, (2dc, 1ch) in each chain loop, slip stitch into first dc.

Round 3 1dc, then work 1dc in each stitch of the previous round, slip stitch into first dc.

Round 4 2ch, then work 1tr in each stitch, slip stitch into the top of the first treble.

4. Make a handle

Continue from where you finished the bag top and 60ch. Count 28 stitches around the bag top from the first chain and slip stitch the other end of the chain into the top of the treble. Turn and work 2ch, then slip stitch into the second stitch along the bag top, then work 1tr in each chain back across to the other side. Slip stitch into the second treble from the chain, making sure the handle is not twisted. Cut the yarn and pull it through the last loop to fasten.

5. Make another handle

Count 28 stitches from the end of the first handle and join the yarn, then repeat step 4 to make a second handle.

6. Finish the bag

Finish off the bag top by working a round of 1dc in every stitch around the inside edges of both handles and across the front and back of the bag top, then around the outside edge of each handle and across the top of the bag side. Weave in the ends of the yarn.

Dye the bag using the vegetable dye of your choice (see page 188). We used onion skins to create a tan color. To achieve the ombré effect, dye the whole bag in yellow-onion-skin dye for 1 hour, then the bottom two-thirds for an additional 1 hour, then dye only the bottom third in red-onion-skin dye for 1 hour.

Create the base of the bag with a flat circle, then work 1 dc, 5ch loops to form the distinctive mesh sides.

CROCHET TERMS

ch . . . . .chain
dc . . . . .double crochet
　　　　　　　　　(US single crochet)
tr . . . . .treble crochet
　　　　　　　　　(US double crochet)

Garden journal cover

An embroidered slipcover for your garden journal means you can insert a new journal in the same cover every year, or make a new slipcover each year and keep a gorgeous collection of garden records. Label the journal with the date each year or each season.

What you'll need

❋ 20-cm (8-in) square of neutral linen fabric
❋ Water-soluble fabric marker or tailor's chalk
❋ Embroidery hoop (optional)
❋ Crewel embroidery needle
❋ Stranded embroidery thread in various colors
❋ Fat quarter (usually 45 x 55 cm/18 x 22 in) of main fabric
❋ Fat quarter (usually 45 x 55 cm/18 x 22 in) of contrasting fabric
❋ 30 x 40 cm (12 x 16 in) of stiff fusible fabric stabilizer
❋ Metal label holder, from scrapbooking supply stores
❋ Split pins (optional)
❋ Fabric scissors, embroidery scissors, and basic sewing supplies
❋ Sewing machine and sewing thread to match fabrics
❋ Iron and ironing board

1   In the center of the linen fabric, trace the embroidery design (see page 204) using water-soluble fabric marker or tailor's chalk. The easiest way to do this is to photocopy the design and tape it and the fabric to a window. Don't sketch in all the details: just pick out the major lines of the design.

2   Mount the fabric in an embroidery hoop, if you are using one. When using a hoop, work on small sections at a time and move the hoop as needed. Don't leave the fabric in the hoop when not stitching, as the fabric can become permanently stretched and the stitches flattened.

3   You can use any embroidery stitches you like and are familiar with. We've used two strands of embroidery thread and outline stitch for most of the outline work. Satin stitch is good for smooth vegetables such as tomatoes and carrots, while French knots make great cauliflowers and broccoli. Carrot leaves are feather stitch, while the cabbage is bullions. Embroider the letters in backstitch. Add as much detail as you like.

4   When the stitching is complete, rinse the embroidery in lukewarm water to completely remove all traces of the fabric marker or chalk. Lay the embroidery flat and allow it to dry. Iron your embroidery, laying it face down on a soft towel or blanket and pressing gently so as not to flatten the decorative stitches.

5   Cut a strip of contrasting fabric 2.5 cm (1 in) wide, then cut into four pieces. Pin and machine-stitch one strip to each side of the embroidered linen, using a 6-mm (1/4-in) seam allowance. Trim the linen and press the seam allowance toward the border, pressing from the back only. Pin and stitch the two remaining strips of fabric to the bottom and top edges of the embroidered linen and finish off as before.

You should now have a border all around the embroidered linen, and the whole area should measure about 12 x 15 cm (about 5 x 6 in). This will fit a spiral-bound art journal approximately 5¾ x 8¼ in. If your journal is a different size, adjust the measurements accordingly.

6   Cut a rectangle of the main fabric measuring 24 x 34 cm (about 9½ x 13½ in). From the right end of this rectangle, cut a 3-cm (1¼-in) vertical strip. Now cut a 12-cm (4¾-in) vertical strip and set the other two pieces aside.

7   Cut a horizontal 4-cm (1½-in) strip from the top of the 12-cm (4¾-in) length and a horizontal 6-cm (2⅓-in) strip from the bottom. (You can make the strips 5 cm (2 in) each if you prefer.) Discard the middle piece. Pin and machine-stitch these two pieces of main fabric to the top edge and bottom edge of the border fabric respectively. Press the seams outward.

8   Pin and stitch the 3-cm (1¼-in) strip to the right edge of the central panel as before, and pin and stitch the remaining piece of main fabric to the left edge of the panel. You will now have the outer cover complete.

9   Cut the fusible stabilizer into a rectangle 22.5 x 34 cm (about 9 x 13 in). Following the manufacturer's instructions, iron the stabilizer onto the back of the cover.

10 Cut two pieces of contrasting fabric 22.5 x 20 cm (9 x 8 in). Fold each in half vertically with wrong sides together and press. Lay the cover right side up and place a folded contrasting flap piece on top of each end, so the raw edges align and the folded edges are facing toward each other across the middle of the cover. Pin the flaps to the cover fabric around all three raw edges and machine-stitch right around the outer edge of the cover, 6 mm (1/4 in) from the edge. Finish the raw edges with a zigzag or overlocking stitch.

11 Snip off the corners of the fabric down to the stitching line. Turn the cover right side out so that the seams are hidden inside the end pockets. Slip-stitch the hem on the top and bottom edges between the pockets, catching the zigzagged edges to the stabilizer. Press carefully on the wrong side.

12 Use split pins or hand stitching to secure a metal label holder on the front cover below the embroidered panel. Write the year on a small piece of card stock and slip it in. Slide the covers of your journal into the pockets and start writing.

These removable slipcovers can be reused each year to keep your garden journal looking neat and attractive.

TIP

These instructions and measurements fit a spiral-bound art journal approximately 5³/₄ x 8¹/₄ in. The completed cover will measure 21.5 x 33 cm (about 8¹/₂ x 13 in).

Assemble the cover piece by piece, pinning and stitching the border in contrasting fabric around the central panel of embroidered linen, then adding the side pieces, which are in the main fabric.

Plantable paper

Embed seeds in handmade paper to give your stationery a dual purpose.

What you'll need

* ✳ Recyclable scrap paper
* ✳ Bowl
* ✳ Blender or food processor
* ✳ Food coloring (optional)
* ✳ 32 x 26-cm (12½ x 10½-in) aluminum roasting pan (baking dish)
* ✳ Aluminum window screen mesh
* ✳ Vegetable seeds
* ✳ Old towels and dish towels
* ✳ Iron

When the paper is dry, cut or tear it into shapes and use it to decorate your stationery. Use any small vegetable seeds, such as broccoli, scallion, lettuce, or carrots. Be sure to include information about the type of seeds and planting instructions when you send off your cards.

TIPS

* ✳ If you want to write directly on the plantable paper, add 1 tablespoon of liquid starch to the pulp; this will help keep the ink from bleeding.

* ✳ If the plantable paper has curled, place the paper on a damp dish towel and iron with a cool iron to press it flat again.

1 Tear or shred the recyclable paper into small pieces, then put in a bowl and cover with water. Soak the paper for about ½–1 hour.

2 Place the soaked paper in a blender or food processor and cover with water. Blend the paper until it forms a thick, sludgy pulp. The pulp will be slightly gray because of any ink that was on the paper. If you wish, you can add 2–3 drops of food coloring to tint the pulp.

3 Cut a piece of mesh a tiny bit bigger all around (about 1 mm more) than the base of the pan so the mesh will sit in the pan just slightly raised above the bottom. Put the mesh in the pan and half-fill with water. Add the pulp and stir to make an even suspension of particles. Sprinkle with about 1 tablespoon of seeds.

4 Carefully lift the mesh out and hold it above the tray for a few seconds to allow water to drain through the paper pulp. You should have a layer of pulp 2 mm (less than ⅛ in) thick covering the entire screen. Carefully transfer the screen to a dish towel lying on a bench or flat surface and allow it to drain more.

5 Lay a thick towel on a flat surface and put the dish towel with the screen and paper onto it. Lay a second towel over the top of the paper and use an iron set on low heat to gently press more water out of the paper. When steam begins to rise, stop ironing.

6 Gently lift the paper from the screen, lay it on a dry dish towel, and let dry completely; this will probably take a day or so. When the paper is dry, cut or tear it into shapes and use it to decorate cards.

Make your own seed-encrusted paper with some simple equipment from your kitchen and the hardware store.

Table setting

Embrace the beauty of fresh seasonal produce in table settings with creative arrangements that guests will love. A tonal palette, scale, and texture are key.

Vegetables bring a rustic element to table settings. Limit your selection to four or five types within a tonal palette. Try these seasonal combinations to create striking centerpieces and place settings.

Spring Globe artichokes, cauliflower, brussels sprouts, cabbage, fennel
Summer Tomatoes, eggplant, cabbage, bell pepper, zucchini
Autumn Winter squash, kale, summer squash, garlic, broccoli
Winter Carrots, Swiss chard, brussels sprouts, fennel

Vessels and containers

Get creative—look in the cupboards for inspiration. A mix of jars, cups, plates, and platters will give variety of height and size, and you can use them to show off produce that might otherwise wilt in water. For a more rustic setting, try wooden crates or a piece of burlap to frame hardier produce in your centerpiece.

Place settings

Individual place settings add a personal touch to the table. Look for small vegetables such as garlic to tie to name cards with twine or ribbon. Seed packets are a lovely way of personalizing each setting.

What you'll need

✳ Vessels and containers—a large central platter, small crates, jars, etc.
✳ Twine, toothpicks, and/or reusable adhesive, for securing the arrangement
✳ Produce—select seasonal produce with variations in size and texture but within a tonal palette
✳ Seed packets or vegetable markers—these make great place cards

ABOVE: Garlic, a vegetable marker, and a seed packet create a layered place setting. Choose small produce that will sit well out of water for individual settings.

Winter squash with kale, pattypan squash, garlic, and broccoli create a rustic, autumnal centerpiece in complementary shades of green, mustard, and yellow.

If you prefer, arrange the vegetables in a vessel such as this wooden crate.

Cross-stitch peas

Crisp, fresh shades of green bring to life this embroidery of a single pod, split open to reveal the sweet, plump peas within. It's almost good enough to eat.

What you'll need

* 30-cm (12-in) square of 28-count evenweave fabric in a neutral color
* Stranded embroidery thread in the colors shown on page 205
* No. 24 tapestry needle
* Embroidery scissors and fabric scissors
* Embroidery hoop (optional)
* Pins
* Steam iron, ironing board, and press cloth
* 15-cm (6-in) square of 6-mm (¼-in) foam core board for mounting (optional)

1 Before you begin the embroidery, temporarily neaten all the raw edges of the evenweave fabric to prevent fraying while you stitch.

2 Fold the fabric in half and finger-press a crease. Starting from one edge, use spare thread to make large running stitches along the crease, following the weave of the fabric. Fold the fabric in half in the opposite direction and repeat, so that you can easily find the center of the fabric in order to place the embroidery design.

3 Begin stitching the embroidery in the center, as marked on the chart on page 205. Use two strands of embroidery thread and make stitches across two threads of the evenweave fabric.

4 When all the cross-stitches are complete, work the backstitch marked on the chart, using dark forest green (DMC 905). Work the backstitch in one strand of thread for the lines on the pea pod and two strands for the tendrils.

5 Carefully wash the finished embroidery in lukewarm water with a little dish-washing detergent, then rinse. Pin the fabric on a flat surface (such as an ironing board) to dry. Slightly stretch the wet fabric as you pin it, but keep the threads of the fabric straight. When it is dry, press it carefully from the back, using a steam iron and a press cloth.

6 Take the embroidery to a professional framer to have it mounted and framed. Or, if you wish to do it yourself, stretch it gently and evenly over a square of foam core and work lacing stitches evenly across the back of the board to hold the fabric taut. Frame as desired.

You could mount this embroidery in a wooden embroidery hoop that's large enough to frame the whole design. Simply trim away the excess fabric at the back of the hoop and use string or a ribbon to hang it on the wall.

Choose a traditional stretching and framing option or go for the simple three-dimensional display that we've used, with a vintage frame and a ribbon. The soothing shades of green in this embroidery design will suit many styles of decor.

Begin stitching the embroidery in the center of the fabric, as marked on the chart on page 205.

Bunting

Decorate your entertaining area and the yard with some pretty bunting, or use it to mark out the border of your vegetable patch.

What you'll need

* Fat quarters (usually 45 cm x 55 cm/18 x 22 in) of coordinating cotton fabrics
* 5 m x 2.5-cm (15 ft x 1-in) bias tape, or make your own
* Cardboard, ruler, and pencil
* Tailor's chalk or soft pencil
* Pinking shears and pins
* Sewing machine and sewing thread
* Iron and ironing board

1   Draw a triangle on cardboard and cut it out to make a template. The size of the triangle is completely up to you. Just make sure that it's a triangle with one shorter side for the top and two equal longer sides for the point.

2   Fold the fabric with right sides out and place the template on the fabric, checking the position of any motifs or patterns in the fabric. Trace around the template using tailor's chalk or a soft pencil. Trace as many triangles as you need, leaving at least 1.5 cm (½ in) between each.

3   Pin the two layers of fabric together inside the traced triangles. Machine-stitch along the traced lines of each pair of triangles.

4   Using pinking shears, cut out the triangles just outside the stitching lines. Lay the triangles out in the order that you want to attach them to the binding tape.

5   Open the bias tape on one side and, leaving at least 30 cm (1 ft) at each end, pin the seam allowance of the bias tape across the top of each triangle in the desired order, allowing a gap of at least 2.5 cm (1 in) between each one. (The distance between them is completely up to you.) Machine-stitch along the seam allowance of the bias tape to attach the triangles.

6   Fold the bias tape over the top of the triangles so the folded edges of the tape meet and machine-stitch along the edge of the tape through all layers.

TIPS

* Make as many triangles as you need to create your desired length of bunting. A good size for the triangle template would be 15–20 cm (6–8 in) long and 10–15 cm (4–6 in) wide.

* A fat quarter is what you get when a yard, or sometimes a meter, of fabric is cut in half across the fabric's width then cut in half vertically. It measures approximately 45 x 55 cm (18 x 22 in) and is a good way of buying small but useful quantities of printed cotton (quilting) fabrics.

After tracing around the template, pin the two layers of fabric together. Stitch on the traced lines before you cut out the shape.

Open out the bias binding tape and pin it with edges aligned across the top of each triangle. Stitch along the tape's fold line.

When you lay out the finished triangles, try different arrangements to see what looks best, and only then start pinning the triangles onto the tape in the final order.

The size of the triangles and the distance between them is completely up to you. Use some of your favorite scraps of fabric to make the bunting, which will brighten your space indoors or out.

Vegetable stamps

There are many beautiful and arresting patterns to be found in vegetable cross sections. Here we've used celery and okra to create truly original wrapping paper, and we used celery and radicchio for gift tags.

What you'll need

* Your choice of vegetable with interesting cross section
* Stamp pads
* Plain wrapping paper, art paper, and blank cards
* Cutting board and kitchen knife
* Paper towels
* Old dish towel

1 Cut the vegetable crosswise to reveal the cross section. We used the base of a bunch of celery. Stand, cut side down, on paper towels to blot up some of the excess moisture.

2 Cover the cut side of the vegetable with stamping ink. Make a few practice stamps on scrap paper to work out how much ink you need and how much pressure to apply.

3 Lay a folded dish towel under the paper or card to be stamped. The layers of the towel soften the surface and allow the vegetable to press more evenly onto the paper. Stamp a repeat pattern all over the paper to create gift wrap, and stamp a single motif onto a blank card to make a matching gift tag.

4 When dry, use the paper to wrap a gift, and write a message in the card.

Also …

Vegetables for stamping
These vegetables create wonderful patterns:

* celery
* okra
* radicchio
* brussels sprouts
* bell peppers
* carrots (for polka dots)

TIP
After you've used it several times, the stamping end of the vegetable might become a little soggy. Simply use a sharp knife to trim off a very thin slice of the cross section, and you've got a fresh stamp to work with!

Press the stamp pad against the end of the vegetable and move it around if necessary to get even coverage.

A bunch of celery cut about 5 cm (2 in) from the base makes a large rose-shaped stamp (as shown on the large parcel), and okra's cross section produces small round flower shapes all over the paper (as shown on the small parcel, far left). The parcel in front is decorated with celery stamped in green. On the cards, radicchio (top) and celery (bottom) make striking single motifs.

Jar toppers, tags, and labels

Fill sterilized jars with homemade relish, pickles, and other produce from your garden. Let your creativity blossom in toppers, tags, and labels for the jars.

What you'll need

✳ Fabric, colored or printed paper, string, ribbon, yarn, and elastic bands
✳ Ready-made tags or thin card stock (optional)
✳ Plain paper
✳ Gloss medium and varnish (decoupage medium)
✳ Small paintbrush
✳ Pinking shears
✳ 2-ply (lace) cotton yarn and a 3-mm (US size C–2/UK size 11) crochet hook
✳ Water-soluble fabric marker
✳ Needle and sewing thread
✳ Scissors, pencil, and craft knife
✳ Embroidery thread and needle

Tags and labels

1 Use ready-made tags bought from a craft store, or cut your own from thin card stock. Cut out labels from plain paper. You could also create the tags and labels on a computer and print them out: This is especially handy if you've got a lot of jars to label. Tie tags around the neck of the jars using string, narrow ribbon, or colored yarn.

2 Using a paintbrush, apply a thin coat of gloss medium and varnish to the front of the label and allow it to dry. The label may curl up when it's wet and gradually flatten out as it dries. When it is dry, apply a coat of gloss medium and varnish to the back of the label and adhere it to the clean, dry jar. Paint another layer of medium over the front of the label, taking it over the edges and onto the glass. (Remove excess medium from around the label edges with a damp cloth.) When it is completely dry, apply another coat of medium in the same way and leave it to dry.

Paper lid toppers

1 Choose a piece of colored or printed paper (old wrapping paper works well, or you can download and print paper designs from the Internet). Trace around the jar lid to be covered, then cut out just inside the circle. Don't forget to take into account any rim of the lid that you don't want covered. Using a paintbrush, apply gloss medium and varnish to the patterned side of the paper and allow to dry.

2 Cover the jar lid as well as the back of the paper circle with gloss medium and varnish. Stick the paper down and apply another coat of medium over the circle, taking it over the edges. When it is completely dry, apply a second coat of medium in the same way and leave it to dry.

Fabric and paper caps

Using pinking shears for fabric or scissors for paper, cut a circle or square of fabric or paper 2–3 cm (about 1 in) larger than the jar lid. Place the fabric or paper over the lid and fasten with string, ribbon, or elastic bands. Smooth the paper down and crease the edges neatly to get that fresh-from-the-deli look.

Crocheted cap

1 Using 2-ply cotton yarn and a 3-mm crochet hook, crochet a ring of 4 chain stitches or a magic loop and work 6dc into the ring. Slip stitch into the first dc. Work one round of 2dc into every stitch. For the second round, work 1dc, then 2dc into the next stitch. For the third round, work 2dc, then 2dc into the next stitch. Continue increasing the number of stitches between increases in the same manner until you have made a circle just slightly smaller than the lid of the jar (our last row was 7dc, 2dc into the next stitch).

2 Work one round of 1dc in each stitch, then one round of 1tr—on this round, decrease by two stitches if necessary so total number of stitches is divisible by 4. Work a third round of 1tr.

3 To make a scalloped edge, miss the first stitch in the next round, then work 5tr into next stitch. Miss the next stitch, then slip stitch into next stitch. Miss one stitch, 5tr into next stitch, miss one, slip stitch into next stitch, and so on until the round is complete. Slip stitch into the last stitch of the previous round and finish off.

4 Weave a ribbon through the middle round of treble stitches and tie the cap on the jar.

Embroidered cap

1 Trace around the jar lid on a piece of fabric, then draw another line 2–3 cm (about 1 in) out from the first traced line. Cut out the circle with pinking shears, or use fabric scissors and make a small hem with needle and sewing thread.

To make gifts from your vegetable garden's bounty, attach labels to the clean, dry surfaces of jars. Cover the plain lids with fabric, paper, ribbon, and string.

2   Draw the outline of a vegetable motif in the centre of the circle. Either stitch the outlines and main features only using outline stitch or back-stitch, or work a cross-stitch design in colors.

3   Add a lacy edge, if desired. Use purchased lace or crochet your own using 2-ply cotton and a 3-mm hook. Work a chain long enough to go around the outer edge of the circle. Work one row of 1dc in every stitch, then ★ 3ch, miss one stitch, slip stitch in next stitch ★; repeat to the end. Finish off and sew the edging to the circle.

CROCHET TERMS

ch . . . . .chain

dc . . . . .double crochet
                (US single crochet)

tr . . . . .treble crochet
                (US double crochet)

For the crocheted cap's scalloped edge, miss one stitch, 5tr into next stitch, miss one stitch, and slip stitch into next stitch. Repeat until the round is complete.

Crafts templates

*Appliqué apron
and oven mitt*

Garden journal cover

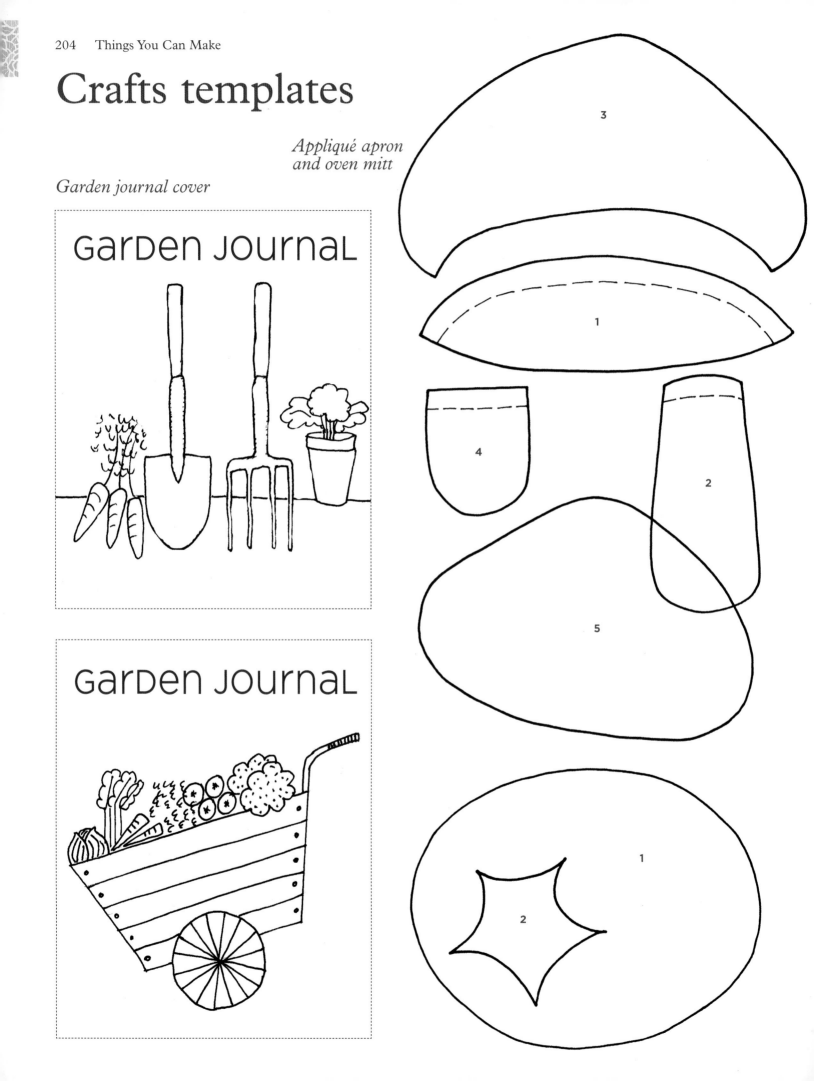

straight grain of fabric

Reversible gardening hat
Enlarge this template by 200%.

Cross-stitch peas

▲	DMC…369	◺	DMC…934
■	DMC…471	☐	DMC…989
●	DMC…704	◆	DMC…3346
◉	DMC…904	◀	DMC…3347
✕	DMC…905	◖	DMC…3348
◢	DMC…906	◹	DMC…3345

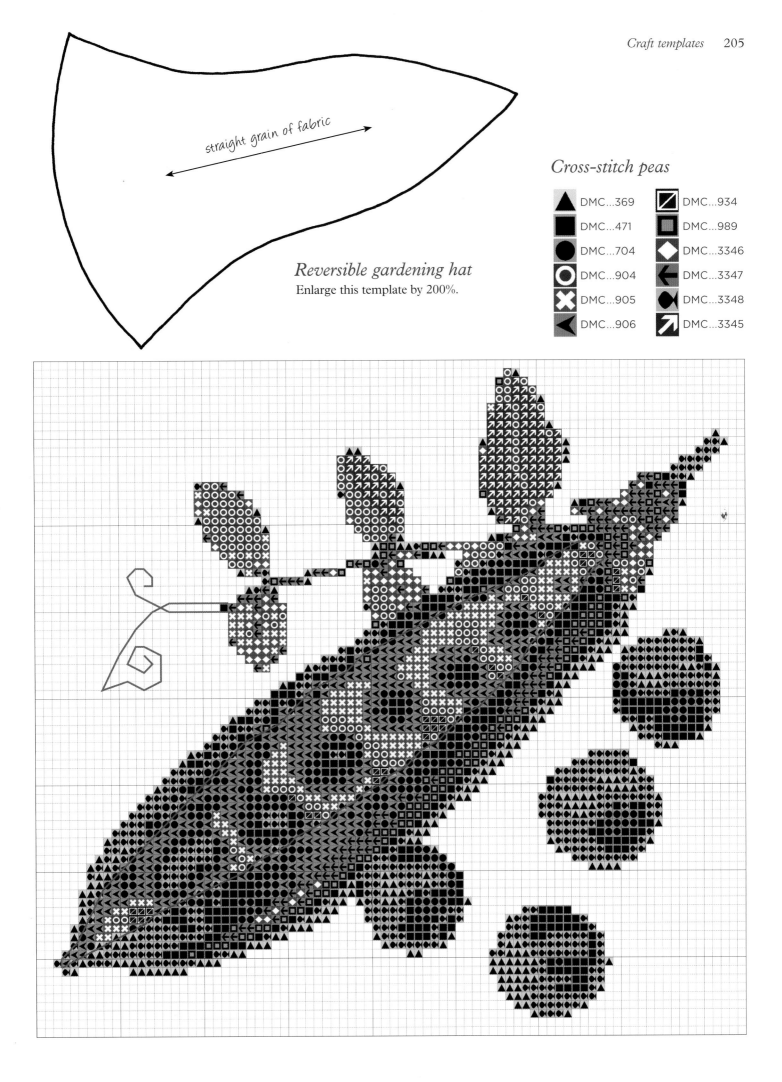

Chicken and vegetable soup with dumplings

Clear chicken soup has been used for centuries to nurture the sick, and there may be a scientific basis for this: Apart from the steam, which helps clear the head, chicken soup contains several anti-inflammatory substances. This recipe includes matzo dumplings in traditional Jewish style.

PREPARATION. . . . . . 20 MINUTES, PLUS COOLING TIME
COOKING . . . . .4–6 HOURS, PLUS 30 MINUTES
SERVES. 4

1 whole chicken (about 1.6 kg/3½ lb),
   broken into pieces
3 whole onions, peeled
4 large carrots, halved lengthwise and cut into
   2-cm (¾-in) slices
2 parsnips, halved lengthwise and cut into
   2-cm (¾-in) slices
4 stalks celery, cut into 2-cm (¾-in) slices
½ bunch dill (about 6 stalks), tied firmly
   with string
½ bunch flat-leaf parsley (about 12 stalks),
   tied firmly with string

Matzo dumplings
1 cup (100 g/3½ oz) matzo meal or finely
   ground water crackers
2 eggs
½ cup (125 ml) olive oil

Choose a large pot that fits the chicken quite snugly. Put onions, carrots, parsnips, celery, dill, and parsley in pot, top with chicken, and add about 12–16 cups (3–4 liters) water to cover.

Cover with lid and simmer over low heat 4–6 hours, or overnight.

Strain stock into a large bowl and refrigerate so that fat hardens for easy removal, then skim off fat. When chicken is cool enough to handle, remove chicken meat from bones, shred into bite-size pieces, and set aside with cooked vegetables. Discard dill, parsley, and chicken bones.

Meanwhile, to make matzo dumplings, mix matzo meal or ground water crackers, eggs, oil, and ¼ cup (60 ml) water—or you could use some of the chicken stock—in a large bowl. Refrigerate mixture 20 minutes, or until firm. Wet your hands a little and roll into balls.

To serve, reheat skimmed chicken stock in a large pot. Drop matzo dumplings into stock and simmer 20–30 minutes, until tender and cooked all the way through. If desired, add reserved vegetables and chicken meat to stock, or put vegetables and meat on a serving dish so people can help themselves.

TIPS
Either egg noodles or rice vermicelli is a traditional addition to this soup instead of matzo dumplings.

Matzo meal is made from finely ground matzo crackers. It is available at some supermarkets and specialty food stores stocking kosher foods.

EACH SERVING PROVIDES
828 calories, 57 g protein, 52 g fat (11 g saturated fat),
35 g carbohydrate (11 g sugars), 7 g fiber, 348 mg sodium

Corn chowder with cornbread

Corn is high in folate, the other vegetables in this nutritious soup add vitamin C, and the milk adds calcium. The beautiful yellow cornbread is a wholesome and tasty addition.

PREPARATION. . . . . .20 MINUTES
COOKING . . . . .35 MINUTES
SERVES. 8

1 tablespoon olive oil

2 slices bacon, coarsely chopped

2 large onions, diced

2 large carrots, diced

2 stalks celery, diced

350 g (12 oz) potatoes, peeled and diced

6 cups (1.5 liters) low-sodium chicken stock

2 cups (400 g) corn kernels

2 cups (500 ml) low-fat milk

⅛ teaspoon freshly ground black pepper

Pinch of cayenne pepper

Cornbread

Butter for greasing

1½ cups (225 g) all-purpose flour

1¼ cups (185 g) polenta or cornmeal

4 teaspoons baking powder

2 tablespoons sugar

1 teaspoon salt

1 egg

1¼ cups (310 ml) milk, chilled

¼ cup (60 ml) vegetable oil

To make the cornbread, preheat oven to 200°C (400°F) and grease a 20-cm (8-in) square cake pan.

Sift together flour, polenta or cornmeal, baking powder, sugar, and salt in a large bowl. Put egg, milk, and oil in a separate small bowl and beat until well combined. Make a well in the center of the dry ingredients. Pour in egg mixture all at once and, using a fork, stir just until wet and dry ingredients are combined—do not overmix.

Pour batter into prepared cake pan and bake 20–25 minutes, until cornbread is lightly browned and pulls away slightly from the sides of the pan. Transfer to a wire rack and let cool 10 minutes. Cut into large squares and keep warm.

Meanwhile, to make the chowder, heat oil in a large, heavy-bottomed saucepan over medium heat. Add bacon and cook until browned, about 4 minutes. Remove with a slotted spoon and set aside to drain on paper towels.

Add onions, carrots, and celery to pan and cook 5 minutes, or until softened.

Stir in potatoes and stock and bring to a boil. Reduce heat to low and simmer, partially covered, stirring occasionally, about 10 minutes, or until vegetables are tender.

Add corn kernels and return soup to boil. Simmer, uncovered, an additional 5 minutes.

Remove from heat and, using a ladle or slotted spoon, transfer about 2½ cups vegetables to food processor or blender. Process to a smooth puree.

Add vegetable puree and milk to saucepan and simmer about 3 minutes. Season with pepper and cayenne. Garnish with reserved bacon and serve with warm cornbread.

EACH SERVING PROVIDES
364 calories, 15 g protein, 14 g fat (3 g saturated fat),
44 g carbohydrate (13 g sugars), 4 g fiber, 1197 mg sodium
(includes cornbread)

Asian broth of noodles, greens, and mushrooms

Mushrooms are highly nutritious, but each type has its own health benefits, so use a variety in this recipe—button mushrooms, cremini, shiitake, enoki, shimeji, or oyster mushrooms.

PREPARATION. . . . . .10 MINUTES
COOKING . . . . .10–12 MINUTES
SERVES. 4

1 tablespoon canola oil or peanut oil

2-cm (¾-in) piece fresh ginger,
   peeled and julienned

3 cloves garlic, crushed

6 scallions, white part cut into 3-cm (1-in) pieces,
   green part thinly sliced

400 g (14 oz) mixed mushrooms, such as button,
   shiitake, oyster, cremini, enoki, or shimeji, stems
   trimmed, large mushrooms halved or quartered

2 tablespoons (40 ml) Chinese rice wine
   (optional)

2 cups (500 ml) water or low-sodium
   vegetable stock

¼ cup (60 ml) soy sauce

¼ cup (60 ml) oyster sauce

60 g (2 oz) rice vermicelli, cellophane noodles, or
   other transparent noodles

½ cup (about 15 g) cilantro sprigs

Heat oil in a wok or large frying pan over high heat. Add ginger and garlic and stir-fry 1–2 minutes.

Add white part of scallions and stir-fry a further 1–2 minutes.

Add large varieties of mushrooms, such as button, shiitake, oyster, or cremini, and stir-fry 2 minutes. Add small varieties of mushrooms, such as enoki, shimeji, and oyster, and stir-fry 2 minutes.

Add Chinese rice wine, if using, water or stock, soy sauce, and oyster sauce. Add rice vermicelli or other noodles and bring to a boil.

Stir in green part of scallions and cilantro sprigs and serve immediately.

TIPS

Chicken or fish can be added to this soup for a complete main meal. Combine Chinese rice wine, soy sauce, and oyster sauce in a bowl and marinate chunks of chicken or fish for 20 minutes. Remove from marinade, add to wok with white part of scallions, and stir–fry until outside of chunks look just cooked, then proceed with the recipe.

Packets of transparent noodles may be labeled cellophane noodles, vermicelli noodles, glass noodles, or bean-thread noodles. You can use any of these in this recipe. Prepare according to the instructions on the packet.

EACH SERVING PROVIDES

162 calories, 7 g protein, 6 g fat (<1 g saturated fat),
20 g carbohydrate (7 g sugars), 4 g fiber, 1770 mg sodium

Watercress soup

The watercress that gives this soup its green color is part of
the reason it's packed with antioxidants and vitamins. Arugula
or spinach works well instead of the watercress, too.

PREPARATION . . . . 10 MINUTES
COOKING . . . . .25 MINUTES
SERVES 4–6

2 tablespoons olive oil or canola oil
1 onion, finely diced
2 leeks, white and green parts, thinly sliced
2 bunches watercress (about 200–300 g/7–10 oz
    total), very finely chopped, a few sprigs
    reserved for garnish
2 large potatoes, peeled and diced
3 cups (750 ml) low-sodium chicken or
    vegetable stock or water
¾ cup (180 ml) low-fat evaporated milk
    or buttermilk
Freshly ground black pepper

Heat oil in a large, heavy-bottomed
saucepan over medium heat. Add onion and
leeks and cook gently over a low heat about
5 minutes, until translucent—do not allow
them to color.

Add three-quarters of watercress as well
as potatoes and stock or water. Bring to
a boil over high heat, then reduce heat to
low and simmer about 10 minutes, until
potatoes are tender.

Add remaining watercress and cook about
2–3 minutes, just until wilted.

Use a handheld stick blender to puree soup
until completely smooth, or puree in a food
processor or blender. Return puree to pan
if using a food processor or blender. Add
evaporated milk or buttermilk and heat
gently—do not allow it to boil.

Serve sprinkled with freshly ground black
pepper to taste and reserved watercress
sprigs.

TIP
For an even smoother, silkier version of this soup,
push the puree through a coarse mesh strainer
before adding the evaporated milk or buttermilk
and reheating. This soup can also be served chilled.

EACH SERVING PROVIDES
198 calories, 10 g protein, 10 g fat (2 g saturated fat),
17 g carbohydrate (8 g sugars), 5 g fiber, 577 mg sodium

Borscht

Traditional beet soup tastes good with a dollop of crème fraîche and rye bread on the side. Chopped greens—such as beet greens, kale, or Swiss chard—add flavor and nutrients.

1 tablespoon vegetable oil

1 onion, finely chopped

1 carrot, diced

2 large beets (400 g/14 oz total),
 cut into small chunks

4 cups (1 liter) low-sodium beef stock

1 large potato, peeled and cut into chunks

1 clove garlic, crushed

2 cups (90 g) chopped greens, stems trimmed

Salt and freshly ground black pepper

100 g (3½ oz) crème fraîche or sour cream for
 garnish

Rye bread for serving

PREPARATION. . . . . .20 MINUTES
COOKING . . . . .40–50 MINUTES
SERVES. 4

Heat oil in a large, heavy-bottomed saucepan over medium heat. Add onion, carrot, and beet and cook, stirring occasionally, 10 minutes, until vegetables are beginning to soften. Add 1 cup (250 ml) water, cover, and bring to a simmer. Reduce heat to medium-low and cook 15–20 minutes, or until vegetables are tender.

Pour stock into another large saucepan and add potato. Bring to a boil over high heat, then reduce heat to medium and cook 5–10 minutes, until potatoes are tender. Add beet mixture and bring back to a simmer.

Add garlic and greens to pan, cover, and simmer 5 minutes, until greens have wilted. Turn off heat and let stand 10 minutes.

Season soup to taste with salt and pepper. Ladle into individual bowls and top each with a dollop of crème fraîche or sour cream. Serve with rye bread.

EACH SERVING PROVIDES
263 calories, 11 g protein, 16 g fat (8 g saturated fat),
21 g carbohydrate (13 g sugars), 5 g fiber, 1237 mg sodium

Ribollita

Tuscan kale is the traditional green used in this soup, although any type of kale will work.

PREPARATION. . . . . 20 MINUTES, PLUS
OVERNIGHT SOAKING TIME
COOKING . . . . .1 HOUR 30 MINUTES
SERVES. 6

1 cup (200 g) dried cannellini beans

1 bay leaf

1 tablespoon olive oil

1 onion, finely chopped

2 carrots, diced

3 stalks celery, chopped

2 cloves garlic, crushed

8 cups (2 liters) low-sodium chicken or vegetable stock

410-g (15-oz) can chopped tomatoes

3 cups (60 g) coarsely shredded kale or Swiss chard

6 thick slices day-old Italian-style bread, torn into pieces

Salt and freshly ground black pepper

Soak cannellini beans overnight in a large bowl of water. Drain, then cook with bay leaf in a large saucepan of boiling water about 1 hour, until tender. Drain and discard bay leaf.

Heat olive oil in a large, heavy-bottomed saucepan. Add onion, carrots, and celery and cook over medium heat, stirring occasionally, about 10 minutes, until very soft and lightly golden. Add garlic and cook, stirring constantly, 1 minute.

Add stock and tomatoes to the pan. Cover and bring to a boil, then reduce heat and simmer, slightly uncovered, 10 minutes. Stir in cooked cannellini beans and kale or Swiss chard and cook an additional 10 minutes, until greens have wilted. Stir in bread, season to taste with salt and pepper, and serve.

TIP
Replace the dried cannellini beans with a 400-g (14-oz) can cannellini beans, rinsed and drained, for a quicker meal.

EACH SERVING PROVIDES
218 calories, 12 g protein, 5 g fat (<1 g saturated fat), 33 g carbohydrate (9 g sugars), 7 g fiber, 1190 mg sodium

Oven-roasted onion soup

This French classic, made with caramelized onions and topped with cheesy toast, is always a popular choice. Gruyère has a lovely, nutty flavor and melts beautifully, but if you can't find it, use Swiss cheese instead.

PREPARATION. .20 MINUTES
COOKING . . . . .1 HOUR 20 MINUTES
SERVES. 4

1 kg (2 lb) onions, thinly sliced
1½ tablespoons olive oil
1 tablespoon sugar
Salt and freshly ground black pepper
1 tablespoon chopped fresh thyme or
   1 teaspoon dried thyme
½ cup (125 ml) dry white wine
5 cups (1.25 liters) low-sodium vegetable stock
4 thick baguette slices
⅓ cup (40 g) grated Gruyère or Swiss cheese

Preheat oven to 220°C (420°F). Toss onions with oil, sugar, and salt and pepper to taste in a large bowl until well coated. Spread in a large ovenproof baking dish and drizzle with 2½ tablespoons (50 ml) water. Cover with foil and roast 30 minutes, then remove foil and return pan to the oven to roast an additional 10 minutes. Sprinkle with thyme and roast, stirring frequently, an additional 20 minutes, until onions are tender.

Put the baking dish on stove top over high heat. Add wine and cook, stirring with a wooden spoon and scraping onions and sediment from the bottom of the pan, for 2 minutes, or until the wine is syrupy.

Transfer onions and pan juices to a large saucepan. Stir in stock, bring to a boil, then reduce heat and simmer 15 minutes, until flavors are blended.

Meanwhile, preheat the broiler. Put baguette slices on a baking sheet and toast 2 minutes on each side.

Ladle soup into four ovenproof bowls. Float a slice of toast in each bowl and sprinkle with cheese. Put bowls on a broiler pan or in a shallow baking dish and broil 2 minutes, or until cheese is melted and bubbling. Serve immediately.

TIP
It's not essential to use wine in this soup, although it does boost the flavor. You can simply use more vegetable stock instead if you prefer.

EACH SERVING PROVIDES
357 calories, 11 g protein, 13 g fat (3 g saturated fat),
45 g carbohydrate (22 g sugars), 5 g fiber, 1706 mg sodium

Soups

You can use almost any vegetable in a soup, and soups are a great way to use leftover vegetables. They can be dressed up for a dinner party or be simple and rustic for a casual Sunday night dinner. A lot of soups freeze well and are great to have on hand for those nights when you don't have time to cook.

FROM LEFT: Fresh tomato soup, Asian green soup with tofu, and roasted butternut squash soup.

Fresh tomato soup

Heat 1 tablespoon olive oil and 1 tablespoon butter in a large saucepan over medium heat until butter melts. Add 1 chopped yellow onion and fry 3–4 minutes, or until soft. Add 2 crushed garlic cloves and cook one more minute. Add 2 kg (4 lb) peeled chopped tomatoes, 3 tablespoons tomato paste, and 4 cups (1 liter) chicken or vegetable stock and bring to a boil. Reduce heat to medium-low and simmer 5 minutes. Using a handheld stick blender or food processor, puree soup until smooth. Season with salt and freshly ground black pepper, then ladle into warm bowls. Garnish with roughly torn fresh basil. **Serves 4**

Salsify soup

Scrub and peel 400 g (14 oz) salsify. Cut into 1-cm (½-in) pieces and immediately put in a bowl of water with the juice of 1 lemon. Melt 30 g (1 oz) butter in a large saucepan. Add 1 sliced leek and cook over medium-low heat 4 minutes, until soft. Add 2 crushed garlic cloves and cook, stirring, 1 minute. Drain salsify and add to pan with 4 cups (1 liter) chicken stock. Bring to a boil, reduce heat slightly, and simmer 20 minutes, until tender. Halve 1 boneless chicken breast lengthwise and thinly slice. Add to pan and simmer 3–4 minutes, until cooked through. Serve soup sprinkled with chopped fresh parsley. Use peeled and sliced Jerusalem artichokes if salsify is not available. **Serves 4**

Arrowhead and won ton soup

Combine 5 cups (1.25 liters) chicken stock, 1 tablespoon soy sauce, and 1 teaspoon sesame oil in a large saucepan and bring to a boil. Add 150 g (5 oz) peeled, halved, and sliced arrowheads and 2 small peeled and sliced carrots and cook 2 minutes. Add 16 small won tons and simmer 5 minutes. Serve topped with sliced scallions. You can replace the arrowhead with 150 g (5 oz) water chestnuts, peeled and halved horizontally, or use a 230-g (8-oz) can water chestnuts, drained and halved. **Serves 4**

Asian greens soup with tofu

Put 5 cups (1.25 liters) vegetable stock, 2 star anise, 1 cinnamon stick, a peeled and sliced 3-cm (1-in) piece fresh ginger, 2 crushed garlic cloves, 1 red chili pepper, and 1 teaspoon brown sugar in a large saucepan. Cover and bring to a simmer, then cook 10 minutes, until flavors infuse. Strain, return liquid to pan, and reheat. Meanwhile, cut 1 large bunch bok choy or other Asian greens to separate stems from leaves. Slice stems and shred leaves. Add stems to pan and simmer 2 minutes, then add 300 g (10 oz) chopped firm tofu and shredded leaves. Cook 2 minutes, until leaves wilt. Serve soup with lime wedges on the side. **Serves 4**

Roasted butternut squash soup

Preheat oven to 190°C (375°F). Peel and seed 1.5 kg (3 lb) butternut squash. Cut into large chunks and put on an oiled baking sheet. Spray with olive oil cooking spray and bake 1 hour, or until lightly browned. Heat 1 tablespoon olive oil in a large saucepan. Add 1 chopped onion and cook over medium heat 5 minutes. Stir in 2 crushed garlic cloves and 1 teaspoon ground cumin and cook 1 minute. Remove pan from heat. Add squash and 3 cups (750 ml) vegetable stock. Blend with a handheld stick blender until smooth, then reheat. Garnish with chopped fresh chives. **Serves 4**

Minestrone

Heat 1 tablespoon olive oil in a saucepan over medium heat. Add 1 finely chopped onion and 3 chopped bacon slices. Cook 3–4 minutes. Add a 680-g (24-oz) can tomato puree, 4 cups (1 liter) beef stock, and 3 cups (750 ml) water. Bring to a boil. Add 1 cup (150 g) dried elbow macaroni and cook, stirring occasionally, 8 minutes, until pasta is almost al dente. Add 3 diced zucchini, 150 g (5 oz) green beans cut into thirds, and a 400-g (14-oz) can cannellini beans, rinsed and drained. Stir well. Cook 2–3 minutes, or until vegetables are tender. Ladle into bowls and top with torn fresh basil leaves and grated Parmesan. **Serves 4**

Bean, pea, and mixed leaf salad

This beautiful salad is the essence of spring. Serve it with chicken or fish and boiled new potatoes tossed in butter.

PREPARATION. . . . . .25 MINUTES
COOKING . . . . .10 MINUTES
SERVES. 6–8

150 g (5 oz) snow peas, trimmed

200 g (7 oz) green beans, trimmed

300 g (10 oz) fresh peas in the pod, shelled

1 cup (50 g) mixed salad greens

4 slices prosciutto or pancetta, cut or torn into bite-size pieces

3 radishes, trimmed and thinly sliced

200 g (7 oz) goat cheese, crumbled

Salt and freshly ground black pepper

Dressing

2 tablespoons extra virgin olive oil

1 tablespoon balsamic vinegar

Salt and freshly ground black pepper

Bring a medium saucepan of water to a boil, and prepare a bowl of ice water. Add snow peas to pan, return to a boil, and cook 1 minute. Lift out with a slotted spoon or tongs, allowing water to drain off, then plunge into ice water. Lift out and drain on paper towels.

Return water to a boil and replenish ice water. Repeat with beans; cook 2 minutes, then plunge into ice water and drain.

Return water to a boil and replenish ice water. Add peas to pan and cook 3 minutes. Drain in a sieve, refresh in ice water and drain. The vegetables should be bright green and tender-crisp.

To make the dressing, whisk oil and vinegar in a small bowl. Season with salt and pepper to taste.

Arrange blanched snow peas, beans, and peas and mixed greens on a platter. Scatter prosciutto, radishes, and goat cheese over the top and drizzle with dressing. Season with salt and pepper to taste and serve immediately.

TIP
For the best flavor, choose small or baby green beans if you can get them. If you buy fresh peas already shelled, you will need 150 g (5 oz). You could also use 150 g (5 oz) frozen peas, which only need to be cooked 1 minute.

EACH SERVING PROVIDES
193 calories, 11 g protein, 13 g fat (5 g saturated fat),
8 g carbohydrate (4 g sugars), 4 g fiber, 472 mg sodium

Cucumber and pear salad

Good edible flowers to use in this salad include borage, violets, chive flowers, calendula, roses, and nasturtiums. Always make sure you are using unsprayed flowers—if not grown yourself, then purchased from a food store rather than a florist.

PREPARATION . . . . 15 MINUTES
SERVES 6

2 Lebanese or other small cucumbers
2 ripe Asian pears
75 g (2½ oz) soft goat cheese, crumbled
2 tablespoons fresh dill sprigs
Edible flowers for garnish

Dressing
1½ tablespoons extra virgin olive oil
3 teaspoons white balsamic vinegar
Salt

Use a mandoline or vegetable peeler to cut cucumbers lengthwise into thin ribbons. Quarter pears lengthwise, discard cores, and cut into thin slices. Arrange cucumber ribbons and pear slices on a large serving platter or shallow bowl.

Scatter goat cheese over cucumbers and pears and sprinkle with dill.

To make the dressing, whisk oil and vinegar in a small bowl until evenly combined and season with salt to taste.

Drizzle dressing over salad. Garnish with flowers and serve immediately.

TIP
If you can't find white balsamic vinegar, you can use white wine vinegar and add a few drops of honey. Raspberry vinegar would also be lovely in this salad.

EACH SERVING PROVIDES
120 calories, 3 g protein, 8 g fat (3 g saturated fat),
8 g carbohydrate (8 g sugars), 2 g fiber, 177 mg sodium

Beet and mozzarella salad

The crimson-striped leaves and yellow and red baby beets in this salad provide color and plenty of antioxidants. A horseradish dressing adds a little heat and pungency.

200 g (7 oz) beet greens
1 bunch yellow baby beets, trimmed
   and thinly sliced
1 bunch red baby beets, trimmed
   and thinly sliced
1 Lebanese or other small cucumber, thinly sliced
2 fresh mozzarella balls (about 100 g/3½ oz
   each), torn into bite-size pieces
¼ cup (5 g) fresh mint leaves
2 tablespoons fresh dill sprigs

Dressing
2 tablespoons olive oil
2 tablespoons lemon juice
1 teaspoon superfine sugar
2 teaspoons prepared horseradish
Salt and freshly ground black pepper

PREPARATION . . . . 15 MINUTES
SERVES 4

Arrange beet greens, yellow and red beets, cucumber, mozzarella, mint, and dill on a serving platter.

To make the dressing, put oil, lemon juice, sugar, and horseradish in a small bowl. Season with salt and pepper to taste and whisk until well combined.

Drizzle dressing over the salad and serve.

EACH SERVING PROVIDES
323 calories, 18 g protein, 22 g fat (9 g saturated fat),
15 g carbohydrate (13 g sugars), 6 g fiber, 600 mg sodium

Mixed tomato salad with basil oil

Use a range of different types, sizes, and colors of tomatoes, which look beautiful on a platter. For the best flavor, avoid supermarket tomatoes: rather, buy them from a farmers' market—or, even better, try growing them yourself if possible.

PREPARATION. . . . . 20 MINUTES, PLUS STANDING
SERVES. 4–6

1 cup (70 g) firmly packed fresh basil leaves
⅓ cup (80 ml) extra virgin olive oil
600 g (1¼ lb) mixed tomatoes in a variety
   of types, sizes, and colors
1 small red onion, halved and very thinly sliced
200 g (7 oz) feta cheese, crumbled into large
   chunks (optional)
2 tablespoons pine nuts, toasted
Freshly ground black pepper

Put basil in a heatproof bowl and pour enough boiling water over it to cover. Let stand just 30 seconds, then lift basil out with tongs, let water drain off, and plunge into a bowl of ice water. Leave 1 minute, then remove and drain on paper towels, pressing with more paper towels to absorb any excess water.

Transfer basil to a small food processor or blender, add oil, and process until leaves are finely chopped. Put a mesh strainer over a bowl and line the strainer with a layer of cheesecloth. Pour basil oil mixture into the strainer and let stand until oil has filtered through, removing any particles. You should have a lovely clear, green oil.

Thickly slice large tomatoes and halve or quarter small tomatoes. Arrange on a platter with onion and feta, if using. Drizzle with oil and sprinkle with pine nuts. Season with pepper to taste and serve.

TIPS
To toast pine nuts, preheat oven to 180°C (350°F). Spread pine nuts on a baking sheet and bake in oven about 3 minutes, until lightly browned. Watch closely, as they can burn easily.

Aim for about five different types of tomatoes, choosing from such varieties as Oxheart, Kumato, Annamay, Merlot, Orenji, Lajaune, Orange Roma, Zebrino, and Pink Roma.

EACH SERVING PROVIDES
236 calories, 3 g protein, 24 g fat (3 g saturated fat),
4 g carbohydrate (4 g sugars), 3 g fiber, 12 mg sodium

Bitter greens salad

This salad is a wonderful accompaniment to any meat or poultry dish, especially ones that are particularly rich. To serve it as its own course, add some crumbled blue cheese and sliced pear.

PREPARATION. . . . . .20 MINUTES
SERVES. 8

½ cup (50 g) walnuts
1 head chicory (about 750 g/1½ lb)
1 head radicchio (about 500 g/1 lb)
1 small head frisée (about 400 g/14 oz)
2 Belgian endive (about 300 g/10 oz total)

Dressing
3 tablespoons extra virgin olive oil
1½ tablespoons white wine vinegar
1 teaspoon Dijon mustard
½ teaspoon honey
Salt and white pepper

Preheat oven to 180°C (350°F). Spread walnuts on a baking sheet and bake about 4 minutes, until fragrant and lightly toasted. Cool and chop roughly.

Cut chicory stems off where leaves begin and discard. Put leaves in a sink or large bowl of cold water and soak 3–4 minutes, occasionally moving with your hand to dislodge any grit. Drain and dry in a salad spinner or on a clean dish towel.

Discard outer leaves of radicchio and frisée, then wash and dry as for chicory. Roughly tear radicchio and chicory leaves. Separate leaves of frisée and Belgian endive. Arrange all the greens on a large serving platter or in a shallow dish. Scatter with toasted walnuts.

To make the dressing, combine oil, vinegar, mustard, and honey in a small screw-top jar, seal tightly, and shake well to combine. Season with salt and pepper to taste.

Just before serving, drizzle dressing over the salad and toss to coat.

EACH SERVING PROVIDES
75 calories, 4 g protein, 5 g fat (<1 g saturated fat),
4 g carbohydrate (1 g sugars), 4 g fiber, 107 mg sodium

Apple and fennel salad with toasted hazelnuts

The aniseed freshness of fennel and the sweet crispness of apple combine with hazelnuts and peppery watercress in this refreshing salad. Toasting the hazelnuts intensifies their flavor and crunchiness.

2 small bulbs fennel, with fronds
(about 225 g/8 oz each)
1 large red apple
2 cups (60 g) watercress sprigs
⅓ cup (45 g) hazelnuts, toasted

Dressing
2 tablespoons lemon juice
3 tablespoons extra virgin olive oil
Salt and freshly ground black pepper

PREPARATION. . . . . .10 MINUTES
SERVES. 4

To make the dressing, put lemon juice and oil in a small bowl. Season with salt and pepper to taste and whisk to combine well.

Trim root ends from fennel bulbs and set aside fronds for a garnish. Cut fennel into quarters, then thinly slice and put in a large salad bowl.

Cut apple into quarters and remove core. Thinly slice apple quarters, leaving skin on for added color. Add to bowl with watercress and hazelnuts.

Drizzle dressing over salad and toss well. Garnish with reserved fennel fronds and serve.

VARIATIONS
For a more substantial salad, add some cooked shrimp or pieces of barbecued or smoked chicken.

Scatter with ⅓ cup (35 g) shaved Parmesan.

Replace hazelnuts with walnuts, pecans, or macadamia nuts.

Instead of a red apple, use a green apple or ½ green apple and ½ red, leaving the skin on.

EACH SERVING PROVIDES
245 calories, 4 g protein, 21 g fat (2 g saturated fat),
11 g carbohydrate (11 g sugars), 6 g fiber, 203 mg sodium

Dips

Prepare a range of attractive cut-up raw vegetables for dipping. Look for vegetables in season. For a spring party, trim a bunch of asparagus, scrub a bunch of baby carrots, trim and halve a bunch of radishes, and cut some baby fennel into thin wedges. Trim and halve some zucchini flowers; one per person. Arrange vegetables on a platter and serve with the dips you've prepared.

Red bell pepper and pomegranate dip

Heat 1 tablespoon extra virgin olive oil in a small frying pan. Fry ½ cup (40 g) fresh whole-grain or sourdough bread crumbs and 1 teaspoon crushed cumin seeds, turning frequently, until lightly golden and aromatic. Remove from heat and drain on paper towels. Roughly puree 1 roasted and peeled red bell pepper, ⅔ cup (65 g) walnuts, 1 teaspoon finely chopped garlic and ½ teaspoon (or more to taste) hot chili paste in a food processor or blender. Add the cumin-and-bread-crumb mixture, 2 teaspoons pomegranate molasses (available from Middle Eastern and specialty food stores), 2 tablespoons lemon juice, and ¼ cup (60 ml) extra virgin olive oil and process to combine. Taste and season with salt and extra pomegranate molasses and lemon juice if desired. Store covered in refrigerator until ready to serve. It will keep for up to 2 weeks. **Makes 1 cup**

Onion dip

Heat 1 tablespoon olive oil in a large frying pan over medium heat. Add 2 finely chopped sweet onions, such as Vidalia onions, and season with salt and freshly ground black pepper. Cook, stirring frequently, 12–15 minutes, or until golden brown. Cool to room temperature. Put onions, 1 cup (250 g) low-fat sour cream, 60 g (2 oz) reduced-fat cream cheese brought to room temperature, 1½ teaspoons white wine vinegar, and ¼ cup (15 g) finely chopped fresh chives in a medium bowl. Stir to combine and season with salt and pepper. Chill dip about 1 hour, until slightly thickened, or cover and refrigerate for up to 2 days. **Makes 1 cup**

Eggplant baba ghanoush

Roughly chop flesh of a 1-kg (2-lb) roasted and peeled eggplant. Put eggplant flesh, ½ cup (125 g) plain Greek-style yogurt, 2 tablespoons lemon juice, 2 tablespoons tahini, 1 crushed garlic clove, and ¼ teaspoon salt in a bowl. Stir to combine. If desired, scatter with chopped fresh flat-leaf parsley and drizzle with olive oil, then serve. **Makes 1 cup**

Cucumber tzatziki

Put 2 cups (500 g) plain yogurt in a sieve lined with cheesecloth over a bowl and let stand 5–10 minutes to drain. Put drained yogurt in a separate bowl; discard the liquid. Meanwhile, peel, halve, and seed 1 cucumber, then coarsely grate cucumber flesh and squeeze out excess moisture with your hands. Put drained yogurt, grated cucumber, 1 crushed garlic clove, 1 tablespoon finely chopped fresh chives, 2 tablespoons olive oil, and 1½ tablespoons lemon juice in a bowl and stir to combine well. Season with salt. Cover and refrigerate for a day before serving to allow flavors to develop. **Makes 2 cups**

Scallions in crème fraîche

Combine 200 g (7 oz) crème fraîche or sour cream, 4 finely chopped scallions, 2 tablespoons each chopped fresh dill, mint, and flat-leaf parsley, and 2 tablespoons lemon juice in a bowl. Season to taste, then cover and refrigerate until ready to serve. It will keep for up to 3 days in the refrigerator. **Makes 1 cup**

Roasted carrot dip

Preheat oven to 200°C (400°F). Scatter 1 kg (2 lb) coarsely chopped carrots and separated unpeeled cloves of 1 garlic head in a single layer in a roasting pan lined with parchment paper. Drizzle ⅓ cup (80 ml) olive oil over the vegetables, season with salt and freshly ground black pepper, and roast until golden and very tender, 1–1¼ hours. Cool to room temperature. Squeeze garlic flesh from skins. Put carrots and garlic in a food processor or blender. Add ½ cup (125 g) plain yogurt and finely grated zest and juice of 1½ lemons, season with salt and freshly ground black pepper, and process until smooth. Add ¾ cup (180 ml) olive oil in a steady stream while processing. Store covered in refrigerator until ready to serve. It will keep for 2–3 days. **Makes 2 cups**

FROM LEFT: Eggplant baba ghanoush, red bell pepper and pomegranate dip, and scallions in crème fraîche.

Tarte tatin of heirloom tomatoes

The easiest way to make sure your tart has a lovely crisp, light base is to bake it upside down. Traditionally made with apples as a dessert, tarte tatin is also delicious with a filling of tomatoes or onions as a light main meal.

PREPARATION. . . . . .10 MINUTES
COOKING . . . . .25 MINUTES
SERVES. 4–6

2 tablespoons olive oil
500 g (1 lb) mixed heirloom tomatoes, halved vertically or cut into similar-size pieces
2 tablespoons red wine or balsamic vinegar
¼ cup (40 g) lightly packed brown sugar
1 sheet frozen puff pastry, thawed
100 g (3½ oz) goat cheese
10 small fresh basil leaves
Freshly ground black pepper

Preheat oven to 225°C (435°F).

In an ovenproof frying pan (about 22–25 cm/8½–10 in diameter), gently warm olive oil over a low heat. Arrange tomato halves or pieces in pan, cut side down. Start with the largest pieces, then fill in the gaps with smaller pieces. Pile any remaining pieces on top.

Cook tomatoes about 10 minutes, or until smaller tomatoes are completely soft and juices are bubbling around the sides of the pan.

Mix together vinegar and brown sugar in a small bowl, then pour evenly over tomatoes in pan. Remove pan from heat.

Cut pastry into a round that is slightly larger than the pan. Working quickly, place pastry on top of tomatoes and tuck edges inside pan so that pastry covers tomatoes completely (some juices will still escape). Bake in oven 15 minutes, or until pastry is crisp and golden.

Holding the pan handle, shake pan firmly back and forth to make sure whole tart is loose. Invert a large plate over pan and, holding plate and pan very firmly, flip pan over to release the tart onto plate. Use a spatula to free any tomato that is still stuck to the pan.

Crumble goat cheese over tart and scatter with basil leaves and pepper to taste. Serve warm or at room temperature.

TIP
Cut out any hard white cores from the heirloom tomatoes.
If you don't have goat cheese, use feta or fresh buffalo mozzarella.

EACH SERVING PROVIDES
387 calories, 9 g protein, 26 g fat (12 g saturated fat),
29 g carbohydrate (14 g sugars), 2 g fiber, 323 mg sodium

Avocado mold

Jelled avocado mousse, encasing a ricotta and salmon filling, makes for a slightly decadent starter on thick slices of crusty bread. For a light lunch, cut into wedges and serve with a leafy green salad.

PREPARATION. . . . . .1 HOUR, PLUS CHILLING TIME
AND OVERNIGHT SETTING TIME
SERVES. 8

Vegetable oil for greasing
3 large ripe avocados, roughly chopped, plus
   1 ripe avocado, sliced, for garnish
2 cloves garlic
Grated zest and juice of 2 limes
Salt and freshly ground black pepper
Dash of Tabasco or other hot sauce
3 teaspoons (10 g) powdered clear gelatin
¾ cup (180 ml) heavy whipping cream

Ricotta salmon filling
375 g (13 oz) ricotta cheese
¼ cup (60 ml) light cream
5 g (1½ teaspoons) powdered clear gelatin
200 g (7 oz) smoked salmon, finely chopped
Salt and freshly ground black pepper
2 egg whites

Lightly oil a 6-cup (1.5-liter) mold or 20-cm (8-in) shallow cake pan. Put roughly chopped avocado, garlic, lime zest, and half the lime juice in a food processor or blender. Puree until smooth, then season with salt, pepper, and Tabasco or other hot sauce.

Sprinkle gelatin over ¼ cup (60 ml) water in a small saucepan and dissolve over a low heat. Let cool slightly. Transfer avocado puree to a bowl and stir in gelatin to combine well.

Chill avocado mixture in refrigerator until just beginning to thicken. Put cream in a medium bowl and beat with an electric mixer until it holds soft peaks, then fold through avocado mixture. Spoon three-quarters of mixture over base and sides of the oiled mold or pan, leaving a cavity for the filling. Cover with plastic wrap and refrigerate, along with remaining avocado mixture, while preparing the filling.

To prepare the filling, put ricotta and cream in a food processor or blender and process until smooth. Sprinkle gelatin over ¼ cup (60 ml) water in a small saucepan and dissolve over a low heat. Cool slightly, then stir into ricotta mixture to combine well.

Fold smoked salmon through ricotta mixture and season with salt and pepper to taste.

Put egg whites in a large clean bowl and whisk with an electric mixer until stiff, then carefully fold through ricotta and salmon mixture. Spoon this filling into center of avocado mold. Spoon remaining avocado mixture over the top and smooth the surface. Cover with plastic wrap and refrigerate until set, preferably overnight.

About 10 minutes before serving, dip mold into hot water, then turn out onto a serving plate. Dip sliced avocado in remaining lime juice to prevent discoloration, then place around the mold to decorate. Refrigerate until ready to serve.

EACH SERVING PROVIDES
420 calories, 16 g protein, 39 g fat (16 g saturated fat),
3 g carbohydrate (2 g sugars), 2 g fiber, 697 mg sodium

Roasted cauliflower with pomegranate

Roasting cauliflower with a sprinkling of spices is easy and gives a lovely nutty flavor. Pomegranate, mint, and a yogurt dressing add Middle Eastern flavors, good for a light lunch.

PREPARATION . . . . 30 MINUTES
COOKING . . . . 30 MINUTES
SERVES 6

Olive oil for greasing
1 head cauliflower (about 800 g/28 oz), leaves
   and thick stalks discarded, cut into small florets
½ teaspoon ground cumin
½ teaspoon ground coriander
Salt
Light olive oil spray
½ cup (125 ml) plain yogurt
1 tablespoon lemon juice
1½ tablespoons finely chopped fresh mint
¼ cup (40 g) pomegranate seeds
Small fresh mint leaves for garnish

Preheat oven to 180°C (350°F) and lightly oil a large baking sheet. Arrange cauliflower in a single layer on sheet. Put cumin and coriander in a small sieve and sprinkle evenly over cauliflower. Season with salt to taste and spray with olive oil spray.

Roast 15 minutes, then rearrange florets, moving those on the outside of the tray to the center and vice versa. Roast an additional 15 minutes, or until tender and lightly golden. Remove from oven and cool slightly.

Meanwhile, combine yogurt, lemon juice, and chopped mint in a small bowl and season with a pinch of salt.

Arrange cauliflower on a serving plate and drizzle with yogurt dressing. Sprinkle with pomegranate seeds and small mint leaves and serve.

TIP

To get the seeds from a pomegranate, cut in half horizontally and put in a large bowl of water. Use your fingers to pry out the seeds under water. They will sink to the bottom while the white membrane will float. Pour off the water and any white membrane, then drain the seeds and pat dry on paper towels. A medium pomegranate will yield about 1 cup (160 g) seeds—the excess seeds can be stored in the refrigerator for 3-4 days.

EACH SERVING PROVIDES
61 calories, 4 g protein, 3 g fat (<1 g saturated fat),
5 g carbohydrate (5 g sugars), 3 g fiber, 133 mg sodium

Onion and shallot pastries

Red onions and shallots are particularly well suited to rapid baking, as they don't lose any of their flavor or crispness. Serve these pastries with a green salad.

Butter for greasing

2 small red onions (200 g/7 oz total), thinly sliced

4 large shallots, halved

4 tablespoons olive oil

2 teaspoons superfine sugar

16 sprigs fresh thyme

Salt and freshly ground black pepper

250 g (8 oz) frozen ready-made puff pastry, thawed

1 egg, lightly beaten

PREPARATION. . . . . 15 MINUTES
COOKING . . . . .20 MINUTES
SERVES. . . . . 4 (MAKES 4 TARTS)

Preheat oven to 220°C (425°F/Gas 7) and grease a large baking sheet. Put onions, shallots, oil, sugar, leaves from 4 sprigs of thyme, and salt and pepper to taste in a medium bowl and toss to combine.

Lightly flour work surface, then cut pastry in half and roll out each piece to form a rectangle about 30 x 15 cm (12 x 6 in). Cut two large rounds from each piece with a 13–15-cm (5–6-in) saucer as a guide and put on prepared baking sheet.

Brush beaten egg over pastry rounds, taking care not to let it trickle over the edges.

Pile a quarter of the onions and shallots in the center of each round, leaving a border of about 2 cm (³⁄₄ inch) around the edge. Put 3 sprigs of thyme on top of each tart.

Bake in oven 20 minutes, or until puffed and golden brown. Serve hot.

EACH SERVING PROVIDES
442 calories, 6 g protein, 34 g fat (11 g saturated fat), 28 g carbohydrate (5 g sugars), 2 g fiber, 461 mg sodium

Grilled vegetable terrine

This makes a lovely picnic treat served at room temperature. Buy a good-quality basil pesto, or better still, make your own when basil is in season.

PREPARATION. . . . . 30 MINUTES, PLUS STANDING TIME
COOKING .1 HOUR 20 MINUTES
SERVES. 6

Olive oil for greasing

1 large red bell pepper, seeded and cut lengthwise into flat pieces

600 g (1¼ lb) sweet potato, cut horizontally into 5-mm (¼-in) slices

3 zucchini, cut lengthwise into 5-mm (¼-in) slices

1 large eggplant, cut horizontally into 5-mm (¼-in) slices

4 tablespoons olive oil

1 cup (130 g) semi-dried tomatoes, chopped (see page 108)

200 g (7 oz) feta cheese, crumbled

5 eggs

½ cup (125 ml) light cream

Salt and freshly ground black pepper

½ cup (125 g) good-quality pesto for serving

Crusty bread for serving

Preheat oven to 160°C (320°F). Lightly oil a 20 x 10-cm (8 x 4-in) loaf pan, then line base and long sides with parchment paper.

Preheat the broiler and line a baking sheet with foil. Arrange bell pepper pieces on sheet and broil until skin has blackened and blistered. Remove, cover with foil, and set aside to cool, then peel off skin.

Preheat grill pan to medium-high. Toss sweet potato and 1 tablespoon oil in a large bowl, then grill about 3 minutes on each side, until tender and lightly browned. Toss zucchini and 1 tablespoon oil in the bowl and grill 1–2 minutes on each side, until tender and lightly browned. Toss eggplant and remaining oil in the bowl and grill 2 minutes on each side, until tender and lightly browned.

Arrange zucchini slices across the base and up the sides of prepared loaf pan. Top with all the bell peppers, then a layer of half the sweet potato. Scatter tomatoes and feta over sweet potato.

Whisk eggs and cream together in a medium bowl and season with salt and pepper to taste. Pour half the egg mixture over the vegetables and feta in the pan. Cover with a layer of eggplant, then top with a layer of the remaining sweet potato. Pour the remaining egg mixture over the top.

Bake 1 hour, or until set. Remove from oven and let stand in the pan 15 minutes, then turn out onto a serving plate. Cut into slices and serve with pesto and crusty bread.

TIP
When assembling the ingredients in the loaf pan, trim and arrange the vegetables to make an even layer if possible.

EACH SERVING PROVIDES
476 calories, 16 g protein, 38 g fat (14 g saturated fat), 21 g carbohydrate (12 g sugars), 4 g fiber, 586 mg sodium

Escalivada

Escalivada comes from a Catalan word meaning "to roast over embers." This oven-roasted version is a quick, easy alternative if you don't have a charcoal grill.

PREPARATION. . . . . .10 MINUTES
COOKING . . . . 1 HOUR
SERVES. 4–6

1 red bell pepper
1 yellow bell pepper
2 ripe tomatoes
2 red onions
1 eggplant (about 400 g/14 oz)
1 head garlic
4 baby leeks or thick scallions, fleshy
   white part only
1 tablespoon chopped fresh thyme leaves
   for garnish

Dressing
3 tablespoons extra virgin olive oil
Salt and freshly ground black pepper

Preheat oven to 180°C (350°F). Put whole red and yellow bell peppers, tomatoes, red onions, eggplant, and head of garlic on a baking sheet—do not peel, core, or cut any of the vegetables. Cook 40 minutes.

Add leeks or scallions and bake an additional 20 minutes, or until all vegetables are very soft and slightly blackened.

When cool enough to handle, peel and core bell peppers. Peel and seed tomatoes and peel red onions. Scoop eggplant flesh out of skin with a large spoon. Cut peppers and eggplant flesh into long strips about 1–2 cm ($1/2$–$3/4$ in) wide. Cut tomatoes and red onions into wedges. Peel outer layer from leeks or scallions. Reserve any juices. Arrange the vegetables on a serving platter.

To make the dressing, use a sharp serrated knife to cut whole roasted garlic head horizontally at the widest point. Squeeze garlic flesh into a small bowl, add oil and some of the reserved vegetable juices as desired, and season with salt and pepper to taste.

Drizzle dressing over roasted vegetables, garnish with thyme leaves, and serve.

TIP
Escalivada is easy to prepare on an outdoor grill and is traditionally served as a first course or a side dish with barbecued or roasted meats.

EACH SERVING PROVIDES
198 calories, 5 g protein, 15 g fat (2 g saturated fat),
12 g carbohydrate (10 g sugars), 8 g fiber, 177 mg sodium

Ratatouille

Ratatouille is extremely versatile and can be used in many ways. It is a delicious one-pot vegetable accompaniment to any meat, fish, or chicken, or it can be used as a pasta sauce or as a vegetarian meal with the addition of kidney beans or chickpeas. It will freeze for up to three months, so it makes a good stand-by base for a meal.

PREPARATION . . . . .20 MINUTES
COOKING . . . . 30 MINUTES
SERVES 6

2 tablespoons olive oil
1 onion, chopped
2 cloves garlic, crushed
1 red bell pepper, diced
2 zucchini, halved lengthwise and sliced
1 eggplant, diced
5 ripe tomatoes, cored and chopped
2 tablespoons shredded fresh basil leaves
    plus whole leaves for garnish
Salt and freshly ground black pepper

Heat oil in a large, heavy-bottomed saucepan over medium heat. Add onion and sauté 7 minutes, or until soft and golden. Add garlic and cook an additional minute.

Add bell pepper and cook 2 minutes, stirring occasionally. Add zucchini and eggplant and stir until well combined.

Stir in tomatoes and bring to a boil. Reduce heat to low and partially cover with a lid. Simmer, stirring occasionally, 20 minutes, or until the vegetables are tender. Stir in shredded basil and season with salt and pepper to taste. Serve hot or warm, garnished with extra basil leaves.

TIP
If your tomatoes aren't super ripe, you can enrich the dish by adding 1 tablespoon tomato paste, or replace the tomatoes with an 800-g (28-oz) can chopped tomatoes. When seasoning tomato-based dishes, a good pinch of sugar often rounds out the flavor.

VARIATION
To make a vegetarian meal, add a 400-g (14-oz) can chickpeas or red kidney beans, rinsed and drained, toward the end of cooking. Stir and heat through, then serve with crusty bread.

EACH SERVING PROVIDES
94 calories, 3 g protein, 7 g fat (<1 g saturated fat),
6 g carbohydrate (6 g sugars), 4 g fiber, 114 mg sodium

Roasted Jerusalem artichokes

These low-starch tubers have a mildly sweet, nutty flavor, reminiscent of a potato, artichoke, and water chestnut in one. Roasted Jerusalem artichokes are particularly good.

1 tablespoon olive oil

60 g (2 oz) butter

500 g (1 lb) Jerusalem artichokes, scrubbed and halved lengthwise

Juice of 1 lemon

6 sprigs fresh thyme

Pinch of salt

PREPARATION . . . . .5 MINUTES
COOKING . . . . 50 MINUTES
SERVES . . . . 4 AS A SIDE DISH

Preheat oven to 200°C (400°F). Warm oil in a heat-resistant baking dish over medium heat. Add butter, and when it froths, put in Jerusalem artichokes, cut side down. Shake pan to avoid sticking.

Pour lemon juice over artichokes. Scatter with thyme sprigs and season with salt.

Roast 50 minutes, turning once, until Jerusalem artichokes are golden on the cut side and tender in the center when tested with a skewer. Serve hot.

EACH SERVING PROVIDES
220 calories, 3 g protein, 17 g fat (9 g saturated fat),
14 g carbohydrate (4 g sugars), 4 g fiber, 265 mg sodium

Fava bean and ricotta pastizzi

This version of the Maltese savory pastries uses purchased frozen puff pastry rather than the traditional handmade phyllo-like pastry. The fava beans make a flavorful alternative to the traditional pea filling.

PREPARATION . . . . . . 40 MINUTES, PLUS COOLING TIME
COOKING . . . . .20–25 MINUTES
SERVES . . . . 4–6 (MAKES 24 PASTIZZI)

3 sheets frozen puff pastry, thawed
  but still chilled
1 egg, lightly beaten

Filling
1 kg (2 lb) whole fava beans in the pod
  or 500 g (1 lb) frozen fava beans
1 tablespoon olive oil
3 scallions, sliced
2 cloves garlic, crushed
2 teaspoons finely grated lemon zest
200 g (7 oz) ricotta cheese
2 teaspoons finely chopped fresh dill
Salt and freshly ground black pepper

If using whole beans in the pod, split pods open and take out beans. Put fresh or frozen beans in a large saucepan of boiling water and cook 3 minutes. Drain well, and when cool enough to handle, remove tough outer skins. To do this, pierce a small opening in the skin at one end with your thumbnail or a knife and slip the tender bright green inner bean out. Put beans in a large bowl and roughly mash with a fork.

Heat oil in a frying pan or saucepan over medium heat and cook scallions and garlic 2–3 minutes, until tender. Add to beans along with lemon zest and mix well. Cool completely, then add ricotta and dill and mix to form a rough paste. Season with salt and pepper to taste.

Put a pastry sheet on the work surface and roll up tightly, starting from the long end. Lay outer edge of this pastry roll on the end of another pastry sheet, overlapping by about 1 cm (½ in), and continue rolling up. Repeat with remaining sheet to form a single large roll. Trim off any slightly dry ends if necessary. Using a sharp knife, cut pastry roll into slices 1 cm (½ in) thick. If the pastry has become too soft, refrigerate until firm.

Preheat oven to 200°C (400°F) and line two baking sheets with parchment paper. Using a rolling pin, roll a pastry slice into a round about 10 cm (4 in) in diameter—roll it between two pieces of parchment paper or lightly dust with flour beforehand to prevent sticking. Repeat with all remaining pastry slices. Put 1 level tablespoon fava bean mixture across a pastry round and fold over pastry to enclose, then pinch edges to seal. Stand upright on a prepared tray. Repeat with remaining pastry rounds and filling.

Brush pastizzi lightly with beaten egg. Bake 15–18 minutes, until well browned. Serve warm or at room temperature.

EACH SERVING PROVIDES
663 calories, 19 g protein, 41 g fat (20 g saturated fat),
57 g carbohydrate (2 g sugars), 6 g fiber, 868 mg sodium

Baked vegetables with spiced rice stuffing

This recipe uses a variety of vegetables stuffed with a lightly spiced rice mixture. Diners can choose the vegetables they prefer or share a little of each one. Serve as a side dish with grilled steak or by itself as a light vegetarian meal.

PREPARATION. . . . . .45 MINUTES
COOKING . . . . .1 HOUR 35 MINUTES
SERVES. . . . . .4–6 AS A LIGHT MEAL,
8 AS A SIDE DISH

4 onions (about 150 g/5 oz each)

2 tablespoons olive oil

1¼ cups (250 g) long-grain white rice

2 cloves garlic, crushed

2 teaspoons ground cumin

2 teaspoons ground coriander

2 tablespoons tomato paste

1¼ cups (310 ml) low-sodium vegetable or chicken stock

2 eggplants (about 200 g/7 oz each)

2 zucchini (about 150 g/5 oz each)

4 small red bell peppers (about 200 g/7 oz each)

¼ cup (35 g) currants

2 tablespoons pine nuts, toasted

Salt and freshly ground black pepper

Fresh cilantro leaves for garnish

Plain yogurt for serving

Preheat oven to 200°C (400°F) and line two large baking sheets with parchment paper. Cut a 1.5-cm (about ½-in) slice off the top of the onions and remove the skin. Cut a small slice off the bottom of onions so they sit flat. Use a melon baller to scoop out the insides, leaving a wall two layers thick. Carefully put hollowed-out onion shells in a medium saucepan of boiling water, reduce heat to low, and simmer 10 minutes. Lift out onion shells, drain, and cool. Meanwhile, finely chop scooped-out onion flesh.

Heat 1 tablespoon oil in a large, heavy-bottomed saucepan over medium heat. Add finely chopped onion and cook about 4 minutes, or until soft. Add rice and cook, stirring, 1 minute. Add garlic, cumin, and coriander and cook, stirring, 30 seconds. Stir in tomato paste. Add stock, cover, and bring to a boil. Reduce heat to low and simmer gently, 8 minutes. Turn off heat, cover with a lid, and let stand 5 minutes. Uncover and fluff the grains with a fork.

Meanwhile, halve eggplant lengthwise. With a sharp knife, score a line around the cut side of each half about 6 mm (¼ in) in from the edge. Score the flesh within the line in a crisscross pattern. Use a melon baller or teaspoon to scoop out the flesh, then set aside the hollowed-out eggplant shells. Repeat with zucchini. Finely chop eggplant and zucchini flesh and set aside. Cut the tops off the bell peppers and remove seeds and membranes.

Heat remaining oil in a large, deep frying pan over medium-high heat. Cook eggplant and zucchini flesh about 5 minutes, until soft. Add to rice with currants and pine nuts and use a fork to mix through. Season with salt and pepper to taste.

Spoon mixture into vegetable shells and stand on prepared baking sheets. Cover loosely with foil and bake 30 minutes, then swap trays between top and bottom shelves and bake an additional 30 minutes, or until vegetables are tender. Garnish with cilantro leaves and serve with yogurt on the side.

EACH SERVING PROVIDES
503 calories, 15 g protein, 16 g fat (2 g saturated fat),
76 g carbohydrate (21 g sugars), 11 g fiber, 451 mg sodium

Pea and ricotta fritters

These simple fritters make a nutritious snack by themselves or a light lunch when served with a salad of arugula leaves or snow-pea shoots.

PREPARATION. . . . . 10 MINUTES
COOKING . . . . 25–30 MINUTES
SERVES. . . . . 4 (MAKES 12 FRITTERS)

2 cups (300 g) fresh or frozen peas
1 tablespoon chopped fresh mint leaves
2 tablespoons chopped fresh dill
Finely grated zest of 1 lemon
2 eggs, lightly beaten
150 g (5 oz) ricotta cheese
3 tablespoons all-purpose flour
Salt and freshly ground black pepper
2 tablespoons olive oil
Lemon wedges for serving

Bring a large saucepan of water to a boil. Add peas and cook 4–5 minutes, until tender. Drain and roughly mash.

Add mint, dill, lemon zest, eggs, ricotta, and flour. Season with salt and pepper to taste and stir until just combined.

Heat 1–2 teaspoons oil in a large nonstick frying pan over medium heat. Put 2 heaping tablespoons of batter in pan and spread out to form a fritter. Cook in batches of three or four, 3 minutes on each side, or until golden and cooked through. Transfer to a plate lined with paper towels and keep warm. Repeat to use up remaining mixture.

Serve fritters with lemon wedges on the side.

TIP
To make smaller fritters for serving as finger food at a party, use 1 heaping tablespoon of batter for each fritter and cook 1½–2 minutes each side.

EACH SERVING PROVIDES
239 calories, 12 g protein, 16 g fat (5 g saturated fat),
11 g carbohydrate (2 g sugars), 4 g fiber, 260 mg sodium

Braised baby vegetables

Gently braising whole baby vegetables will preserve their nutrients and intensify their flavors. Reducing the cooking juices in the final stage creates a nutrient-rich, glossy sauce.

2 tablespoons butter or olive oil

4 baby leeks (250 g/8 oz), trimmed

250 g (8 oz) baby parsnips, trimmed

250 g (8 oz) baby carrots, trimmed

8 small white onions or shallots, trimmed and peeled

½ cup (125 ml) low-sodium vegetable stock

1 teaspoon sugar

1 bay leaf

Pinch of freshly ground black pepper

PREPARATION . . . . 15 MINUTES
COOKING . . . . 20–25 MINUTES
SERVES 4

Melt butter or oil in a large saucepan or flameproof casserole over medium heat. Add leeks, parsnips, carrots, and onions or shallots and stir to coat with butter or oil.

Add stock, sugar, bay leaf, and pepper and stir. Bring to a boil, then cover and reduce heat to low. Simmer 10 minutes, or until vegetables are just tender. Transfer to a large heatproof dish and keep warm.

Increase heat to high and boil liquid 2–3 minutes, or until bubbling and reduced to a thick, syrup-like glaze. Pour glaze over vegetables and toss to coat, then serve.

TIP
When baby vegetables aren't available, use standard-size vegetables and cut them into even chunks. Add the grated zest and juice of 1 orange at the same time as the stock to enrich the flavor.

EACH SERVING PROVIDES
146 calories, 3 g protein, 8 g fat (5 g saturated fat),
15 g carbohydrate (11 g sugars), 5 g fiber, 259 mg sodium

Swiss chard quiche

Swiss chard is an excellent vegetable to grow yourself. You can harvest as many or as few leaves as you like, and if you have a glut, this recipe uses up plenty of leaves. Don't be alarmed by the volume of leaves that it calls for, as Swiss chard reduces considerably when cooked.

PREPARATION. . . . . . 35 MINUTES, PLUS CHILLING TIME
COOKING . . . . 1 HOUR 10 MINUTES
SERVES. 6–8

1¼ cups (190 g) all-purpose flour
90 g (3 oz) chilled butter, diced
Approximately 4 tablespoons ice water

Filling
1 large bunch Swiss chard (about 1 kg/2 lb)
1 tablespoon olive oil
1 onion, chopped
½ cup (60 g) grated Gruyère or Cheddar cheese
4 eggs
1 cup (250 ml) light cream
⅓ cup (80 ml) milk
Salt and freshly ground black pepper

Combine flour and butter in a large bowl. Use your fingertips to rub butter into flour until mixture resembles bread crumbs. Using a nonserrated knife or a pastry blender, mix ice water into breadcrumb mixture until evenly moistened, adding more water if necessary.

Gather dough into a ball and turn out onto a lightly floured surface. Using a rolling pin, roll out pastry to fit a 23-cm (9-in) round tart pan with a removable bottom and 2.5-cm (1-in) sides. Line the pan with pastry and trim edges. Refrigerate 20 minutes. Preheat oven to 180°C (350°F).

Remove pan from refrigerator and stand on a baking sheet. Loosely cover chilled pastry with parchment paper and fill with pie weights, uncooked rice, or dried beans. Bake 15 minutes. Remove paper and weights and cook an additional 15 minutes, until pastry shell is dry and lightly golden. Cool completely before filling. Reduce oven temperature to 160°C (320°F).

While the pastry shell is cooking, prepare the filling. Tear Swiss chard leaves from stems, wash well, and shake moisture from leaves. Heat a large, deep frying pan over medium heat and add chard in batches, cooking just until wilted. Remove from pan and set aside to cool, then squeeze with your hands to remove as much liquid as possible. Roughly chop leaves.

Heat oil in the frying pan over medium heat and cook onion, stirring occasionally, about 5 minutes, or until soft. Spread onion over cooked pastry shell, then evenly spread chard on top. Sprinkle with Gruyère or Cheddar.

Whisk together eggs, cream, and milk in a medium bowl. Season with salt and pepper to taste, then pour into pastry shell. Bake 40 minutes, or until quiche is set and golden. Serve hot or warm.

EACH SERVING PROVIDES
540 calories, 15 g protein, 41 g fat (24 g saturated fat),
27 g carbohydrate (4 g sugars), 4 g fiber, 614 mg sodium

Cucumber sandwiches

This is the quintessential English teatime delicacy. Make sure that you use the freshest, thinnest slices of bread you can, and cut the cucumber into wafer-thin slices.

PREPARATION. . . . . 10 MINUTES
SERVES. . . . . 6 (MAKES 24 TRIANGLES
OR 18 FINGER SANDWICHES)

12 thin slices white bread
60 g (2 oz) butter, softened
1 Lebanese or other small cucumber
Salt
Extra cucumber slices for garnish

Spread each slice of bread very thinly with butter. This prevents the cucumber's moisture from soaking into the bread.

Thinly slice cucumber, then pat dry with paper towels. Arrange a layer of cucumber slices on 6 bread slices. Lightly season with salt and top each with a bread slice.

Cut crusts off sandwiches, then cut sandwiches into neat triangles or fingers. Garnish with extra cucumber slices, arrange on a serving platter, and serve immediately.

VARIATIONS
Purists might be horrified, but you can vary the basic sandwich in several ways. Just remember to keep the fillings very delicate so the sandwiches hold together.

✳ Add a thin layer of watercress for a slightly peppery bite.

✳ Add a thin layer of smoked salmon. To this you could also add a tiny squeeze of lemon juice.

✳ Spread bread with softened cream cheese rather than butter for extra creaminess—it goes particularly well with smoked salmon.

✳ Scatter with finely snipped fresh herbs, such as chives, mint, or dill.

✳ Blot thin slices of tomato between paper towels to absorb excess moisture, then place tomatoes on top of the buttered bread slices before you add the cucumber.

EACH SERVING PROVIDES
126 calories, 2 g protein, 9 g fat (5 g saturated fat),
10 g carbohydrate (<1 g sugars), <1 g fiber, 284 mg sodium

Baked beets

For perfect tenderness, bake the beets very slowly at a low temperature. This dish is good with roast pork or roast duck. It also goes well with barbecued lamb chops.

PREPARATION. . . . . .20 MINUTES
COOKING . . . . .3 HOURS – 3 HOURS 30 MINUTES
SERVES. 4

8 baby beets (about 400 g/14 oz total)
60 g (2 oz) butter
4 scallions, thinly sliced
1 tablespoon snipped fresh chives
2 teaspoons chopped fresh flat-leaf
   parsley

Preheat oven to 150°C (300°F). Carefully wash beets, taking care not to pierce or bruise skin. Wrap each in a square of greased foil and put in a baking dish. Bake in oven 3–3½ hours, or until skins come away easily when rubbed gently.

Remove beets from oven, unwrap foil, and when cool enough to handle, peel carefully and cut into quarters.

Melt butter in a large frying pan over medium heat. Add beets, scallions, chives, and parsley and toss gently to coat. Transfer to a warmed serving dish and serve.

VARIATION
Add ½ cup (125 ml) light cream to pan after transferring beets to serving dish. Bring cream to a boil over medium heat and cook 1 minute, then pour over beets. Cut 2 sweet gherkins into very thin strips and sprinkle over the top.

EACH SERVING PROVIDES
155 calories, 2 g protein, 12 g fat (8 g saturated fat),
9 g carbohydrate (9 g sugars), 3 g fiber, 164 mg sodium

Steamed Asian vegetables

This is a side dish packed with vitamins. It makes a wholesome meal served with steamed rice.

PREPARATION. . . . . 15 MINUTES
COOKING . . . . .5–8 MINUTES
SERVES. 4

400 g (14 oz) carrots, cut into sticks
3 cups (375 g) small cauliflower florets
3 cups (180 g) small broccoli florets
250 g (8 oz) green beans, trimmed and halved
350 g (12 oz) zucchini, cut into sticks
4 baby bok choy, quartered

Sweet soy dipping sauce
2 tablespoons kecap manis (sweet soy sauce)
1½ tablespoons oyster sauce
2 teaspoons Chinese rice wine
1 teaspoon sesame oil

To make sweet soy dipping sauce, combine kecap manis, oyster sauce, rice wine and sesame oil in a small bowl. Set aside.

Fill a large wok or saucepan with about 2 inches of water. Cover and bring to a boil. Scatter carrots, cauliflower, broccoli, and beans in a steamer basket. Carefully set basket above boiling water—the water should not touch the base of the basket. Cover and steam 2 minutes.

Scatter zucchini and bok choy in a second steamer basket, put it on top of first basket, and steam an additional 2–3 minutes, or until all vegetables are just cooked. Alternatively, if only one steamer basket is available, scatter zucchini and bok choy on top of vegetables already cooking and steam an additional 3–5 minutes, until just tender.

Using a dish towel, carefully remove baskets and divide vegetables among serving bowls. Serve immediately with sweet soy dipping sauce.

TIP
You can add ginger, garlic, diced firm tofu, and other vegetables, such as asparagus, fennel, and mushrooms, to the steamer basket. Replace the dipping sauce with lemon or lime juice, tahini, or satay sauce.

EACH SERVING PROVIDES
119 calories, 9 g protein, 1 g fat (<1 g saturated fat),
19 g carbohydrate (17 g sugars), 10 g fiber, 872 mg sodium

Roasted potatoes and root vegetables

Whether you're planning a dinner of lamb, beef, pork, or chicken, there's no better accompaniment than roasted potatoes—and any combination of root vegetables alongside them.

4 baking potatoes
3 carrots
3 parsnips
3 small rutabagas or turnips
3 beets
Olive oil for drizzling
Salt and freshly ground black pepper

PREPARATION . . . . .10 MINUTES
COOKING . . . . .45 MINUTES
SERVES 6

Preheat oven to 210°C (410°F). Wash and scrub all vegetables, then pat dry with paper towels. Peel potatoes and cut in half. Top and tail carrots and parsnips, then peel and halve lengthwise. Peel rutabagas or turnips and quarter. Leave beets whole, with skin on.

Put all vegetables in a large roasting pan, drizzle generously with olive oil, and season well with salt and pepper to taste.

Roast 30 minutes, then turn vegetables over and roast an additional 15 minutes, or until golden and tender. Serve hot.

TIPS
Root vegetables such as parsnips, turnips, rutabagas, and carrots are at their peak in late autumn and winter. Store them in the crisper in the refrigerator.

Kohlrabi is a great addition to this dish. Steam the bulb 5 minutes, then roast 45 minutes.

VARIATION
In summer, try Provence-style roasted vegetables. Trim and halve some zucchini, red and green bell peppers, pattypan squash, and red onions; toss with olive oil, salt, pepper, and fresh thyme. Bake in a baking dish in an oven preheated to 180°C (350°F) for 45 minutes.

EACH SERVING PROVIDES
142 calories, 5 g protein, 1 g fat (<1 g saturated fat), 28 g carbohydrate (13 g sugars), 7 g fiber, 167 mg sodium

Stuffed zucchini flowers

Zucchini flowers are easy to work with but should always be handled gently and cooked right away. The flowers add a lovely sweetness to the crunchy batter and creamy ricotta filling within.

PREPARATION. . . . . 30 MINUTES
COOKING . . . . .20 MINUTES
SERVES. . . . . 4–6 (MAKES 24)

150 g (5 oz) ricotta cheese

2 tablespoons finely grated Parmesan

2 anchovies, drained and finely chopped

1 clove garlic, crushed

1 teaspoon chopped fresh thyme leaves

Freshly ground black pepper

24 small zucchini with flowers attached

1 cup (150 g) self-rising flour or 1 cup all-purpose
   flour mixed with 1½ teaspoons baking powder
   and ¼ teaspoon salt

1 cup (250 ml) chilled club soda

Vegetable oil, for deep-frying

Salt

Lemon wedges for serving

Put ricotta, Parmesan, anchovies, garlic, and thyme in a medium bowl and mash together with a fork until evenly combined. Season with pepper to taste.

Gently open a zucchini flower and fill with ricotta mixture. Adjust petals so that the flower returns to its former shape and twist the end to seal. Repeat with the remaining flowers and filling.

Sift flour into a mixing bowl and make a well in the center. Gradually pour in club soda, stirring continuously to incorporate flour. Mix until just combined—if you overbeat it, the batter won't be light and fluffy.

Half fill a deep fryer or large saucepan with oil and heat over medium-high heat until a cube of bread dropped in the oil becomes crisp in 15 seconds. Working in batches of three or four at a time, dip each zucchini and its stuffed flower into batter, letting excess drain off. Gently drop into oil and deep-fry about 2 minutes, until crisp and lightly golden. Using a slotted spoon, transfer to a baking sheet lined with paper towels and keep warm. Working quickly, repeat with the remaining zucchini flowers.

Sprinkle with salt and serve with lemon wedges.

TIPS

Only cook three or four at a time. If you try to cook too many at once, the temperature of the oil will drop, resulting in batter that is heavy and oily rather than light and crisp.

To prepare a zucchini flower, hold the flower in your hand and make a split along the petals with your thumbs, then use your fingertips to snap off and discard the stamens inside (see page 000). Don't snap off the stamens until just before you're ready to fill the flower, as the flower will quickly wilt without them.

EACH SERVING PROVIDES
441 calories, 13 g protein, 30 g fat (6 g saturated fat),
31 g carbohydrate (5 g sugars), 6 g fiber, 661 mg sodium

Shrimp and vegetable tempura

In Japanese cuisine, tempura is a form of deep-frying that uses seafood and vegetables. You can use any firm vegetables.

PREPARATION . . . . 15 MINUTES
COOKING . . . . 15–25 MINUTES
SERVES 4

1½ cups (225 g) all-purpose flour
¼ cup (30 g) cornstarch
Pinch of baking soda
1 cup (250 ml) chilled club soda or water
1 egg, lightly beaten
Vegetable oil for deep-frying
1 carrot, cut diagonally into 5-mm (¼-in) slices
¼ small winter squash, peeled, seeded, and thinly sliced
1 red bell pepper, seeded and cut into 8 strips
1 small eggplant, cut into 5-mm (¼-in) slices
12 green beans, trimmed
300 g (10 oz) uncooked shrimp, peeled and deveined, tails left on
Soy sauce and wasabi for serving

Sift ¾ cup (110 g) flour, cornstarch, and baking soda into a medium bowl and make a well in the center. Pour in club soda or water and egg. Using chopsticks, whisk gently until just combined—the batter should be lumpy; be careful not to overmix. Put bowl inside a larger bowl of ice water to keep batter chilled.

Pour enough oil into a deep fryer, wok, or large saucepan to reach a depth of about 6.5 cm (2½ in). Heat oil over medium-high heat to 190°C (370°F)—test with a candy thermometer—or until a cube of bread dropped in the oil browns in 10 seconds.

Pat dry carrot, squash, bell pepper, eggplant, and beans with paper towels. Put remaining flour on a plate.

Working with a quarter of the vegetables at a time, coat each individual piece in flour, shaking off any excess. Then dip each piece in batter, shaking off any excess. Deep-fry 2–3 minutes, or until pale golden. Do not overcrowd the pan, as this will lower the temperature of the oil and result in soggy batter. Using a slotted spoon, transfer vegetables to a baking sheet lined with paper towels and keep warm. Repeat with the remaining vegetables.

Working in batches and holding shrimp by the tail, coat each shrimp in flour and shake off any excess, then dip in batter and shake off any excess. Deep-fry 3–4 minutes, or until shrimp is pale golden. Transfer to a second baking sheet lined with paper towels and keep warm. Repeat with the remaining shrimp.

Transfer vegetables and shrimp to four plates or a platter and serve immediately with soy sauce and wasabi on the side.

TIP
Firm vegetables, such as asparagus, strips of carrot or bell pepper, green beans, or slices of eggplant, onion, potato, and zucchini, are suitable for tempura. Vegetables with a high water content, such as cucumber, cabbage, lettuce, and tomato, are not suitable.

EACH SERVING PROVIDES
457 calories, 26 g protein, 13 g fat (2 g saturated fat),
57 g carbohydrate (7 g sugars), 5 g fiber, 210 mg sodium

Vegetable purees and mashes

A puree and a mash could really be interchangeable—puree being a more refined version of the humble mash. To make your puree even more velvety smooth, you could pass it through a food mill or fine sieve after pureeing. Reheat gently in a saucepan or in the microwave. Just remember to season. **All these recipes serve 4.**

Parsnip and pear puree

Peel and dice 500 g (1 lb) parsnips. Put in a large saucepan and cover with water. Bring to a boil and cook 10 minutes, then add 1 peeled, cored, and chopped pear and cook an additional 5 minutes, or until very soft. Drain and return to low heat to evaporate excess water. Transfer to a food processor or blender and process until smooth. Add 30 g (1 oz) soft butter and a pinch of nutmeg. Process until combined and season to taste. Drizzle with 1/4 cup (60 ml) cream and garnish with a sprinkling of nutmeg.

White bean and rosemary puree

Rinse and drain two 410-g (15-oz) cans cannellini beans. Put in a food processor or blender with 1 chopped garlic clove, 2 tablespoons each lemon juice and extra virgin olive oil, and 1 teaspoon chopped fresh rosemary. Process until smooth and season to taste. Garnish with a little extra fresh rosemary.

Minted pea puree

Add 2 cups (300 g) frozen peas to a saucepan of boiling water. Return to a boil and cook 2 minutes. Drain and put in a food processor or blender with 30 g (1 oz) soft butter, 2 tablespoons chopped fresh mint, and 2 teaspoons finely grated lemon zest. Process until smooth and season to taste. If desired, garnish with fresh mint leaves or extra lemon zest.

Beet puree

Preheat oven to 200°C (400°F). Wash 4 beets and trim tops. Wrap all together in a large sheet of foil and put on a baking sheet. Roast 1 hour, or until very tender. Cool slightly, then slip off skins. Roughly chop beet flesh and put in a food processor or blender with 1/2 cup (125 g) plain yogurt, 1 chopped small garlic clove, and 1 tablespoon balsamic vinegar. Process until smooth and season to taste. Top with a swirl of yogurt.

Perfect mashed potato

Peel 800 g (1¾ lb) baking potatoes and cut into 5-cm (2-in) chunks. Put in a large saucepan and cover with water. Bring to a boil and cook 15 minutes, or until very soft. Drain and return to low heat to evaporate excess water. Mash potatoes, then add 60 g (2 oz) soft butter and ⅓ cup (80 ml) warmed milk. Beat with a wooden spoon until smooth and light. Season with salt and white pepper. Serve with a little knob of butter on top.

Sweet potato mash with sage

Preheat oven to 200°C (400°F). Put 2 400-g (14-oz) whole orange sweet potatoes on a baking sheet and roast 45 minutes. Add 5 whole unpeeled garlic cloves and cook an additional 15 minutes, until tender. Cool slightly, then split sweet potatoes and scoop out flesh into a bowl. Squeeze garlic flesh from the skins into the bowl. Add 2 tablespoons extra virgin olive oil and 2 teaspoons chopped fresh sage. Mash well and season to taste. Serve garnished with a few fresh sage leaves.

Spiced carrot mash

Peel 500 g (1 lb) large carrots and cut into 3-cm (1-in) chunks. Steam over a saucepan of boiling water 10 minutes, or until soft. Transfer to a bowl and roughly mash. Add 1 teaspoon honey, ½ teaspoon ground cumin, a good pinch of ground cinnamon, and a pinch of cayenne pepper, if desired. Stir well with a wooden spoon to combine and season to taste. Serve sprinkled with toasted sesame seeds.

Celeriac mash

Peel 1 kg (2 lb) celeriac and cut into 3-cm (1-in) pieces. Put in a large saucepan and cover with water. Bring to a boil, then cook 25 minutes, until very soft. Drain well. Mash celeriac, then add ¼ cup (60 ml) cream and 2 teaspoons Dijon mustard. Beat with a wooden spoon until almost smooth. Season with salt and white pepper. Drizzle with a little extra cream if desired.

FROM LEFT: Beet puree, minted pea puree, sweet potato mash with sage, and perfect mashed potato.

Spiced vegetables with red lentil dal

Serve these vegetables and dal with steamed basmati rice or some warmed naan bread and a refreshing raita made from of plain yogurt mixed with chopped cucumber.

PREPARATION. . . . . 30 MINUTES
COOKING . . . . 30 MINUTES
SERVES. 4–6

Spiced vegetables

1 teaspoon mustard seeds
1 teaspoon cumin seeds
2 tablespoons vegetable oil or ghee
1 onion, chopped
2 cloves garlic, crushed
2 teaspoons grated fresh ginger
1 long green chili peppers, seeded and chopped
1 teaspoon ground turmeric
1 teaspoon garam masala
2 large tomatoes, chopped
1 small cauliflower (800 g/28 oz), cut into florets
1 large carrot, roughly chopped
300 g (10 oz) fresh peas, shelled and blanched, or 1 cup (150 g) frozen peas
1/2 teaspoon salt
1/3 cup (10 g) roughly chopped fresh cilantro leaves for garnish

Red lentil dal

1 cup (200 g) red lentils
1/2 teaspoon cumin seeds
1 tablespoon vegetable oil or ghee
1 onion, chopped
2 cloves garlic, crushed
2 teaspoons grated fresh ginger
1/2 teaspoon ground coriander
1/2 teaspoon garam masala
1/2 teaspoon ground turmeric
1/4 teaspoon ground cayenne
1/2 teaspoon salt

To make the spiced vegetables, heat a large, deep nonstick frying pan over medium heat. Add mustard seeds and cumin seeds and toast, stirring continuously, about 30 seconds, or until fragrant. Add oil or ghee and onion and cook, stirring occasionally, 5 minutes, or until soft and lightly golden.

Stir in garlic, ginger, and chili pepper and cook, stirring, 1 minute. Stir in turmeric, garam masala, and tomatoes. Cover pan and reduce heat to low. Cook 5 minutes, or until tomatoes are soft and pulpy. If too dry, add 1/2 cup (125 ml) water.

Add cauliflower, carrot, and peas to the pan. Cover and cook about 7 minutes, stirring occasionally, until tender. Season with salt.

While the spiced vegetables are cooking, make the dal. Rinse lentils in a strainer under cold running water, then drain. Transfer to a medium saucepan and add 2 cups (500 ml) water. Bring to a boil, then reduce heat to medium-low and simmer, stirring occasionally to ensure the lentils don't stick to the pan, about 8 minutes, until very soft and the mixture is thick.

Meanwhile, heat a small non-stick frying pan over medium heat and toast cumin seeds, stirring continuously, about 30 seconds, or until fragrant. Add oil or ghee and onion and cook, stirring occasionally, 5 minutes, or until soft and lightly golden. Add garlic, ginger, coriander, garam masala, turmeric, and cayenne and cook, stirring, 1 minute.

Add onion and spice mixture to cooked lentils, stir to combine, and season with salt.

Serve dal and spiced vegetables garnished with fresh cilantro leaves.

EACH SERVING PROVIDES
363 calories, 21 g protein, 16 g fat (2 g saturated fat),
34 g carbohydrate (10 g sugars), 15 g fiber, 663 mg sodium

Tagliatelle with mushroom medley

Choose a variety of exotic and wild mushrooms for this feast of fungi. Their flavors are complemented by Marsala in a dish that fits perfectly in a well-balanced diet—the result is very pleasing without being laden with cream, the ingredient that usually makes mushroom sauces overly rich.

PREPARATION. . . . . 15 MINUTES, PLUS
15 MINUTES SOAKING TIME
COOKING . . . . 30 MINUTES
SERVES. 4

10 g (⅓ oz) dried porcini mushrooms
90 ml (3 fl oz) boiling water
2 tablespoons extra virgin olive oil
3 shallots, sliced
250 g (8 oz) button mushrooms, sliced
⅔ cup (150 ml) Marsala
500 g (1 lb) tagliatelle
1 clove garlic, finely chopped (optional)
500 g (1 lb) mixed mushrooms, such as shiitake,
    oyster, cremini, chanterelles, or other wild
    mushrooms, sliced or halved
250 g (8 oz) tomatoes, peeled,
    seeded, and chopped
2 teaspoons fresh thyme leaves or
    1 teaspoon dried thyme
Salt and freshly ground black pepper
2 tablespoons chopped fresh flat-leaf parsley
    for garnish

Put dried porcini mushrooms in a small heatproof bowl and cover with boiling water. Soak 15 minutes, then drain, reserving the soaking liquid. Slice mushrooms, discarding any tough stalks.

Heat 1 tablespoon olive oil in a large, heavy-bottomed saucepan over medium heat. Sauté shallots until tender and golden, about 3 minutes. Add button mushrooms and cook an additional 8–10 minutes, or until all juices have evaporated.

Stir in Marsala and the reserved soaking liquid from porcini mushrooms. Simmer about 10 minutes, or until sauce has reduced by about half.

Meanwhile, cook tagliatelle in boiling water 10–12 minutes, or until al dente.

About 5 minutes before pasta is done, heat remaining oil in a large frying pan over medium heat. Add garlic, if using, mixed mushrooms, and rehydrated porcini mushrooms. Cook 3–5 minutes, shaking the pan often, until mushrooms are lightly cooked.

Stir tomatoes and thyme into button mushroom and heat 1–2 minutes. Add mixed and porcini mushrooms and stir carefully. Season with salt and pepper to taste and remove from heat.

Drain tagliatelle and divide among four warmed bowls or plates. Spoon mushroom sauce over the top, sprinkle with parsley, and serve immediately.

TIP
Most recipes use mushrooms in small quantities, so their nutritional contribution to the diet is limited. But this dish contains a substantial amount of fresh mushrooms as well as dried mushrooms for additional flavor.

EACH SERVING PROVIDES
624 calories, 20 g protein, 11 g fat (2 g saturated fat),
97 g carbohydrate (10 g sugars), 8 g fiber, 174 mg sodium

Buddha's delight vegetable stir-fry

This vegetarian dish is thought to have originated in Buddhist monasteries but is also popular during the Chinese New Year, when people often follow a vegetarian diet. Using a large number of ingredients is considered good luck.

PREPARATION. . . . . 10 MINUTES, PLUS
30 MINUTES SOAKING TIME
COOKING . . . . .25 MINUTES
SERVES 4

4 dried shiitake mushrooms

10 dried tiger lily buds (golden needles) (about 20 g)

15 dried lotus seeds (about 20 g)

¾ cup (about 20 g) dried or 100 g (3½ oz) fresh wood ears or dried black moss

Boiling water for soaking

2 tablespoons canola oil or peanut oil

350 g (12 oz) firm tofu, cut into 1-cm (½-in) slices, halved diagonally

1-cm (½-in) piece fresh ginger, grated

2 large cloves garlic, crushed

1 small head broccoli (about 100 g/3½ oz), cut into small florets

1 carrot, halved lengthwise and thinly sliced on the diagonal

2 stalks celery, thinly sliced on the diagonal

10–12 fresh baby corn or 1 drained 425-g (15-oz) can baby corn, sliced on the diagonal

1 200-g (7-oz) can water chestnuts, drained and thinly sliced

¼ cup (60 ml) oyster sauce

1 tablespoon firmly packed brown sugar or Chinese rock sugar

1 tablespoon sesame oil

Brown rice for serving

Put shiitake mushrooms, tiger lily buds, lotus seeds, and dried black moss, if using dried moss rather than wood ears, in a heat-resistant bowl. Pour boiling water over the mixture to cover generously. Soak 30 minutes, then drain. Coarsely chop shiitake mushrooms and black moss. Cut any tough ends off lily buds. Tie each lily bud in a knot in the traditional Chinese fashion, if desired. Set aside.

Meanwhile, heat 1 tablespoon of the oil in a large nonstick frying pan over medium heat and cook tofu triangles until golden and crisp on all sides, about 10–15 minutes. Keep warm.

Heat remaining oil in a wok or large frying pan over medium heat. Add ginger, garlic, broccoli, carrot, celery, and fresh baby corn, if using, and stir-fry until carrot is just tender, about 5 minutes.

Add water chestnuts, canned baby corn, if using, soaked shiitake mushrooms, tiger lily buds, and lotus seeds, and soaked black moss or fresh wood ears. Stir-fry 5 minutes.

Add oyster sauce, sugar, sesame oil, and 2 tablespoons water and stir to combine well. Toss tofu with vegetables and serve with brown rice.

TIP
Buddha's delight can be made with any mixture of vegetables. You could substitute other mushrooms, nuts, and Asian greens if dried tiger lily buds, lotus seeds, and black moss are not available.

EACH SERVING PROVIDES
335 calories, 16 g protein, 21 g fat (2 g saturated fat), 23 g carbohydrate (10 g sugars), 8 g fiber, 737 mg sodium

Eggplant croquettes

These croquettes are good as part of an antipasto selection. They can also be served with a leafy green salad as a healthful main meal.

PREPARATION . . . . . . 10 MINUTES, PLUS COOLING TIME
COOKING . . . . .20 MINUTES
SERVES . . . . 4 (MAKES 20 CROQUETTES)

1 large eggplant (about 500 g/1 lb),
    cut into large chunks
1 cup (125 g) pine nuts
½ cup (40 g) soft fresh bread crumbs (from about
    2 slices with crusts discarded)
¼ cup (25 g) finely grated Parmesan
2 tablespoons finely chopped fresh flat-leaf
    parsley
1 clove garlic, crushed
1 egg, beaten
2 cups (about 200 g) dried bread crumbs
Olive or canola oil for frying
Plain yogurt and lemon wedges for serving

Put eggplant in a large saucepan, cover with water, and top with a small plate to keep eggplant submerged. Bring to a boil, reduce heat to medium, and cook 10 minutes, or until very soft. Drain, then cool.

Meanwhile, toast pine nuts in a nonstick pan until golden, about 2–3 minutes.

When eggplant is cool enough to handle, squeeze with your hands to remove any excess liquid. Chop finely, then mash well in a large bowl.

Add toasted pine nuts, soft bread crumbs, Parmesan, parsley, garlic, and egg and stir to combine well.

Put dried bread crumbs on a plate. Form mixture into 20 small patties, then roll in dried bread crumbs.

Heat oil in a large, deep frying pan over medium heat. The oil should come about ⅛ inch up the sides of the pan. Fry croquettes in batches, turning occasionally, 4–5 minutes, until golden and crisp all over. Drain on paper towels and serve with yogurt and lemon wedges.

VARIATIONS
Replace the eggplant with zucchini or fennel, pine nuts with almonds, and Parmesan with other hard cheeses.

EACH SERVING PROVIDES
662 calories, 19 g protein, 46 g fat (5 g saturated fat),
43 g carbohydrate (6 g sugars), 6 g fiber, 520 mg sodium

Steak and beet salad

Soft, tangy goat cheese complements beets and steak beautifully, but it could be replaced with feta. If you can only get large beets cook them for an hour and cut into small pieces once cooled.

8 baby beets (400 g/14 oz total), trimmed,
    small leaves reserved
500 g (1 lb) rib-eye or strip steak, about 2.5 cm
    (1 in) thick
1 tablespoon olive oil
Salt and freshly ground black pepper
60 g (2 oz) arugula
1½ tablespoons balsamic vinegar
1 tablespoon lemon juice
1 tablespoon extra virgin olive oil
75 g (2¾ oz) soft goat cheese, crumbled
1 tablespoon finely chopped fresh chives

PREPARATION. . . . . . 30 MINUTES, PLUS COOLING TIME
COOKING . . . . 10–45 MINUTES
SERVES. 4

Cook beets in a large saucepan of boiling water 30 minutes, or until tender. Drain and set aside until just cool enough to handle. Slip off skins and slice or cut into 8 wedges each. Put in a bowl of ice water for at least 10 minutes. Drain, then dry with paper towels. Set aside.

Brush both sides of steak with olive oil and season with salt and pepper to taste. Heat a large, heavy-bottomed frying pan over medium-high heat and cook steak 5 minutes on each side for medium rare and 6–7 minutes on each side for medium. Transfer to a warm plate, cover loosely with foil, and let rest 5 minutes.

Put beets in a large bowl with reserved beet greens and arugula.

Whisk together vinegar, lemon juice, and extra virgin olive oil in a small bowl, then drizzle over beets and salad greens.

Divide salad among four plates, then scatter with goat cheese and chives. Slice steak against the grain, top each salad with several slices, and serve.

EACH SERVING PROVIDES
324 calories, 32 g protein, 17 g fat (6 g saturated fat),
10 g carbohydrate (10 g sugars), 3 g fiber, 361 mg sodium

Ghiveci: Romanian vegetable stew

"Ghiveci" is a Romanian word meaning "patchwork" or "hodgepodge." You can use any combination of vegetables in season to make this robust stew, a Romanian tradition.

PREPARATION. . . . . .10 MINUTES
COOKING .1 HOUR 20 MINUTES
SERVES. 8

100 ml (3½ fl oz) olive oil

1 onion, roughly chopped

1 large carrot, halved lengthwise and cut into
   1-cm (½-in) slices

1 kohlrabi, peeled and diced

1 zucchini, halved lengthwise and cut into
   1-cm (½-in) slices

1 bell pepper, seeded and cut into
   2-cm (¾-in) pieces

1 small eggplant, diced

2 potatoes, diced

2 cups (about 250 g/8 oz) cauliflower florets

¼ small green or red cabbage, finely shredded

100 g (3½ oz) fresh or frozen peas or green
   beans, cut into 2.5-cm (1-in) lengths

3 tomatoes, peeled and chopped, or
   1 410-g (15-oz) can chopped tomatoes

2 stalks fresh dill, finely chopped

½ teaspoon dried thyme

1 teaspoon sweet paprika

Juice of 1 lemon

5 stalks fresh flat-leaf parsley, finely chopped

Heat oil in a large flameproof casserole over medium heat. Sauté onion, carrot, and kohlrabi until onion is translucent, about 10 minutes.

Preheat oven to 150°C (300°F).

Add zucchini and bell pepper to casserole and stir well to coat with oil. Add eggplant and stir well to combine, then cook 10 minutes—do not stir—until vegetables are slightly browned.

Add the potatoes, cauliflower, cabbage, peas or beans, tomatoes, dill, thyme, paprika, lemon juice, and half the parsley and stir to combine.

Cover and bake 1 hour, or until potato is tender. Uncover, increase oven temperature to 200°C (400°F) and bake an additional 10 minutes, until vegetables on top look caramelized.

Serve topped with remaining chopped parsley.

TIP
For a fresher, greener ghiveci, add the peas or green beans and herbs during the final 10 minutes of cooking. This dish is excellent with roast meat or chicken but can also make a vegetarian main meal if you add a 400-g (14-oz) can chickpeas or cannellini beans, rinsed and drained, along with the potatoes.

EACH SERVING PROVIDES
177 calories, 5 g protein, 12 g fat (2 g saturated fat),
14 g carbohydrate (6 g sugars), 6 g fiber, 30 mg sodium

Vegetarian sliders

Sliders are really just small burgers, so they make great party food or a fun midweek meal. The texture of vegetable-based patties is always softer and more fragile than patties made from meat, so handle these carefully when cooking.

PREPARATION. . . . . 30 MINUTES
COOKING . . . . 20 MINUTES
SERVES. . . . . 8 AS A MAIN DISH (MAKES 16)

1 tablespoon olive oil, plus extra
 for frying

1 small onion, finely chopped

2 cloves garlic, crushed

2 teaspoons ground coriander

2 teaspoons ground cumin

2 zucchini (250 g/8 oz), grated

350 g (12 oz) orange sweet potato, peeled
 and grated

1 400-g (14-oz) can chickpeas, rinsed and drained

175 g (6 oz) haloumi cheese, grated

1½ cups (120 g) fresh bread crumbs

16 small rolls, split and toasted

1 avocado (300 g/10 oz), sliced

2 tomatoes (250 g/8 oz), sliced

16 small Boston lettuce leaves

Sour cream and sweet chili sauce for serving

Heat 1 tablespoon olive oil in a large, deep frying pan over medium heat. Add onion and cook 5 minutes, until soft. Add garlic, coriander, and cumin and cook, stirring, 30 seconds. Remove from the heat.

Put zucchini on a clean dish towel and gather up the ends. Twist over the sink to squeeze out as much liquid as possible. Return pan to the heat. Add zucchini and sweet potato and cook, stirring occasionally, 5 minutes, until vegetables are softened.

Put mixture in a food processor or blender, add chickpeas, and process to form a coarse paste.

Transfer paste to a large mixing bowl. Add haloumi and ½ cup (40 g) bread crumbs, season with salt and pepper to taste, and stir to combine well.

Shape a level ¼ cup of the mixture into a patty about 5 cm (2 in) in diameter. Repeat with remaining mixture.

Spread remaining bread crumbs on a plate. Press both sides of each patty into bread crumbs to coat lightly.

Heat 3 mm (⅛ in) oil in a large frying pan over medium heat. Cook patties in batches about 2 minutes on each side, or until golden. Transfer to a plate and keep warm while cooking remaining patties.

Serve on the rolls with avocado, tomato, lettuce, sour cream, and sweet chili sauce.

EACH SERVING (1 SLIDER) PROVIDES
227 calories, 8 g protein, 10 g fat (3 g saturated fat),
26 g carbohydrate (4 g sugars), 3 g fiber, 570 mg sodium

Three-bean chili

This dish calls for three types of beans. Aim for a combination of three different colors. We used red kidney beans, black beans, and cannellini beans.

PREPARATION. . . . . .15 MINUTES,
COOKING . . . . .30–60 MINUTES
SERVES. 6–8

1 400-g (14-oz) can or 100 g (3½ oz) dried white beans, such as cannellini or navy

1 400-g (14-oz) can or 100 g (3½ oz) dried red beans, such as such as kidney or azuki

1 400-g (14-oz) can or 100 g (3½ oz) dried black beans

2 tablespoons olive oil

4 teaspoons chili powder

1 teaspoon ground cumin

2 onions, chopped

1 clove garlic, crushed

1 green bell pepper, seeded and diced

1 teaspoon dried oregano

1 teaspoon sugar

Salt and freshly ground black pepper

½ cup (125 ml) red wine

1 410-g (15-oz) can chopped tomatoes

Sour cream, fresh cilantro leaves, lime wedges, and corn chips for serving

If using canned beans, rinse and drain. If using dried beans, soak and cook according to package directions.

Heat oil in a large, heavy-bottomed saucepan over medium-high heat. Stir in chili powder and cumin and cook 1 minute. Add onions, garlic, and bell pepper and cook, stirring frequently, 5 minutes, or until softened.

Stir in oregano, sugar, and salt and pepper to taste and cook 1 minute. Add wine and tomatoes, stir to combine, and cook 2–3 minutes.

Add cooked or canned beans and bring to a boil. Reduce heat to low and simmer, stirring occasionally, 20 minutes.

Spoon into individual serving bowls and serve with a dollop of sour cream, cilantro leaves, a lime wedge, and a bowl of corn chips on the side.

EACH SERVING PROVIDES
135 calories, 4 g protein, 7 g fat (<1 g saturated fat),
11 g carbohydrate (6 g sugars), 5 g fiber, 286 mg sodium

Alsace-style cabbage with pork

While it might seem counterintuitive to cook cabbage for more than a few minutes, this recipe's longer cooking time, as well as the addition of apples, renders a sweet and tender vegetable that is perfect with pork.

PREPARATION . . . . .25 MINUTES
COOKING . . . . .35 MINUTES
SERVES 6

½ red cabbage (800 g/1¾ lb)
30 g (1 oz) butter
1 onion, halved and thinly sliced
2 Granny Smith apples, peeled, cored, and grated
⅓ cup (80 ml) chicken stock or water
2 tablespoons red wine vinegar
1 tablespoon sugar
¼ teaspoon ground nutmeg
1 stick cinnamon or pinch of ground cinnamon
Salt and freshly ground black pepper
6 thick pork loin cutlets, loin chops, or rib chops, trimmed of fat
1 tablespoon olive oil
300 g (10 oz) steamed green beans for serving

Discard outermost layer of cabbage leaves and cut cabbage in half. Remove and discard core and any thick ribs. Finely shred the cabbage.

Melt butter in a large, heavy-bottomed saucepan over medium-low heat. Add onion and cook, stirring occasionally, 5 minutes, until soft and lightly golden.

Add cabbage, apples, stock or water, vinegar, sugar, nutmeg, and cinnamon to pan. Cover and cook 30 minutes, until tender. Season with salt and pepper to taste.

Meanwhile, rub both sides of pork with oil and season with salt and pepper.

Heat a heavy-bottomed frying pan over medium-high heat. Cook pork 3 minutes, then turn and cook the other side an additional 3 minutes. Transfer to a warm plate, loosely cover with foil, and let rest 5 minutes.

Serve pork with red cabbage and steamed green beans.

EACH SERVING PROVIDES
375 calories, 49 g protein, 12 g fat (5 g saturated fat),
14 g carbohydrate (13 g sugars), 7 g fiber, 310 mg sodium

Stir-fried pork with Thai eggplant

This stir-fry uses the round white or green eggplant common in Thai cooking (see page 46), as well as that cuisine's distinctive combination of ingredients—chili paste, fish sauce, sugar, and kaffir lime leaves. Serve with steamed jasmine rice.

2 tablespoons vegetable oil

1 clove garlic, crushed

375 g (¾ lb) pork tenderloin, cut into thin strips

1 tablespoon chili paste

1 tablespoon low-sodium vegetable stock or water

2 tablespoons fish sauce

2 teaspoons sugar

250 g (8 oz) Thai eggplant, halved
or quartered lengthwise and sliced

6 kaffir lime leaves, finely shredded

2 large red chili peppers, halved, seeded, and
thinly sliced

PREPARATION. . . . . 15 MINUTES
COOKING . . . . .7–8 MINUTES
SERVES. 4

Heat oil in a wok or large frying pan over high heat. Add garlic and fry 30 seconds, until golden.

Add pork and stir-fry until lightly browned. Add chili paste and stock or water and stir to combine. Stir in fish sauce and sugar and cook until bubbling.

Stir in eggplant, kaffir lime leaves, and chilies and cook an additional 2 minutes. Serve immediately.

EACH SERVING PROVIDES
215 calories, 22 g protein, 12 g fat (2 g saturated fat),
5 g carbohydrate (4 g sugars), 3 g fiber, 1051 mg sodium

Potato gnocchi with tomato sauce

Use only beautifully ripe tomatoes for this sauce. You can enrich it with a spoonful of tomato paste if you think it needs a little more color and depth of flavor.

PREPARATION . . . . 45 MINUTES
COOKING . . . . ABOUT 1 HOUR
SERVES 6

1 tablespoon olive oil
1 onion, finely chopped
2 cloves garlic, crushed
1 kg (2 lb) ripe tomatoes, chopped
1 teaspoon dried oregano
½ teaspoon dried red pepper flakes (optional)
Salt and freshly ground black pepper
Pinch of sugar
Fresh basil leaves and finely grated Parmesan for
   serving

Potato gnocchi

1 kg (2 lb) baking potatoes
1 egg, lightly beaten
1 cup (150 g) all-purpose flour
Salt

Heat oil in a medium saucepan over medium heat. Add onion and cook about 5 minutes, or until softened. Add garlic and cook, stirring, 30 seconds. Add tomatoes, oregano, and dried red pepper flakes, if using, and cook 20 minutes, or until pulpy. Use a handheld stick blender or a food processor or blender to puree until smooth. Season to taste with salt, pepper, and sugar. Set aside.

Meanwhile, to make the potato gnocchi, scrub potatoes and put in a large saucepan. Cover with cold water, put the lid on, and bring to a boil. Remove lid and cook about 30 minutes, or until tender when pierced with a knife. Drain, and as soon as potatoes are cool enough to handle, remove skins using a small paring knife. For best results, press potatoes through a potato ricer to get a smooth, fluffy pile of potato. Or mash with a fork or potato masher to remove any lumps, but don't overwork it or it will become gluey.

Put potato in a large mixing bowl, fold in the egg and flour, and season to taste with salt. Gather dough into a ball.

Divide dough into four portions. Using your hands, roll one portion out on a lightly floured work surface to form a long sausage shape about 2 cm (¾ in) thick. Cut into 2-cm (¾-in) pieces. Gently roll each piece into a rough oval shape and press gently with the tines of a fork to create ridges. Repeat with remaining dough.

Bring a large saucepan of water to a boil. Add a quarter of the gnocchi and cook 2–3 minutes, or until the dough rises to the surface and floats. Lift out with a slotted spoon and transfer to a baking sheet. Keep warm while cooking remaining gnocchi.

Reheat the tomato sauce. Divide gnocchi among four bowls, spoon the sauce over the gnocchi and sprinkle with basil and Parmesan.

TIP
Make sure you don't knead the dough or overhandle it.
A light touch means light gnocchi.

EACH SERVING PROVIDES
259 calories, 10 g protein, 5 g fat (<1 g saturated fat),
44 g carbohydrate (4 g sugars), 7 g fiber, 229 mg sodium

Creole-style gumbo

Gumbo, a stew that originated in Louisiana, draws influences from French cuisine as well as Native American, West African, and Spanish cooking. Okra contains a sticky gum that blends into the sauce and helps thicken it.

PREPARATION. . . . . .25 MINUTES
COOKING . . . . ABOUT 40 MINUTES
SERVES. 6

50 g (1¾ oz) butter

2 tablespoons all-purpose flour

1 yellow onion, finely chopped

1 large green bell pepper, chopped

3 stalks celery, chopped

3 cloves garlic, crushed

400 g (14 oz) ripe tomatoes, chopped

200 g (7 oz) okra

2 cups (500 ml) low-sodium chicken or fish stock

1½ tablespoons Creole seasoning (see tip below)

1.2 kg (2½ lb) uncooked shrimp, peeled and deveined

Steamed white rice for serving

Fresh flat-leaf parsley leaves and sliced scallions for garnish (optional)

Combine 30 g (1 oz) butter and flour in a small, heavy-bottomed saucepan. Cook, stirring, over medium-low heat 5 minutes, until the mixture turns a rich golden brown color. Remove from heat and set aside.

Heat remaining butter in a large heavy-bottomed saucepan. Add onion, bell pepper, and celery and cook over medium-low heat 10 minutes, until very soft and just lightly golden. Stir in garlic and cook 1 minute. Add tomatoes and cook, stirring occasionally, an additional 5 minutes, until pulpy. Stir in the reserved roux (the butter and flour mixture).

Trim tops from okra and cut horizontally into even slices about 6 mm (¼ in) thick. Add to pan with stock and Creole seasoning. Cover and bring to a simmer over medium-low heat, then simmer 20 minutes.

Add shrimp, return to a simmer, and cook 3 minutes, until shrimp change color and are cooked through—don't overcook them.

Serve the gumbo on rice and sprinkle with parsley and scallions, if desired.

TIP
If you can't buy a ready-made Creole seasoning blend, make it yourself. Mix 2 teaspoons paprika, 1 teaspoon garlic powder, ½ teaspoon each salt, freshly ground black pepper, onion powder, and cayenne pepper, and ¼ teaspoon each dried oregano, thyme, and basil.

EACH SERVING PROVIDES
329 calories, 44 g protein, 11 g fat (5 g saturated fat), 12 g carbohydrate (4 g sugars), 3 g fiber, 737 mg sodium

Leek and chicken pies

This is a winning combination—the sweetness and subtlety of leeks paired with chicken. Serve the pies with mashed or baked potatoes and a leafy green salad.

PREPARATION . . . . . 30 MINUTES, PLUS COOLING TIME
COOKING . . . . 40 MINUTES
SERVES 6

2 leeks
1 tablespoon olive oil
1 kg (1 lb) boneless, skinless chicken thighs,
    cut into bite-size pieces
45 g (1½ oz) butter, plus extra for greasing
1½ tablespoons all-purpose flour
1½ cups (375 ml) milk
Salt and freshly ground black pepper
1 teaspoon fresh thyme leaves
6 sheets pâte brisée, thawed
1 egg, lightly beaten

Trim ends from leeks, then cut off dark green tops, leaving white and pale green part. Halve lengthwise and rinse out any grit under cold running water. Pat dry with paper towels. Cut into 5-mm (¼-in) slices.

Heat oil in a large, nonstick frying pan over medium-high heat. Cook chicken in four batches, about 4–5 minutes each batch, stirring occasionally, until well browned and cooked through. Transfer to a bowl and set aside.

Reduce heat to medium and add leek to pan. Cook 2 minutes, until softened. Transfer to the bowl with the chicken.

Melt butter in the same pan, then sprinkle with flour. Cook, stirring, 1 minute. Add milk a little at a time, stirring between each addition until smooth and well combined. Add the sauce to chicken and leeks and stir to combine. Season with salt and pepper to taste, and stir in thyme. Cool slightly, stirring often to release the heat. Refrigerate until just cold.

Preheat oven to 190°C (370°F) and lightly grease six 1-cup (250-ml) pie pans. Cut a 12-cm (5-in) round from 1 sheet of pastry as close to one corner as possible. Cut a 16-cm (6½-in) round from the leftover pastry, using a small piece of scrap pastry to patch the slight gap in the larger piece. Repeat with remaining pastry sheets.

Line each pie dish with one of the larger rounds of pastry. Fill with chicken mixture. Top each with a smaller pastry round, crimping or pressing the edges together with a fork to seal. Brush lightly with egg. Using a fork, prick a few steam holes in the top.

Bake 25 minutes, until tops of pies are golden brown.

EACH SERVING PROVIDES
1100 calories, 45 g protein, 67 g fat (33 g saturated fat),
80 g carbohydrate (6 g sugars), 4 g fiber, 1007 mg sodium

Chili crab

This spicy crab stir-fry is made with fresh chilies, ginger, and a tangy sauce. Serve with steamed rice and a crisp salad.

PREPARATION . . . . 10 MINUTES
COOKING . . . . 15 MINUTES
SERVES 4

4 300-g (10-oz) uncooked crabs, such as blue crabs, Dungeness crabs, or rock crabs
2 teaspoons peanut oil
2 cloves garlic, crushed
2 small red chili peppers, seeded and finely chopped
2 teaspoons finely grated fresh ginger
4 scallions, thinly sliced
½ cup (15 g) fresh cilantro leaves, chopped
1 teaspoon salt (optional)
1 long red chili pepper, seeded and thinly sliced, for garnish

Chili sauce
½ cup (125 ml) low-sodium fish, chicken, or vegetable stock
¼ cup (60 ml) ketchup
2 tablespoons sweet chili sauce
2 tablespoons hoisin sauce
1 tablespoon fish sauce
¼ cup (60 ml) Chinese rice wine
2 teaspoons sugar

Lift the flap under the body of each crab with your thumb, then twist it off and discard it. On the side opposite the eyes, insert your fingers and thumb between the top and bottom shells. Pull off the top shell and discard. Remove and discard the spongy, finger-like white gills. Cut the body, with legs and claws still attached, into quarters.

To make the chili sauce, combine stock, ketchup, sweet chili sauce, hoisin sauce, fish sauce, rice wine, and sugar in a bowl.

Heat oil in a large wok or frying pan over medium-high heat. Stir-fry crabs, tossing occasionally to cook evenly, 6–7 minutes. Add garlic, chopped chilies, and ginger. Stir-fry 1 minute, until fragrant. Add chili sauce and stir-fry 3–4 minutes, until sauce boils and thickens slightly and crabmeat is white. Stir in three-quarters of scallions and cilantro. Taste and add salt, if desired.

Garnish with remaining scallions, cilantro, and sliced chili. Serve.

EACH SERVING PROVIDES
183 calories, 15 g protein, 4 g fat (<1 g saturated fat),
18 g carbohydrate (14 g sugars), 2 g fiber, 1165 mg sodium

Vietnamese rice paper rolls

Filled with shrimp, noodles, vegetables, and mint, these rice paper rolls are evocative of the flavors of Vietnamese cooking. They are served cold, usually accompanied by the traditional nuoc cham dipping sauce. They can be prepared in advance, making them a good option for entertaining.

75 g (2½ oz) rice vermicelli

1 tablespoon low-sodium soy sauce

½ teaspoon sesame oil

16 15-cm (6-in) round rice paper wrappers

1 cup (30 g) fresh mint or cilantro leaves

8 cooked jumbo shrimp, peeled, deveined, and halved lengthwise

¼ iceberg lettuce, finely shredded

1 small carrot, grated

1 small Lebanese or other small cucumber, seeded and cut into thin matchsticks

2 cups (180 g) bean sprouts, trimmed

8 scallions, green part only, halved

PREPARATION. .20 MINUTES
SERVES. . . . . 4 (MAKES 16 ROLLS)

Soak noodles according to package instructions. Drain well and toss in a large bowl with soy sauce and sesame oil.

Pour warm water into a separate shallow bowl. Working with 1 rice paper wrapper at a time, dip it into water 20–30 seconds, or until it softens, then drain on paper towels. Lay on a clean work surface. Put 1–2 mint leaves followed by some noodles in the lower third of the rice paper. Top with a shrimp half, some lettuce, carrot, cucumber, bean sprouts, and 1 scallion piece. Fold over the bottom end of the wrapper, then fold over the two sides to cover the filling. Neatly roll up to enclose the filling and make a log.

Repeat with remaining wrappers, noodles, and vegetables to make 16 rolls. Serve.

TIP

To make the traditional accompaniment, nuoc cham dipping sauce, combine ¼ cup (60 ml) lime juice, ¼ cup (60 ml) fish sauce, 2 tablespoons sugar, 1 red Thai chilli, seeded and finely chopped, 1 clove garlic, crushed, and ¼ cup (60 ml) water in a medium bowl. Stir well, then set aside until ready to serve.

EACH SERVING PROVIDES
327 calories, 18 g protein, 2 g fat (<1 g saturated fat), 60 g carbohydrate (5 g sugars), 4 g fiber, 506 mg sodium

Roast lamb with baby spring vegetables

This very simple dish is the epitome of spring. Vary the vegetables to suit what is available—beans could be replaced with peas, and pattypan squash could be replaced with zucchini. If you can't get slender asparagus, cut thick spears in half lengthwise.

PREPARATION. 30 MINUTES,
PLUS MARINATING TIME
COOKING . . . . 15 MINUTES
SERVES. 4

2 tablespoons olive oil

2 cloves garlic, crushed

2 teaspoons finely grated lemon zest

4 racks of lamb (about 3–4 ribs and 175 g/6 oz each), Frenched

Salt and freshly ground black pepper

400 g (14 oz) new potatoes (about 50 g/ 1¾ oz each), scrubbed and quartered

1 bunch baby carrots (250 g/8 oz)

150 g (5 oz) baby green beans, trimmed

6 pattypan squash (175 g/6 oz each), quartered

1 bunch slender asparagus spears (125 g/4 oz), trimmed

30 g (1 oz) butter, at room temperature

1 tablespoon finely shredded fresh mint

Combine oil, garlic, and lemon zest in a shallow glass or ceramic baking dish. Add lamb and turn to coat both sides in the mixture, then marinate in the refrigerator 30 minutes or up to 4 hours.

Preheat oven to 200°C (400°F).

Heat a large, heavy-bottomed frying pan over high heat. Brown lamb, then transfer to a baking sheet. Season with salt and pepper. Roast in the oven 15 minutes for medium rare. Set aside on a warm plate, covered loosely with foil, to rest 5 minutes.

While lamb is cooking, put potatoes in a medium saucepan and cover with cold water. Cover with a lid and bring to a boil. Remove lid and cook 10 minutes, or until tender. Drain.

At the same time, bring a large saucepan of water to a boil. Cut leafy tops from carrots, leaving about 1 cm (½ in) of green stem, and peel neatly. Add carrots to boiling water and cook 2 minutes, then add beans and cook an additional minute. Add squash and asparagus and cook an additional 2 minutes. Drain vegetables well, then return to the pan. Add drained potatoes and toss with butter and mint. Season with salt and pepper to taste.

Slice the lamb into individual chops and serve with the vegetables.

EACH SERVING PROVIDES
405 calories, 27 g protein, 26 g fat (9 g saturated fat),
20 g carbohydrate (6 g sugars), 7 g fiber, 308 mg sodium

Eggplant and lamb moussaka

This Greek favorite is an excellent example of a perfect pairing—eggplant and lamb. Beef could be substituted for lamb if preferred. Kefalotyri is a hard, salty Greek cheese, for which Parmesan can be substituted if necessary.

PREPARATION. . . . . 30 MINUTES
COOKING . . . . .1 HOUR 45 MINUTES
SERVES. 6

4 large eggplants (about 350 g/12 oz each)
½ cup (125 ml) olive oil
1 onion, finely chopped
2 cloves garlic, crushed
½ teaspoon ground allspice
½ teaspoon ground cinnamon
750 g (1½ lb) ground lamb
2 tablespoons tomato paste
1 410-g (15-oz) can chopped tomatoes
½ cup (125 ml) low-sodium beef stock
1 teaspoon dried oregano
Salt and freshly ground black pepper

Topping
2½ cups (625 ml) milk
1 bay leaf
50 g (1¾ oz) butter
⅓ cup (50 g) all-purpose flour
½ cup (80 g) grated kefalotyri cheese
2 eggs, lightly beaten

Cut eggplant into 1-cm (½-in) slices. Heat 2 tablespoons oil in a large, deep frying pan over medium heat and cook eggplant in batches about 2 minutes on one side. Brush lightly with oil before turning to cook on the other side, about 2 minutes. Add more oil to the pan as needed. Set aside on paper towels.

Heat remaining oil in pan over medium heat and add onion. Cook, stirring occasionally, 5 minutes, until soft and lightly golden. Add garlic, allspice, and cinnamon and cook, stirring, 30 seconds. Add lamb and cook, breaking up any lumps with a wooden spoon, about 5 minutes, or until browned.

Stir in tomato paste, tomatoes, stock, and oregano and bring to a simmer. Reduce heat slightly and cook, stirring occasionally, 30 minutes, or until liquid has reduced and thickened. Season with salt and pepper to taste and set aside.

Preheat oven to 180°C (350°F). To make the topping, combine milk and bay leaf in a small saucepan and bring to a simmer. Turn off heat and let stand 5 minutes for the flavor to infuse.

Meanwhile, melt butter in another saucepan over medium heat. Add flour and cook, stirring, 1 minute. Add milk gradually, stirring between each addition until smooth. When all milk has been added, bring to a simmer and cook 2 minutes. Add ⅓ cup (60 g) kefalotyri and stir until melted. Set aside to cool slightly, stirring occasionally to release the heat. Add eggs and stir to combine well.

To assemble, lightly grease a 10-cup (2.5-liter), 20 x 26-cm (8 x 10½-in) ovenproof baking dish. Arrange a third of the eggplant in a layer in the base of the dish. Spread half the meat mixture over it, then make another layer of eggplant. Top with remaining meat mixture, then remaining eggplant. Spread topping over final eggplant layer and sprinkle with remaining kefalotyri.

Bake 45 minutes, or until golden brown. Let stand 15 minutes before serving.

EACH SERVING PROVIDES
658 calories, 41 g protein, 46 g fat (17 g saturated fat),
22 g carbohydrate (15 g sugars), 7 g fiber, 695 mg sodium

Pommes frites and steak

Steak frites is a French bistro mainstay. Starchy rather than waxy potatoes are best suited to making french fries. Cooking them twice ensures a crispy outside and a light, fluffy center.

PREPARATION. . . . . . 30 MINUTES, PLUS COOLING TIME
COOKING . . . . 25–35 MINUTES
SERVES. 4

Vegetable oil for deep-frying
1 kg (2 lb) baking potatoes, peeled and
    cut lengthwise into 1.5-cm (½-in) spears
4 150-g (5-oz) sirloin steaks, about 2 cm
    (¾ in) thick
1 tablespoon olive oil
½ cup (125 ml) white wine
½ cup (125 ml) low-sodium beef stock
1 teaspoon cracked black peppercorns
⅓ cup (80 ml) cream
Steamed peas or green beans or lightly dressed
    green salad for serving

Pour in enough vegetable oil to half-fill a large, heavy-bottomed saucepan or deep fryer. Heat over medium heat until a small cube of bread sizzles constantly when dropped in the oil.

Meanwhile, spread out potato spears on a clean dish towel and pat to absorb excess moisture. Working in three or four batches, lower chips into oil and cook about 5 minutes, until just starting to take on some color. Lift out with a wire scoop or slotted spoon, allow excess oil to drain back into the pan, and transfer potatoes to paper towels to drain. Repeat with remaining potatoes. Leave to cool and dry out—they can be refrigerated, uncovered, for up to 4 hours.

When ready to serve, reheat oil for deep-frying over medium-high heat. Cook chips in batches about 4 minutes, or until crisp and golden brown. Drain on paper towels and season with salt.

Meanwhile, heat a large, heavy-bottomed frying pan over medium-high heat. Brush steaks with olive oil and cook 2 minutes on each side for medium rare. Set aside on a warm plate, covered loosely with foil, to rest 5 minutes.

Add wine and stock to frying pan, stirring and scraping the bottom of the pan. Bring to a boil and cook about 2 minutes, or until reduced by half. Reduce heat to medium and stir in pepper and cream. Simmer about 2 minutes, until thickened slightly. Drizzle sauce over steak and serve with potatoes and peas, green beans, or a salad.

TIPS
For best results, use a frying or candy thermometer (available from most cookware shops). Do the first stage of cooking with the oil at about 130°C (265°F), then the second stage of cooking at 180°C (350°F). Be sure not to overcrowd the pan.

If you want to serve the potatoes all at once, keep cooked fries warm in a 160°C (320°F) oven. Spread in a single layer on a baking sheet.

EACH SERVING PROVIDES
598 calories, 38 g protein, 32 g fat (12 g saturated fat), 34 g carbohydrate (2 g sugars), 4 g fiber, 221 mg sodium

Steamed fish with ginger and sprouts

This traditional Chinese way of serving a large whole fish is rich in antioxidants from the ginger and scallions. Serve the fish with steamed jasmine rice and a dish of stir-fried vegetables, with extra shredded scallions on the side.

PREPARATION. . . . . 10 MINUTES
COOKING . . . . 20 MINUTES
SERVES. 4

1 large whole fish (about 1 kg/2 lb),
    such as snapper, bream, mackerel, or cod,
    cleaned at the fish market
½ cup (45 g) bean sprouts, trimmed
4 scallions, finely shredded
5-cm (2-in) piece fresh ginger, peeled and finely
    shredded
Juice of 1 lemon
Freshly ground black pepper
⅓ cup (80 ml) low-sodium soy sauce
1 tablespoon sesame oil

Rinse fish and pat dry with paper towel. With a sharp knife, make three or four diagonal cuts down to the bone on each side of fish.

Fill a large wok or saucepan with about 2 inches of water. Bring to a boil, then reduce heat so that water is at a simmer. Line a large bamboo or metal steamer with a circle of parchment paper. Snip paper in a few places to allow steam to come through.

Put fish on parchment paper in the steamer. Scatter bean sprouts, scallions, and ginger over fish. Drizzle with lemon juice and season with pepper.

Carefully place steamer above simmering water—the water should not touch the base of the steamer. Cover and steam about 20 minutes, until fish is just cooked.

Meanwhile, put soy sauce and sesame oil in a small bowl and whisk to combine. Transfer fish to a warmed serving plate, pour the soy mixture over it, and serve.

TIPS
You could make this recipe with 4 evenly sized fish fillets. Reduce the steaming time to about 10 minutes, depending on the thickness of the fillets—check often to avoid overcooking the fish.

Shredding is a technique in which the food is cut into very thin, matchstick-like shreds. You first cut the food into slices, then stack a few slices on top of each other and cut them lengthwise into very fine strips. This technique is often used for preparing ginger.

EACH SERVING PROVIDES
261 calories, 43 g protein, 8 g fat (2 g saturated fat), 4 g carbohydrate (2 g sugars), <1 g fiber, 909 mg sodium

Red velvet cupcakes

Red velvet cakes are often loaded with food coloring to give a reddish hue to the chocolate batter. In this case, fresh beets do the trick.

PREPARATION. .15 MINUTES, PLUS COOLING TIME
COOKING . . . . .1 HOUR 20 MINUTES
MAKES 24

5 beets (500 g/1 lb each)
½ cup (125 ml) buttermilk
175 g (6 oz) butter, at room temperature
1 cup (200 g) firmly packed brown sugar
3 eggs
1 teaspoon vanilla extract
2 cups (300 g) self-rising flour
⅓ cup (40 g) unsweetened cocoa powder
1 teaspoon baking soda
Sugared rose petals for garnish

Cream cheese frosting
250 g (8 oz) cream cheese, at room temperature
1½ cups (185 g) confectioners' sugar, sifted
1 teaspoon lemon juice

Preheat oven to 200°C (400°F). Trim tops from beets and wash the skins. Securely wrap each beet in foil, put on a baking sheet, and cook 1 hour, or until very tender. (To test, unwrap and pierce with a small sharp knife). When cooked, unwrap beets and let stand until cool enough to handle. Peel off skin. Roughly chop flesh, then puree with buttermilk in a food processor or blender until smooth.

Reduce oven temperature to 180°C (350°F). Line two standard-sized 12-muffin pans with paper liners.

Put butter and brown sugar in a medium bowl and beat with an electric mixer 5–8 minutes, or until pale and creamy. Add eggs one at time, beating well after each addition. Add vanilla extract and beat to combine.

Sift together flour, cocoa powder, and baking soda into a large mixing bowl, then make a well in the center. Add butter mixture and beet puree. Fold together until just combined—do not beat. Spoon into paper liners.

Bake cupcakes 20 minutes, or until they spring back when lightly touched in the center. Transfer to a wire rack and cool.

To make the frosting, put cream cheese in a medium bowl and beat with an electric mixer until smooth. Add confectioners' sugar a little at a time and beat until smooth, then beat in lemon juice.

Spread frosting over cooled cupcakes and top each with a sugared rose petal.

TIP
Try to choose similar-sized beets so they take the same time to cook. Wear gloves when peeling off skin, as the juice will stain.

EACH SERVING (1 CUPCAKE) PROVIDES
164 calories, 4 g protein, 5 g fat (3 g saturated fat),
27 g carbohydrate (18 g sugars), 1 g fiber, 182 mg sodium

Surprise chocolate mousse

Avocado in a dessert may be surprising, but it makes a dairy-free version of chocolate mousse that contains only good fats and very little added sugar. It tastes rich and chocolaty, yet is packed with antioxidants.

PREPARATION. . . . . 15 MINUTES, PLUS 10 MINUTES
SOAKING TIME AND 1 HOUR CHILLING TIME
SERVES. 4

¾ cup (135 g) pitted dates
1 large ripe avocado, roughly chopped
1 tablespoon maple syrup
⅓ cup (40 g) unsweetened cocoa powder
1 teaspoon vanilla extract
Fresh mint leaves for garnish

Put dates in a heatproof bowl. Cover with boiling water and soak 10 minutes, or until softened. Drain, reserving soaking liquid.

Put dates in a food processor or blender and process until smooth. Add avocado and process until smooth. Add maple syrup, cocoa powder, and vanilla extract and process until well combined, adding about 2 tablespoons of the reserved soaking liquid to achieve the desired consistency.

Spoon mousse into four ½-cup (125-ml) dessert glasses. Refrigerate 1 hour, or until chilled. Serve garnished with mint leaves.

TIP
Use good-quality cocoa powder to ensure that the mousse has a rich chocolate taste.

EACH SERVING PROVIDES
269 calories, 4 g protein, 15 g fat (4 g saturated fat),
30 g carbohydrate (27 g sugars), 5 g fiber, 33 mg sodium

Trio of melon sorbets

You will need a 1-kg (2-lb) piece of watermelon and a whole cantaloupe and honeydew, each weighing approximately 1.2 kg (2¼ lb), to make the three sorbets in this recipe.

1½ cups (345 g) superfine sugar

5 cups (700 g) coarsely chopped seedless watermelon

5 cups (700 g) coarsely chopped cantaloupe

5 cups (700 g) coarsely chopped honeydew melon

3 egg whites

PREPARATION. . . . . . .15 MINUTES, PLUS COOLING TIME
AND 6 HOURS CHILLING TIME

SERVES. 8

Put 1½ cups (375 ml) water and sugar in a medium saucepan and stir over medium heat, without boiling, until sugar dissolves. Bring to a boil. Reduce heat to low and simmer, without stirring, 10–12 minutes, or until slightly thickened but not colored. Remove sugar syrup from heat and cool to room temperature.

Meanwhile, process watermelon in a food processor or blender until smooth, then strain into a shallow stainless-steel bowl. Clean the food processor and repeat this process with the cantaloupe, then the honeydew, straining each fruit into a separate bowl. Pour one-third of the cooled sugar syrup into each bowl and stir to combine.

Cover each bowl with foil and freeze 3 hours, or until fruit mixture is almost set.

Chop each fruit mixture coarsely with a knife. Put the watermelon mixture and 1 egg white in the clean food processor and process until smooth. Return to its bowl. Clean the food processor and repeat this process with the cantaloupe mixture, then the honeydew, returning each mixture to its original bowl. Cover and freeze an additional 3 hours, or until firm.

Remove from freezer and let stand at room temperature 15 minutes before serving.

EACH SERVING PROVIDES
247 calories, 3 g protein, <1 g fat (0 g saturated fat),
57 g carbohydrate (57 g sugars), 2 g fiber, 68 mg sodium

Brazilian carrot cake with chocolate glaze

The intense chocolaty glaze on this cake really makes it something special.

PREPARATION. . . . . . 25 MINUTES, PLUS COOLING TIME
COOKING . . . . 1 HOUR
SERVES. 8–10

Butter for greasing
2 cups (300 g) all-purpose flour
1 tablespoon baking powder
1½ cups (345 g) superfine sugar
2 cups (250 g) grated carrot (about 3 carrots)
¾ cup (180 ml) vegetable oil
3 eggs
1 teaspoon vanilla extract

Glaze
1 tablespoon (20 g) butter
⅓ cup (80 g) superfine sugar
⅓ cup (40 g) unsweetened cocoa powder
¼ cup (60 ml) milk

Preheat oven to 180°C (350°F). Lightly grease a 22-cm (8½-in) round cake pan and line the base of the pan with parchment paper.

Sift flour and baking powder into a large mixing bowl. Stir in sugar and make a well in the center.

Process carrot, oil, eggs, and vanilla extract in a food processor or blender until smooth. Pour into the dry ingredients in the mixing bowl and fold together lightly until just combined. Pour mixture into the prepared pan.

Bake 40 minutes. Cover with foil and bake an additional 20 minutes, or until the cake springs back when lightly touched. Cool in the pan 5 minutes before turning out onto a wire rack to cool completely.

To make the glaze, combine butter, sugar, cocoa powder, and milk in a small saucepan. Stir over low heat until melted and smooth. Increase heat to medium, bring to a boil, and cook 2 minutes, until slightly thickened. Cool 10 minutes, stirring occasionally to release the heat. Spread glaze over the cooled cake.

EACH SERVING PROVIDES
600 calories, 8 g protein, 27 g fat (6 g saturated fat),
82 g carbohydrate (53 g sugars), 3 g fiber, 108 mg sodium

Cassava cake

If you can't find fresh cassava, look for frozen cassava in Asian supermarkets. If it isn't already grated, thaw completely, then use the grater attachment on a food processor for best results.

PREPARATION. . . . . 30 MINUTES, PLUS COOLING
COOKING . . . . 50 MINUTES
SERVES. . . . . 8–10 (MAKES 15-16 SQUARES)

Butter for greasing
1 kg (2 lb) grated fresh or frozen cassava,
    thawed if frozen
1 cup (230 g) superfine sugar
½ cup (60 g) grated mild Cheddar cheese
400 ml (14 fl oz) canned coconut milk
¾ cup (180 ml) evaporated milk
½ cup (125 ml) sweetened condensed milk
2 eggs
60 g (2 oz) butter, melted
1 cup (230 g) firmly packed brown sugar
Fresh or toasted coconut shavings for garnish

Preheat oven to 180°C (350°F). Grease a 30 x 23 x 4.5-cm (13 x 9 x 2-in) baking pan.

Put cassava, sugar, and Cheddar in a large mixing bowl. Whisk together coconut milk, evaporated milk, condensed milk, and eggs in a separate bowl. Pour into the large mixing bowl, add melted butter, and stir until evenly combined. Pour mixture into prepared pan and smooth the surface.

Bake 45 minutes, until cake feels firm when gently touched in the center. Remove from oven and cool.

Meanwhile, put 1 cup (250 ml) water and the brown sugar in a small saucepan over low heat and stir until sugar dissolves. Increase heat to high and bring to a boil, then cook 4–5 minutes, or until thick and syrupy. Set aside to cool.

Pour the syrup over the cake and spread evenly over the top. Garnish with coconut shavings and cut into squares to serve.

TIP
To prepare coconut shavings, pierce the small "eyes" of a whole fresh coconut with a skewer. Reserve any coconut water that drains out for another use. Put coconut on a baking sheet and bake in an oven preheated to 200°C (400°F) 20 minutes. Cool slightly, then holding coconut upright in one hand, use a hammer to tap around the shell's "equator," or middle. It should crack apart neatly. Slide a nonserrated knife between flesh and shell to pry out large pieces of flesh. Shave with a vegetable peeler. To toast the shavings, spread on a baking sheet and bake in an oven preheated to 160°C (320°F) about 5 minutes—watching carefully—until golden.

EACH SERVING PROVIDES
708 calories, 9 g protein, 25 g fat (18 g saturated fat),
110 g carbohydrate (74 g sugars), 7 g fiber, 190 mg sodium

Spicy sweet potato cheesecake

This cheesecake combines foods native to the Americas, such as maple syrup, pecans, and sweet potato, for a spicy autumn dessert.

PREPARATION. . . . . 10 MINUTES, PLUS
2 HOURS CHILLING TIME
COOKING . . . . 1 HOUR 25 MINUTES
SERVES. 10–12

EACH SERVING PROVIDES
578 calories, 9 g protein, 39 g fat (11 g saturated fat),
50 g carbohydrate (33 g sugars), 5 g fiber, 186 mg sodium

1 large sweet potato (750 g/1½ lb), peeled and cut into 2-cm (¾-in) chunks
¼ cup (60 ml) canola oil
2 teaspoons ground cinnamon
1 teaspoon ground nutmeg
1 teaspoon ground ginger
⅔ cup (140 g) firmly packed brown sugar
2 cups (240 g) roughly chopped pecans
½ cup (75 g) all-purpose white or whole-wheat flour
½ cup (60 g) rolled oats
¼ cup (45 g) crystallized ginger
75 g (2½ oz) chilled butter, diced
250 g (8 oz) cream cheese, at room temperature
2 eggs
½ cup (125 ml) maple syrup

Preheat oven to 180°C (350°F). Line a baking sheet and a 23-cm (9-in) springform cake pan with parchment paper.

Toss sweet potato and oil in a large bowl to coat. Add cinnamon, nutmeg, and ground ginger and toss to coat. Spread on prepared baking sheet. Bake 10–15 minutes, or until soft. Cool.

In the same bowl, combine ⅓ cup (70 g) sugar and 1½ cups (180 g) pecans. Add a little oil, if needed, to moisten. Set aside.

In a food processor or blender, process remaining sugar, pecans, flour, oats, and crystallized ginger until finely ground. Add butter and process until just combined. Press mixture firmly into springform pan to cover base and 2 cm (¾ in) up the sides. Bake 10 minutes.

Meanwhile, wipe out food processor. Add sweet potato mixture and cream cheese and puree until smooth. Add eggs and maple syrup and blend until well combined. Pour over base and bake 30 minutes. Scatter pecan sugar mixture over cheesecake, reduce oven to 150°C (300°F), and bake an additional 30 minutes, or until set. Refrigerate at least 2 hours.

Zucchini bread

Zucchini has little flavor but helps to keep this bread moist. You can double or triple the recipe and freeze the extra loaves.

Butter for greasing

1 cup (120 g) chopped pecans

1¾ cups (260 g) all-purpose flour, sifted

1½ teaspoons baking powder

½ teaspoon salt

½ teaspoon baking soda

1 teaspoon ground cinnamon

125 g (4 oz) butter, at room temperature

¾ cup (165 g) sugar

2 eggs

1½ cups (200 g) grated zucchini, squeezed to remove excess moisture

⅓ cup (80 ml) buttermilk or plain yogurt

¼ teaspoon almond extract (optional)

PREPARATION. . . . . . 20 MINUTES, PLUS COOLING TIME
COOKING . . . . 1 HOUR 10 MINUTES
SERVES. . . . . 8–10 (MAKES 1 LOAF)

Preheat oven to 180°C (350°F). Lightly grease a 23 x 12.5-cm (9 x 5-in) loaf pan and line with parchment paper.

Spread pecans on a baking sheet and toast in oven about 7 minutes, until lightly browned. Cool nuts, then roughly chop and set aside.

Meanwhile, sift together flour, baking powder, salt, baking soda, and cinnamon into a large mixing bowl. Stir to combine.

Put butter in a large bowl and beat with an electric mixer until light and creamy. Gradually add sugar and beat well. Add eggs, one at a time, beating well after each addition. Add flour mixture a little at a time, beating only just enough to incorporate it— the batter should not be smooth.

Put zucchini, buttermilk, and almond extract, if using, in a small bowl and stir to combine. Add to cake batter with reserved pecans and fold to combine.

Spoon mixture into prepared loaf pan. Bake about 1 hour, until a skewer inserted in the center comes out clean. Cool 10 minutes in the pan before carefully turning out onto a wire rack to cool completely. Cut into slices to serve.

EACH SERVING PROVIDES
446 calories, 8 g protein, 27 g fat (10 g saturated fat),
46 g carbohydrate (22 g sugars), 3 g fiber, 374 mg sodium

Preserving vegetables

Preserving vegetables is much easier than it seems. To sterilize jars and lids, wash thoroughly and dry in a low oven, or run through the dishwasher on a high temperature setting. To prevent shattering, always make sure jars are hot before adding a hot mixture. Seal jars tightly, and though it might seem obvious, don't forget to label and date them. Keep in a cool, dark pantry for a couple of weeks for the flavors to develop, and always refrigerate once opened.

Onion jam

Halve 2 kg (4 lb) red onions lengthwise, then slice thinly. Heat 2 tablespoons olive oil in a large, deep, wide saucepan. Add onions and cook over medium heat, stirring often, about 20 minutes, until soft. Add 2 cups (440 g) sugar and 2 cups (500 ml) white vinegar and stir until dissolved. Bring to a simmer and cook 1 hour, stirring frequently, until liquid has evaporated and mixture is sticky. Season with salt and freshly ground black pepper. Transfer to sterilized jars and seal. Keep for up to 1 month once opened. **Makes 4 cups**

FROM LEFT: Broiled red bell pepper, onion jam, and pickled red cabbage.

Spicy tomato jam

Roughly chop 1 kg (2 lb) ripe tomatoes. Peel, core, and coarsely grate 2 green apples. Put tomatoes, apples, 1 teaspoon finely grated fresh ginger, and 1 teaspoon chopped red chili pepper in a large saucepan. Bring to a boil, then reduce heat slightly and simmer 10 minutes, until pulpy. Add 1 cup (250 ml) white vinegar and 1 cup (220 g) sugar and stir to dissolve. Return to a simmer and cook 45 minutes, until thick. Stir mixture occasionally, more often closer to the end of cooking time. Transfer to sterilized jars and seal. Keep for up to 1 month once opened. **Makes 2 cups**

Pickled red cabbage

Toss 500 g (1 lb) finely shredded red cabbage with ¼ cup (50 g) salt in a large bowl to combine. Cover and refrigerate overnight. Rinse cabbage well in a colander, then spread out on a clean dish towel and pat dry. Combine 2 cups (500 ml) white vinegar, 1 cinnamon stick, 4 whole allspice, 1 teaspoon whole cloves, and 2 teaspoons dill seeds in a stainless steel or enamel saucepan. Bring to a boil, stirring to dissolve sugar, then set aside to cool and allow flavors to infuse. Pack cabbage into sterilized jars and pour cooled, strained vinegar into jars to cover completely. Seal. Use within 2 months. **Makes 3 cups**

Pickled onions

Dissolve ¼ cup (50 g) salt in 4 cups (1 liter) water in a glass or ceramic bowl. Peel 1 kg (2 lb) pearl onions and add to bowl. Let stand overnight. Rinse and dry well. Combine 3¼ cups (810 ml) white vinegar, ½ cup (115 g) superfine sugar, 2 teaspoons black peppercorns, 2 teaspoons mustard seeds, and 2 bay leaves in a stainless steel or enamel saucepan. Bring to a boil, stirring to dissolve sugar, then set aside to cool and allow flavors to infuse. Pack onions into sterilized jars and pour cooled, strained vinegar into jars to cover completely. Seal. Use within 2 months. **Makes 6 cups**

Pickled vegetables

Combine 4 cups mixed vegetables (washed, peeled, or prepared as necessary and cut into bite-size pieces) in a large bowl. Carrots, pickling cucumbers, bell peppers, fennel, cauliflower, and onions are good choices. Sprinkle with ¼ cup (50 g) salt and toss to combine. Cover and refrigerate overnight. Rinse and dry well. Combine 3 cups (750 ml) white wine vinegar, ⅓ cup (75 g) sugar, 1 teaspoon coriander seeds, 1 teaspoon black peppercorns, 6 whole cloves, and ½ teaspoon dried red pepper flakes in a stainless steel or enamel saucepan. Bring to a boil, stirring to dissolve sugar, then set aside to cool and allow flavors to infuse. Pack vegetables into sterilized jars and pour cooled, strained vinegar into jars to cover completely. Seal. Use within 2 months. **Makes 4 cups**

Broiled red bell peppers

Preheat broiler and line a large baking sheet with foil. Cut 6 large red bell peppers into flat pieces, arrange on the sheet, and broil until skin is black and blistered. Set aside, covered loosely with foil, to cool. Peel off skin and cut flesh into pieces. Put 1 cup (250 ml) white wine vinegar, ¼ cup (55 g) sugar, and 2 teaspoons salt in a small saucepan and stir over medium heat to dissolve sugar. Pack peppers into sterilized jars. Bring vinegar to a boil, then pour into jars to cover. Seal. Use within 2 months. **Makes 3 cups**

Preserving vegetables

continued

Mixed vegetable relish (ajvar)

Preheat oven to 200°C (400°F). Put 8 large red bell peppers and 1 eggplant on 2 baking sheets. Roast 45 minutes, until soft and red pepper skin is black. Set aside, covered loosely with foil, to cool. Peel off pepper skins and discard seeds, cores, and membrane. Halve eggplant lengthwise and scoop out flesh. Put red pepper and eggplant flesh, 2 garlic cloves, and 2 tablespoons red wine vinegar in a food processor or blender and process to a rough puree. Keep in covered container in the refrigerator for up to 1 week, or freeze for up to 3 months. **Makes 3 cups**

Carrot relish

Combine 1 kg (2 lb) peeled and grated carrots, 1 chopped onion, 2 crushed garlic cloves, 2 cups (440 g) sugar, and 2 cups (500 ml) cider vinegar in a large saucepan. Stir over low heat until sugar has dissolved. Tie $\frac{1}{2}$ teaspoon coriander seeds, $\frac{1}{2}$ teaspoon dill seeds, and 1 cinnamon stick in a piece of cheesecloth and add to pan. Bring to a simmer and cook 40 minutes, stirring occasionally, then more often toward the end of cooking, until liquid has evaporated. Discard spice pouch. Transfer to sterilized jars and seal. Keep for up to 1 month once opened. **Makes 3 cups**

Corn relish

Use a small sharp knife to cut the kernels from 4 corncobs. Finely dice 1 onion and 1 red and 1 green bell pepper. Heat 1 tablespoon vegetable oil in a large saucepan. Add peppers and cook over medium-low heat 5 minutes, until softened. Stir in 1 crushed garlic clove and cook about 30 seconds. Add corn, $1\frac{1}{2}$ cups (375 ml) white wine vinegar, 1 cup (220 g) sugar, 1 tablespoon mustard powder, 1 teaspoon salt, and a pinch of ground turmeric. Bring to a boil, reduce heat, and simmer 15 minutes. Combine 3 teaspoons cornstarch with 3 teaspoons water in a small bowl to make a paste, then stir into the corn mixture. Cook 5 minutes, or until thickened. Transfer to sterilized jars and seal. Keep for up to 1 month once opened. **Makes 4 cups**

Eggplant chutney

Finely dice 2 large eggplants and put in a colander. Sprinkle generously with salt and toss to coat. Let stand 20 minutes. Rinse and pat dry with paper towels. Heat 1/2 cup (125 ml) vegetable oil in a large saucepan. Add 1 finely chopped onion and cook over medium heat 5 minutes, until soft. Add 1 tablespoon finely grated fresh ginger and 3 crushed garlic cloves. Cook, stirring, 1 minute. Add 1 tablespoon ground cumin, 1 teaspoon cayenne pepper, and 1/4 teaspoon ground turmeric and cook, stirring, 30 seconds. Add eggplant and cook, stirring occasionally, until soft. Add 1/2 cup (60 g) raisins and 1 cup (250 ml) white wine vinegar, bring to a boil, then reduce heat slightly and simmer 5 minutes. Add 1/2 cup (110 g) sugar and stir until dissolved, then cook an additional 5 minutes, or until thickened. Transfer to sterilized jars and seal. Keep for up to 1 month once opened. **Makes 4 cups**

Tomato pasta sauce

Heat 2 tablespoons olive oil in a large saucepan. Add 2 chopped onions and cook over medium heat 5 minutes, until softened. Add 4 crushed garlic cloves and cook, stirring, 1 minute. Add 1.5 kg (3 lb) peeled, seeded, and chopped ripe tomatoes. Bring to a boil, reduce heat to medium-low, and stir in 2 teaspoons dried basil. Simmer 30 minutes, until sauce has reduced and thickened. Season with salt, freshly ground black pepper, and a good pinch of sugar. Keep in the refrigerator for up to 1 week or divide into usable portions and freeze for up to 3 months. **Makes 4 cups**

FROM LEFT: Corn relish, eggplant chutney, and tomato pasta sauce.

Index

Page numbers in **bold** print refer to main entries.

Acknowledgments

The publishers wish to thank the following individuals, companies and organizations for their help during the preparation of *The Ultimate Book of Vegetables*.

The Diggers Club (www.diggers.com.au); Lechelle Earl, Onions Australia (www.onionsaustralia.org.au); Outback Pride and Australian Gourmet Merchants (www.outbackpride.com.au); Sutton Forest Country Store; Cathie Lonnie (health and beauty recipe testing); Kate Nixon (text p. 195); Jane Strode (vegetable purchasing).

Locations Allan Humphries (balcony); Anne Kaleski (Wahroonga garden); Lewis/Sarsfield garden; Turramurra Lookout Community Garden; Southern Adelaide Local Health Network (rooftop garden); Mickey Robertson, Glenmore House, Camden.

Special thanks to Adina Gherman, Yulia Humphries, Alex Park and Sylvia Valk for their help with Romanian, Russian, Korean and Estonian recipes, respectively.

Photography Credits

Any images not listed in the photography credits are the copyright of Reader's Digest.

8-9 Reader's Digest; 10 All Reader's Digest with the exception of (L) Corbis; 11 All Reader's Digest with the exception of (R) Corbis and (L) Shutterstock; 13 (L) Getty Images; 18 (T) Shutterstock; 18 (C) Corbis; 18 (B) Alamy; 21 (T) Shutterstock; 22 Shutterstock; 23 (T) Shutterstock; 29 (T) Shutterstock; 31 (B) The Picture Desk/Art Archive; 34 (T) Alamy; 34 (B) The Picture Desk/Art Archive; 39 (T) Alamy; 41 Getty Images; 44 (TL, TC, BR) Corbis; 44 (TR, BL, BC) Shutterstock; 45 (TL, TR, BR) Shutterstock; 45 (TC, BR) Getty Images; 45 (BC) Alamy; 46 (B) Getty Images; 48 Corbis; 49 (R) Shutterstock; 51 (B) Getty Images; 52 (T) Getty Images; 53 (B) Shutterstock; 54 (L) Wikipedia; 54 (R) Mary Evans Picture Library; 56 (T) Corbis; 56 (C) Alamy; 58 (R) iStockphoto; 59 (T) Mary Evans Picture Library, (L) Corbis, (R) istockphoto; 61 (T) Shutterstock; 63 (B) Corbis; 65 (T) Getty Images; 67 (T) Mary Evans Picture Library, (B) Corbis; 68 (B) Getty Images; 69 (B) Corbis; 73 Getty Images; 76 (B) Mary Evans Picture Library; 77 (B) Getty Images; 80 (T) Getty Images; 81 (T) Getty Images; 82 (T) Garden World Images; 83 (T) Getty Images; 84 Getty Images; 85 (B) Corbis; 86 (R) Shutterstock; 87 (B) Alamy; 89 (T) iStockphoto, 89 (B) Getty Images; 91 (T) Getty Images; 92 (T) The Picture Desk/Art Archive, (B) Shutterstock; 94 (R) Alamy; 95 (L) Corbis, (R) Shutterstock, (B) Wikimedia; 99 (B) Getty Images; 104 (R) Corbis; 108 (T) Shutterstock; 108 (L) Alamy; 110 Shutterstock; 111 (CL) iStockphoto, (C, CR) Alamy, (BL, BC) Shutterstock, (BR) Garden World Images; 116 (R) Getty Images; 117 (T) Alamy; 120 Diggers Club; 121 (T) Corbis, (B) Getty Images; 122 Alamy; 123 (B) iStockphoto; 124 Alamy; 125 (T) Corbis, (B) Shutterstock; 126 (TL) iStockphoto, (TC) Garden World Images; (TR) Shutterstock, (CL, CR, BL, BR) all Shutterstock; 127 (T) Garden World Images, (B) iStockphoto; 128 (L) Corbis, (R) Garden World Images; 129 (T) Alamy; 130 (L) Corbis, (R) Alamy; 131 (T) Alamy, (B) Getty Images; 132 (T) Shutterstock, (B) Ecolicious; 133 (L) Shutterstock, (R) istockphoto, (B) Shutterstock; 134 (L) Shutterstock, (R) Getty Images, (T) Alamy, (B) Garden World Images; 136 (T) Getty Images, (B) Shutterstock; 137 (TL) iStockphoto, (TR) Alamy, (BL, BR) Shutterstock; 138 (TL) Alamy, (BL) Shutterstock; 139 (TL) Shutterstock, (TR) Alamy, (BL, BR) Shutterstock; 140 Getty Images; 141 (T) Shutterstock; 142 Alamy; 143 (R) Getty Images; 144 (L) Alamy, (R) Garden World Images; 145 (T) Alamy, (B) Diggers Club; 146 Garden World Images

Weights and measures

Sometimes conversions within a recipe are not exact but are the closest conversion that is a suitable measurement for each system. Use either the metric or the imperial measurements; do not mix the two systems.

The Ultimate Book of Vegetables

Consultants and Writers Suzie Ferrie, Sari Harrar, Melody Lord, Margaret McPhee, Deborah Nixon, Tracy Rutherford, Sophie Thompson

Designer Vivien Valk
Project Manager Deborah Nixon

Photographers
Andre Martin (A-Z of Vegetables; Things you can make; chapter openers; p. 143 top left);
Steve Brown (recipes and how-to boxes in A-Z of Vegetables; Health and beauty; Cooking with vegetables; title page and p. 21, p. 147, p. 183 bottom right, p. 186 left);
Maree Homer (p. 190);
Chris L. Jones and Natasha Milne (locations);
RD photographs (recipes on pages 46, 55, 58, 60, 71, 79, 81, 107, 229, 242, 256, 257, 260, 286, 287, 295, 298)

Stylists
Kate Nixon (A-Z of Vegetables; Things you can make; chapter openers; p. 143 top left);
Trish Heagarty (recipes and how-to boxes in A-Z of Vegetables; Health and beauty; Cooking with vegetables; title page and p. 21, p. 147, p183 bottom right, p186 left)

Food Preparation
Nick Eade; Kirsten Jenkins

Copy Editor Bronwyn Sweeney
Photographic Coordinator Amanda McKittrick
Proofreader Susan McCreery
Indexer Diane Harriman
Production Controller Martin Milat

The Ultimate Book of Vegetables was first published in 2014 by Reader's Digest (Australia) Pty Limited, 80 Bay Street, Ultimo NSW 2007, Australia

Copyright © 2015 by The Reader's Digest Association, Inc.

ISBN 978-1-62145-222-5

National Library of Australia Cataloguing-in-Publication entry
Title: The ultimate book of vegetables.
ISBN: 978-1-922085-29-0 (hardback)
Notes: Includes index.
Subjects: Vegetable gardening. Cooking (Vegetables). Medicinal plants.
Dewey Number: 635

We are interested in receiving your comments on the contents of this book. Write to:
The Reader's Digest Association, Inc.
Adult Trade Publishing
44 South Broadway
White Plains, NY 10601

Visit us on the web at RD.com or ReadersDigest.ca (in Canada)

Printed in China

1 3 5 7 9 10 8 6 4 2